British politics
a reader

Edited by
Martin Burch and Michael Moran

Manchester University Press

Selection and editiorial material © Manchester University Press 1987

Published by Manchester University Press,
Oxford Road, Manchester M13 9PL

British Library cataloguing in publication data
British politics : a reader.
  1. Great Britain   Politics and
  government   1979 –
  I. Burch, Martin   II. Moran, Michael, *1946 –*
  320.941   JN231

ISBN 0 7190 2302 5 paperback
            2301 7 hardback

Typeset in Great Britain
by W A Print Services
Printed and bound in Great Britain by
Biddles Ltd, Guildford and King's Lynn

Contents

Preface

This collection of edited articles and extracts from books is intended for use as a supplementary text by students on 'A' level and introductory degree courses on British politics. Textbooks and lectures communicate the necessary institutional detail, but any good course will go beyond this kind of description. In politics, more than in most subjects, issues arising from events in the world around us impinge on the classroom and lecture theatre. Learning about British politics therefore also involves becoming acquainted with themes and issues dominating practical argument. The necessity is particulary pressing in the case of Britain where rapid change and a succession of crises have produced great debates among observers about the nature of our system. No single textbook can communicate the range of these arguments. That is why students have traditionally been sent to the library to read the diversity of views reflected in the literature. But the reality of life in most schools and colleges now makes this difficult. Cuts in library funding, legal restrictions on photocopying and the sheer pressure of numbers on introductory courses make it exceptionally hard for students to obtain material. The purpose of this reader is to make available some of the best recent interpretations of key issues in British politics.

Our selection is both eclectic and partial. We have been guided by the belief that, since textbooks and lectures will provide the basic factual material, a 'reader' should open up possibilities for discussion and also put the reader in touch with some of the most recent research. The pieces chosen have been selected because they are up to date and provoke thought and argument. We make no claim to comprehensiveness. The function of the book is utilitarian. In an ideal world students would have instant access to all books and journals on a reading list; but the reality of library provision is far from this ideal. The hard – pressed teacher should find that each of the extracts included here can be used to form the basis for a class discussion.

We have abridged all the selections. Interpolations are indicated by the use of square brackets, which, have, however, been kept to a minimum, largely being used to explain unfamiliar terms or to make grammar consistent with our abridgements. Excisions are shown by three dots(...), which should help readers to understand the extent and nature of editing. References are presented at the end of each selection and have been kept in the same form as original. For this reason they are not presented in a uniform way throughout the book.

We would like to acknowledge the assistance of Marilyn Dunn and Karen Hall who kindly coped with typing some tricky manuscripts. Without their help and co – operation the reader could not have been so efficiently put together in keeping with our publisher's deadline.

Martin Burch
Michael Moran

August 1986

Acknowledgements

The editors and publishers wish to thank the following who have kindly given permission for the use of copyright material:

George Allen & Unwin Ltd for 'The Politicization of Local Government' by J. Gyford from *Half a Century of Municipal Decline* by M. Loughlin *et al.*, 1985.

Basil Blackwell Ltd for 'Police and Public Order' by J. Alderson, Vol.63 (4), 1985 and 'The development of the Thatcher Government's grand strategy for the Civil Service: a public policy perspective' by G. K. Fry, Vol. 62 (3), 1984 from *Public Administration;* and 'Behavioural changes: backbench independence in the 1980s' by P. Norton, from *Parliament in the 1980s,* ed. P. Norton, 1985.

Butterworth Scientific Ltd for 'Pluralism and the new corporatism' by R. Martin, Vol.XXXI (1), 1983 and 'The discipline of the New Democracy: Mrs Thatcher's domestic statecraft' by J. Bulpitt, Vol.XXXIV (1) from *Political Studies.*

Cambridge University Press for 'Overload, ungovernability and delegitimation: the theories and the British case' by A. H. Birch, Vol. 14 (2), 1984, 'The rise of the career politician in Britain - and its consequences' by Anthony King, Vol. 11, 1981 and 'Continuity and change in British central local relations: the "Conservative threat" ' by R. A. W. Rhodes, Vol. 14, April 1984 from *British Journal of Political Science.*

Collins Publishers for extracts from *The Politics of the Judiciary* by J. A. G. Griffith, 1985.

Fourth Estate for extracts from 'Capital: the neglected face of power?' by D. Marsh and G. Locksley, from *Pressure Politics*, ed. D. Marsh, Junction Books, 1983.

Hamish Hamilton Ltd and Sphere Books Ltd for extracts from

Whitehall: Tragedy and Farce by Clive Ponting, copyright © Clive Ponting 1986.

Little, Brown & Co. for extracts from 'Political culture in Great Britain: the decline of the civic culture' by Dennis Kavanagh from *The Civic Culture Revisited*, ed. G. Almond and S. Verba, 1980.

Macmillan Publishers Ltd for extracts from *Britain in Decline* by Andrew Gamble, 2nd edition, 1985.

New Socialist for 'Fleet Street: its bite on the ballot' by P. Dunleavy, *New Socialist*, January 1985.

New Society for 'Who are the Social Democrats?' by H. Dorning, *New Society*, 8 September 1983.

Oxford University Press for 'Changes in the Labour Party leadership' by H. Drucker, Vol.34 (3) 1981, 'Women's role in contemporary British politics: impediments to Parliamentary candidature' by J. S. Rasmussen, Vol.36 (3) and 'Understanding electoral change in Britain' by A. Heath, R. Jowell and J. Curtice, Vol.39 (1) 1986 from *Parliamentary Affairs*; and extracts from *Liberal Party Politics* by V. Bogdanor, Clarendon Press, 1983 and *Change in British Society* by A. H. Halsey, 1981.

The Political Studies Association for extracts from 'Thatcherism, liberalism, and Tory collectivism', by Robert Leach, *Politics*, Vol.3 (1), 1983.

The Policy Studies Institute for 'The quality of Cabinet government in Great Britain' by Peter Henessy, *Policy Studies*, Vol.6 (2), October 1985.

Every effort has been made to trace all the copyright holders but if any have been inadvertently overlooked the publishers will be pleased to make the necessary arrangements at the first opportunity.

Part one

The context of politics

Introduction

Political activity does not exist in isolation. It is shaped by a wider set of factors than the purely political. The size, terrain and history of a country plus the way its people organise their economic and social lives all influence political attitudes and actions. And, while the exact relationship between each one of these influences and the political is a matter of much debate, there can be no doubt that non – political factors are important. So any attempt to understand British politics needs to consider the wider forces that serve to shape what people do in the political sphere.

There are many approaches to studying this wider context. We have limited our selection to three pieces which cover a wide range of viewpoints. In particular they provide insights into the changing nature of the economy and social structure and suggest the political consequences that might flow from these. Gamble (1.1) examines the consequences of Britain's decline as a major imperial and economic power. The motif of decline has been emphasised by many observers. Some see Britain as a nation living in the past which has lost its sense of confidence and purpose. Its leaders are often said to place too high a value on the accepted way of doing things and to be over – resistant to new forces and ideas. Increasingly the debate has centred on whether and to what extent the British can adapt to modern circumstances. To many the 'accepted ways' no longer appear adequate in the face of considerable economic and social pressures.

Gamble emphasises the necessity of viewing changes in Britain over a long period and against the background of changes within a broader set of international relationships. He speaks about the 'hundred years decline' beginning in 1880 when Britain began to fall behind other nations in terms of world status, power and economic development. Of course in the economic sphere the decline about which Gamble and others speak is not absolute, but relative. That is to say that the British economy has expanded more or less on a year – to – year basis, yet when we look at the extent of this expansion in comparison to that of other countries Britain is seen to have done less well than her major competitors. So it is a decline in economic position, influence and competitive performance.

By placing Britain within the context of the world economy Gamble stresses that Britain's problems are not unique but are a particular manifestation of difficulties that are prevalent elsewhere. He also argues that the economic difficulties which Britain faces began to reach severe proportions in the mid – 1970s following the termination of what he calls the 'long boom'. The implication is that the consequences of the increasing rapidity of economic decline have manifested themselves with growing severity in the political sphere. To substantiate this point Gamble argues that in recent years there has been a weakening in the unity of the nation state, political instability has increased, and the social basis of party affiliation has been transformed.

The extract from Halsey (1.2) draws attention to the social context of British politics. He provides a view of the class structure defined in terms of occupation, income and wealth. He shows that while there has been a rise in the general standard of living throughout the century, inequality still persists. Even so there has been a 'slow and unsteady progress towards a more equal distribution of wealth', but this trend has had only a marginal impact on the overall picture. Consequently in social class terms Britain remains a deeply divided society. More particularly he notes that the element of wealth which assists the acquisition of political power 'has a most impressively unequal distribution'. This emphasis upon continuity in income and wealth distribution is qualified in part and Halsey does show that there have been some important changes in the social map of Britain. Amongst these he includes the growth of female employment; the shrinking of income differentials between skilled manual and clerical (non – manual) employees; and the development of service industry employment.

In 1.3 Birch provides an examination of some of the theories about the political consequences of the kind of social and economic changes which have been noted by Halsey and Gamble.

Although he looks at theories which apply to a number of countries he specifically assesses the validity of these in relation to Britain. He concentrates on three sets of writings which he labels neo – conservative, liberal economists and neo – Marxist. All these writings emphasise the fragility of the British system of politics and variously suggest that it is facing a potential crisis in terms of its capacity to handle change. Birch considers how well these generalisation stand up to hard analysis in the light of the evidence. In conclusion he questions the pertinence of these theories to the British case and emphasises the adaptability of the system and its great flexibility in the face of adversity.

The piece by Birch offers an interesting contrast to the arguments put forward by Gamble. Both approach similar issues, but from different political perspectives. To Gamble the capacities of the political system to manage problems and to satisfy the demands of various sections are increasingly strained towards crisis point as the economy continues to register difficulties. Birch accepts that contextual changes have altered the problems of governance, yet he does not accept the arguments about the inevitable weakening of established politics. Of course, as all these pieces demonstrate, the situation is open to a variety of interpretations and arguments. Nevertheless all illustrate that British politics in the 1980s has to take place in a much more constrained and much less certain context than at almost any time since 1945. An awareness of the past emphasises the continuity of the system and its capacity for peaceful change, while economic and social developments suggest that the adaptability of British politics is undergoing a severe test. We can only speculate as to whether its capacity for survival can be maintained in the years ahead.

1.1 *Andrew Gamble*

The politics of economic decline

From *Britain in Decline,* 2nd ed., Macmillan, London 1985, pp.3-44.

To speak of British decline is to isolate a national economy and a state that are British and are declining. But decline should not be confused with decay, nor with a process of internal decomposition. During its rise to world power the British state abandoned self-sufficiency and became dependent for its survival on the wider world economy. British decline is not therefore primarily an internal question of morals and customs, but depends on perceiving the British state and national economy within the world political and economic order, which Britain helped to construct and of which the British economy remains an integral part. Britain's successes and failures are accordingly measured against the successes and failures of other states in the world system, and much of the writing on decline is a deliberate attempt to identify what is peculiar to British experience...

1 Britain and the world economy

During the past hundred years Britain has succumbed to its major rivals. The failure to meet the challenge appears all the stranger because at no time has Britain suffered military defeat or occupation. What Britain did suffer progressively was industrial and commercial defeat, and this steadily undermined British military predominance. In the years since 1880 Britain has passed through three main phases of decline.

This 'hundred years decline', however, was not continuous, nor were its effects always cumulative. The first phase of decline was between 1880 and 1914, when Britain first suffered major competition from industrial rivals, and shortcomings in British industry began to be noticed. A major but unsuccessful challenge to the ruling free-trade policy of the British state was mounted by Joseph Chamberlain and the Social Imperialists. The second phase — between the two world wars — saw a much weakened Britain attempting and failing to rebuild its world power, but managing to avoid the worst effects of the world slump of the 1930s. The internal challenge of the Labour movement was contained for the moment, and the lesser challenge of Fascism resisted. In the third phase after 1945 Britain, now subordinate financially and militarily to the United States, and shorn of a substantial part of its accumulated wealth, was forced to withdraw from its empire, and failed to grow or invest at the same rate as other capitalist national economies during the long post-war boom. As a result its position grew steadily more vulnerable.

The period of decline has seen Britain change from a position of world leadership and dominance to one of weakness and dependence, its fortunes increasingly linked to a world economic system over which the British state could exert less and less control. For a long time the seriousness of Britain's position was concealed by the prosperity and buoyancy of the post-war western economy. But with the downturn in the 1970s a new phase opened both in the history of the world economy and in Britain's decline. Britain entered it with heavy burdens and facing daunting tasks.

2 The long boom

A major world recession erupted in 1974-5. It marked the decisive end of the longest and most rapid period of continuous expansion world capitalism has ever enjoyed, and opened a period of much more uncertain and uneven economic progress. Because the boom was so prolonged and so general there is a paradox in speaking of British 'decline' since 1945, since in absolute terms the British economy had never been so prosperous, nor had it ever expanded so fast.[1] This boom was unannounced and largely unexpected, but once it was properly under way many came to believe it could be a boom without end. The general downturn that began at the end of 1973 was not widely accepted at first as the turning point it has since been acknowledged to be.

The widespread predictions made after 1945 of an early return to the slow growth, stagnant demand and high unemployment of the 1930s proved false because of major changes which the world war had brought about. It created a new set of investment opportunities, new social relations between capital and labour, and new political relations between the leading capitalist states, which helped to create for almost twenty-five years a most favourable environment for accumulation. These conditions were fortuitous in the sense that no central authority designed them or planned them...

The great post-war expansion that finally ended in 1973 rested on conditions that released the springs of capitalist advance.[2] A wide range of new investment opportunities emerged, particularly in cars, electronics, and construction, which boosted average profitability in a wide band of industrial sectors. There was a plentiful supply of labour, and in many countries, particularly in those which had suffered Fascist rule, labour was weakly organised. There were also many new supplies of labour as yet untapped in agriculture, amongst women, and in less developed regions of the world economy, and there were abundant and cheap supplies of energy and raw materials. Political regimes were now quite ready to extend government involvement in the economy and to remove many costs and insecurities from the shoulders of individual enterprises.[3]

But there was another condition which was crucial... Responsibility for maintaining the conditions for the functioning of the world market was accepted by no one. Yet from the beginning the prosperity of capitalist economies depended crucially on the delicate networks of the world economy, its markets and its division of labour, and on the free flow of goods, capital and labour.[4]

In the history of world capitalism this responsibility has been borne by two states, Britain and the United States, because each for a time was the unchallenged industrial and financial centre of the world economy. The United States after 1945 took over the role Britain had been performing with increasing difficulty, and set out to rebuild the shattered international monetary system and trading network of the capitalist world...

The reasons why the boom has now ended lie in the circumstances of its success. The intensive exploitation of the new investment opportunities eventually led to their exhaustion. No new technological systems of the same scope have yet appeared which might form the leading sectors of a future expansion. Supplies of cheap labour that are easily or safely available have been used up, and in the advanced western states the working class is now highly

organised and highly paid. State expenditure and state involvement in the economy have been pushed to the point where they
have created everywhere a fiscal crisis of expenditures outrunning
revenues, and accelerating inflation. Finally, the very success of
the United States in creating the conditions in the world economy
for the boom led directly to the recovery of rivals, particularly
Germany and Japan, and the closing of the productivity gap between them and the United States. The levels of American foreign
investment and overseas military spending were only supportable
indefinitely so long as the allies of the United States agreed to
finance them. Their refusal caused the downfall of the dollar and
the eventual disintegration in 1971 of the international monetary
system which the Americans had designed and upheld after the
war.[5] It signalled the end of a phase of development of world capitalism which the recession in 1974-6 confirmed...

When Britain is placed in the context of the world economy, its
apparently peculiar and special problems often lose their uni-
queness and are seen to be problems shared by all the leading capitalist states. Periods of boom and periods of recessions affect all
economies. So do changes in prices of primary commodities and
energy. There are significant differences between states, but these
arise within a context of common institutions and common structures, such as the increasing scale of industrial enterprises; the application of science to production; the widening of the market to
embrace all occupations, social groups and nations; the great expansion of the state; the growth of trade unions and the establishment of mass democracy. These have generated many common
problems, of which the most important in recent years has been to
find ways to fund state expenditures, which have risen inexorably
and apparently irreversibly in every state, and at the same time to
contain the inflation which has become since the war a permanent
feature of western capitalist economies.[6] The key to both has long
been seen as engineering a faster rate of growth, because it ef-
fortlessly generates higher tax revenues and permits demands to
be more easily reconciled with resources at lower levels of inflation. But it is precisely growth that can no longer be relied upon or
stimulated in the old ways. In the 1970s Britain's leisurely relative
decline in economic performance threatened to turn into something potentially much more serious.

3 The measurement of decline

British decline can only be understood, and in some sense only perceived, when it is related to the world economy which Britain once dominated and to which it has remained chained long after its dominance has passed away...   •

The steady slide of the British economy, from a position of commanding superiority to a condition where some observers have begun to speculate whether Britain could be the first developed capitalist economy to become underdeveloped, prompts obvious questions. Why have the British been unable to organise a recovery? Why has there been no political reorganisation capable of enabling Britain, once it had fallen behind, to catch up? Why has the decline been so remorseless? Where is British nationalism? The decline has now been proceeding for a hundred years, half the period that industrial capitalism has existed in Britain. The panic that swept the British press and British ruling circles at the turn of the century about the rise of German and American industry, produced a stream of arguments and complaints very similar to those of the 1960s and 1970s[7]...

It is clear that the problem goes deeper than incorrect or insufficient policies, since so many technical remedies have been tried, so far without great success. Whenever any particular feature of the British economy or British state is isolated and proclaimed to be the factor holding back the economy from performing more successfully, contrary evidence has never been long in coming to throw doubt on its importance.

Awareness of the nation's relative economic decline has come to dominate contemporary British politics. According to Martin Wiener 'the leading problem of modern British history is the explanation of economic decline'[8]...

The extent of the slide has been remarkable. From being the leading economy in western Europe in 1950 Britain had declined by 1980 to be one of the poorest. British output and productivity were little better than half the levels in comparable economies. The size of the gap that has opened in such a short time is astonishing. Pollard estimates that if present trends were to continue, Britain would be overtaken by Greece, Portugal and Spain, and that the British economy would not reach the *present* level of national income enjoyed by the Federal Republic of Germany until 2051[9]...

The problems are more intractable in the 1980s than they were in the 1960s. Between 1979 and 1981 the economy was no longer merely in relative decline but actually began contracting. On some estimates unemployment reached 20 per cent of the labour force,[10] manufacturing output shrank to the levels of the mid-1960s and the public finances were under severe strain.

But has Britain actually declined? Is the decline real? Here there is an immediate paradox. The decline in Britain's world status and world power has been accompanied not by falling but by rising material wealth. The mass of British people were considerably better off in 1973 when Britain finally entered the EEC, as one of its poorer members, than they had been in 1900 when British power and economic superiority, though challenged, were still pre-eminent. Moreover, the performance of the British economy has steadily improved as the century has gone on. The annual rate of growth increased from 1 per cent between 1900 and 1913 to 2.3 per cent between 1922 and 1938 to 3.2 per cent between 1957 and 1965. The annual productivity increase in the same three periods was 0 per cent, 1.1 per cent and 2.4 per cent.[11] The period of loudest clamour about British decline actually turns out to be the period when the British economy has grown faster than at any time since 1870.

Is this decline? What has to be remembered are the different senses which are entangled in the word. Britain's decline can be most clearly perceived in the absolute decline of British dominance of the world economy — military, financial, and industrial. Britain's leading role was heavily qualified after the First World War. After the Second World War Britain, although still a world power, was no longer a major one, and its position dwindled still further as it shed its Empire and attempted to negotiate entry into the EEC. Decline as a process in British politics refers first to this loss of world power, the painful transition to a greatly reduced role and a greatly diminished capacity, and the corresponding alteration in national perspectives which had to result.

The second process involved in Britain's decline is not an absolute decline at all, but the relative economic decline that is apparent when British national economic performance is compared with that of its major industrial rivals, particularly the other states in the EEC, and Japan...

The striking fact is not that the British economy showed no growth, but that its rate of growth was less than that of the most technologically advanced economy, the United States. Whereas Germany, Japan and France all significantly closed the technological gap between themselves and the United States, Britain failed to do so. If anything the gap grew greater.[12]

The annual rate of growth of the British economy both in terms of output and output per head were significantly below all other major capitalist countries in the second decade of the long boom (see Table 1). Such a performance naturally had its effect upon the international growth league. In terms of Gross Domestic Product per head Britain slipped from ninth in 1961 to thirteenth in 1966 and fifteenth in 1971. By 1976 Britain was eighteenth, having fallen behind not just the United States, Canada and Sweden, but Iceland, France, Finland, Austria, and Japan as well.[13]

The most serious aspect of this relative decline which has often been highlighted is the erosion of the United Kingdom's position in world manufacturing. The British share in world manufacturing output fell from 9.6 per cent in 1960 to 5.8 per cent in 1975.[14] Britain consistently failed to match the levels of productivity growth achieved in other countries (see Table 2)...

Table 1   Rates of growth of GDP (Gross Domestic Product) 1962 – 72
(annual percentage rates)

	GDP	GDP *per capita*
France	4.7	5.7
West Germany	3.6	4.5
Italy	3.9	4.6
Japan	9.2	10.4
United States	3.0	4.2
United Kingdom	2.2	2.7

Source: OECD National Accounts 1961–72.

A major factor contributing to this has been the persistently low levels of investment in Britain, generally about half the levels of investment in manufacturing of Britain's major competitors. One study in 1978 estimated that the fixed assets per worker in manufacturing in the United Kingdom were only £7500, compared with £23 000 in West Germany and £30 000 in Japan.[15] Whereas in 1870 Britain enjoyed the highest productivity level amongst the major capitalist economies, by 1970 Britain had one of the lowest.

Table 2   Phases of productivity growth (GDP per man-hour), 1870–1976
(annual average compound growth rates)

	1870–1913	1913–50	1950–76
France	1.8	1.7	4.9
Germany	1.9	1.2	5.8
Italy	1.2	1.8	5.3
Japan	1.8	1.4	7.5
United States	2.1	2.5	2.3
United Kingdom	1.1	1.5	2.8

Source: A. Maddison, 'The Long Run Dynamics of Productivity Growth',
in W. Beckerman (ed.) *Slow Growth in Britain* (Oxford University Press,
1979), p. 195.

Table 3   Shares in the value of world exports of manufactures, 1950–79
(percentages)

	1899	1929	1937	1950	1960	1970	1977	1979
United Kingdom	33.2	22.9	21.3	25.5	16.5	10.8	9.3	9.7
France	-	-	-	9.9	9.6	8.7	9.9	10.5
Germany	-	-	-	7.3	19.3	19.8	20.8	20.8
Japan	-	-	-	3.4	6.9	11.7	15.4	13.6
United States	-	-	-	27.3	21.6	18.5	15.9	15.9

Sources: London and Cambridge Economic Service, *The British
Economy, Key Statistics* (London, 1970) and NIESR *Quarterly Bulletin,*
May 1980.

The failure to maintain superiority in productivity and in
manufacturing has caused a steep fall in the importance of the
British economy in the world economy and in its share of world
trade (see Table 3). The significance of this table is not that the
British share has declined, which might only be of arithmetical significance, but that the shares of Germany and Japan not only expanded greatly but were then maintained at a much higher level.
The French share also remained constant...

The effects of all this on the British economy have become increasingly sharp in the 1970s. Unemployment has climbed steeply
in Britain and inflation has accelerated whilst industrial output has
stagnated. British performance has again been noticeably worse

than most other major capitalist economies. Its level of unemployment was, until 1980, about average, but its record on prices and output was significantly below [average]...

4 The debates of the intellectuals

Decline re-emerged as a major problem for economic policy and as a major issue in political debate in the 1960s... In the political economy debate about the causes of decline, the starting-point is 'why has British decline been so untouched by frequent changes of policy and government?'. Why does the decline persist? Why has the political system been paralysed by it and increasingly thrown into considerable turmoil as each new experiment has run its course and ended in failure? Second there is the comparative dimension. All the approaches in political economy are directly interested in the question, 'what makes Britain special?'. What are the particular weaknesses and features which account for the remarkable divergence of performance in economies which are otherwise so similar and so closely integrated with one another? Four main perspectives can be identified. They present different diagnoses of the fundamental problem Britain faces:

1. a market order fettered by social democracy;
2. a political system deadlocked by unresolved conflicts over the distribution of income and the control of industry;
3. a political culture antagonistic to modern industry;
4. a world state unable to promote domestic modernisation.

A market order fettered by social democracy
...Decline is explained as an effect of various kinds of rigidities which prevent markets from functioning as they should. Many liberal economists disclaim any belief in ideal markets or perfect competition; nevertheless their analytical technique is to assume that markets do naturally clear at a price which creates full employment of resources, and to study the obstacles which prevent this from happening. The major obstacles in post-war Britain which allegedly condemned the economy to slow growth — and more recently to accelerating inflation and rising unemployment — are the size of the public sector, the character of government interventions in the economy, and the monopoly powers of private 'coercive groups', notably trade unions...

The key issue is the failure of the state to keep within its proper limits. By encroaching on the market order and seeking to determine market outcomes the state destroys the delicate mechanism which maximises economic efficiency. By transferring private decisions to the public realm the state turns economic decisions into political ones which encourage group conflict and competition between the parties which generates excessive expectations in the electorate. By disbursing collective welfare payments and subsidies it makes citizens dependent on government and erodes personal responsibility. By expanding public services and public employment and by constantly increasing its borrowing and its taxes, the state 'crowds out' private investment, destroys incentives, and becomes an ever-heavier unproductive burden on the wealth-creating market sector.[16]

The major reason why governments have intervened more and more with the market order is union power. Unions are not held responsible for inflation — only governments can increase the money supply. But unions are held directly responsible for helping to create the political conditions in which governments resort to inflation. Unions are directly responsible therefore for unemployment and economic decline. The post-war commitment to full employment and the substantial increase in public expenditure and taxation are regarded by social market theorists as arising from the need to appease the unions and marked a decisive shift in political and economic power in favour of the labour movement...

From this analysis it follows that restoring the economy to full employment and promoting expansion requires the curbing of union power, the reduction of public expenditure and taxation, and the reintroduction of sound money as the principal object of government stabilisation policy.[17] The condition for the restoration of sound money is not technical but political. Only when governments no longer feel an obligation to respond to an increase in unemployment by increasing demand can a sound money policy succeed. This means that a political consensus has to be forged which sets strict limits to the role of government. Governments are charged with protecting the market order (that is, money, contracts, property rights) and preventing the emergence of private coercive groups, but must disclaim direct responsibility for either employment or growth...

A deadlocked political system

The second approach emphasises not the imperfections of markets
but the weakness, incompetence or malign influence of political
institutions. The problem lies not in the fact of intervention by the
state (which is considered necessary and desirable) but the in-
conclusive, inadequate or harmful character of that intervention.
How can government/industry relations be so reconstituted that a
more effective national economic performance becomes possible?
It is taken for granted in this approach that a close partnership between government and industry and significant involvement and intervention in private sector decision-making is essential for the
successful working of a modern capitalist economy... The
'deadlocked state' approach takes as its models France and Japan
and argues that it is the failure of Britain to evolve similar co-
operation between government and industry that is responsible for
decline.[18]

There are a number of variants of this approach. One of the
most influential in recent years has been the adversary politics
thesis.[19] This asserts that governments have failed to create either
a stable environment for decision-making in private and nationalised industry, or to sustain long-term policies aimed at expansion.
A principal cause is the adversary style of party conflict in Britain.
The consensus between the parties is regarded as policy coinci-
dence rather than a genuine ideological consensus. Both parties remain wedded to opposed ideologies and tied to the two major
producer-groups, unions and private capital...

It is argued that this adversary conflict between the parties and
the alternation of the parties in government roughly every five
years since 1959 has produced significant discontinuities in
economic policy. Each party in opposition has drawn up policies
heavily influenced by its ideologues. On winning office it has proceeded to implement its radical policies, overturning the policies
of its predecessor. In mid-term each government has then found it
needed the policies and institutions it had discarded. It adopts
them and begins to pursue sensible policies but before these can
bear fruit it loses office at the general election, and the other party, its ideological batteries recharged, returns for a new
experiment.[20]

A different version of the thesis argues that the harmful effects
of adversary politics as it is practised in Britain, are not limited to
discontinuity in policy.[21] As important are the continuitites in

policy they produce. The British adversary style of politics produces ritualised party conflict over a few well-publicised issues while enforcing silence on many substantive policy questions. By this means the fundamental conflict between labour and capital which has lain at the heart of twentieth-century British politics was not resolved, merely displaced. The consequence has been the failure of the British political system to generate effective evaluation and correction of economic policy. The disastrous foreign economic policy of the post-war period, with its associated stop–go stabilisation policy, survived every change of government unscathed.

This version of the adversary politics thesis focuses on the shortcomings of the democratic procedures for evaluating and implementing policy. Its arguments are buttressed by other variants of this approach. One common theme is pluralistic stagnation. Here the argument is that the very success, longevity and continuity of the British political system has encouraged the proliferation of special interest groups. On one account these have steadily encroached on markets preventing them from functioning efficiently and severely limiting the practical options of government policy.[22] Another account argues that the producer interests were elevated into 'governing institutions' and formed a partnership with government which assisted the containment and defusing of industrial conflict over primary issues of ownership and control and its replacement by ritualised and often rhetorical conflict over lesser issues.[23] While this sustained social order and political stability, and smoothed the full participation of the labour movement in the state, it had costs. Many fundamental questions of economic policy were not addressed because of the need for governments to work through the institutions...

The idea of a deadlocked state has also been developed by those who have castigated particular institutions, usually the Treasury, for the overall conduct of economic policy. Frequent targets are the 'Treasury view' and its resistance to correction and insulation from outside pressures[24] and the centralised and arbitrary procedures of British Government. A much more open style of policy-making, a much greater scope for democratic participation, would have disturbed the maintenance of the consensus priorities which over thirty years had such damaging results...

Many socialist writers argue that it is the relative defensive strength of the British working class which is the crucial factor in explaining the backwardness of the British economy.[25] This strength, they argue, can be measured by a number of indicators — the extent of trade union organisation, its historical traditions and continuity, the internal unity of trade unions, and the degree to which trade unions have established shop-floor organisations. On all these criteria the British Labour movement appeared to have a much stronger bargaining position than its counterpart in other countries. Its defensive power as a corporate interest created a major obstacle to any modernisation programme pursued by central Government and lowered the return on new investment. The political failure either to harness or to break this organised defensive power is regarded as the chief cause of the continuing decline.

An anti-industrial political culture

The third approach states that Britain's relative economic decline is to be explained by Britain's peculiar political culture and peculiar civil society: the complex of attitudes and values which have created a social climate in England that has acted as a constant break to industrialism.

Two main features of this culture are singled out. There is first the culture of the ruling class which it is argued never came fully to reflect the values and attitudes of the industrial bourgeoisie.[26] The industrialists eventually accommodated themselves to the social and political order of the ruling land-owners. They did not challenge and overturn it; hence the persistence of aristocratic institutions, life-styles and aspirations; hence the ambivalent attitude towards industry and the identification of the enduring values of the patria with the countryside and pre-industrial England; hence the lower status of business, trade and applied knowledge; hence the continuing importance of title, rank, hierarchy, and status, and the obstacles in the path of an open, meritocratic and egalitarian system. Arguments such as these have been used to explain the poor 'quality' of British management and to infer that most British talent has gone into the professions of finance or the media or the public sector, rarely into industry[27]...

A second theme, not always wholly compatible with the first, is that a major source of the 'anti-industrial spirit' in England is the culture of the Labour movement.[28] Labour it is alleged has fostered a climate of egalitarianism which has discouraged risk-taking, reduced rewards for enterprise and responsibility, undermined the essential values of a market order — such as thrift, initiative and self-reliance... Social democracy has encouraged a culture of redistribution and entitlement rather than one of growth and incentive.

The main problem with such theories is their vagueness. They become catch-all explanations. Nothing escapes their grasp, yet it is very difficult to assess the representativeness or the significance of much of the evidence they present. Often the thesis is tautological — every economic or social change is automatically explained in terms of some shift in the political culture.[29] Proponents of such theories often forget the rapidity with which traditions and attitudes can be transformed, and they often neglect the scale of the industrial and social changes which Britain has undergone in the twentieth century...

A world state

One major difficulty with all the explanations so far considered is that although they often have a comparative aspect they still tend to treat Britain's problems primarily as an internal affair.

But the decline has been relative and only exists when the British economy is seen as part of a much larger world economy. This opens a new window on the problem, for its directs attention to the manner in which the British economy has been integrated into the world economy as the key explanation of why relative progress turned into relative firm decline...

The value of relating Britain's economic problems to their proper international context is that it provides a framework for handling and evaluating the various kinds of evidence that exist about the reasons for the backwardness of the British economy. By focusing on the peculiar history of the British state, its remarkable overseas expansion, and its emergence at the centre of the world economy, it is possible to identify the specific legacies that this period of world dominance left behind and which underwrote the policies, the institutions and the attitudes which have blocked the kind of programme that could have halted decline.

Two legacies have been crucial. The first is the degree of external dependence, of the openness of the British economy which was accepted from the middle of the nineteenth century onwards because of its obvious advantages for an economy whose industries enjoyed a substantial lead in productivity over all its foreign rivals. It led to the flourishing of finance and commerce, and imparted an international orientation to state policy and to the key sectors of the British economy and to the ideological outlook of British politicians and intellectuals.

The second legacy was the successful way in which internal challenges were met and new demands and interests accommodated. A series of compromises with organised labour preserved institutional continuity and the international orientation of the state and the openness of the economy. The political forces that might have implemented a successful programme of reconstruction were contained and diverted. The fettered market order, the deadlocked political system, and the anti-industrial political culture are all expressions of this containment. What made the containment possible was the vast and varied strengths of the British State and the metropolitan Establishment which administered it.[30]

In this explanation of decline, therefore, the rapid relative economic decline after 1950 is traced to the demise of Britain as a world state, a state no longer at the centre of the world economy but still possessed of the legacies of its period of world leadership and still eager to retain as many aspects of its world role as possible. The crucial policy error was the failure to recognise the scale of adjustment of the British economy that was required if the national economy was to prosper as a successful region of the new American-dominated world economy.[31]

Between 1950 and 1970 the relations between state and economy show two main trends; first, the increasing internationalisation of the British economy, and the weakening of domestic manufacturing; second, the entrenchment domestically of social democratic priorities in stabilisation policy and industrial policy. In the 1950s this compromise between the internationally-oriented metropolis and internal social democracy appeared to many the final achievement of the British system. In the 1970s it began to crumble because the relative decline it had produced made it impossible to sustain an open economy with the gains of social democracy. In the 1970s, internationalisation began to gather pace. Its key aspect is the ability of businesses not just to trade internationally, but to operate internationally, and therefore independently of the British national economy.[32] This ability had long been possessed by many of the businesses of the City. Leading sectors of industry acquired it in the 1950s and 1960s. Many more businesses gained it in the 1970s. The complete lifting of exchange controls in 1978 and 1979 was symbolic of the whole direction of post-war foreign economic policy.

5 The political impact

As British national power has declined, so many internal problems have come to loom much larger because the handling of them has become more intractable. They included the racial tensions that have accompanied the permanent settlement of immigrant workers from the Commonwealth, exploited by political movements like the National Front, and the renewal of armed conflict in Ulster. But in addition to these, the failure to manage the economy successfully has had considerable impact upon the political system itself. Ireland was never successfully integrated into the United Kingdom, but the union of England, Scotland and Wales did not face any serious challenge in two hundred years until the rise of nationalist movements in the late 1960s. The disintegration of the British multinational state had never been seriously considered before. The nationlist parties suffered major setbacks at the elections in 1979 and in the referenda that preceded them, but the underlying reason for their rise remains — an increasing unwillingness in those nations to permit Welsh and Scottish futures to be forever linked to that of England and determined by England.

Decline has also had a major impact on the party system and the authority of the state. The British system tends outwardly to display a sharp conflict between two evenly matched adversaries, but inwardly it relies upon an informal consensus on policy, which depends upon the leaders of both parties, when they are in government, acting within limits of the politically practicable as these are perceived and defined by the state's permanent agencies. The construction of such a party system is a fairly elaborate procedure. It broke down under the strains of the First World War and was painfully reconstructed around a Conservative/Labour axis, but is now under serious threat again...

A major cause of this political instability, and the growing disaffection of more and more voters from the major parties, came from the repeated failure of the two parties to achieve the targets of their economic policy, and the increasing rating of governments' performance in terms of economic indicators. Partly because of the kind of electoral competition in which the parties engaged, partly because of government assuming overall responsibility for economic prosperity and performance, the state of the economy became the central political issue and a crucial determinant of every government's electoral fortunes.

The failure of either party, despite intentions, to reverse or even halt decline, and the steady worsening of Britain's economic problems, seriously undermined the stability of the two-party system. This had two further consequences. It led to a marked polarisation between the parties in ideological terms, which has now gone beyond the adversary rhetoric of the formalised party battle. It also undermined the authority of the state and public institutions over which governments preside. The competence of the civil service, the impartiality of the media, the relevance of the universities, the professionalism of business, the representativeness of the trade unions, even the spirituality of the Church, have all come under serious attack. The secrecy and lack of openness in government, the cult of amateurism, the magic circles of insiders, which once were celebrated as strengths and factors of cohesion, are now more often denounced as handicaps and evils. The British governing class has long been under attack, but never has it been in such disarray. As its reputation declines so the ideological attack on the policy consensus, which the governing class has always endeavoured to maintain, mounts. A New Right and a New Left have arisen in the past twenty years, which between them have broken the ideological torpor of British politics and have made space for new political movements and demands. Both liberal political economy and socialist political economy had remarkable revivals, and out of them came alternative strategies and alternative scenarios for the British economy. Politics has become interesting again in Britain, and turbulent.

At the heart of the new ideological ferment lies the plight of the British economy. Left and Right attacks on the consensus long preceded the recession, but they have been greatly amplified by it. British problems are not unique to Britain, but because they have been exacerbated by the long national decline, the political effort of coping with them has become more difficult and more necessary. In the 1970s there was a growing feeling that only major social and political changes would suffice, for technical solutions were then practically exhausted... The modernisation strategy of the 1960s with its perspective of partnership between classes and between government and industry remains, but it is now relatively enfeebled. Two new strategies for modernisation have arisen to challenge it — the *social market strategy,* developed by the New Right in the Conservative party, and the *alternative economic* strategy, developed by the Left in the Labour party. These strategies arose as alternatives to what were regarded as the failures of the Wilson and Heath governments... Where there is a high degree of consensus on fundamentals, the role of strategy is muted, since no major changes of the framework of policy are envisaged. For much of the post-war period Britain was governed within a social democratic consensus, and the bid to overcome Britain's economic weakness had to take place within its constraints. This gave rise to a number of *modernisation* programmes. Launched in the 1960s by the Conservative government under Harold Macmillan, 'modernisation' was carried forward by the new Labour administration of Harold Wilson after 1964. A final bold attempt to make it succeed was undertaken by the Conservative government under Edward Heath after 1970...

Notes

1 See P. Deane and W. A. Cole, *British Economic Growth* (Cambridge University Press, 1967), and W. W. Rostow, *The World Economy* (London: Macmillan, 1978), ch. 28.

2 The nature of the long boom and the forces which undermined it are explored from different standpoints in E. Mandel, *Late Capitalism* (London: New Left Books, 1975), P. Sweezy and H. Magdoff, *The Dynamics of the Capitalist Economy* (New York: MR Press, 1972), and Rostow, *The World Economy*.

3 See Paul Mattick, *Marx and Keynes* (London: Merlin, 1969).

4 See M. Barratt-Brown, *The Economics of Imperialism* (Harmondsworth: Penguin, 1972).

5 The downfall of the dollar is analysed by R. Segal, *The Decline and Fall of the American Dollar* (New York: Bantam, 1974).

6 See the discussion in Paul Bullock and David Yaffe, 'Inflation, the crisis and the post-war boom', *Revolutionary Communist,* Nos. 3-4, November 1975, pp. 1.45; and in Andrew Gamble and Paul Walton, *Capitalism in Crisis* (London: Macmillan, 1976).

7 There are two detailed studies of the reaction to the challenge: R. Heindel, *The American Impact on Great Britain, 1898-1914* (New York: Octagon, 1968), and R. J. S. Hoffman, *Great Britain and the German Trade Rivalry, 1975-1914* (New York: Russell, 1964).

8 M. Wiener, *English Culture and the Decline of the Industrial Spirit, 1850-1980* (Cambridge University Press, 1981).

9 Sidney Pollard, *The Wasting of the British Economy* (London: Croom Helm, 1982).

10 For the calculations see *Labour Research,* January 1983, Vol. 72, No. 1.

11 M. Prest and D. Coppock, *The UK Economy,* table 1.14, p. 50.

12   See S. Gomulka, 'Britain's Slow Industrial Growth', in W. Beckerman (ed.), *Slow Growth in Britain* (Oxford University Press, 1979), pp. 166-93.
13   See D. McKie and C. Cook, *Election Guide* (London: Quartet, 1978), pp. 57-8.
14   F. Blackaby, *De-Industrialisation* (London: Heinemann, 1978), p. 243.
15   F. E. Jones, 'Our manufacturing industry: The missing £100,000 million', *National Westminster Bank Review,* May 1978, pp. 8-17.
16   Bacon and Eltis, *Britain's Economic Problem;* IEA, *The Dilemmas of Government Expenditure* (London: IEA, 1976).
17   IEA, *Is Monetarism Enough?* (London: IEA, 1980).
18   A. Shonfield, *Modern Capitalism* (Oxford University Press, 1964).
19   See in particular S. E. Finer, *Adversary Politics and Electoral Reform* (London: Wigram 1979); and for a critique, R. Rose, *Do Parties Make a Difference?* (London: Macmillan, 1981).
20   See M. Stewart, *The Jekyll and Hyde Years* (London: Dent, 1977).
21   D. Ashford, *Policy and Politics in Britain* (Oxford: Stockwell, 1981).
22   M. Olson, *The Rise and Fall of Nations* (Oxford: Blackwell, 1982).
23   K. Middlemas, *Politics in Industrial Society* (London: Deutsch, 1979).
24   Pollard, *The Wasting of the British Economy.*
25   See Andrew Glyn and Bob Sutcliffe, *Workers, British Capitalism, and the Profits Squeeze* (Harmondsworth: Penguin, 1972) and David Purdy, 'British capitalism since the war', *Marxism Today,* September 1976, Vol. 20, No. 9, pp. 270-7, and October 1976, Vol. 20, No. 10, pp. 310-18.
26   Wiener, *English Culture and the Decline of the Industrial Spirit.*
27   M. Postan, *An Economic History of Western Europe, 1945-64* (London: Methuen, 1967); M. Shanks, *The Stagnant Society* (Harmondsworth: Penguin, 1961).
28   T. Nairn, *The Breakup of Britain* (London: New Left Books, 1977); K. Joseph, *Stranded on the Middle Ground* (London: CPS, 1976).
29   S. Beer, *Britain Against Itself* (New York: Norton, 1982).
30   Nairn, *The Breakup of Britain.*
31   Blank, 'The politics of foreign economic policy', *International Organisation,* Vol. 31, No. 4, 1977, pp. 673-722.
32   R. Rowthorn, 'Imperialism in the 1970s: unity or rivalry' in H. Radice (ed.), *International Firms and Modern Imperialism* (Harmondsworth: Penguin, 1975).

1.2 *A. H. Halsey*

Society and class

From A. H. Halsey, *Change in British Society,* Oxford University Press 1981, pp. 21-42

'A class-ridden society'; that is the common judgement on Britain made by social observers, whether delivered as praise or condemnation... Why is it that, though Britain has become a rich country, social inequality is a continuing feature of its internal life?

In looking for an answer to this question we shall be carried to the centre of the debate about Britain among sociologists. My first task is to assemble a clear vocabulary. Fortunately this has been emerging in post-war sociological writing.

When sociologists speak of a structure of inequality they refer to the ways in which power and advantage form a stratified system of relations. By power they mean the resources which individuals or groups use to have their will, irrespective of the will of others. A board of directors can close a plant: a union can strike. By advantage, they mean control over things which are valued and scarce, such as the wealth of a millionaire, or the skill of a surgeon. Power and advantage are convertible. Together they define the character of strata and the relations between them in a stratification system. This system has three dimensions or forms of organization through which power and advantage are distributed.

The three dimensions are class, status, and party. Classes—for example, professional people or factory workers—are formed socially out of the division of labour. They make up more or less cohesive and socially conscious groups from those occupational groups and their families which share similar work and market situations. Status is formed out of the no less fundamental tendency of human beings to attach positive and negative values to human attributes, and to distribute respect or honour and contempt or derogation accordingly: status groups, for example peers of the realm or vagrants, form as social networks of those who share similar social prestige or life-style. Parties form out of the organized pursuit of social objectives; they are political parties, pressure groups, associations, and unions of those who consciously share a planned movement for the acquisition of power. In short, classes belong to the economic, status groups to the social, and parties to the political structure of society.[1]

Status and party will concern us in my third and fourth chapters. Here and now my task is to see how far inequality can be explained by class. But again, there is a welter of confusing terms. One thing is broadly agreed. Britain held a special historical place as the first industrial nation, which made it in the nineteenth century the classic home of an urbanized industrial working class or proletariat. But there agreement ends, and there is sharp debate about its older and its more recent history of a shifting balance of power and advantage.

A proletariat implies a bourgeois or capitalist class, and here it is essential to appreciate the long pre-industrial history of a landed aristocracy and gentry into which that capitalist class was absorbed. With due allowance for its sustained willingness and capacity to assimilate new elements, it may be said that an essentially hereditary medieval estate was slowly transformed into a fully developed class, retaining its hereditary character in a period stretching from late medieval times almost to our own day. There was no overt political revolution of the bourgeoisie. Control of state power and cultural advantage was virtually unbroken in the long journey from agrarian feudalism to industrial capitalism. The muddle of adjectives to denote classes comes from this history so that the terms upper, leisured, middle or middling, and lower are verbal deposits from the earlier pre-industrial age. It was the nineteenth-century analysts of industrial society who identified classes as capitalist, bourgeois, proletarian, and working. So the peculiarity of the British case is the mixture of confusing terms, reflecting history rather than logic. One consequence is that, in trying to name the classes which have evolved out of industrialism, Britons frequently divide themselves not into an upper and a lower but, absurdly, into a middle and a working class.

But the essential point is that in industrial society the anatomy of class is displayed in the occupational structure.[2] Groups and individuals differ first according to the terms on which they can sell their skills and their labour on the market, and second according to the actual conditions of their work–its autonomy, or lack of it, its intrinsic satisfactions, and its attendant amenities. True, the British retain the archaic customs of an honours system through which they translate occupational achievement into feudal rank. They pretend, in other words, that power and advantage derive not from activity in the labour or capital markets, but from birth and breeding. True, too, that part of all social inheritance is immutable: birth gives us a family of origin, sex, race, and nationality. Some medieval estates–an extreme form of status–were legally hereditary. Class, too, in its fully developed form, shares this hereditary quality: but its foundation is in the market, not the law. An individual may move between classes in his own lifetime. The rise and fall of classes themselves is a broader and usually longer historical process through changes in the economy and polity which may be intended or unintended, violent or peaceful. Whether we follow the original Marxist orthodoxy and hold that legal ownership of the means of production is the crucial distinction or whether, with later writers like Dahrendorf,[3] we prefer to concentrate on authority in the organization of work, classes emerge out of occupational structure, and power and advantage are unequally distributed between them.

It is this definition of class in terms of occupation, which is widely used in European sociology, that I shall be using in this [chapter]... it will usually suffice to distinguish three classes–the middle. lower-middle, and working classes.

The first stratum can be taken to mean what most people mean by the *middle class:* professional, managerial, and administrative occupational groups and higher technicians, and their wives and children–the 'service class'. The second stratum is a heterogeneous *lower-middle class* of non-manual employees, small proprietors, self-employed artisans–the petite bourgeoisie or lower-middle class–but also lower-grade technicians and supervisors of manual workers who might be thought of as a 'blue-collar élite'. The third stratum is the *working class*–industrial manual workers, and agricultural workers whether skilled, semi-skilled, or unskilled. Nevertheless, the reader should be aware that more refined class schema may be used, and indeed would be necessary, to identify groups with more homogeneous market and work situations.[4]

At the beginning of the century the occupational division of labour in Britain was such that over three-quarters of the employed and self-employed population were engaged in manual work. Of these, 28.7 per cent were skilled, 34.3. per cent semi-skilled, 9.6 per cent unskilled, and 1.8 per cent were self-employed artisans in 1911. Above these manual workers stood a white collar and professional class, more confidently divided then than now into the upper-middle class and lower-middle class. And above these stood the tiny group of a few thousand–the group which Lord David Cecil termed 'the governing class' of his grandfather's day. By mid-century the proportion of manual workers had fallen below two-thirds and since then it has fallen still further to roughly a half. So the first impression is of a gradual movement away from what might be called a proletarian society: and this transformation has been gathering pace in recent decades.

By 1971, as John Goldthorpe and Catriona Llewellyn have described it,[5] the occupational structure was more differentiated and more balanced. In the middle there were now three main blocks of comparable size, each accounting for one-fifth to one-quarter of the total. There were first the semi-skilled manual workers, second the skilled manual workers, and third the clerical and sales workers. Flanking these three groups were three other small groups, each between 7 per cent and 15 per cent of the total–on the one side the unskilled workers, and on the other the professional and technical workers and the administrative, managerial, and supervisory staff.

These twentieth century shifts of occupational structure, from the shape of a pyramid to that of an electric light bulb, are characteristic of advanced industrial societies in general. They are shown for Britain in Table 1, which was constructed by Goldthorpe and Llewellyn. Behind them lies economic transformation: from small to large scale; from manufacturing to so-called tertiary sector activity; from personal dealing to bureaucracy; from handling things to manipulating words and numbers; and from private to public organizations.

Some sociologists interpret these trends as involving the development of a middle mass of technical and clerical employees with a consequent decline of class antagonisms, and with the spectre of polarized capitalist society in retreat.[6] But before drawing such inferences about Britain, it is prudent to notice what is perhaps the outstanding feature of occupational change, namely the growth of women's employment outside the home. Male and female involvement in the economy have run different courses over the period

Table 1.[1] Distribution of economically active population by occupational category in, Great Britain, 1911-71, males (M) and females (F) shown separately.

Standardised census occupational category	1911 M	1911 F	1921 M	1921 F	1931 M	1931 F	1951 M	1951 F	1961 M	1961 F	1971 M	1971 F
					percentage by column							
Self-employed and higher-grade salaried professionals	1.5a	1.0a	1.6	0.9	1.7	1.0	2.8	1.0	4.5b	1.1b	6.1	1.4
Employers and proprietors	7.7	4.3	7.7	4.7	7.6	4.4	5.7	3.2	4.8c	3.0c	5.2	2.9
Administrators and managers	3.9	2.3	4.3	2.1	4.5	1.6	6.8	2.7	7.5c	2.6c	9.9	3.3
Lower-grade salaried professionals and technicians	1.4a	5.8a	1.8	6.3	1.8	6.0	3.0	7.9	4.0b	9.2b	5.5	10.8
Inspectors, supervisors and foremen[d]	1.8	0.2	1.9	0.3	2.0	0.4	3.3	1.1	3.8	0.9	4.5	1.2
Clerical workers	5.1	3.3	5.1	9.8	5.1	10.3	6.0	20.3	6.5	25.5	6.1	28.0
Sales personnel and shop assistants[e]	5.0	6.4	4.1	7.5	5.9	8.2	4.0	9.6	3.9	10.0	3.9	9.4
Skilled manual workers (inc. self-employed artisans)	33.0	24.6	32.3	20.3	30.1	19.2	30.3	12.7	32.3	10.8	29.4	9.3
Semi-skilled manual workers[f]	29.1	47.0	24.5	40.0	23.4	41.4	24.3	33.6	22.8	30.9	21.2	27.3
Unskilled manual workers[f]	11.5	5.1	16.7	8.1	17.9	7.5	13.8	7.9	9.9	6.0	8.2	6.4
Total active population (Thousands)	12,926	5,424	13,635	5,698	14,760	6,263	15,584	6,930	15,992	7,649	15,609	8,762

[1] This table was constructed by J. H. Goldthorpe and Catriona Llewellyn.

Notes

(a) Divided according to 1921 ratios. (The 1911 census did not distinguish between self-employed and salaried professionals.)

(b) Divided on the assumption of a linear trend in the ratios from 1951-1966 (sample census).

$$\frac{\times 61}{\text{Total } 61} = \frac{\times 51}{\text{Total } 51} \times \frac{\times 66}{\text{Total } 66} + \frac{2}{3} = \frac{\times 51}{\text{Total } 51}$$

(The 1961 Census did not distinguish between Self-employed and Salaried professionals.)

(c) Numbers in Groups 3 and 4 divided according to a ratio arrived at by plotting trend lines for these groups from 1951 to 1961, i.e. $P_{61} = P_{51} + \frac{2}{3}(P_{66} - P_{51})$. (The 1961 Census did not distinguish between Employers and Managers).

(d) Of manual workers.

(e) Includes supervisory personnel and also a small number of self-employed workers.

(f) Includes self-employed workers.

Sources:

The basic source is the Occupational Tables of the Censuses of Population for England and Wales and Scotland. We have, however, drawn to a large extent on the re-working of Census data by earlier investigators although modifying their procedures somewhat, and correcting what appear to be several minor errors. In various respects, therefore, our figures differ from those of our predecessors where they might appear comparable, but not to any very significant degree.

For 1911 to 1951 we began with the work of Guy Routh, *Occupation and Pay in Great Britain, 1906-60* (Cambridge University Press, 1965), Table 1, pp. 4-5, taken together with the further information provided in Appendix A. pp. 155-7.

For 1961 we have drawn on the work of G. S. Bain, *The Growth of White Collar Unionism*, (Oxford, 1970), Table 2A. 1, p. 191; and of Bain, Robert Bacon, and John Pimlott, 'The Labour Force' in A. H. Halsey (ed.), *Trends in British Society since 1900*, (Macmillan, 1972), Tables 4.1 and 4.5, pp. 113-4.

we are considering. As may be seen from Table 1, in 1911 both sexes were divided between manual and non-manual jobs three-quarters to one-quarter. Subsequently, the female labour force has both grown and shifted substantially into non-manual work, so that by the 1970s three-fifths of the employed women were non-manual while three-fifths of the men were still manual workers. And even the small shift to non-manual jobs among men has mostly taken place since the Second World War. What is more important about it is that the increasing numbers of higher-level professional and managerial positions have largely gone to men, while women have filled the even faster expanding array of lower white-collar jobs.

Thus, if we attach relatively greater importance from the point of view of class formation to the pattern of male employment–and this makes sense because the class, status, party, and other group affiliations of families have been principally determined by the occupational position of husbands and fathers–then the changes have been quite undramatic. The one significant change is the expansion of the professional and managerial stratum. Ralph Dahrendorf calls this the 'service class', those who provide a bridge between the rulers and the mass of the people by acting as the agents of public and private authorities.[7] In this same view the burgeoning middle mass is largely female. We know little about its impact, if any, on the degree of class polarization in Britain.

So much for a preliminary view of stratification using a simple conception of class. Now let us look at collective prosperity. At the outset, the reader should be warned against taking official estimates of the national income or the gross national product–those modern talismans of national virility–as ultimate measures of the wealth of a nation. They are the gifts of bureaucracy rather than social science. These economists' sums tell us roughly what are the products of the *occupational* division of labour: but there is a larger *social* division of labour which includes the exchanges in families, and the services of the Samaritans, as well as the fiddles unrecorded by the Inland Revenue. There is, in short, another economy of vast dimension. It was, for example, only by the fiat of the Victorian economist Alfred Marshall, that the paid labour of charwomen is counted as part of the national product, while the work of housewives is not.[8] If we were to reckon the whole output of the social division of labour it is most likely that our sterling numbers would be more than doubled. Nevertheless, if we assume that output from the two economies are in less than completely inverse relation, the official figures can be used to indicate trends. They tell us that since 1900 the United Kingdom has at least tripled its gross national product in real terms.[9]

In any case, there is general agreement that British levels of living have risen throughout the century... Yet inequality persists after a long period of economic growth. From this point of view the picture of prosperity looks very different. The assumption of growing affluence is not beyond question. The old poverties of lack of property, low pay, poor health, inadequate education, and bad housing still disfigure, and many would say disgrace, the powerful engine of production which we call industrial society...

[The registered unemployed are] heavily concentrated in the working class and within that class among the young, the old, the sick, and the disabled. Over five million Britons depend on the Supplementary Benefits Commission. In other words, over five million are living in the government's own estimate of the poverty line. And there are more below it who do not claim their due.

How, then, are income and wealth shared among the population? Let us begin with two relatively simple statistics. In Britain now the richest 1 per cent still own one-fifth and perhaps as much as one-quarter of all personal wealth.[10] Income is less unequally distributed, but here again recent official estimates show that, in 1976-7, the richest 1 per cent took home about the same amount as the poorest 20 per cent.[11] They each had, in other words, more than twenty times as much income. These are quite spectacular inequalities.

The trend over the past fifty years has been one of slow and unsteady progress towards a more equal distribution of personal income. By the early 1970s the top 10 per cent of income receivers were taking about one-quarter of total income, and this one-quarter share was also the amount being taken by the bottom half of income receivers. If we look at non-manual earnings a trend towards decreasing inequality is also to be seen. That trend can be traced at least as far back as the 1920s and it is still going on. Between 1970 and 1978 the ratio of non-manual to manual earnings fell from 1.32 to 1.25.

The trends in distribution of income from 1959 [are outlined in] Report No. 5 of the Royal Commission on the Distribution of Income and Wealth.[12] The Commission summarizes them as follows:

Over the whole of the period from 1959 to 1974/5, the share of the top 1 per cent has declined continuously: the share of the next 2-5 per cent has declined but not continuously; the share of the 6-10 per cent group has shown little change. The share of the top 10 per cent as a whole in the before tax distribution has fallen from 29.4 per cent of total income in 1959 to 28.0 per cent in 1967 and to 26.6 per cent in 1974-5. Over the same period (1959 to 1974-5) the share of the top 1 per cent has fallen from 8.4 to 6.2 per cent of total income. The decline in the income share of the top 10 per cent as a whole is balanced by a corresponding increase in the overall share of the remaining 90 per cent, within which only one decile–61-70 per cent–did not increase. Approximately three-fifths of this increase accrued to the remaining 40 per cent of tax units in the top half of the distribution. Their share increased from 47.5 per cent to 49.2 per cent of total income between 1959 and 1974-5 while, over the same period, the share of the bottom 50 per cent of tax units increased from 23.1 per cent to 24.2 per cent of total income.

More recent figures for 1976-7 show only marginal changes in the distribution, though a continuing decline to 5.5 per cent in the share of the top 1 per cent. But we have yet to consider the redistributive activity of the State. The impact of taxes and transfers is a complicated one and much debated. It operates, as R. M. Titmuss pointed out,[13] through three loosely related systems of state intervention–fiscal policy, the social services, and occupational welfare. Essentially these political interventions can only be understood as collective action to change the unacceptable outcome of market exchanges: and that means the outcome of class... Social policy itself has been powerfully shaped by class. For example, the fiscal system has been no simple extension of progressive taxation from its introduction in 1907. By 1976/7 before tax the richest 10 per cent took 26.2 per cent of income, and this was reduced to 23.1 per cent by taxation. At the lower end, the poorest 10 per cent took 2.5 per cent before tax, and this was increased to 3.0 per cent after tax.[14] These figures can scarcely be interpreted as evidence of a hugely redistributive 'welfare' state. Welfare, it would appear, is largely self-financed for the bulk of the population. The activity of the state makes for no dramatic reduction of market inequalities.

Similarly, the social services are not to be thought of as a steady development of 'class abatement' through politics. In education, for example, throughout the twentieth century, a policy of expansion has been frequently justified as a means to equality of opportunity. But in spite of a slight tendency to more equal investment in the school education of children from different classes, the

development of further education more than counter-balanced
this equalizing effect because it was concentrated on middle-class
children. If we compare boys born between 1913 and 1922 with
those born between 1943 and 1952 (and standardize the figures by
putting them into 1958 prices), it turns out that the average son of
a professional or managerial family had seven times as much spent
on him as the son of an agricultural labourer in the earlier period,
and six times as much in the later period. A comparison of these
First War and Second War children in absolute terms shows that
the average professional son got an extra £566 a year for education
after school, and the agricultural labourer's son an extra £103 a
year as a result of the intervening expansion of educational opportunity.

Again, the third system of occupational welfare is more of a
complement than a counterweight to class inequality. Occupational pensions are earnings-related. Sick pay and pension arrangements are better for non-manual than for manual workers.
And there has been a considerable growth of tax-deductable fringe
benefits since the war with the effect of increasing inequality between highly paid executives and the rest.

In the argument up to this point we have documented continuing, if slowly decreasing, income differences: and we have shown
that they are related to class. But the more challenging task is to
explain them. For orthodox Marxists the distribution of capital is
crucial: it fundamentally defines the class structure. Professor
Westergaard and Miss Resler, who have produced a voluminously
and soberly argued empirical account from the Marxist standpoint, conclude that it was the exceptional circumstances of war
which produced lasting effects on the contrasts in income and
wealth. They insist, however, that the two wars

formed no part of a continuous trend toward equalization, and that they
entailed only modest redistribution... Disparities may indeed have widened since the 1950s. They certainly did not narrow significantly, from the
early 1950s to the early 1970s under governments of either political
shade.[15]

Moreover, these authors find the root cause of continuing inequality in the condition of property-less labour of most people:
and this in turn they attribute primarily to the concentration of
property ownership. 'It is for that reason above all,' they argue,
that capitalism can make no claim to a steadily more equal spread
of wealth. Inequality is entrenched in its institutional structure.'[16]

Liberal theorists, for their part, do not deny the inequality of distribution of personal wealth. But they do not accept the importance that Marxists attach to it, and would contest the further Marxist theory that status and power in society are derived from it. Instead, they begin by arguing the significance of trends towards a more equal spread of both wealth and income. Argument about the exact measure of the distributions themselves is relatively unimportant. The various authorities would agree that the proportion of personal wealth held by the richest 1 per cent of the population before the First World War was about 70 per cent. By the mid 1930s it was reduced to 56 per cent, and by 1960 to 42 per cent. Subsequent official figures are on a slightly different basis. They show the percentage held by the top 1 percent of people as moving down from 37 per cent in 1962, to 24 per cent in 1977. At first glance, then, these figures would appear to contradict Westergaard and Resler, and to show a strong and steady trend towards equality. But essentially Westergaard is right because the redistribution has very largely been a spread of wealth to the richest 5 per cent instead of 1 per cent, and much of it reflects arrangements for gifts *inter vivos*–gifts between the living as distinct from those bequeathed at death. In this way rich families have passed on their wealth and legally avoided tax.

The technicalities leave room for further arguments about the exact degree of concentration of private wealth and its long-run trends. But if following R. H. Tawney, we distinguish between property for power, by which I mean property that carries with it control over the lives of other people, and property for use, possessions that free a man from other people's control, then we can reasonably say that, throughout the period we can collectively remember, three-quarters of the British have been virtually propertyless in that area which covers the central part of life and occupations–how men and women earn a living and how they relate themselves most fully and creatively to their fellows. A tiny minority has monopolized wealth, and an even tinier minority of that minority has monopolized property for power.

At the same time, of course harking back to the fact of rising affluence, we should not ignore the social significance of the spread of property for use. Most of the under-40s take a wide range of amenities and consumer durables for granted. Only the over-40s remember those primitive instruments of washing day–the poss-stick and the dolly-tub.

To sum up a formidable ledger of evidence, we can say that distributions through the capital and labour markets were dramatically unequal at the opening of the century. Wealth, part of which is property for power, was always more unequally spread than income. And both distributions have remained unequal around a rising average level. Over and above such wealth for use as housing and personal possessions, property for power still has a most impressively unequal distribution. But the trend to a relatively more equal sharing of income has increasingly dominated the structure of inequality as a whole because the labour market distributes much more income than does the capital market. In 1976 income from employment accounted for well over two-thirds of all income. The self-employed accounted for less than one-tenth, and so did unearned income from rent, dividends, and interest payments. On the evidence so far, then, the problem is to decide whether to attach more importance to the remaining inequality, or to the expanded material freedom which has attended the rising norm. The judgement will turn on whether one is impressed by absolute or by relative riches.

In either case, we have still not fully explained the inequality of a rich society. The question of how it has survived can again be put in class terms by quoting what J. B. Priestley had to say on his journey through England in 1933, when he came to Jarrow–a wholly working-class town.

Wherever we went there were men hanging about, not scores of them but hundreds and thousands of them. The whole town looked as if it had entered a perpetual penniless bleak Sabbath. The men wore the masks of prisoners of war. A stranger from a distant civilization, observing the condition of the place and its people, would have arrived at once at the conclusion that Jarrow had deeply offended some celestial emperor of the island and was now being punished. He would never believe us if we told him that in theory this town was as good as any other and that its inhabitants were not criminals, but citizens with votes.[17]

Jarrow provides one example of the remarkable absence of resentment against class inequality. In an attempt to explain this feature of British society, W. G. Runciman has put forward the theory of relative deprivation.[18] On this theory, satisfaction or resentment is not a function of inequality as documented by economists, but of a man's assessment of his position relative to other people with whom he compares himself. In Runciman's view the period from the end of the First World War up to 1962, against a background of trends towards the equalization of class, status, and power in Britain, working-class status resentment increased, and class resentment fluctuated, but at a remarkably low level. Working men compared their lot with other people in the working class and not with non-manual groups, who, incidentally, were just as likely to feel deprived despite their objective advantages. In the decades before 1962 there was seldom a close correlation between class inequality and resentment of it. Both World Wars raised expectations and lifted the horizons of working-class people. But the egalitarian hopes thus engendered receded in both post-war periods. The economic depression of the 1930s inhibited comparisons between manual wages and white-collar salaries. After the Second World War there was widespread belief that a programme of class redistribution was taking place when in fact it was not. Runciman's 1962 survey showed that resentment was still low among working men and their wives because they compared themselves, in the traditional way, with those near to them in the factory and the neighbourhood. They did not compare themselves with barristers, or the residents of Mayfair. Relative deprivation was in fact more likely to be felt by middle-class than by working-class people.

Repeating the survey thirteen years later in 1975, W. W. Daniel found that the same patterns of restricted social horizons of comparison were still present.[19] Several years of serious inflation and still more years of high publicity to pay claims and incomes policy, had not significantly altered them. Most importantly, the more recent survey showed that people cared not so much about how other people were getting on as about how they saw their own financial position this year compared with last year. It seems that government policy for 'gentling the masses' is more likely to be successful if it looks to economic growth for all, rather than to redistribution between unequally placed groups.

So far, then, we have explained the continuing inequality of a rich society mainly in terms of the slow growth of prosperity and the limited social horizons of the relatively poor. This explanation, however, still leaves open the question of whether we can properly call the inequalities we have found class inequalities. If we follow post-Marxist and liberal theorists and define class in terms of occupational structure rather than capital ownership and if, further, we treat the family rather than the individuals as the unit of the class system, we shall have to recognize that many inequalities are of status rather than of class-those between men and women, or between older and younger people, or between ethnic groups. For example, if we take the average earnings of all white males to be 100, the comparable figure for coloured men is 88. Nor is this inequality of earnings between ethnic groups to be explained in class terms. Within classes the differentials are still to be found except among the lower paid groups of semi-skilled and unskilled workers and personal service workers.[20]

Class, we may conclude, remains fundamental to stratification in Britain but it does not tell us the whole story.

Notes

1 This division of social organization derives from Max Weber. See H. Gerth and G. W. Mills, *Essays from Max Weber,* Kegan Paul, 1948, pp. 180-95. See also J. H. Goldthorpe and P. Bevan, 'The Study of Social Stratification in Great Britain 1946-76', *Social Science Information,* 1977, Vol. 16 (3/4), pp. 279-334.

2 See F. Parkin, *Class Inequality and Political Order,* Paladin, 1972 (first published by MacGibbon and Kee, 1971).

3 R. Dahrendorf, *Class and Class Conflict in Industrial Society,* Routledge and Kegan Paul, 1959.

4 For example, the Oxford Mobility Study, discussed briefly in Chapter 3 and more extensively in Chapter 6 below, has made a 36 and a 7-fold classification based on J. H. Goldthorpe and K. Hope, *The Social Grading of Occupations: A New Approach and Scale,* Oxford University Press, 1974. Note is also made below of the Registrar General's classification of five social classes (with a further division of Class III into its non-manual and manual components).

5 J. H. Goldthorpe and C. Llewellyn in their 'Class mobility in Britain: three theses examined', *Sociology,* Vol. 11, No. 2, pp. 257-87, May 1977. Table 2.1 is reproduced from this source.

6 See, for example, Daniel Bell, *The Goming of Post-Industrial Society,* Basic Books, Inc., 1973, Chapter 2.

7 R. Dahrendorf, 'Recent Changes in the Class Structure of European Societies', *Daedalus,* Winter, 1964, pp. 225-70.

8 Cf. Colin Clark, 'The Economics of Housework', *Bulletin of Oxford Institute of Statistics,* Vol. 20 (2), May 1955, pp. 205-11.

9 For details and guidance through the difficulties of measurement see A. H. Halsey, *Trends in British Society Since 1900,* Macmillan, 1972; and for later figures see *Social Trends,* a publication of the Government Statistical Service which is an invaluable source of material data on British social structures.

10 See *Social Trends,* No. 10, 1979, Table 6-30.

11 J. Westergaard and H. Resler, *Class in a Capitalist Society: A Study of Contemporary Britain,* Heinemann, 1975, p. 43, use a figure of 30 per cent rather than 20 per cent. They are referring to 1960.

12 *Royal Commission on the Distribution of Income and Wealth,* Report No 5 (Third Report on the Standing Reference). Cmnd 6999, London, H.M.S.O., 1977.

13 See R. M. Titmuss, *Essays on the Welfare State,* Unwin University Books, 1958, pp. 34-55.

14 *Social Trends,* No. 10, 1979, Table 6.19.

15 Westergaard and Resler, op. cit., p. 118.

16 Ibid., p. 119.

17 J. B. Priestley, *English Journey,* Heinemannn, 1934. Penguin edition, 1977. p. 296

18 W. G. Runciman, *Relative Deprivation and Social Justice,* Routledge and Kegan Paul, 1966. Runciman uses the word power to mean what I refer to as party.

19 W. W. Daniel, *The P.E.P. Survey on Inflation,* P.E.P. Broadsheet 553, July 1975.

20 *Social Trends,* No. 8, 1977, Table 5.10.

1.3   *A. H. Birch*

Theories of political crisis

From 'Overload, ungovernability and delegitimation: the theories and the British case', *British Journal of Political Science, Vol.14, No.2, 1984, pp. 135—60.*

The concept of 'overload' was introduced into the vocabulary of political science in 1975, in two publications which appeared almost simultaneously in the United States and Britain. One was by Michel Crozier in a 'report on the governability of democracies' entitled *The Crisis of Democracy;*[1] the other by Anthony King in *Political Studies.*[2] Both authors took the same general line: that there had been a rapid growth in public expectations about what benefits could be provided by government in Western democracies, that many of these expectations had inevitably been disappointed, and that the result was a serious decline of public confidence in government... It was suggested by King that this development had made Britain more difficult to govern and by Crozier, more generally, that Western democracies might be moving towards a condition of ungovernability.

These publications drew attention to the issues in a succinct manner... However, neither King nor Crozier has written about the problems in length. For theories about how and why the phenomena to which they gave the label of 'overload' have developed, and what their consequences are likely to be, we must look to three other groups of writers, who did not always use the term themselves. The first is the group of American writers who have come to be known as the neo—conservatives, the second is a group of liberal economists [and] the third is a group of neo—Marxist writers... The primary object of this paper is to outline and criticize the contributions of these three groups of theorists... A second object is to examine some aspects of recent British politics in terms of the theories, to see how far they illuminate British experience.

1:   The theories reviewed

The neo—conservatives

The basic position of all writers in this school is that the liberal
policies followed in the United States since 1960 have, in Lipset's
words, 'frequently created more problems than they have solv-
ed.'[3] They have encouraged people to have excessive ideas about
their 'rights' and to attach far too much importance to equality.
Moreover, they have weakened the traditional ties of family and
community, leaving people dependent upon help from government agencies. The enlarged role of the state has placed too much
strain on political institutions and has led to a withdrawal of confidence in them which weakens the whole democratic system...

Beyond this, there are several main themes in the literature
(now very large) which are found in various permutations and
combinations, and may be summarized briefly. First, Daniel Bell
(displaying once again his ability to coin a slogan) has written
about the 'cultural contradictions of capitalism'.[4] We are told that
the emphasis on acquisition has been transmuted into hedonism.
The Protestant ethic has given way to the consumer society...

Secondly, Kristol, Moynihan and others have complained about
the growth of a 'new class' of social workers, bureaucrats and intellectual consultants, who are said to have a large influence on national policy and a personal commitment to expanding the role of
government...[5] The people who shape opinion and advise governments are said to be disproportionately liberal in their policy preferences.

Thirdly, Bell and Huntington have said that the growth of
expectations and the accompanying development of sectional demands have led to constant group conflict and battles over every
budget, together with a decline in support for political parties and
the executive agencies of government. There is too much articulation through single—issue pressure groups, but not enough aggregation by political institutions and parties... Huntington calls
these developments 'the democratic distemper',[6] and maintains
that an aspect or consequence of them is a withdrawal of public
confidence from politicians and the political system.

Fourthly, Kristol has pointed out that those younger Americans
who dislike the values of the consumer society have not returned
to the older virtues, but have instead embraced a new form of

morality which undermines the values necessary to the successful working of the capitalist system.[7]

The assumptions of this group of writers can be described as individualistic and voluntaristic. The implication of the propagandist flavour of their work is that the regrettable developments they describe need not have taken place and could yet be put into reverse by a combination of wise leadership and changes in individual values...

How much importance should be attached to this body of writing? As political propaganda, it is always urbane and intermittently persuasive... However, its wider generalizations are more dubious. For one thing, it is just not clear that the United States has experienced an expansion of governmental activities sufficient to justify expressions of alarm by academics, as distinct from expressions of regret by politicians. In comparative terms, it is remarkable as the only advanced industrial state which accepts no general governmental responsibility for health services. In fiscal terms, it has suffered relatively little from overload. Usher's statistics show that between 1960 and 1978 government expenditures in the United States increased from 30 per cent of GNP to 33 per cent, whereas the equivalent proportions in Canada rose from 30 per cent to 42 per cent, and in the United Kingdom from 40 per cent to 50 per cent.[8]

Another problem about this literature is a certain looseness of logic in the arguments adduced to demonstrate the deleterious effects of the various developments mentioned on the American capitalist and democratic systems. Thus, it is historically true that American social values are less puritanical than in the past, but the relationship of this development to economic performance is a very complex and difficult question to answer. The difficulties are enhanced by the fact that American economic growth in the post—war period, while not very different from the rate of growth in the first forty years of the century, has been significantly slower than that of less puritanical societies like France and Italy...

Again, it is entirely reasonable for commentators to express concern that the processes of representative government may be distorted by the growth of populist single—issue pressure groups. But if this is to go beyond concern and become a theory with predictive value about the future of American democracy, it has to be established that the development is a secular trend rather than a passing phase, and that it undermines democratic procedures and

values. These points have not been established. The new groups
are not without precedent. The moralistic fervour of the Right to
Life Movement is doubtless worrying, but it is not very different
from that of the Anti – Saloon League, and has not yet been so influential. The old elitist and sectional groups continue to
operate...

The apparent decay of the US party system is certainly serious,
for parties are needed to achieve consistency in policy outputs and
responsibility to the general electorate. But the casual relationships between this development and the other developments have
not been made clear by neo – conservative theorists... There is no
evidence that the apparent decline in public esteem for the institutions of national government is related to either the decay of the
party system or the expansion of government activities... Nor does
this decline necessarily undermine political authority, unless
authority is defined simply in terms of esteem.

For all these reasons, the explanatory power of neo – conservative theories is limited. They have identified several trends in
American politics which appear to comprise a syndrome, and
which collectively give valid cause for concern. But they have not
established the relationships between these trends with the clarity
that is needed if their theories are to have predictive value, let
alone if they are to comprise a model of democratic decline in the
Western world.

The liberal economists
In this context the most important of the liberal economists is
Samuel Brittan, whose seminal paper of 1974 opened with the fol-
lowing words:

The conjecture to be dicussed in this paper is that liberal representative democracy suffers from internal contradictions, which are
likely to increase in time, and that, on present indications, the
system is likely to pass away within the lifetime of people now
adult. This idea has now become commonplace; and any interest it
has must lie in the supporting argument.[9]

The supporting arguments put by Brittan consisted of an extension and modification of the arguments advanced by Joseph
Schumpeter in 1942...[10] [Schumpeter believed] that state enterprises in a democracy should be kept free of party politics, on the
lines of the BBC in Britain. Brittan argues that in the long run the

competition for votes and power in a liberal representative democracy will inevitably lead politicians to bring state enterprises into the bidding. The consequence of this is that groups of workers will realize that governmental decisions can affect their livelihood in the most direct way, and as more and more enterprises are brought within the scope of party politics, so more and more expectations will be generated about the benefits government can provide. Many of these will inevitably be disappointed.

Another of Schumpeter's conditions [for successful democracy] was what he called 'democratic self – control'.[11] People must not make excessive demands on their leaders and must not try to control politicians directly, between elections. Brittan argues that restraint in making demands cannot be expected, because the advantages to be gained from specific concessions will benefit groups of citizens directly whereas the advantages of restraint are 'public goods' such as price stability or faster economic growth, 'which are thinly diffused amongst the whole population'.[12] Moreover, the competition for votes will undermine the sense of restraint that might be expected of political leaders. 'The temptation to encourage false expectations among the electorate becomes overwhelming to politicians. The opposition parties are bound to promise to do better and the government party must join in the auction'.[13]

When unrestrained demands by voters and pressure groups go along with competitive bidding for votes by politicians, the combination endangers sound economic policy – making. The problem is likely to be exacerbated by the readiness of sectional groups possessing economic power, notably trade unions, to employ it for political ends. The predictable consequence is said to be uncontrolled inflation, which undermines the social stability necessary to the maintenance of the democratic system... [For Brittan] the decay of democracy could be averted if there were a general change in values, in the form of either 'a genuine revulsion against materialism'[14] or a retreat from egalitarianism. Unlike Bell and Kristol, Brittan welcomes the development of post – industrial values, on the ground that their spread would reduce the competitive pressures under which democratic systems are beginning to break. His liberal and individualistic assumptions apparently exclude any suggestion that people (or their political and union representatives) might become more public – spirited, willing to forgo individual advantage for the interests of the community. He therefore has to pin his hopes on the possibility of changes in individual aspirations...

The vulnerable point of the Brittan thesis is that it does not show that liberal democracy is self – destructive except in so far as it generates rapid inflation, and [it does] not show that it generates rapid inflation except in special conditions that are not created simply by individual motivations. It may possibly be true as a generalization that individual workers tend to be self – seeking and short – sighted in regard to wage levels and related issues, but it does not follow that the organizations through which their demands are channelled will necessarily reflect and embrace these attitudes. How trade unions behave depends on their strength, their internal structure, their leadership, their relations with management and the legal and institutional framework within which they press their claims. It would be quite misleading to predict their behaviour by aggregating the individual preferences of their members. And the institutional factors involved are contingent and local rather than inevitable and universal.

I would say that liberal democracy is under pressure to generate rapid inflation if its governments are confronted by trade unions which are simultaneously powerful, legally privileged, controlled by militant leaders, and short – sighted in regard to the effects of their behaviour on the economy. Whether this situation will obtain depends on the state of industrial relations rather than on the extent of democracy. The situation obtained in Britain between 1971 and 1979, but it does not follow that all liberal democracies will have similar problems... There are no good grounds for generalizing from the British experience of the 1970s, and there is no reason to accept Brittan's view that there is a general democratic disease which 'has simply progressed further in Britain than in the United States or in continental Europe'.[15]...

Neo – Marxist contributions

The first basic proposition is that in Western industrial societies the capitalist system is (for a time) legitimized in the eyes of workers by the liberal – democratic state. In the words of Claus Offe, this process of legitimation can be defined as one by which 'the capitalist state manages, through a variety of institutional mechanisms, to convey the image of an organization of power that pursues common and general interests of society as a whole, allows equal access to power, and is responsive to justified demands'.[16] This image disguises the dominant role of the capitalist class in society and in the formation of state policy, but it would be an over – simplification in the modern age to regard the state as no more than an agent of that class. It would be more accurate to say that the advanced capitalist state, in its democratic form, has a relative autonomy from the capitalist class.

A second proposition is that within this kind of state the political values of the capitalist class enjoy what Gramsci called an 'ideological hegemony', so that they both set out the main terms of political debate and indicate the channels and limits within which political conflict is normally confined. Nicos Poulantzas put the point in the following terms: 'The dominance of this ideology is shown by the fact that the dominated classes live their conditions of political existence through the forms of dominant political discourse: this means that often they live *even their revolt* against the domination of the system within the frame of reference of the dominant ideology'.[17]

A third point is that the liberal – democratic state adopts various policies and tactics to protect both its own legitimacy and that of the social order. An essential policy is to develop welfare services so as to shelter disadvantaged groups from the inevitable hardships resulting from the operations of capitalism. A protective tactic is for the state to ensure that those forms of social conflict which are most likely to upset sizeable groups take place outside the institutions of the state itself. Thus, group conflicts over taxation or import duties are resolved in Parliament but conflicts over wage levels, which upsets the losers much more directly, take place in other arenas. It is true that these conflicts are resolved in a framework of rules which are to some extent determined by the state, but so long as no significant group challenges the rules themselves the state is protected from the wrath of losing groups in the bargaining process. The point is to safeguard the appearance (or illusion) of state neutrality in class conflicts...

Fourthly, it is claimed that in the late capitalist state this whole system of legitimation has begun to break down. A major reason for this is that pressures within the system have led to the extension of social benefits in one form or another to virtually the whole population, which eventually creates a fiscal crisis by overloading the burden of public expenditure... This crisis cannot be dealt with by reducing social expenditures, partly for electoral reasons and partly because any determined move in this direction by a govern-

ment willing to risk an electoral defeat would lead to a withdrawal
of public support from the state that could rightly be called a process of delegitimation, and might destabilize the whole political
system...

In economic terms, the growth of social expenditure puts
pressure on both private consumption and capital accumulation.
The pressure on private consumption leads to inflationary wage
demands. If the demands are granted, and accompanied by a corresponding expansion of the money supply, the resulting inflation
will generate demands for increased social benefits from disadvantaged groups like pensioners. Rapid inflation also reduces the rate
of saving and jeopardizes economic growth, so that a vicious circle
develops, citizens lose confidence in the ability of the
liberal – democratic state to protect their interests, and that state
consequently loses its power to legitimize the capitalist system.

Offe and Habermas agree that the advanced capitalist states are
rapidly approaching this point, but they have somewhat different
views about the significance of various recent developments and
about what may be expected. From Offe's perspective, what is
most significant is the growth of new forms of economic and
political conflict, which are not vertical between classes but hori-
zontal between groups and sections. These may include conflicts
between depressed and relatively prosperous regions of a country,
conflicts between skilled workers and unskilled, conflicts between
young and old, conflicts between ethnic minorities and the dominant community.[18]

At the same time, these and similar conflicts are no longer confined to the channels regarded as legitimate in a liberal – democratic state. Offe does not specify the alternative channels, but it
may be surmised that he is thinking of conflicts in the streets, conflicts on the factory floor and conflicts taking place in private
negotiations about public issues in what are sometimes called the
institutions of the corporate state. And the significance of this development is that the outcomes of these conflicts are apt not to be
regarded as legitimate by the losers or the general public, because
there exists no normative political theory by which they can be
justified.[19]

In Habermas's formulation, the most significant problems are
to be found in the realm of values and motivations rather than in
the direct expression of group conflicts. Habermas is impressed
with the burdens that various recent developments have put on the

ability of the state to take policy decisions that will command general assent. This is obviously a problem in connection with the fiscal and budgeting dilemmas that have been created by the growth of social expenditures. But it is also a problem in connection with several new areas of political decision created by the application of legislative controls or reforms to types of behaviour that were previously unregulated or governed by tradition or settled by the church...[20]

It would seem that [Habermas] is saying that a readiness to accept state decisions on taxes or tariffs or foreign policy as legitimate because they are reached through representative institutions will not necessarily extend to similar decisions on welfare policies or divorce or educational reforms, which will only be accepted as legitimate if they appear justified in terms of some wider set of values in society. If agreement on these wider values does not exist the result will be what Habermas calls a 'motivational crisis', which he defines as a discrepancy between the motives and values required by the political and economic system and those produced by the socio – cultural system.[21] This kind of crisis, partly caused by rigidity in the socio – cultural system, is responsible for the 'sharpening of legitimation difficulties into a legitimation crisis'.[22]

If this argument about new areas of political decision is compared with Offe's point about new channels for the expression of political demands and the resolution of conflicts, it must be said that Offe's argument is more convincing. It is clearly true, as a generalization, that the employment of mass demonstrations, political strikes and similar tactics cannot easily be justified in terms of existing normative theory. It has recently been argued that people should adjust their values to accommodate such types of action,[23] but the evidence suggests that people are slow to do so.[24] The logic of Habermas's argument is not nearly so clear. He does not explain exactly what it is about the issues he mentions that makes it difficult to gain acceptance for a political resolution of them. If these new areas of political decision share certain characteristics which distinguish them from more traditional areas, these characteristics need to be defined.

Moreover, the historical evidence does not seem to support Habermas's viewpoint. State decisions on moral and social questions are not really a novelty: Western democracies experienced fierce arguments in earlier periods about such issues as aid to church schools, religious education in state schools, compulsory education, divorce laws, and the legality of birth control, all of which questions were eventually settled by parliamentary votes...

In his concern about motivations, Habermas also lays a good deal of stress on changing values among the younger generation. Habermas, like the American neo – conservatives, feels that the spread of post – industrial values is undermining the culture appropriate to a capitalist society, though not for the same reason. While the Americans fear that these new values will further erode the work ethic and the habit of personal saving, Habermas thinks that they will increase the difficulty of legitimizing economic inequality. One of the basic problems of capitalist society is how to distribute socially produced wealth inequitably and yet legitimately.[25] If people cease to believe that superior skill and industry justify higher rewards, the problem will be exacerbated. Neither Habermas nor the Americans pay any attention to Brittan's very different point, that the growth of post – industrial values, by reducing the emphasis on material satisfactions, may ease the pressure for inflationary wage increases and thus help to stabilize the system in a period of economic difficulties.

Each of these points is logical in its own context and terms, but to a large extent Brittan's argument cancels out Habermas's. While younger people in the grip of post – industrial values may not think that hard work justifies superior economic rewards, it is difficult to believe that they will feel so strongly about the existence of economic inequality that their protests will destabilize the system...

In summary, this critical review of the main theoretical writings does not yield any simple or sweeping conclusion, such as that one of the main theories is true and the other two are false. It shows that several of the arguments advanced by the theorists are loosely formulated, or limited in their relevance to particular places and periods. However, it also suggests that the writings contain a fair number of hypotheses and speculations that deserve further examination in the light of practical experience.

II: The British case

Britain is a better country than most in which to examine the relevance of these theories to practical politics. It has suffered more than most other countries from the problems of overload. Rose and Peters concluded their analysis of fiscal overload in six industrial countries (Britain, France, West Germany, Italy, Sweden and the United States) by saying: 'Whatever technique is used, Italy, Sweden, and Britain all are facing big troubles now'.[26] Some of their findings may usefully be recalled.

Fiscal overload may be defined as a condition in which the cost of public services grows more quickly than the GNP, to the point at which it takes up more than the increase in national income in a given year, thus causing a decline in private consumption. In various studies, Rose and Peters have shown that the proportion of workers dependent on government employment or contracts in Britain in 1975 (38 per cent) was second only to that in Sweden;[27] that the proportion of the national product devoted to public policy in Britain in the 1970s (49 per cent) was second only to that in Sweden;[28] that private consumption in the years 1951 – 77 fell more often in Britain (in eight out of the twenty – six years) than in any of the other five states;[29] and that British public expectations about their personal prosperity in the forthcoming year were more pessimistic than expectations in any of the other five countries in 1975 and 1976, though not quite so pessimistic as the Italians had become by 1977.[30]

It is not necessary to make sweeping claims about what these figures prove. In the context of the present article, all that need be (and is) claimed is that these statistical indicators, when considered in conjunction with the descriptive evidence provided by Anthony King, establish that Britain is a suitable country for a brief examination of the relevance of the theories under discussion.

A similar claim can be made about ungovernability and delegitimation. As Rose has pointed out, the idea of ungovernability should not be taken literally, for no modern industrial society can survive without government.[31] It is, however, possible to identify indicators of a decline in governmental authority and effectiveness, which may be taken as evidence of a trend towards the delegitimation of a particular regime. First, there may be a measurable decline in public confidence in the regime. Secondly, there may be evidence that people are turning away from the normal channels of representative government, either to press their demands through direct action or to retreat into indifference and evasion of civic responsibilities. Thirdly, political conflict may become violent, leading to a breakdown of public order.

There is evidence of all three trends in Britain. Dennis Kavanagh has examined some of the ample evidence of a decline in public confidence in government...[32] Secondly, there has been a marked increase in direct action of all kinds, accompanied by a readiness to justify it in theoretical terms. Some of it has been inside the law and some of it outside. A 1973 survey showed that 18 per cent of British citizens believed they would be justified in breaking law 'to combat excessive rent, tax, or price increases', while 16 per cent thought it right to break the law 'to further strikes and oppose legal regulation of industrial relations'.[33] Thirdly, there has been an increase in violent conflict, with repeated attacks on the police, culminating in the 1981 riots in twenty – seven urban areas.

There are countries where political authority is weaker and political violence more endemic, Italy being an obvious example among Western industrial societies. But the British evidence gains in significance from the fact that it shows a very recent deterioration from a position that has for long been held up to the world as an example of excellent relations between citizens and their government.

The relevance of theory
A. *Neo – conservative theories* 1. Bell's conjectures about the cultural contradictions of capitalism are difficult to apply. If taken literally, they seem to be of little relevance to contemporary British problems. The Protestant ethic motivated north – country and Scottish entrepreneurs in the early and middle decades of the nineteenth century, but has been of little importance in the twentieth century. It might, of course, be observed that Britain lost its economic leadership of the world in the very period when this ethic was fading, but it would be a bold person who tried to establish a causal connection between these developments...

Perhaps the most positive way of interpreting these conjectures is in the very loose sense (also suggested by Habermas) that success in operating a capitalist system depends partly on non – economic motives, not supplied by the system itself. The spectacular post – war success of Japan and West Germany can then be related to the determination of their peoples to recover from defeat, and the high growth rates of other West European countries can be attributed in some small measure to their experience of German occupation, which produced both a determination to make up for lost years and a greater sense of solidarity between social classes than did Britain's isolation... Looked at in this very loose way, it can be said that Daniel Bell's theories teach us something about the relationship of cultural factors and values to economic performance, and are therefore indirectly relevant to the problems of overload.

2. The hypothesis about the growth of a 'new class' [of government employees and consultants] is also difficult to apply, in part because it has not been formulated in a precise way by neo – conservative theorists. If it is meant that the growth of social services has produced a large number of social workers and civil servants who have a vested interest in the continuance of growth in these areas, this is true, but it is also a truism. I know of no evidence that they have had any more influence on British government policy than other groups of public servants wanting expansion in their departments...

3. Huntington's ideas about the 'democratic distemper' may be partially relevant to Britain. Single – issue pressure groups are numerous in Britain, as in the United States, and in the past two decades they have tended to press their claims with more vigour and militancy than was previously common. However, their impact on the political system has been different. Whereas in the United States they are said to have distorted the representative process and contributed, among other factors, to the decay of the party system, in Britain they have not had these effects. The two main parties have lost members, but the British party system remains healthy. Party discipline in Parliament is less rigid than it was before the 1970s, but the strength of the government has not been seriously undermined by this development.

What has happened is that many single – issue groups have taken to direct action. Demonstrations have been numerous and militant, leading to violent clashes between rival groups and with the police. Squatters, opponents of highway construction, nuclear disarmers, anti – apartheid groups, anti – immigrant groups and others have enlarged the arena of political action. The control and powers of the police have become matters of sharp political controversy. In these ways, the authority of various official agencies has been challenged, and to some (perhaps slight) extent weakened.

B. *The theories of liberal economists* 4. The evidence is mixed and sketchy regarding Brittan's proposition that in the long run politicians in a liberal democracy will be unable to resist the

pressures to use their control of state enterprises for partisan purposes. The eight major enterprises can be placed on a continuum
in this respect. At one end, it seems clear that the BBC, British
Airways and the Gas Board have not been contaminated. The
Steel Board has also acted according to economic criteria. The closure of the smaller and less efficient plants between 1979 and 1983
caused protests, but was made inevitable by the world – wide
surplus of capacity and was partly planned during the life of the
Callaghan Government. The position of the Central Electricity
Generating Board is slightly ambiguous. It was free from con-
tamination until the 1974 Labour Government succumbed to
pressure from the National Union of Mineworkers (henceforth
NUM) to order the Board to build an enormous coal – fired
generating plant in north – east England, not needed as there is
already excess capacity in the generating industry, so as to ensure
jobs for miners over the next twenty years. It seems unlikely that a
Conservative government would have done this, but it was a matter of pressure politics rather than electoral politics, as the mining
constituencies are all safe Labour seats.

Moving along the continuum, the policies of the National Coal
Board, British Leyland and British Rail have been subject to partisan controversy throughout much of their lives as state enterprises...

The general conclusion about Brittan's proposition must
therefore be that British experience provides relatively little support for it. There is no doubt a temptation for politicians to intervene in the running of state enterprises for partisan purposes,
but the British record indicates that in most cases politicians have
been able to resist it.

5. The Brittan argument about the inability of democratic politicians to control inflationary pressures was always limited to Britain
and countries with similar patterns of industrial relations. Its validity even in Britain has now been destroyed by the Conservative
Government's monetary and economic policies and by its decision
to change the law so as to reduce the power of trade unions in
future strikes. This is not to say that the Government should be
given all the credit for the reduction in inflation, which owes a
good deal to the world recession and the reduction in non – oil
commodity prices. The point is that a democratic government has
shown itself willing to do two things which Brittan thought highly
unlikely, if not inconceivable: first, it has been willing to accept

the heavy costs, in terms of bankruptcies and unemployment, of monetary and economic policies designed to reduce inflation; secondly, it has had the courage to curtail the powers of trade unions against the vociferous opposition of union leaders. The result of the June 1983 election suggests that the Conservative Party has suffered very little from these policies in electoral terms, and in these circumstances the Brittan hypothesis must now be discarded.

C. *Neo – Marxist theories* 6. The theories of neo – Marxists are... influenced by shades of the traditional Marxist faith that capitalism is both morally objectionable and doomed to be overthrown. Thus, Habermas bases several of his arguments on the assumption that the inequalities of reward in a capitalist system are unjustifiable and will be resented, without thinking it necessary to produce any justifications for this assumption. Elsewhere Habermas declares, in the middle of his discussion of the relationship of cultural values to the growing legitimation crisis, that this crisis will occur *even if* the state succeeds in organizing a rate of economic growth sufficient to overcome the problems that have led to the recognition of a coming crisis. The reason for this surprising assertion is that this growth would take shape as a function of 'private goals of profit maximization', and 'in the final analysis, *this class structure* is the source of the legitimation deficit'.[34] ... This seems to be a pure piece of Marxist faith which, if accepted, makes the rest of his analysis somewhat superfluous. It is better to ignore it and focus on the detailed arguments...

7. Habermas's thesis about the problems for authority in democratic systems created by the extension of state decisions to new areas of activity has little relevance to Britain. As noted earlier, it is not clear that the areas he mentions (family life, education and moral issues) are actually new to politics, for they were all the subject of poltical conflicts in the nineteenth century. And where new issues are involved the British system has generally been little disturbed by them...

8. Habermas's point about changing values among the young is very interesting. It anticipated Inglehart's work on the same topic and is compatible with Inglehart's findings.[35] How much relevance it has to Britain is unclear. Post – industrial values have gained less hold in Britain than in any of the societies covered by Inglehart's surveys. The contrast with Germany is illuminated by the relative

electoral success of the Greens compared with the abject failure of their British equivalent, the Ecology Party, whose candidates gained only 1.1 per cent of the vote in the constitutencies they contested in the 1979 election.

It may be helpful, however, to consider Inglehart's original hypothesis about changing values without necessarily accepting his elaboration of it. Inglehart's basic proposition was that rapid changes in economic circumstances lead to changes in life – style which in turn produce changes in value systems. Impressed by the changing life – styles of American university students, he related these changes to the development of new, soft, tender – minded value orientations.

Now, as it happens, the life – styles of British university students have changed very little in the post – war period, because the grants on which they depend have not at all kept pace with the general improvements in living standards. In the 1980s, as in the 1950s, students can afford lodging, cheap food, beer, public transport and camping holidays, but can rarely afford good food, wine, cars or hotels. One should not therefore expect radical changes in value systems among students. The groups who have experienced the most radical changes in life – styles in post – war Britain are working – class teenagers who do not go on to further education or training. In the 1950s these young workers were very poor while in the sixties and seventies they became prosperous... The social values of these groups are very different both from those of their parents' generation and from those of the well – educated environmentalists of America and West Germany whom Inglehart and Habermas had in mind.

The very rapid growth of unemployment among unskilled teenagers since 1979 has deprived them of the means to buy the consumer goods that they have come to think essential to their life – styles. Social workers interviewed by the author after the civil disturbances of July 1981 said that these unemployed teenagers could see no moral objection to helping themselves to the gear they had been brought up to expect... The tenuous hold that traditional liberal values now have on unemployed young people in Britain is also illustrated by 1981 polls which showed that 44 per cent of them believed that 'violence to bring about political change can be justified' (with 41 per cent disagreeing and 15 per cent uncertain), that 28 per cent thought the riots of July 1981 were justified, and that 40 per cent thought that 'Commonwealth immigrants should be sent back to where they came from'.[36]

In conclusion

This article has been based on the assumption that hypotheses and speculations about contemporary political developments should be greeted neither with enthusiasm nor with suspicion, as if they were passing fashions, but should rather be treated to the same kind of critical examination that we apply to established theories. It must be admitted that the theories under discussion have not stood up all that well to the examination. Some of them have been shown to be loosely formulated and to have logical weaknesses, while other appear to lack the universal validity that, explicitly or implicitly, has been claimed for them. They are applicable to other countries, but not to Britain, or applicable to Britain in the mid – seventies, but not in the early eighties. They fall considerably short of being scientific propositions, and have only a limited and patchy predictive value... What we have a right to expect from political theories is not predictive value, but explanation value... The main contributions that theorists can make to the explanation (as distinct from the justification or condemnation) of contemporary events are to develop scenarios, to identify syndromes, to publicize their insights about motivation, and to hypothesize about casual relationships. The theorists under review have all made interesting contributions of these kinds, which need not be recapitulated. That some of the hypotheses appear to be refuted by the evidence does not particularly matter. As Popper has pointed out, conjecture and refutation is the main process by which the frontiers of human knowledge are extended.[37] The invalidation of the hypothesis is itself a contribution to understanding.

Turning to contemporary events, it is remarkable that the concept of overload, introduced only in 1975, is now universally accepted. Virtually every government in Western Europe, irrespective of party affiliation, is now attempting to reduce the proportion of national income devoted to public services, or at least to check its growth. Politicians have also become noticeably more cautious about making promises.

The question of ungovernabililty is more open. Clearly Western democracies have become more difficult to govern in the past ten years than they were between 1950 and 1973. Whether the difficulties are greater than they were earlier in the century is another matter... What seems clear, however, is that the capacity of these

regimes for system maintenance is very impressive...
In Britain the capacity for system maintenance is truly
remarkable. In the past ten years, the system has coped with the
prolonged crisis in Northern Ireland, the challenge of Scottish and
Welsh nationalism, the defeat of a government by industrial action, the experience of 25 per cent inflation in twelve months, the
growth of mass unemployment and an unprecedented set of urban
riots. It will probably continue to cope, but it is nevertheless salu-
tary to note that no social scientist predicted the 1981 riots, or can
be sure that similar outbreaks will not recur on a larger scale.

Notes

1 Michael Crozier, Samuel Huntington and Joji Watanuki, *The Crisis
   of Democracy* (New York: New York University Press, 1975).
2 Anthony King, 'Overload: Problems of Governing in the 1970s',
   Political Studies, XXIII (1975), 284 – 96.
3 I. L. Horowitz and S. M. Lipset, *Dialogues on American Politics*
   (New York: Oxford University Press, 1978), p. 46.
4 Daniel Bell, *The Cultural Contradictions of Capitalism* (New York:
   Basic Books, 1976).
5 Irving Kristol, *Two Cheers for Capitalism* (New York: Basic Books,
   1978), pp. 27 – 30.
6 S. P. Huntington. 'The Democratic Distemper', *The Public Interest,*
   XLI (1975), 9 – 38.
7 Kristol, *Two Cheers for Capitalism,* pp. 47 – 9 and 62 – 3.
8 Dan Usher, *The Economic Prerequisite to Democracy* (New York:
   Columbia University Press, 1981), p. 78.
9 Samuel Brittan, 'The Economic Contradictions of Democracy',
   British Journal of Political Science, v (1975), 129 – 59, p. 129.
10 Joseph Schumpeter, *Capitalism, Socialism, and Democracy* (New
   York: Harper, 1942).
11 Schumpeter, *Capitalism, Socialism, and Democracy,* p. 294.
12 Brittan, 'The Economic Contradictions of Democracy', p. 145.
13 Brittan, 'The Economic Contradictions of Democracy', p.140.
14 Brittan, 'The Economic Contradictions of Democracy', p. 157.
15 Samuel Brittan, 'The Economic Tensions of British Democracy', in
   R.E. Tyrell, ed., *The Future that Doesn't Work* (New York:
   Doubleday, 1977), p. 143.
16 Claus Offe, 'The Theory of the Capitalist State and the Problem of
   Policy Formation', in L. N. Lindberg, R. Alford, C. Crouch and C.
   Offe, eds, *Stress and Contradiction in Modern Capitalism* (Lex-
   ington, Mass.: D. C. Health, 1975), p. 127.
17 Nicos Poulantzas, *Political Power and Social Classes* (first in
   Paris, 1968; London: New Left Books and Speed and Ward,
   1973), p. 223.

18 Claus Offe, 'Political Authority and Class Structures', International Journal of Sociology, II (1972), particularly pp. 94 – 105.

19 Claus Offe, 'The Separation of Form and Content in Liberal Democratic Politics', Studies in Political Economy III (1980), pp. 8 – 11.

20 See Jurgen Habermas, 'What Does a Crisis Mean Today? Legiti – mation Problems in Late Capitalism', *Social Research,* XL (1973). 643 – 67, p. 658, and *Legitimation Crisis* (first pub. Frankfurt, 1973; Boston: Beacon Press, 1975), pp. 71 – 2.

21 Habermas, 'What Does a Crisis Mean Today?', p. 660.

22 Habermas, *Legitimation Crisis,* p. 74.

23 See, for instance, S. H. Barnes, M. Kaase and K. R. Allerbeck, *Political Action* (Beverly Hills, Calif.: Sage Publications, 1979).

24 See David Sanders and Eric Tanenbaum, 'Direct Action and Political Culture: The Changing Political Consciousness of the British Public', *European Journal of Political Research,* XI (1983), 45 – 61.

25 See Habermas, *Legitimation Crisis,* p. 20.

26 Richard Rose and Guy Peters. *The Juggernaut of Incrementalism* (Glasgow: University of Strathclyde Studies in Public Policy, No. 24, 1978), p. 33.

27 Richard Rose and Guy Peters, *Can Government Go Bankrupt?* (New York: Basic Books, 1978), p. 258.

28 Rose and Peters, *The Juggernaut of Incrementalism,* p. 19.

29 Rose and Peters, *The Juggernaut of Incrementalism,* p. 14.

30 Rose and Peters, *Can Government Go Bankrupt?.* p. 247 and Richard Rose, ed., *Challenge to Governance* (Beverly Hills: Sage Publications, 1980), p. 162.

31 Richard Rose, *Ungovernability; Is There Fire Behind the Smoke?* Glasgow; University of Strathclyde Studies in Public Policy, No. 16, 1978), p. 1.

32 Dennis Kavanagh, 'Political Culture in Britain: The Decline of the Civic Culture', in Gabriel Almond and Sidney Verba, eds, *The Civic Culture Revisited* (Boston; Little, Brown, 1980.

33 Alan Marsh, *Protest and Political Consciousness* (Beverly Hills: Sage Publications, 1977), p. 53.

34 Habermas, *Legitimation Crisis,* p. 73.

35 See Ronald Inglehart, *The Silent Revolution: Changing Values and Political Styles Among Western Publics* (Princeton, N.J.: Princeton Univeristy Press, 1977).

36 MORI national poll for Granada Television, reported in *Sunday Times,* 6 September 1981.

37 See Karl Popper, *Conjectures and Refutations* (London: Routledge & Kegan Paul, 1963).

Part Two

Political culture and participation

Introduction

The British political system can be characterised as a form of representative democracy: a system in which the public elect representatives to the various institutions of government with the task of expressing their wishes and protecting their interests. This is an idealised model of British politics. It implies that politicians and policy makers are sensitive to public opinion and that the institutions of the State are subordinate to the popular will. In practice the system is much less representative and responsive than this idealised view suggests. As we will see in later readings there are many instances in which the democratic nature of the system seems not to apply. However, the aspiration of the system to be democratic implies that any examination of British politics must consider the nature of public attitudes and opinions and the manner and extent of public involvement.

Examining public attitudes and opinions is fraught with difficulties. There are a great variety of publics with a large range of viewpoints and it is a matter of interpretation as to which public's opinions can be considered important and influential. Opinions and attitudes can also change, sometimes quite dramatically. Moreover it is not clear as to what forces shape opinion; whether they are a manifestation of deeper economic and social factors or simply the product of the persuasive powers of politicians and the media. Studying mass involvement through the analysis of voting may seem an easier task. Nevertheless there is much debate about how to collect and understand information about electoral behaviour. The selections in this section reflect these difficulties of interpretation and method. As in Part 1, all indicate the potentials for and constraints upon change in British politics.

The issue of change in relation to public attitudes towards both the system of politics and the operations of governments is analysed in the first extract by Kavanagh (2.1). He reviews the changes that have taken place in British political culture — which he defines as 'a set of attitudes to political objects' — since the publication in 1963 of the cross—national study by Gabriel Almond and Sidney Verba, *The Civic Culture*. Like many other observers at the time they emphasised the moderate attitudes of those taking part in British politics, the high degree of consensus amongst the population concerning political procedures, and the deference that was shown to rulers. It was argued that these supportive attitudes contributed to the creation of a highly stable and effective political system.

Kavanagh reviews a wide range of evidence drawn from both attitude surveys and from the observation of political activity over the intervening two decades. He shows that there have been important alterations in public attitudes. He postulates that public deference towards political leaders has declined, and he argues that this, coupled with the growth of regional politics and more disruptive styles of political action, implies a weakening of the sense of national community and a fracturing of the consensus about the acceptable procedures of political action. He is cautious, however, when it comes to drawing conclusions about the consequences of these changes for the stability of the political system. He notes that amongst those who are politically competent and active there appear to be far higher levels of ideology and mistrust of government than was the case in the 1960s. Kavanagh argues that where these developments are combined there is an enhanced potential for protest. He concludes that while there is evidence of greater political dissatisfaction, the object of most of this dissatisfaction has been directed against particular governments rather than the system itself. Nevertheless the 'civic culture' is undoubtedly less established than when Almond and Verba undertook their survey.

The question of how attitudes and opinions are formed is touched on in the piece by Dunleavy (2.2). He looks at the influence of the press on the electoral support for the Conservative and Labour parties. Drawing on survey data relevant to the 1983 General Election, he suggests that the political impact of the press is often underestimated. He criticises what he terms the 'liberal orthodoxy' for its contention that the apparent bias of the press in favour of the Conservative Party can be discounted as a major influence on public opinion and voting behaviour. According to this orthodox view the Conservative bias of the press is offset by the more balanced operation of other mass media such as television and radio. While there is a lack of evidence that the Press does have any influence on political attitudes, Dunleavy questions these arguments and by using empirical evidence drawn from the 1983 General Election attempts to show that the influence of the Press on the way in which people vote is much greater than is usually allowed. He contends that press bias may have had some consequences for the decline in Labour support in the 1970s and 1980s.

A broader range of evidence on voting is examined in the contribution by Heath, Jowell and Curtice (2.3). They consider the changes that have taken place in voting behaviour over the 1970s with particular emphasis upon the 1983 General Election. They note two major developments — a fall in support for Labour coupled with a rise in support for the Liberals and, later, the Alliance (Liberal and Social Democratic parties). They go on to examine two of the major accepted explanations for these changes. First the notion that changes in working—class support have contributed to Labour's weakening — the notion of 'class dealignment'. Secondly, the idea that there has been a growth of protest voting from which the Alliance has been the principal beneficiary. In examining these explanations the authors offer a reassessment of the definition of class and conclude that an explanation of Labour weakness and Alliance growth based on the withering away of class support is not tenable. Rather, the class composition of the electorate has itself been changing. So while Labour has been retaining support amongst the working class, as a proportion of the electorate the working class is much smaller. The authors proceed to argue that the Alliance's vote is not wholly one of protest. There are some indications, especially on the evidence of the 1983 poll, that the Alliance vote has begun to firm up around a particular cluster of attitudes and a particular set of electors.

The final extract by Rasmussen (2.4) considers the experience and prospects of women candidates in general elections since 1951. His analysis raises questions as to how and why women have been excluded from most of the formally important positions in the political system. Rasmussen concludes that the fault does not lie with the electorate. Voting figures over the period suggest that there has been no significant public bias against female candidature. Rather, the difficulty is to be found in local selection committees who appear to exhibit a bias against selecting women as candidates for Parliament. Rasmussen's findings suggest that there has been little change in this regard, at least since the 1950s and possibly earlier. Not only does he illustrate the inpenetrability of the British system to new forces, but he also raises questions about the apparent lack of impact of the women's movement at least in the area of Parliamentary candidature.

2.1 *Dennis Kavanagh*

The decline of the 'civic culture'?

From 'Political culture in Great Britain: the decline of the civil culture' in G.. A. Almond and S. Verba (eds.), *The Civic Culture Revisited,* Little Brown, Boston 1981, pp. 124 – 73.

The publication in 1963 of *The Civic Culture* was a signal contribution to the empirical study of political culture and a pioneer effort in cross—national survey research[1]. It was based on the first nationwide academic sample survey of political attitudes in Great Britain and was also the first to examine them in a comparative context...

Britain has of course long been regarded as a model stable democracy, and the qualities of the political culture have often been advanced as a major explanation for the system's stability and effectiveness. Much emphasis has been placed on the pragmatism and moderation of the political elites, the widespread consensus about the political procedures, and the deference to rulers. *The Civic Culture* is an important part of this tradition: it has been regularly cited because it both purveyed these views and also provided empirical evidence to support them. The recent intensification of challenges to many established ideas about the British political system and its political culture, however, makes it appropriate that we should reassess the work at this time...[2]

A nation's political culture is in a constant state of evolution, though the nature and extent of the change are difficult to measure. The difficulty is compounded in the case of *The Civic Culture* because we are dealing with the relatively short period from 1959 to the present. The fact that the label "traditionally modern"is frequently applied to British politics suggests that the culture is a complex mix of values derived from different points in history and that change in the British culture has usually involved the subtle fusion of new and old values. On many values there is, unsurprisingly, much continuity. But the present cultural mix reflects an altered emphasis on such values as deference, limited government, liberty, public participation, Britain's role as a world power, and the symbols of parliament, empire, and national identity.[3]

The political culture is a set of attitudes to political objects. In a study of change the most important dimensions are the affective and evaluative orientations. For purposes of limiting the range of this chapter we shall focus on attitudes to three broad areas, each of which was regarded as salient by Almond and Verba. These are:

1. *The political system and community*.[4] This concerns such questions as how much pride the British take in their system of government. Is it able to generate loyalty apart from its outputs and benefits for citizens? How much attachment is there to a shared British identification? What is the nature of partisanship and ideology? How much trust is there in the government?

2. *Subjective political competence*. This has two aspects. First, how confident is the individual as a *citizen?* How confident is he that he can influence the political parties and election process? How would he go about trying to exercise influence? Does he view the system as being responsive to his demands? Has there been a decline in deference? To what extent has the sense of political competence been taken over by a mood of protest? Second, how confident is he as a *subject?* This deals with such topics as the individual's assessments of the local and central government officials who enforce the laws and regulations.

3. *Support for the political system*. To what extent have changes in satisfaction with outputs and benefits been translated into different levels of allegiance to the system?...

Attitudes toward the system and community

Political pride

The Civic Culture was impressed by the high levels of support among the British population for the political system. The legitimacy of the institutions was not based merely on satisfaction with the outputs... When asked to indicate the features they were most proud of in their country, nearly half the British sample spontaneously mentioned the system of government and political institutions, a proportion higher than that in any other country except the United States. Much other evidence confirmed A. L. Lowells's assessment that 'the typical Englishman believes that his government is incomparably the best in the world.'[5]

More recent evidence, however, suggests that there has been growing dissatisfaction with the way the system works and with the policies it produces. The 'what's wrong with Britain' literature in the early 1960s dealt mainly with the economy and society; now, however, there is more criticism of the political institutions, particularly of the two—party system and the centralization of decisions in London. The large—scale *Attitudes Survey*, conducted for the Royal Commission on the Constitution in 1970, reported 'some general feeling of dissatisfaction' with the 'system of running Britain' and also a widespread feeling for some change.[6] Nearly half (49 percent) favored some change in the arrangements and only 5 percent thought that things could not be improved; this dissatisfaction was widespread regardless of the respondent's political interest, activity, or social background. At the time the commission found the evidence of dissatisfaction difficult to evaluate and thought its task would have been easier 'if public opinion had crystallised a little further.'[7] But political trends and other survey data in succeeding years have, if anything, only confirmed their interpretation.

Unpublished data from the Essex Survey of the 1974 general elections reflects the ambivalent views about parties and politicians. A substantial minority (nearly 30 percent) expressed only negative views (not satisfactory, unhappy, very unhappy), which was a higher proportion than those expressing only positive views. Examination of Gallup Poll ratings also shows a decline in popular satisfaction with party leaders. An index of the leaders' joint popularity may be constructed by combining the percentages of those thinking that both party leaders are handling their jobs well. In the early 1960s the index often exceeded 100 percent; it fell to a record low of 61 percent in 1968 and then hovered around the 75—80 mark until 1974. Comparative surveys also suggest a lower level of political satisfaction in Britain compared to other Western states.[8] In sum, the survey evidence, fragmentary though it is, bears out this sense of dissatisfaction.

A strong consensus on procedures for resolving political differences is characteristic of the British. Agreement on the 'rules of the game' was documented by Robert Putnam in the course of his lengthy, tape—recorded interviews with British MPs (members of Parliament) and Italian *deputati*. He found a high degree of

satisfaction with the system among British MPs, with only a fifth
wishing for substantial changes in the system compared to three – -
quarters of the Italians.[9] There was also agreement on the meaning of democracy as a system resting essentially on competition
between parties. Putnam reasonably concluded that this procedural consensus and the close fit between the realities and ideas in
Britain legitimated the system, among the elite at least, in contrast
to the Italian situation where there was little consensus on the interpretation of democracy. Since 1970, notwithstanding this elite
attachment to the system, there have been a number of constitutional innovations. There has also been intense debate about the
advantages of importing such devices as proportional representation, federalism, and a bill of rights. The innovations may be
regarded as further signs of British adaptability, but there is now
less agreement on what constitute the rules of the political game.

Many social scientists have stressed the role of the British
monarchy in developing a sense of community and allegiance to
authority. According to Shils and Young, for example, the monarchy plays 'a part in the creation and maintenance of moral consensus,'[10] Successive polls have demonstrated that the public reacts
positively to the monarchy, though few regard it as playing an important political role. The queen is viewed as playing a figurehead
or ceremonial role in society... There is some evidence that the
monarchy still adds something to the authority and legitimacy of
the system. A study of attitudes to monarchy found that pro-
monarchists are more likely than antimonarchists to support the
regime and comply with its basic political laws.[11]

Partisanship

Almond and Verba were impressed by the positive nature of
political partisanship in Britain and particularly by how very few
respondents allowed differences over politics to affect personal
relationships. Most voters belong to friendship groups containing
supporters of a party different from one they support, and a
steady majority of voters favor the principle of parties alternating
their control of government.[12] Apart from the issue of Irish Home
Rule in 1914, the differences between the parties have not strained
the fabric of the society of the constitution.

One explanation for this moderate partisanship lies in the kind
of image and appeals the parties have put forward in the postwar

years. There has been a convergence in the social backgrounds of the Labour and Conservative front benches as both have become more meritocratic and middle class. The decline of the work-ing – class element in the Labour cabinets (half of Attlee's postwar cabinet had been manual workers compared to only one in Wilson's 1970 cabinet) was paralleled by a similar erosion of the aristocracy on the Conservative side. *Embourgeoisement* of parliamentarians has meant that Labour MPs are increasingly be-ing drawn from the ranks of the professions and university gra-duates. In the interwar years, 72 percent of Labour MPs were drawn from the working class, in 1945 one – half, and in 1974 only 28 percent.

The weakening of the class basis of party representation was reflected in the electorate's view of politics. Butler and Stokes found that only a fifth of the electorate based their choice of party on class concerns, and that the image of party politics as represent-ing opposed class interest was declining among voters who entered the electorate in the 1960s.[13] Indeed, a growing number of voters saw little to choose between the parties...[14]

The decline in partisanship among voters is associated with a weakening of the class basis of party support and an apparent fall in class consciousness. By October 1974 only one – half the elec-torate identified with the party of its social class (i.e., manual workers for Labour, and nonmanual for Conservative). Ivor Crewe reports a blurring of class and party in the minds of many voters and also a fall from 1970 in the proportion of voters assign-ing themselves to a social class without prompting by the inter-viewer (from 50 percent to 43 percent)... The decline in the electoral importance of class has continued, indeed accelerated, in spite of the return by the main parties in the 1970s to ideological and class – related issues. As the main survey study of the 1974 election comments, 'the electorate was well aware of the return to the politics of class conflict — and did not like it.'[15]

There is some evidence of a greater interest in ideology. Young MPs, for example, are more ideological than their predecessors in terms of possessing a coherent, comprehensive set of beliefs.[16] On the Labour side this has coincided with a tendency for younger, newer MPs to be drawn from more white – collar occupations, particularly the teaching profession. But there is no evidence that this mood has been followed by the voters. Butler and Stokes found that only one – sixth of the electorate meaningfully use the

terms *left* and *right* to describe the parties. A cross – national
survey, asking questions on left/right evaluations of the parties,
found that Britain was markedly less ideological than West Germany, Austria, the Netherlands, and the United States.[17]

Trust
We lack good evidence of trust in the British system of government which, on the surface, is a good indicator of diffuse support.
It is also particularly difficult to talk with any confidence about the
extent or nature of any change in this area. Some of Almond and
Verba's unreported data showed a larger degree of cynicism
toward British politicians in 1959.[18] A more recent survey confirmed this skepticism about the motives of MPs; 58 percent agreed
with the view that 'people become MPs for their own gain

Table 1 *Trust in Government*

Generally speaking, would you say that this country is run by a few big interests concerned only for themselves, or that it is run for the benefit of all the people?	48% Few big interests 37% All the people 15% Don't know
How much do you *trust* the Government in Westminster to do what is right?	7% Just about always 32% Most of the time 47% Only some of the time 10% Almost never 4% Don't know
When people in politics speak on Television, or to the Newspapers, or in Parliament, how much, in your opinion, do they tell the truth?	3% Just about always 22% Most of the time 60% Only some of the time 10% Almost never 4% Don't know
How much do you trust a British Government of either party to place the needs of this country and the people *above* the interests of their own political party?	7% Just about always 28% Most of the time 45% Only some of the time 15% Almost never 5% Don't know

Source: Alan Marsh, *Protest and Political Consciousness* (London:
Sage, 1978), page 118.

and to further their own ambitions' while only 20 percent disagreed, and many were particularly likely to doubt claims and promises made by MPs at election time and during party broadcasts.[19] We may usefully think of two dimensions of trust: intrinsic trust, or a belief in the honesty and probity of the political authorities; and pragmatic trust, or the belief that government carries out its promises.[20]

Data collected by Alan Marsh in 1974 on these two measures and reported in Table 1 show that only a small minority (10–15 percent) are totally cynical about the conduct of government in Britain. But we also see that for none of the four measures does a majority offer a 'trusting' response. A plurality think that government is run by a few big interests, which are concerned only for their own benefits, and many feel that a government is able to do what is right and give priority to the needs of all the people for only some of the time. There is also a poltical basis to feelings of cynicism toward the system. It is highly developed among those who are dissatisfied with the performance of the government and among those who regard the system as unresponsive to their demands. Without trend data we have no way of knowing whether this low level of confidence represents the normal state of affairs or not. It shows, however, a general lack of trust in the country's leadership and coincides with other indicators of dissatisfaction with the way things are going in Britain.

Community
Our assumptions about the secure sense of national community and integration in Britain and the agreement on the boundaries of the United Kingdom have been undermined in recent years... That religion and nationality were not decisive influences in politics was part of the conventional wisdom until very recently. In recent years, however, changing attitudes in the non–English parts have thrown the future of the United Kingdom as we know it into question... The sense of belonging to a 'British' community is weak outside England. Most Scots and Welsh people identify with their own respective nationalities and most people in Ulster divide their loyalties between Ulster and Ireland.[21] These differences are not new, but hitherto they lacked political significance because they were not expressed in distinctively nationalist political parties and because some five–sixths of the population reside in England. But there has been a recent upsurge of support for nationalist par-

ties. In 1966 such parties collected only 6 percent of the votes outside England and failed to return a single MP. By October 1974
they had captured a third of this vote and twenty – six seats. The
Nationalist party in Scotland, appealing to a separate Scottish
identify and holding out the prospect of an oil – rich Scotland since
the discovery of North Sea oil, saw its share of the Scottish vote
leap from 5 percent in 1966 to 30 percent in 1974 and fall to 19 percent in 1979.

The major challenge to the authority of the British government
today is found in Northern Ireland. Since the partition of Ireland
in 1921 many among the Catholic minority in Ulster have refused
to recognize the Protestant – dominated regime. Catholics and
Protestants have continued to protest their exclusive loyalties to
the Irish Republic and the British Crown respectively, and have remained separate subcultures.[22] In 1968 Catholics began
demonstrations for greater civil rights and Protestants responded
with counterdemonstrations. British troops were sent in 1969 to
keep the peace, but their presence has not stopped the escalation
of violence by the sectarian forces of both sides nor prevented the
spread of terrorism to the mainland. In the years since the disturbances broke out more than 1800 people have died as a result of
violence. The legacy of history and the conflicts of religion and national identity make politics in Ulster distinctive in the United
Kingdom, and it stands as a major qualification to all generalizations about the British political culture. In Britain religion is of little political significance, but it dominates political life in Northern
Ireland. Violence is not a part of British politics, whereas in Northern Ireland, riots, assassinations, and terrorism are everyday oc-
currences.[23] ...

The arrival of a substantial number of coloured immigrants
after 1958 introduced a group of citizens who were visibly different from the rest of the British community. In spite of measures
to limit the numbers of entrants, several surveys have shown that
the great majority feel strongly that there are too many coloured
immigrants and want to end immigration. Enoch Powell has attracted much support from voters of all parties by articulating
fears that the immigrants, notwithstanding their British citizen-
ship, are 'alien' in speech and colour, and a threat to 'the British
way of life'.[24] ... His speeches on the issue in the 1970 elections
swung many voters and may have been decisive in turning the election for the Conservatives.[25] British experience of immigration

election for the Conservatives.[25] British experience of immigration and the imposition of strict controls on entry showed that Britain possessed no magic formula for coping with the tensions of mixed races; the legislation was designed to ease strains by maintaining a predominantly white population. The events also showed the relevance of a person's colour to many citizens' notions of a British community.

Influencing government
Almond and Verba were impressed with the large number of British voters who felt themselves capable of influencing the local and national governments. Subsequent research into political efficacy or competence has shown how complex this concept is. Questions about an individual's perception of the responsiveness of government and other authorities to 'people like me' may actually measure a person's self — confidence rather than his attitudes to the political system. More than two – thirds of Nordlinger's sample of workers, for example, felt that they could do something about an unjust regulation and a similar number were confident of their ability to influence the government; however, only 10 percent claimed to have a 'good deal' of influence on the way the country is run.

The choice of parties and free elections figures prominently in theories of responsive government. Butler and Stokes found that 60 percent of voters showed some understanding that these institutions facilitated popular control. Yet their surveys also showed that there was an increase during the 1960s in those who doubted the abilty of these institutions to make the government responsive to public opinion. In 1963, 50 percent of their sample thought that government paid 'not much' attention to the people; by 1969 the proportion had risen to 61 percent. Another test of competence by the Royal Commission in 1970 revealed that the majority of people had a low level of confidence in their political capability vis – à – vis *local* government. The survey also found that respondents who were dissatisfied with the present system of governing Britain were very likely to feel that people were powerless in the face of government. Other surveys invariably find that respondents, when asked to rank the influence of various groups in government, place 'people like yourself' near the bottom. Marsh's 1974 survey provides the opportunity for direct comparison with the *Civic Culture* findings on strategies of popular influence. He replicated two of the 1959 questions, which asked what citizens would do to try to influence their national and local governments. The attitudes show a striking stability, though there is some increase in the proportions who would 'do nothing' in the face of local or national regulations that were regarded as 'unjust' and there is a small shift to forms of more direct action.[26]

In this context it is interesting that there has been an upsurge of more direct forms of protest and self – assertiveness in recent years. The continued violence and sectarian murders in Ulster, resistance between 1971 and 1974 by trade unions and local authorities to Acts of Parliament, and, most spectacularly, Mr. Heath's dissolution of parliament in the face of the miners' strike against his incomes policy spring to mind as examples. Have these incidents made obsolete our image of the law – abiding English?

A number of explanations have been advanced for this development. Individuals may still be politically competent in the *Civic Culture* sense of the term but with the difference that there is a more frequent resort to extralegal or unorthodox methods beyond those associated with voting, party activity, writing to the press, and so on. Britain may also be a more generally dissatisfied society, in comparison either with other nations or with the past; hence the greater potential for protest. And, finally, it may be that the protestors are actually concentrated among the most dissatisfied and among those who connect the causes of their dissatisfaction to the political system.

Alan Marsh's survey of support for unorthodox forms of political protest is useful in helping our understanding here. His scale for measuring protest potential was based on the respondent's degree of approval for various forms of protest and the likelihood that he would engage in acts of protest. Nearly four – fifths expressed approval for, and willingness to engage in, legal forms of protest (signing petitions, boycotts, and demonstrations). This finding confirms our image of the law – abiding Englishman. One – fifth were an unorthodox minority, ready to engage in illegal acts (rent strikes, blockades, and other forms of violence). Marsh also asked, 'It is *ever* justified to break the law to protest about something you feel is very unjust or harmful?' More than half (56 percent) said Yes and 36 percent said No (8 percent 'don't know'). But this widespread potential for protest was rarely directed against the regime; few of the latent rebels had in mind the overthrow of capitalism or the government. They were more concerned to defend what they regarded as their 'normal' rights, such as their civil liberties, protecting their homes against threat of eviction, resisting threats to living standards, and using industrial action to protect free wage bargaining.

We find something interesting about the character of the protest – oriented minority. Willingness to protest is highest among those who share all three of the following characteristics: (*a*) a high sense of political efficacy, (*b*) cynicism toward the political system, and (*c*) a sophisticated level of ideological and political conceptualization. It is also related to dissatisfaction with perceived government performance and the state of democracy in Britain. Willingness to protest is not therefore a displacement from conventional forms of political participation; rather, it is regarded as an additional means of redress. The protester is like the good citizen in favouring orthodox political behaviour. But because he does not trust the government he believes that only protest will be effective. We have here uncovered one important change in the civic culture. Among the politically competent (or those most expected to support the civic culture in the Almond – Verba survey) there appear to be higher levels of ideology and mistrust and where these are combined there is an enhanced potential for protest.[27]

Political support

The question remains: Do these changes in political values, added to such other features as the retreat from the major parties, demands for devolution and separatism, violence, and so on, indicate some crisis of legitimacy for the British political system? It is notoriously difficult to be sure that respondents are distinguishing between attitudes to the *regime* (the set of procedures and institutions), and the *authorities* (the group of leaders who occupy the important positions at a particular time). It is also tempting to conflate statements of desire for change in particular institutions and incumbents into criticism of the system as a whole. In fact, satisfaction with government outputs or leaders may vary independently of attitudes to the system itself.

In a recent reformulation of his notion of political support, David Easton has distinguished between support that is either *diffuse* or *specific*.[28] The former is a general attachment to the system, is largely independent of the varying performance or outputs of the system, and is relatively enduring. Specific support, on the other hand, is contingent on the individual's perception of the system's performance and may vary greatly even over short periods of time. In spite of the difficulties in operationalizing and measuring the motives on which an individual's support is based and the lack of research into the extent to which citizens actually differentiate the regime from the authorities, the distinction will be useful for our purposes.

Much of the dissatisfaction we have traced is *specific*, that is, it is directed at the political parties, their leaders, and the performance of governments... A good example of this specific support is seen in the correlation in the 1960s between changes in the macroeconomic measures of unemployment and price inflation and the shifts in the popularity of the parties.[29] Voters saw the actions of the government as affecting their prosperity, and changes in their evaluations of the government's economic performance had a major influence on shifts in levels of party support... It is possible, however, that disappointment and consequent loss of specific support for the authorities, if maintained for sufficient time, will carry over and lead to general dissatisfaction with the system or at least to the authority roles. Indeed, we think that something like this has probably happened in Britain over the past decade.

Before pursuing this line of argument, a warning is necessary. We lack satisfactory trend data for accurate assessment of a number of important attitudes to the British system, and where such data exist the changes are usually too small to establish a trend or to warrant firm interpretation... Perceptions of the limitations or failings of the British government, far from reflecting alientation, may simply indicate appropriately modest expectations of what governments and politicians can achieve.[30]

Moreover, such orientations as we have considered may not matter much for regime support. Research into levels of satisfaction with various aspects of life in Britain today found least satisfaction with the quality of democracy. But, compared with such other domains as marriage, family life, and health, most people did not rate the political realm highly in determining the overall quality of life.[31] In spite of the economic depression of the 1970s, life satisfaction has remained high in most West European countries. Survey indicators of life satisfaction show that it has actually increased while the economy declined, largely because satisfaction with face – to – face relationships has more than outweighed dissatisfaction with major institutions like government, business, and unions.[32] The comparative survey evidence shows that more Britons are satisfied with their lot and the way democracy works than are citizens of other West European countries.

There is other evidence of the tenacity of traditional values. Runciman's 1962 survey showed how socioeconomic inequalities had not led to resentment among most of the working class. When making comparisons, less favoured groups usually adopted narrow frames of reference in evaluating their rewards and opportunities, that is, they made comparisons with people like themselves or just a little better off.[33] In 1975 research by W. W. Daniel showed that in, spite of an increasingly egalitarian climate of opinion and more powerful unions, the same restricted comparisons were operating and damping dissatisfaction.[34]

These qualifications warn us to be cautious in our interpretation of the survey data. But such data are only one source of material in assessing attitudes to the system and they have to be related to other sorts of evidence. The data do become plausible when they are linked to such phenomena as the electorate's increasing volatility, declining support for two major parties and transference of support to other parties, and demands for devolution in Scotland. We know that the strong identifiers with parties are more likely than nonidentifiers to support the parliamentary system and party politics, be more interested and active in politics, and believe in the efficacy of the election process.[35] The decline in strong partisanship and the erosion of both working – class deferential Tory and the 'traditionalist' Labour voter has made support for party and government more instrumental, tying it to actual performance...

Conclusion

In 1963 Almond and Verba were optimistic about the prospects for the civic culture in Britain. It was then fashionable to believe that the legacy of the British historical experience and the consequences of further socioeconomic modernization, including the spread of the mass media, greater involvement with voluntary organizations, and a more educated and participatory population, would help the spread of the civic culture. The implicit and benign scenario was that further socioeconomic development would be associated with a less ideological, more participatory, secular, and pragmatic style of politics. These expectations have not been confirmed.

Assessment of change is necessarily tentative; a period of less than two decades is a short term in a country's history and a culture changes slowly. It will require the passage of further time for many recent political events and generational trends to have an impact on the political culture. Although discussion of civic culture in the original volume lacked precision we do feel able to talk about a change in the balance of the cultural mix and a decline in the deferential or supportive elements. The evidence suggests that there is no great popular confidence in the political institutions, though there is also no desire for radical changes. Similarly, while there is no survey evidence to show widespread trust in the political authorities, outright cynicism or support for violence outside the law is confined to a small minority. The dissatisfaction remains more pronounced on the dimensions of the 'output affect' rather than the 'system affect'. There is, in other words, more dissatisfaction with the specific performance of government than with the system as a whole. The recent years of slow economic growth have led to greater social tensions, group rivalries, and growing dissatisfaction with the incumbent authorities. Indeed, apart from the 'exceptional' problem of Ulster, the major challenges to the authority of government in Britain in recent years have arisen in the economic sphere, when trade unions resisted attempts to alter methods of wage bargaining and industrial relations. What does seem clear is that the traditional bonds of social class, party, and common nationality are waning, and with them the old restraints of hierarchy and deference.

Notes

1   Gabriel A. Almond and Sidney Verba, *The Civic Culture: Political Attitudes and Democracy in Five Nations* (Princeton, N.J..: Princeton University Press, 1963).
2   For a review of the changes, see Dennis Kavanagh and Richard Rose, eds., *New Trends in British Politics* (London: Sage, 1977).
3   For an inventory of values and symbols, see the table in Richard Rose, *Politics in England*, p. 56.
4   See Almond and Verba, *Civic Culture*, p.101, for a further discussion of these terms.
5   Lowell, *The Government of England* (New York: Macmillan, 1908). p. 507.

6   *Report of the Royal Commission on the Constitution,*Research Paper 7. *Devolution and Other Apsects of Government: An Attitudes Survey* (London: HMSO, 1973), p. 10.

7   *Report of the Royal Commission on the Constitution 1969 – 1973,* vol. 1. p. 100.

8   See the evidence cited in Dusan Sidjanski, 'The Swiss and Their Politics,' *Government and Opposition,* vol. 6 (1976), p. 316.

9   Robert Putnam, *The Beliefs of Politicians* (New Haven: Yale Univ. Press, 1973), p. 187.

10 Shils and Young, 'The Meaning of the Coronation,' *Sociological Review* 1 (1953): 77.

11 Rose and Kavanagh, 'The Monarchy in Poltical Culture,' *Comparative Politics* 7:552 (1976).

12 See Nordlinger, *The Working Class Tories,* p. 186, and D. Butler and D. Stokes, *Political Change in Britain,* 2nd ed., pp. 32 – 36.

13 D Butler and D. Stokes, *Political Change in Britain,* 2nd ed., pp. 91ff., 117 – 18

14 See also Monica Charlot, 'The Ideological Distance Between the Two Major Parties in Britain,' *European Journal of Political Research 3* (1976): 178 – 88, and David Robertson, *A Theory of Party Competition* (London: Wiley, 1976).

15 Ivor Crewe et al., 'Partisan Realignment in Britain 1964 – 74,' *British Journal of Political Science 7* (1977): 172.

16 Putnam, *Beliefs of Politicians.*

17 Max Kaase and Alan Marsh, 'Pathways to Political Action,' paper presented to International Political Science Association, Edinburgh, 1974.

18 For example, 63 percent agreed that a few strong leaders would do more for this country than all the laws and talk, and 82 percent were doubtful of candidates' promises at election times.

19 Data from specially commissioned survey on *Attitudes to MPs,* Opinion Research Centre, June 1973.

20 See Alan Marsh, *Protest and Political Consciousness* (London: Sage, 1978), p. 118.

21 See Richard Rose, *The United Kingdom as a Multi – National State,* in Rose, ed., *Studies in British Politics,* 3rd ed.   (London: Macmillan & Co., 1974).

22 Richard Rose, *Governing Without Consensus* (London: Macmillan & Co., 1971).

23 Rose, *op cit.,* chap. 14.

24 On race, see Ira Katznelson, *Black Men, White Cities* (London: Oxford Univ. Press, 1973), and Donley T. Studler, 'Political Culture and Racial Policy in British Politics,' *Patterns of Prejudice,* vol. 8 (1974). On Powell, see Studler's 'British Public Opinion, Colour Issues and Enoch Powell,' *British Journal of political Science* 4 (1974), and Douglas Schoen, *Enoch Powell and the Powellites* (London: Macmillan & Co., 1977).

25 See Butler and Stokes, *Political Change in Britain,* 2nd ed., chap. 14.

26 See Alan Marsh, 'Explorations in Unorthodox Political Behaviour,' *European Journal of Political Research 2* (June 1974), and *Protest and Political Consciousness,* pp. 66 – 68.

27 For the fuller argument that cynicism allied to a sense of political competence creates the predisposition to protest, whereas cynicism combined with the sense of powerlessness creates apathy, see William Gamson, *Power and Discontent* (Homewood Ill.: Dorsey, 1968).

28 David Easton, 'The Concept of Political Support,' *British Journal of Political Science* 5 (1975).

29 See C. A. E. Goodhart and R. J. Bhansali, 'Political Economy,' *Political Studies* 17 (1970).

30 See the forceful statements on this point by A. H. Birch and Dennis Kavanagh in *British Journal of Political Science,* vol. 1, no. 4; and vol. 2, no. 1, respectively.

31 See Mark Abrams, 'Subjective Social Indicators,' *Social Trends,* no. 4 (1973).

32 Richard Rose, 'Ordinary People in Extraordinary Economic Cir – cumstances, ' unpublished paper, 1977.

33 Runciman, *Social Justice and Relative Deprivation* (London: Routledge, 1966).

34 W. W. Daniel, *The PEP Survey on Inflation,* PEP Broadsheet 553 (London: PEP, 1975).

35 Ivor Crewe et al., 'Partisan Realignment in Britain.'

2.2 *Patrick Dunleavy*

The influence of the press

From 'Fleet Street: its bite on the ballot', *New Socialist,* January 1985, pp. 24-6.[1]

Structure of Newspaper industry
↓

The liberal orthodoxy cites four reasons why the manifest Tory predomnance in the nation's press monopolies does not significantly damage the fabric of British democracy, nor fatally skew the structure of political communications to Labour's disadvantage.

First, it is claimed that the partisan press is located within a basically pluralistic media system, marked by the countervailing powers of print and broadcast media. Conservative supremacy in Fleet Street is fundamentally constrained by the role of TV and radio, whose news and current affairs outlets must operate within a non-partisan, public service ethic. Their growing importance has created and constantly enlarged a pool of highly professional journalists whose judgments and sense of news values are not open to partisan proprietorial direction. The effect has been to keep the papers 'in line' if they are not to lose all credibility as news sources.

Media pundits used confidently to predict that press partisanship would decline. More readers would turn to 'quality' titles. Newspapers would have to concentrate more on specialist and background news to survive against TV's competition. And Fleet Street was likely to become dominated by large corporations with impersonal management structures, and hence uninterested proprietorial intervention. For a long time, the liberal orthodoxy even claimed that the partisan balance of the press in terms of readerships was relatively equal, because the large circulation *Daily Mirror* supported Labour, offsetting the effect of several smaller circulation Tory dailies. The switch by the *Sun* to fervent Tory support in 1975, and the *Mirror's* circulation losses, at least killed this argument by the time of the 1979 election.

Second, the liberal orthodoxy argues that television news is now the central source of most people's political information. Even the first *Bad News* study [produced by the Glasgow University Media group] gave credence to opinion poll data showing that 70 per cent of people see TV news as their most important channel of information. Television output produced under the public service broadcasting requirement of political balance is also regarded as much more reliable and less biased than press coverage.

Third, liberals play down the possibility of press influence on political alignments by arguing that many readers take little notice of their paper's political coverage, concentrating instead on its racing tips, sports news, cartoons, bingo and other entertainment items. And that even where we can uncover a connection between reading a paper and voting in a particular way, this may simply mean that voters choose a like-minded paper to read, rather than demonstrating that what papers say influences their readers' voting behaviour.

For evidence, they point to the third of *Sun* readers in 1979 who saw their paper as a Labour title; and they then explain away most existing evidence of a correlation between press readership and voting behaviour.

Fourth, the liberal orthodoxy argues that people's press reading habits and voting behaviour are not very closely associated anyway. Sizeable groups of readers regularly vote against their newspaper's political line, especially with the biggest-selling popular titles, the *Sun, Mirror,* and big Sundays.

I want to argue that each link in this four-way defence of the Tory-dominated press status quo is faulty, and consequently that the current one-sidedness of Fleet Street is a major force undermining the fabric of democratic politics in Britain. My critique matches the liberal orthodoxy point for point.

First, there is no substantiated evidence that the supposed countervailing powers of the press and broadcast media are in any kind of tension. What is remarkable about the British media is how unified they are in their selection of items to cover and their assignment of news priorities. Press and broadcast journalists regularly 'cross over' from one medium to another. In fact, the two mediums feed off each other. Political columnists from Fleet Street daily comment on TV and radio, and both channels incestuously study and replicate each other's output. If three or four national papers run a major story it won't be ignored by TV news. The *Bad News* studies demonstrate beyond a shadow of doubt that TV journalists operate completely within an overall climate of professional news values which is quite largely constituted by print journalists and newspaper output.

Notwithstanding the supposed bipartisan requirements of TV and radio coverage, the integration of broadcast journalists into a single system of news production and news values routinely distorts coverage in ways which are biased against the labour movement as a whole, and against the Labour left in particular.

An equally fundamental index of the failure of the 'countervailing powers' argument has been the crashing inaccuracy of the liberal predictions about Fleet Street's development over time. Instead of becoming less partisan, the Conservative popular titles have become firmer propagandists of increasingly rightwing policies, not just at election times but continuously. Far from withering away, the cardboard cut-out journalism of the popular press has begun to invade 'quality' titles like *The Times* and *Sunday Times*...

Second, there is no worthwhile evidence to support the claim that TV news has eclipsed the newspapers' role in supplying political information. The problem with opinion poll data allegedly demonstrating the primacy of television is that a great deal depends on how the questions are phrased. If you force people to nominate a *single* media source as of key importance, they will predominantly cite television news. Quite understandably. Television is a more visually immediate medium; it usually gives urgent news earlier than the newspapers; and the daily pattern of most people's behaviour involves them in seeing items first on the evening news and reading about them afterwards in the following morning's daily paper. It is not surprising, therefore, that in the LSE Election Studies Unit survey, carried out just after the 1983 general election, 63 per cent of respondents nominated TV as their most important source of information and politics. Only 29 per cent chose the newspapers.

However, when we asked instead about the *top two* information sources, the balance between TV news and the press was much more equal. In the sample as a whole 88 per cent included TV news and 73 per cent included the press in their top two sources of political information. Among daily newspaper readers (who made up 84 per cent of the sample), 88 per cent included TV news in their top two sources, and 80 per cent the newspapers. Only among the sixth of the population who do not read a daily newspaper was there a significant differential in the proportion of people nominating TV news (85 per cent) and the national press (35 per cent).

By contrast, both are clearly much more important than other possible information sources, such as radio news (included in their top two sources by only 11 per cent of newspaper readers). Because of the importance given to personal contacts by liberal political science, we particularly prompted people about talking with their families, neighbours or workmates as ways in which they might gather political information. Less than 9 per cent of newspaper readers included any of these personal channels in their top two sources of information about politics.

Third, the liberal arguments about downgrading press influence are contradictory. It cannot simultaneously be true that people pay little attention to the political news and comment in their newspaper, *and* that they select which paper to read partly to fit in with their political views. If the first argument is correct, then partisan self-selection in newspaper readership will be quite rare, and any correlation between readership and voting patterns needs to be taken seriously. On the other hand, if people do select a paper to read on partisan grounds, presumably they will go on to take a great deal of notice of what that paper says on political issues. There can be no *a priori* grounds for discounting press influence.

Fourth, if we assume that choosing a paper is influenced by a large number of factors, of which its political complexion is only one, then the correlation we find between readership patterns and voting behaviour should not be great. In practice, however, there was a very close fit in June 1983 between people's exposure to particular kinds of press influences and the ways in which they voted. [If we look at the] proportion of each individual newspaper's readers who voted Labour at the general election, not surprisingly, the *Telegraph's* readers are the most politically homogeneous group, with no less than 85 per cent voting Tory and only 3 per cent Labour. Conservative preponderance is watered down somewhat among readers of the *Mail, Express, The Times* and *Financial Times* all of which show Tory majorities around the 60 per cent level, falling to 50 per cent among readers of provincial dailies. The *Sun's* predominantly working class readers split much more evenly across all three parties, despite the paper's strident campaigning for Thatcherism, giving only a 6 per cent Tory lead over Labour.

We have classified both the *Guardian* and the *Star* as non-Tory papers (even though the *Star* finally advocated a vote for Thatcher's leadership qualities on the day before polling began). Among both these papers' readers, Labour is the largest party by a small margin over the Alliance. Only the *Mirror* (and *Daily Record)* actively supported Labour, and their readers are the only group to give the party (slender) majority support.

To say more about the political influence of the press, we need to go beyond these figures for individual titles, and look instead at the overall patterns of media influences to which people are exposed. The liberal orthodoxy correctly argues that many people read more than one paper, so that the figures above include some double counting, and may mask the presence of countervailing influences even among the print media. Lastly, of course, just looking at voting patterns for each paper's readers could be misleading unless we control for the obvious tendency for different types of people to read different papers.

[We] meet these criticisms by classifying our survey respondents, both by the overall pattern of media influences to which they were exposed and their social class. Those people who read one or more Conservative daily newspaper, but no non-Tory or Labour titles (34 per cent) [we] include in a 'Tory predominance' category. Those who read a Conservative paper, but also a non-Tory or Labour title (18 per cent) were classified in the 'mixed Tory' category, as were those people who read only a regional daily or evening (12 per cent). Then came the one in six people who do not read a daily newspaper at all. And last are those people who read a non-Tory or Labour paper but not a Conservative title (17 per cent). The [survey] demonstrates that there is a very marked correlation *within* social classes between the pattern of media influences to which people are exposed and their voting behaviour. Manual workers exposed to predominantly Tory influences show a Tory lead over Labour of 17 per cent, whereas manual workers exposed solely to non-Tory media influences showed a Labour lead over the Conservatives of 62 per cent.

Among *all* social classes, the Conservative vote is over 35 percentage points greater among those exposed to predominantly Tory media influences than it is among those exposed to non-Tory influences. The [evidence] shows that the Labour vote decreases by a minimum of 38 percentage points in *all* social classes as we make the same comparison between people exposed to predominantly non-Tory media influences and those exposed to solidly Conservative influences.

The connections between press exposure and voting remain equally strong when we extend the analysis even further to include reference to Sunday newspaper readership. Sunday papers have more limited political significance because they appear much less frequently than dailies, and because the largest circulation titles *(News of the World, Sunday Mirror* and *Sunday People)* assign so little space to political news that they are best regarded as 'non-political', whatever their overt editorial line. Including full reference to patterns of Sunday paper readership scarcely alters the close association of media exposure and voting recorded here.

Our findings suggest that media influences are very closely and precisely associated with the ways in which people vote. Even if we allow for some tendency for people to choose a paper which fits their political leanings, the correlation between press readership and voting is so great that it dwarfs most of the influences on political attitudes to which liberal political science directs our attention. Many people adjust their attitudes on individual issues, anyway, to fit in with their prior decision to support one or another party. The only clear-cut causal variables which can in combination begin to match the importance of media effects are the enduring influence of social class and the newer social cleavages which have grown up around public/private sector conflicts in production and consumption...

1 This article is based on the survey of the 1983 General Election carried out by the author and C. Husbands; see their *British Democracy at the Crossroads: Voting and Party Competition in the 1980s,* London: Allen & Unwin, 1985.

2.3 *Anthony Heath, Roger Jowell and John Curtice*

Electoral change

From 'Understanding electoral change in Britain', *Parliamentary Affairs,* Vol. 39, No. 1, 1986, pp. 150-64.[1]

It is clear that important changes in the level of support for Britain's political parties have occurred in the last two decades. These changes need to be explained. We are fortunate that since 1964 an academic series of post-election surveys of the electorate has been maintained. This series, now widely known as the British Election Surveys, enables us to analyse in a way that is possible in only a few other countries,[2] the process of recent electoral change.

In this article we wish to use that series to examine the validity of two widely quoted explanations for the fall in Labour's, and the rise in the Alliance's, electoral support. We will attempt to demonstrate that each is of only limited validity and then sketch out some alternatives.

The first explanation we wish to examine is the 'class dealignment' thesis.[3] This thesis asserts that class has become a less important influence upon voting behaviour. Many writers suggest that class itself has become a less important feature of social life, with the classes either becoming more similar to each other or else fragmenting into a series of diverse and overlapping social groups.[4] This change is alleged to have had two consequences. Firstly, because it is a non-class party, the change has benefitted the Alliance; as the bond between the middle class and the Conservative Party and that between the working class and the Labour Party weakens, so voters are more inclined to support a third party which does not present either a class based image or espouse avowedly class based policies.

Secondly, the decline of class is said to have hurt the Labour Party to a greater extent than the Conservative Party. Labour is regarded as a party whose raison d'être and appeal is bound up with the existence of a class cleavage. It was founded in 1900 by the trade unions to promote working-class representation in parliament and its early electoral progress was based on the development of a class cleavage. Its continued appeal is based upon the continued potency of explicitly class-based values and images. The Conservative Party's existence, on the other hand, predated the onset of the class cleavage and its appeal is more diffuse, less vulnerable to a fragmentation of the class structure or a decline in class consciousness.[5]

While the 'class dealignment' thesis concentrates on the fall in Labour's share of the vote the second of our explanations concentrates on the rise in Liberal and Alliance support. A Liberal vote, it argues, is primarily a 'protest' vote. Liberal voters are registering not so much their *positive* support for some feature of the Liberal Party as their *rejection* of some aspect of the Conservative or Labour parties. As a consequence, Liberal voters as a group are incoherent in their beliefs and attitudes. Further, their support for the Liberal Party is often fleeting; having registered their protest, Liberal voters often return to their 'normal' party at the next election[6]...

The decline of class voting

In any discussion of the role of class in politics we need first of all to define what we mean by class and consider how we are going to measure it...

Most survey research is, of course, conducted not by academics, but by the polling organisations for most of whom political research is a small part of their business. They have developed a class schema, known as social grade, which aims to distinguish households according to their income and lifestyle. Six social grades are commonly distinguished: A, B, C1, C2, D and E. 'A' grade families, for example, are described as families where the 'head of household is a successful business or professional man, senior civil servant or has considerable private means... In country or suburban areas, 'A' grade households usually live in expensive flats or town houses in the better parts of town.'[7] Such a focus on income and lifestyle may well be appropriate for distinguishing different patterns of consumption in market research, but it is not necessarily appropriate to an analysis of the relationship between class and politics.

Use of the social grade scheme implies that the fundamental divisions in society are based simply upon the income levels associated with particular occupational positions. It is this view, for example, which has led some commentators to believe that increasing affluence would erode Labour's working class base. It ignores, however, the fact that occupations differ not only in the level of income that they enjoy but the conditions under which it is earned. The latter may and indeed does give rise to differences in political behaviour and attitudes.

In order to categorise occupations according to differences in employment conditions we need to concentrate on two important aspects. The first is the degree of security associated with a job. Those with greatest security are those in salaried occupations whose contracts of employment and specialised skills usually provide considerable security against variation in demand for their labour. At the other end of the spectrum stand those who are self-employed and either work on their own or with no more than one or two employees. While they may own their own capital, they are dependent upon their continued ability to maintain a success of their business for their future security of employment. Also with relatively low job security are those in manual occupations. Their jobs are often the first to go in a recession for their skills are not scarce enough for employers to be concerned about their ability to attract replacement labour in the event of a future upturn in their business.

The second important aspect is the degree of authority and autonomy in the workplace. Many professional, managerial and administrative positions often involve the exercise of authority over others and/or leave the individual with considerable freedom in both defining his work tasks and deciding how to execute them. Those in rank and file manual occupations on the other hand are in general not responsible for the work of others and have little or no say in how they do their own work.

Using these two criteria we distinguish the following five classes:[8]
1. The salariat. This consists of managers and administrators, supervisors of non-manual workers, professionals and semi-professionals. These are all occupations which afford a secure basis of employment, typically affording a high income. They either involve the exercise of authority over subordinates or, in the case of semi-professionals, involve a fair degree of discretion and

autonomy.

2. Routine non-manual. This consists of workers such as clerks, sales personnel and secretaries. These are subordinate positions with relatively low levels of income and constitute a kind of white-collar labour force.

3. The petty bourgeoisie. This consists of farmers, small proprietors and own-account manual workers. What they share is the fact of being 'independents' who are directly exposed to market forces and constraints. They also, of course, have direct ownership of their own capital, although in many cases this will be very small in quantity.

4. Foremen and technicians. This is a kind of blue-collar elite, its members being set apart from the mass of wage labour by their supervisory functions or greater amount of discretion and autonomy.

5. The working class. This consists of the rank and file manual employees in industry and agriculture. In some cases, take-home pay may be quite high, particularly if overtime is worked, but the jobs are relatively insecure and are subject to the authority of others.

The distinction between employment conditions and income level becomes clear in Table 1.[9] While the salariat is clearly at the top of the earnings league, the differences in the income levels of the remaining classes are small or non-existent. Yet, as Table 2 shows, the differences in their voting behaviour are quite marked.

Table 1 Class and Income (Relative Incomes: Base—Working-Class Men)

	Men	Women
Salariat	170	119
Routine non-manual	102	72
Petty bourgeoisie	96	72
Foremen and technicians	121	77
Working class	100	66

Table 2 Class and Vote in 1983 (%)

		Cons.	Lab.	Alliance	Others
Salariat	(N = 867)	54	14	31	1
Routine non-manual	(N = 749)	46	25	27	2
Petty bourgeoisie	(N = 245)	71	12	17	0
Foremen and technicians	(N = 220)	48	26	25	1
Working Class	(N = 992)	30	49	20	1

For example, Labour support amongst the routine non-manual class stood at 25% in 1983 compared with 49% amongst the working class.

Our class scheme identifies, in fact, two groups which are hidden or ignored by the social grade scheme. The first is the petty bourgeoisie. They are dispersed across the social grades, but it can be seen that they prove to be the most politically united section of the electorate. Over 70% voted Conservative in 1983. They constitute the bedrock of Mrs Thatcher's support. The second group consists of the foremen and technicians. These are usually included in the C2 social grade along with other 'skilled' manual workers. It is widely believed that skilled manual workers are more pro-Conservative than other manual workers. We find, however, that once we pick out the foremen and technicians (who clearly are more Conservative than their colleagues) skilled workers are no less likely to vote Labour than semi-skilled and unskilled workers. Indeed, in the 1983 post-election survey 51% of skilled workers voted Labour compared with 48% of semi-skilled and unskilled. Our class scheme, then, shows a somewhat different, but also rather stronger, relationship between class and voting than that provided by social grade.

The study of the relationship between class and voting has been handicapped in the past by the use of an inadequate conceptualisation of class. But proponents of the class dealignment thesis have also confused two crucially different meanings of the term 'dealignment'.

In one sense dealignment has a perfectly simple meaning. Fewer working-class people vote Labour and fewer middle-class people vote Conservative. People are, in other words, less likely to vote for the party normally identified with their class position. It is relatively easy to demonstrate that there has been a steady and persistent decline in the proportion voting for their 'natural' class party. If, for example, we dichotomise electors into those in manual occupations and those in non-manual occupations, less than half of the electorate voted for their 'natural' class party in 1983 compared with two-thirds in 1966. We shall term this a decline in the *absolute* level of class voting.

For certain purposes an absolute measure of class voting is entirely appropriate. However there is an important logical difficulty in using class dealignment defined in this way as an explanation of the rise of Liberal and Alliance voting. In measuring the absolute

Table 3. Trends in Class Voting

	Liberal % share of the vote (GB)	% of all voters who voted for their natural class party	% of Conservative and Labour voters who voted for their natural class party
1945	9	62	68
1950	9	62	68
1951	3	67	69
1955	3	65	69
1959	6	61	69
1964	11	63	70
1966	9	66	72
1970	8	60	67
1974 (Feb)	20	55	70
1974 (Oct)	19	54	69
1979	14	55	65
1983	26	47	63

level of class voting, the Liberal and Social Democratic parties are taken to be non-class parties. So if the Liberal or Alliance share of the vote increases, the proportion of the electorate voting for a class party must decrease, and this will in general mean that the absolute level of class voting will also decrease. Table 3 shows that, in the post-war period as a whole, the fluctuations in the Liberal share of the vote rather closely mirror those in the absolute level of class voting. Class voting increased to its highest level in 1951, when the Liberal vote fell to its lowest point. But as Liberal voting grew in 1974 and 1983, so class voting declined.

The difficulty with this, absolute measure of class voting, however, is that it is impossible to determine whether class dealignment is a cause of the rise in third-party voting or a consequence. The two have such a close logical relation with each other that we may be doing no more than redescribing the phenomenon we are trying to explain.

There is, however, a further meaning of class dealignment (one already implicitly used in the existing literature),[10] which does not have this problem. This is *relative* class dealignment. In this sense class dealignment will have occurred if, for example, Labour loses votes amongst the working class while gaining votes amongst the middle class. The ratio of its working class to its middle class vote will have fallen; it will have become relatively stronger in the middle class than it was previously.

We need, then, an appropriate measure of the class alignment which is independent of rises and falls in the absolute strength of the parties. The simplest method is to exclude Liberal voting altogether from the calculations. For example, we could calculate the proportion solely of Conservative and Labour voters who vote on class lines. In other words, we can calculate the proportion of the two-party vote, rather than of the total vote, which is cast for the natural class party.[11] If the Labour party for example gained votes at the Conservatives' expense among non-manual workers but lost votes to the Conservatives among manual workers, this would show up as decline in class voting on this measure, irrespective of what was happening to the Liberal share of the vote.

The third column of table 3 gives the results. It shows remarkable stability in the level of two-party class voting, albeit with a small decline towards the end of the period. True, a significant fraction of the electorate has turned away from these two class parties, but those that remain with them are still tending to vote along class lines. There is no support here for the view that there has been a major, long-term crumbling in the class basis of support for the Labour and Conservative parties.

The class dealignment thesis is then at best an unsteady rock on which to build an explanation of the rise of the Alliance and the fall of the Labour party. If it is unambiguously to be a cause rather than a consequence of changes in party strengths, then class dealignment in the relative as well as the absolute sense would have been expected. This is what might have been anticipated if the class structure itself had been crumbling or fragmenting. But there is no evidence of a gradual and persistent decline in the relative strength of the class/party alignment to match the steady erosion of Labour strength or the secular increase in Liberal support. The 'withering away of class' does not seem to be a good explanation for the decline of Labour or the rise of the Alliance. In place of such a 'social' explanation for the changes, a more 'political' one would seem more promising. As we noted above, the theory of Alliance protest voting has been widely advanced as just such an explanation.

The Alliance as a protest party

A crucial characteristic of Liberal voters, according to the protest theory is that they have little in common with each other. They have not been attracted by any positive quality of the Liberal Party which gives them a common identity. Rather, their behaviour can be better understood by reference to the negative qualities of one or both of the other two political parties. As what they are protesting against varies from one voter to another, so Liberal voting takes on its disparate character[12]... We have analysed the results of our 1983 post-election survey to see how united or divided the current crop of Alliance voters were in 1983. Table 4 compares five of the issues which were important in the 1983 election campaign and shows the extent to which the voters agreed with the policies of their own parties on these issues.

Table 4 Party Agreement: % Broadly Agreeing With Own Party's Position

	Cons.	Lab.	Alliance
Nuclear weapons	62	62	63
Unemployment	56	84	69
Taxation	48	72	65
Nationalisation	82	53	60
Law and order	69	63	62

We can see that there is no single issue on which Alliance voters were solidly behind their party. In contrast, 84% of Labour voters supported their party's policies to deal with unemployment, while 82% of Conservative voters supported the Conservative policies on privatisation. The best that the Alliance could do was on unemployment, with 69% agreement.

On the other hand, we can also see that there were issues on which Labour and Conservative voters were deeply divided. Only 48% of Conservative voters agreed with their party's policies on tax cuts and government spending, and only 53% of Labour voters agreed with their party's policies on nationalisation. Alliance voters were not as divided as this on any issue...

It is by no means clear, then, that Alliance voters were more divided overall than the other groups of voters. They shared no single unifying principle, but nor were they as seriously at odds with party policy as were Conservative and Labour voters. Doubtless, some former Labour voters switched to the Alliance in protest at Labour's policies on nationalisation, but the fact that many stayed loyal to Labour despite their disagreements on nationalisation suggests that protest is only half the story. The other half is that people who switched to the Alliance were generally in sympathy with their new party's overall array of policies.

There is also evidence that, in 1983, there was greater unity and a more distinctive profile to Alliance voters than there had been in the past. We found that the Alliance was not the purely centrist political formation that had been often supposed. Many commentators have thought of the British political parties as set out of different positions along a 'left-right' spectrum. The Labour Party is seen as being towards the left, while the Conservative Party is placed on the right. The Liberals and the SDP lie towards the centre of this spectrum, perhaps with the SDP somewhat to the left of the Liberals.

This left-right spectrum is usually described in economic terms. It can be thought of as measuring differing degrees of government intervention in the economy ranging from full socialism on the left to a completely laissez faire policy on the extreme right. However, there has been an increasing number of non-economic issues in contemporary politics which to a large extent cross-cut the left-right spectrum. For example, there is no logical reason why attitudes to immigration or defence should go with particular attitudes towards the economy. Someone who favours free enterprise, for example, could logically oppose immigration controls just as much as a socialist might. And indeed there is evidence that attitudes towards economic and non-economic issues are only weakly related empirically.[13]

This is important in understanding Alliance voters because we found that they took up rather different positions on the two types of issue. On the economic issues, as might be expected, they tended towards the centre of the left-right spectrum roughly midway between Conservative and Labour voters. But on the non-economic issues–defence, immigration, certain aspects of the welfare state and classic moral issues like the death penalty and free speech for extremists–they tended to be much closer to the Labour voters and further away from the Conservative. This means that there was, in 1983, a much more distinctive ideological profile to the Alliance voters than had commonly been realised. They were not the amorphous collection of voters that had sometimes been supposed but tended to favour a distinct ideological package, one which was relatively 'doveish' or reformist on the non-economic issues but more centrist on the economic issues.

However, comparison with previous election studies suggests that this distinctive profile is a relatively new phenomenon. The picture of the Liberal protest voter does seem to be reasonably accurate of the past but does not appear to explain the growth of Alliance support over the last decade. This can be seen if we compare the ideological character of Liberal voters in 1974 with that of the Alliance voters in 1983.

We can show the changes quite clearly if we draw a two-dimensional map of the voters' attitudes and ideology. The first dimension, running left-right or west-east across the page, is the classic economic one measuring preferred levels of government intervention in the economy. The second, north-south dimension is the non-economic one measuring attitudes towards moral or social issues.

Table 5 Liberal Shares of the Vote in February 1974 (% Voting Liberal)

15	25	22	increase benefits
(236)	(218)	(78)	
17	23	24	no change
(147)	(318)	(128)	
15	18	16	cut benefits
(101)	(294)	(231)	

nationalise   no change   sell off
private   nationalised
companies   industries

(Figures in brackets give cell sizes)

In Table 5 we show the distribution of the Liberal vote across our ideological map in February 1974. The economic dimension is measured by attitudes towards nationalising or privatising industries, the non-economic dimension by attitudes towards the reduction or expansion of social services and benefits.[14] The particular choice of questions to measure each axis is not important; if we had chosen any other items on the two dimensions, we would have acquired similar results.

It will be seen that the level of the Liberal vote in 1974 varies lit-

Table 6 Alliance Shares of the Vote in 1983 (% Voting Alliance)

15 (301)	34 (570)	28 (417)	spend more on services
19 (115)	37 (400)	18 (510)	no change
14 (65)	19 (150)	15 (288)	cut taxes
nationalise private companies	no change	sell off nationalised industries	

(Figures in brackets give cell sizes)

tle from one cell to another. Although the vote is above 20% in the four cells to the north-east of the map and below 20% elsewhere, the differences are not enough to provide any degree of coherence to the Liberal vote. Only just over half the Liberal vote lies in the four north-eastern cells. The traditional characterisation of the Liberal vote as a protest vote certainly appears true at the time of the Liberals' last peak general election performance in February 1974.

The analysis is repeated for the 1983 Alliance vote in Table 6.[15]

We see that the alliance gains between 1974 and 1983 have been almost entirely restricted to three out of the nine cells, giving it a much more concentrated distribution than before. For example, the Alliance failed to make any gains in the top left corner of the map (which we can think of as the Labour corner). Its share of the vote here was only 15% in 1983, exactly the same as in 1974. Similarly there was no change in the bottom right corner (the Conservative corner), where again the Alliance managed only 15% of the votes.

Where the Alliance did gain, of course, was in the very centre (up from 23% to 37%), in the cell immediately to the north (up from 25% to 34%), and, to a lesser extent in the cell to the north-east (up from 22% to 28%). In other words, it was precisely among voters who tended towards the centre on the economic issues but towards the 'doveish' end of the non-economic dimension that the Alliance made most headway.

The change in the ideological profile of the Alliance vote is not the only evidence that there is that a protest-based account of its progress is inadequate. Its vote has apparently also become somewhat less volatile. Although there was a 12% increase in the Liberal vote between 1970 and February 1974, only 64% of 1970 Liberal voters voted for the Liberals again in February 1974. But in the wake of a similar increase between 1979 and 1983, the Liberal retention rate was 72%.

There appears then to have been an important change in the character of the third-party vote since 1974. While Alliance voters still do not identify with the Alliance as strongly as Conservative or Labour supporters do with their parties, and while the Alliance is nothing like as dominant in its heartland as the Conservative and Labour parties are in theirs (their support in both cases was nearly 80%), the Alliance vote has less of an apparent protest character than it formerly did. The growth of third party support since 1974 at least cannot therefore be adequately explained by a protest-based theory. We have, therefore, to account not for a general increase in third party support irrespective of ideological position, but a specific appeal to those with a particular ideology.

Towards an explanation

Having cast doubt upon the validity of two widely supported accounts of recent electoral trends in Britain, what are we to put in their place?...

While the extent and significance of any class dealignment since 1964 is uncertain, what is beyond doubt, almost irrespective of the class schema used, is the change in the shape of the class structure which has occurred. Over the last twenty years Britain has been transformed from a predominantly blue-collar society into a majority white-collar one. As Table 7 shows, on our (narrow) definition the working class has shrunk from being little under half of the electorate to little more than a third, while the salariat and the

Table 7. Class Composition of the Electorate: 1964 and 1983 (%)

	1964 (N = 1475)	1983 (N = 3790)
Salariat	18	27
Routine non-manual	18	24
Petty bourgeoisie	7	8
Foremen and technicians	10	7
Working class	47	34

routine non-manual groups have increased in size by one half and a third respectively.

The significance of this change for the Labour party as a working class party is immediately apparent; its traditional electoral base is shrinking. In order to win the same share of the electorate now as it did in 1964 it has to be much *more* popular within the working class now than it was then. We can get some measure of the disadvantage that Labour has suffered from this change by recalculating what the 1964 election result would have been if each party were as popular within each social class as it was then, but each class were as large as it was in 1983. This calculation produces a Conservative vote $5\frac{1}{2}$% higher than it actually was in 1964, a Liberal vote $1\frac{1}{2}$% higher, and a Labour vote 7% lower than it was. Change in the class structure may, in other words, account for nearly half of the 16% fall in the Labour vote between 1964 and 1983 and indeed virtually all of its decline between 1964 and 1979.

But electoral change, even long-term electoral change, is not simply a consequence of social change. Social change cannot account for the scale of Labour's defeat in 1983. Nor can it account for more than a small fraction of the rise in Liberal/Alliance support. In order to understand the emergence of an Alliance heartland in the north-eastern quadrant of our ideological map, we need to look at political sources of change. For example, values while stable are not immutable; it is open to politicians to seek to persuade the electorate of the correctness of their own ideology. Parties can also change their ideological position, rendering themselves more or less attractive to certain sets of voters.

Both these processes appear to have been at work. It has been widely argued that the electorate has moved to the right.[16] This does indeed appear to have happened on the economic issues.[17] But the electorate has also become more liberal on the non-economic ones. Thus, for example, while only 18% of the electorate favoured abolition of the death penalty in 1966, 37% did so in 1983.[18] Thirty per cent said that the government spends too little on the health service in 1960; in 1983 this figure was 50%.[19] Together, the two trends have produced an increase in the proportion of the electorate lying in the north-east quadrant of the map...

But while the electorate has been moving in one direction, the Conservative and Labour parties have in the opinion of many been moving in another. In 1983 half of the electorate believed that the Labour Party had moved to the left since Mr Callaghan had been leader, while a quarter thought the Conservatives had moved to the right since Mr Heath was leader. Eighty-two per cent believed there was a great deal of difference between the Conservative and Labour parties, compared with only 46% as recently as 1979. The Alliance's success in gaining votes in the north-east quadrant appears to have occurred in part because the ideology of the Conservative and Labour parties had diverged from that of these particular voters.

At the same time there is a scattering of evidence to suggest that the Alliance has become more positively attractive to voters in the north-east quadrant. This change was not simply a consequence of the formation of the Social Democratic Party in 1981, for the increasing concentration of the Liberal/Alliance vote was also evident in 1979 before the SDP's formation. But while only 24% of respondents placed the Liberals in the centre-north or far north-east cell of the map in February 1974, 33% did so in 1983. The proportion who said they did not know where the Alliance stood was also much lower in 1983 than it was for the Liberals in February 1974. The Alliance has thus to some extent created an ideological identity for itself which makes it positively attractive to voters in the north-east quadrant.

Conclusion

We remarked at the beginning that it was being asked whether the main focus of electoral competition in Britain has shifted from being a contest for office to a battle for the role of principal opposition party. We have cast doubt upon two common explanations for the rise of the Alliance and the decline of Labour and sketched out alternatives. What do those alternatives suggest for the future of British politics?

The Labour party clearly has a difficult task ahead of it. The contraction of the working class has resulted in a marked decline in the size of its electoral base and looks set to continue further. Yet that decline on no account doomed the party to a disaster of 1983 proportions. Further, we have argued that political change as well as social change can be important in producing long-term electoral trends. It remains open to the Labour Party to win votes either by persuading the electorate more successfully of the virtues of its ideology or by modifying its policies so as to make them more attractive to the growing north-east quadrant of the electorate.

The new coherence to the Alliance vote, on the other hand, may be deemed to augur well for its prospects. Its future may not simply be dependent on protest votes generated by the continued failure of the other parties. Its strength in its emerging heartland is still only half of the Conservative and Labour parties in theirs; there would thus appear to be considerable potential for further strengthening of its heartland apeal. But further Alliance progress in this quadrant would not simply hurt the Labour party; there were over twice as many Conservative as Labour supporters in the four cells of the north-east quadrant in 1983. Further Alliance consolidation of its heartland may thus come at the especial expense of the Conservatives. At the same time, the Alliance's hold on its new found heartland must be considered uncertain. As we have already indicated, Labour, or the Conservatives, could attempt to regain their lost popularity amongst this group of voters.

Our analysis therefore proscribes no particular future for British electoral politics. Each of the parties has both constraints to overcome and opportunities to seize. History does not repeat itself in any mechanical fashion.

Notes

1 The authors were directors of the 1983 British General Election Study. This article is based upon some of their findings which are reported in full in A. Heath, R. Jowell and J. Curtice, *How Britain Votes* (Pergamon, 1985). The research was generously supported by the Economic and Social Research Council, Pergamon Press and Jesus College, Oxford.

2 For a summary of the history of the series see Heath et al, *op. cit.*, Appendix II. The 1983 survey consisted of interviews with 3,955 respondents conducted between July and October 1983. Respondents were selected using a clustered random sampling design. Further technical details of the survey are given in Heath et al, *op cit.*, Appendix I, and a full methodological report is given in J. Field, *The 1983 British General Election Survey: Methodological Report* (Social and Community Planning Research, 1985). We are grateful to the ESRC Data Archive for supplying the data sets of the earlier election studies.

3 The literature on the thesis is considerable. Amongst the more important works are the following: D. Butler and D. Stokes, *Political Change in Britain* (London: Macmillan, 1974) Ch. 9; I. Crewe, B. Sarlvik and J. Alt, 'Partisan Dealignment in Britain 1964-74', *British Journal of Political Science,* VII (1977); R. Rose, *Class Does Not Equal Party: The Decline of a Model of British Voting,* (University of

Strathclyde Centre for the Study of Public Policy, 1980); I. Crewe, 'The Electorate: Partisan Dealignment Ten Years On' in H. Berrington (ed.), *Change in Britain Politics* (Frank Cass, 1984); D. Robertson, *Class and the British Electorate* (Basil Blackwell, 1984); and M. Franklin, *The Decline of Class Voting in Britain 1964-79* (Clarendon Press, 1985).

4 See, for example, K. Roberts, F. Cook, S. Clark and E. Semenoff, *The Fragmentary Class Structure* (Heinemann, 1977); D. Butler and D. Kavanagh, *The British General Election of 1983* (Macmillan, 1984) p. 8; Robertson, *op. cit.*

5 See, for example, Crewe, 'Partisan Dealignment Ten Years On', p. 199; Robertson, *op, cit.*, pp. 85-6.

6 D. Butler and D. Stokes, *Political Change in Britain* (Macmillan, 1969), ch. 14; J. Alt, I. Crewe and B. Sarlvik, 'Angels in Plastic: The Liberal Surge in 1974', *Political Studies* XXV (1977) and I. Crewe 'Great Britain' in I. Crewe and D. Denver (eds.), *Electoral Change in Western Democracies (Croom Helm, 1985).*

7 *D. Monk, Social Grading on the National Readership Survey* (Joint Industry Committee for National Readership Surveys, London, 1978), p. 9.

8 The class scheme in fact follows very closely that devised by John Goldthorpe. See J. Goldthorpe, *Social Mobility and Class Structure in Britain* (Clarendon Press, 1980). We have simply collapsed together Goldthorpe classes I and II to form the salariat (Goldthorpe himself calls it the 'service class') and classes VI and VII to form the working class.

9 This table is derived from an analysis of the 1979 General Household Survey. The classes used are an approximation to the Goldthorpe scheme based on a collapse of socio-economic groups.

10 See, for example, Crewe's analysis of the difference in 'swing' between Conservative and Labour in each social class between 1979 and 1983 in I. Crewe, 'How to Win a Landslide without Really Trying' in A. Ranney (ed.) *Britain At The Polls 1983* (Duke University Press, 1985), pp. 169-71. A similar analysis of the October 1974-1979 swing is given in I. Crewe 'Why the Conservatives Won' in H. Penniman (ed.), *Britain At The Polls 1979* (American Enterprise Institute, 1981) pp. 278-81.

11 There are some technical problems with the use of this measure of two-party class voting. First, it will not be invariant with respect to the relative popularity of the Labour and Conservative parties themselves. And secondly the manual/nonmanual dichotomy over-simplifies the nature of the class structure. Our own preference is to use loglinear analysis and to employ the full five-class schema described above. When this is done, we again find no evidence of a continuing gradual decline in the relative class alignment. However, the more refined analysis suggests that, in place of the short-term fall at the end of the period shown in table 3, there was instead a decline between 1964 and 1970. For the full details see Heath et al, pp. 29-35. Note also that using very different methods from us, Franklin also

discovers that such class dealignment as has occurred since 1964 was largely confined to the period between 1966 and 1970. Franklin, *op. cit.*

12　On the attitudinal coherence of the Liberal vote see H. Himmelweit, P. Humphreys and M. Jaegar, *How Voters Decide* (Open University Press, 1985), and B. Sarlvik and I. Crewe, *Decade of Dealignment* (Cambridge University Press, 1983) pp. 282-9

13　See, *inter alia,* Heath et al, pp. 71-2, Robertson, op. cit., and M. Rokeach, *The Nature of Human Values* (Free Press, 1973).

14　For details of the question wording see Heath et al, *op. cit.,* p. 132 and pp. 153-4.

15　The question wording of the social services question differs significantly in 1983 from that used in February 1974. See Heath et al, *op. cit.* p. 155. We must therefore be aware of the possibility that these differences affect the validity of the comparison. Measurement of the liberal dimension using attitude towards the death penalty does, however, broadly confirm the increasing concentration of the Alliance vote in the north-east quadrant.

16.　See especially, I. Crewe, 'The Labour Party and the Electorate' in D. Kavanagh (ed.), *The Politics of the Labour party* (London: Allen and Unwin, 1982); and Sarlvik and Crewe, *op. cit.*

17　The evidence is clearest in the case of nationalisation. In 1964 21% favoured privatisation; by 1983 this had doubled to 42%. On other issues the change was probably less sharp. There was, for example, a 9% fall in the proportion of those favouring the redistribution of income and wealth between 1974 and 1983.

18　There have been changes in the wording of the relevant questions over time. For details see Heath et al, *op. cit.,* p. 140.

19　The 1960 figure comes from a Gallup survey of that year and is quoted in Crewe, 'Labour Party and the Electorate'.

2.4 *Jorgen S. Rasmussen*

Women in politics

From 'Women's role in contemporary British politics: impediments to Parliamentary candidature', *Parliamentary Affairs,* Vol. 36, No. 3, 1983, pp. 300-15.

At the close of World War I most British women obtained the right to vote in parliamentary elections. A decade later this right was extended to the rest, as women were enfranchised on the same basis as men. This triumph proved to be largely a hollow victory, however. Women made few political gains during the interwar period. Only five per cent (67) of the candidates in 1935 for the last election prior to World War II were women and only nine of them (little more than one per cent of the total membership of the Commons) were elected. (In 1931, 15 women had been elected). Detailed analysis of the interwar elections provides a dismal view of the political position of women in Britain.[1]

The upheavals of World War II and the problems of postwar reconstruction appeared to offer a major opportunity for the advancement of women. World War II changed perceptions and behaviours relevant to women's—especially wives'—economic role. Not only were women important to the war economy, but no official effort to get them back to the home occurred once the war ended. Instead, they were regarded as a labour pool to cope with the economic problems of reconstruction. Thus in the mid-1940s British women seemed poised for a political break-through corresponding to their new economic activity and the changes in role perception associated with it. As had been true in 1918, the political situation in 1945 was in considerable flux—in the ten years since the last election many people had died, while others had come of voting age, geographic mobility had been considerable and the upheavals of the war had affected basic political attitudes. All this uncertainty created a possibility of new patterns of political behaviour which might provide an opportunity for the political advance of women; unlike the situation in 1918 they did not have to wait until a few weeks before the election to know that they would be permitted to be candidates and thus were not denied the chance to take advantage of the opportunity.

The election did provide some hopeful signs for women. The number of women standing for Parliament—87—was larger than in any previous election; the number of women elected was a record also, half as many again as in 1931. While incumbent women MPs did not fare very well—5 of the 11 standing for re-election were defeated, 18 of the 76 non-incumbents were elected.[2] Despite early advances, however, a break-through never occurred. After an increase of nearly 50% in the next general election, the number of women standing for Parliament dropped off and a quarter of a century passed before the high attained in 1950 was surpassed. The 24 women MPs elected in 1945 grew by only five more during the next 20 years. From a high point of 29 in 1964, it declined to only 19 in 1979—only four more than had been elected in 1931, nearly half a century earlier.

Much of the research which has been done on the role of women in parliamentary elections has tended to be anecdotal, vitiated by a small number of cases, concerned only with some elections or out-of-date. Thus a current, comprehensive study is desirable. Furthermore, by looking at the post-World-War-II period in its entirety, trends can be seen more clearly. Has the role of women in parliamentary elections simply been stagnant or is the lack of progress due to mutually cancelling ebbs and flows? Does the rise of the women's movement in the 1960s appear to have had any impact either in terms of making women more assertive in seeking a political role or by producing a backlash of greater resistance to women among the political elite? As traditional loyalties to the main parties weakened in the 1970s, did the gender of a candidate come to have a significant effect upon voters?

This study focuses on the response to women at two levels: the mass or societal level and the local political elite level. In the first instance, the concern is with what voting patterns reveal about popular attitudes toward women in politics; in the second, with what patterns of candidate adoption demonstrate the attitudes of local party officials to be. This approach permits not only an assessment of the status of women in contemporary British national politics, but also helps to suggest where future advances are most likely.

The 1945 results cannot be compared to the subsequent general election either, since a major redrawing of constituencies occurred before the 1950 election. These boundaries were soon altered themselves. About a third of the constituencies were revised to one extent or another before the 1955 election. The next redrawing did not go into effect, however, until the time of the February 1974 election. For purposes of this analysis the 1951 election can be compared with 1950, but 1955 cannot be compared with 1951. The 1959 election can be compared with 1955 and each of the next three elections can be compared with its predecessor. February 1974 cannot be compared with 1970, but October 1974 and 1979 can be compared with their predecessors. With these qualifications, seven elections spanning 28 years—1951 to 1979—are studied.

The effect of women candidature on voter participation

By 1945 women had been permitted to contest parliamentary elections for nearly 30 years; therefore, one might think that women candidates were a familiar phenomenon to most voters. In the seven general elections from 1918 to 1935, however, more than two-thirds of the constituencies (405 of 595) never had had a woman candidate for any party or even as an independent. And another fifth of the constituencies had seen a women candidate only once...

The electorate has not regarded the opportunity to vote for a woman candidate as an inducement for going to the polls. In none of the seven elections did the average change in turnout in constituencies where a woman stood when none had in the previous election differ from the national change in turnout by more than 0.5 percentage points. Similarly, with one exception, where women candidates withdrew or continued to stand the average change never differed from the national change by more than 0.7 percentage points.

The exception occurred in 1970. In those constituencies where a woman candidate entered, turnout was little affected, falling on average by only 3.4 percentage points compared to the national average decline of 3.8%. Where a woman candidate withdrew, however, the average decline was 5.1%. This appears to suggest that in this one election female candidature did help to sustain electoral participation. In those constituencies, however, where women stood in both 1966 and 1970 turnout declined by 5.3%. Thus it was the entry of a woman candidate—not the continued presence or withdrawal—that was associated with a more moderate decline in turnout...

Women candidature and partisan preferences

If a woman candidate did not affect whether people voted, did she affect how they voted? While the election results alone do not permit an inference of vote switching because of female candidature, nonetheless, they do show that the average woman received fewer votes than did the average man. Furthermore, the figures fail to suggest any trend to correct this 'sex penalty'. During the inter-war period the best election for women candidates was in 1924, when they averaged 85% of the vote received by male candidates. In only five of the 11 post-war elections was this proportion exceeded. Furthermore, it declined in both of the two most recent elections, dropping to only 66% in 1979. This is almost exactly as low as it had been in 1922.

The 1979 figure is somewhat misleading. Since 1970 the number of women standing for minor parties or as independents has been increasing and was especially high in 1979.[3] Since most of these candidates receive only a few votes, they tend to depress the average vote for women candidates. But even if one considers only Conservative, Labour and Liberal candidates, the average woman in 1979 received only three-fourths as many votes as the average man.[4]

The lower average vote for women can be explained in two ways: the electorate is no more willing to accept a woman on equal terms with a man than it was a half century ago or local party selection committees persist—to some extent even more frequently than before the war—in adopting women as candidates primarily in those seats where the party has only limited support. Previous work has suggested that the latter explanation is likely to be the correct one.

The electoral results, however, initially suggest at least a limited resistance to women candidates among the electorate. In every election except 1951 the majority of women replacing men reduced their party's share of the vote. For the entire period, only 43% improved upon what their male predecessor had been able to obtain. On the other hand, the average decline in support was not great—as can be seen in Table 1—ranging from 2.3 per cent points in 1970 to 0.6% in 1964 (the average increase in 1951 was 2.9%). The average decline for all elections was 1.0%.

Table 1: Effect of Women Candidature upon Party's Share of Vote (Average Percentage Point Change)

		All Candidates	Women Enter	Women Exit	Women Continue
1951	Con	4.9	3.6	4.2	4.9
	Lab	3.5	2.9	2.6	2.3
	Lib		*	*	*
	Total		2.9	2.9	2.4
1959	Con	-0.6	-1.5	1.6	*
	Lab	-2.8	-2.5	-3.1	-1.8
	Lib		*	*	*
	Total		-1.5	-0.2	-0.2
1964	Con	-6.2	-4.5	-5.8	-5.6
	Lab	-0.4	0.2	2.1	3.4
	Lib	1.6	1.1	4.4	*
	Total		-0.6	0.2	-0.7
1966	Con	-1.6	*	-2.6	-2.1
	Lab	4.6	*	4.0	4.5
	Lib		*	*	*
	Total		-1.2	-0.4	0.9
1970	Con	4.3	2.6	2.5	5.0
	Lab	-5.2	-5.0	-4.8	-5.6
	Lib	-2.6	-4.6	-3.4	*
	Total		-2.3	-2.5	-0.8
Oct	Con	-2.1	-3.9	-4.3	-3.1
1974	Lab	2.2	1.3	1.1	2.5
	Lib	-4.7	-4.2	-3.4	-3.3
	Total		-1.8	-2.3	-1.0
1979	Con	8.2	7.8	6.9	*
	Lab	-2.4	-3.6	-2.7	-0.1
	Lib	-4.0	-4.7	-4.7	-3.0
	Total		-1.2	-1.0	0.1

(*—fewer than 10 cases)

To a considerable extent, however, the recepton given to entering women candidates was more a reaction to their party label than to their gender. The difference between the average change for entering women and for all candidates of her party in that election ranges from 1.7 to -1.8 percentage points. Entering women candidates did not receive markedly different levels of support. Nonetheless, they did tend to do less well than their party's candidates generally; in only 5 of the 16 instances did an entering woman have a more positive impact on support for her party than did her party's candidates generally. This lagging behind was especially pronounced for the Conservatives and the Liberals—in only one election for each did women help their party more than did all candidates. Although in three of six instances Labour women replacements were a greater benefit, the help provided was quite marginal and tended to be smaller than the margins by which they ran behind their party in the other three elections. Furthermore, over the entire group of elections more than half (56%) of the entering Conservative women candidates polled better than had their male predecessors, while less than half (47%) of the entering Labour women did so. (Only 24% of the entering Liberal women did better).

Significantly, men who replaced women as candidates (see 'exit' column in Table 1) fared just about the same as women who replaced men. Only 42% of the male replacements improved their party's share of the vote, losing an average 0.8 percentage points. These figures are almost exactly the same as for women who replaced men. So also is the proportion of instances—6 of 18—in which a male replacement helped his party's vote more than his party's candidates did generally in a given election.

Perhaps the most instructive comparisons are the intra-party ones. Whatever change occurred in a party's fortunes in a given election should affect men and women equally if gender is not a factor influencing the behaviour of the electorate. The proportion of male replacements improving their party's performance over what had been achieved by a woman in the previous election was 60% for the Conservatives, 42% for Labour, and 21% for the Liberals–almost exactly the same proportions as for women candidates. Furthermore, comparing the figures in the middle two columns shows that in seven instances a woman replacement helped her party's share of the vote more in a given election than a male replacement did, in eight instances the male replacement helped more, and in one instance both had the same effect. Considering only Labour and the Conservatives, the women replacement had the better effect in seven of 12 instances.

Persistence earned a small bonus, as the final column shows. In 52% of the cases in which a party continued to offer a woman candidate (usually the same woman stood again, but in some instances a party replaced one woman with another) its share of the vote increased, although the average gain for the entire period is only 0.1 percentage points. Both figures are somewhat better than the ones for either women or male replacements. Continuing with a woman candidate instead of replacing her with a man made little difference for the Conservatives or the Liberals, but produced markedly better results for Labour–two-thirds of the continuing Labour women increased their party's share compared to only two-fifths of the male replacements.

Comparing the last two columns in the table reveals that continuing women had a more beneficial impact on their party's share of the vote than did male replacements in 12 of the 14 instances in which the number of cases is sufficient to permit comparison. The two best instances were 1970–when continuing Conservative women raised the party's share of the vote on average by 2.5 percentage points more than did male replacements–and 1979–when continuing Labour women lost an average 2.6 percentage points less than did male replacements. To summarise these figures: replacing a man with a woman was no worse than replacing a woman with a man and, having once adopted a woman as candidate, sticking with her in the next election was better than substituting a man. The electorate does not seem to have been deterred from its normal partisan preferences by female candidature.

While changes in a party's share of the vote are readily understood, they may not adequately measure a candidate's success. If a third party in a constituency withdraws in the next election, both the first and second place parties may increase their share of the vote, but if the former gets more of those previously voting for the third party, then the second party really is worse off than before, even though its share of the vote has increased. Since during the post-war period the number of Liberal candidates has fluctuated between 109 and 619 and the number of minor candidates between 33 and 754, this is not a trivial concern. Therefore, calculating ground gained or lost may provide a better measure of success.[5] In some senses, changes in a party's share of the vote is an absolute measure of success, while ground gained or lost is a relative measure. Analysing changes in ground reveals how a woman did compared to other parties' competing candidates, most of whom, of course, were men.

When ground gained is used as the measure of electoral success, the advisability of continuing to offer a woman candidate becomes more questionable and replacing man with a woman entails a small cost. Forty-four per cent of the men who replaced women candidates gained ground for their party, while 41% of the women who replaced men and 43% of the continuing women did so. Each of the three groups lost ground on average overall–women replacements lost 2.3 percentage points, male replacements 1.4, and continuing women 1.1...

For each party over the entire period the proportion of female replacements gaining ground was virtually the same as the proportion of male replacements who did so... In only three of the 16 comparable instances did the average ground gained by a woman replacement surpass that of her party's male replacements for that election.

When ground gained is considered, continuing with a woman rather than replacing her with a man is just barely the preferable strategy... The decline for women from the situation when share of vote is analysed is affected partially by party fortunes. Continuing with a woman candidate remains a good strategy for Labour. The proportion of continuing women gaining ground for Labour, however, is only about 10 percentage points greater than the proportion of male replacements doing so, contrasted with a difference of more than 20 percentage points when changes in share of vote are analysed. For the Conservatives and the Liberals, unlike the findings for share of vote, continuing women candidates are notably less likely than either male or female replacements to gain ground for their party. Only 46% of the continuing Conservative women gained ground, compared to 57% of the Conservative women replacements and 59% of the male replacements. For the Liberals the figures were 18%, compared to 26% and 30%.

Thus analysis of ground gained suggests that the previous finding should be qualified somewhat. While replacing a man with a woman may involve some cost, it is quite minor–not appreciably different than that involved in replacing a woman with a man. Liberal and Conservative voters, however, appear to be somewhat reluctant to support a woman candidate in consecutive elections; their partisan preferences may be somewhat weakened by the candidate's gender. Only the Labour party clearly has an incentive not to replace a woman with a man.

While being able to improve a party's share of the vote and gain ground on opponents is important, the crucial consideration, of course, is to win and retain seats. Since some of the differences discussed above were matters of only a few percentage points, the question must be addressed whether they are sufficiently great to affect the payoff. Are women electoral liabilities–do they cost their party seats?...

In both leading parties replacing a man with a woman was as successful as the reverse substitution.[6] The liability–especially pronounced in the Labour party–was continuing with a woman candidate. When seats changed hands in such cases, women lost more than two-thirds of them. For both parties, male replacements lost 16 seats fewer than continuing women candidates and gained six seats more than they did; substituting a man for a woman meant an average combined gain for the main parties of three seats per election–hardly a major improvement.

A good year for a woman's party is essential if she is to be elected. Only two of the 22 seats gained by a woman replacing a man or by a woman continuing to stand occurred in an election in which her party lost seats. On the other hand, an especially good year for a party cannot be counted upon to bring women into the Commons, witness the lack of success for Labour women replacing men in 1966 and Conservative women replacing men in 1979. Especially bad years for a party seem primarily to have an adverse effect upon women continuing to stand for Labour.

The findings for seats gained or lost appears to contradict the conclusion reached from analysing ground gained or lost–instead of the Labour party being the only party having an incentive not to replace a woman with a man, it is precisely Labour that bears the greatest cost for continuing to offer a female candidate. Since the previous analysis has established that continuing Labour women do not adversely affect their party's share of the vote or strength relative to the other parties, the reason for the apparent contradiction in findings must lie in the nature of the constituencies for which many Labour women are adopted. If many of them were chosen for marginal seats, then they would be able to win when the electorate swung to Labour but would be quite vulnerable to losing their seat when Labour lost popularity. The question of the type of constituencies for which women candidates are adopted is explored more fully in the next section.

In summary, the electorate appears to have been largely indifferent to women candidates. While they did not regard them as a special attraction, equally they did not respond hostilely to them. Continuing women candidates did lose seats, but this was not because they did less well than male replacements in gaining support either absolutely or relative to the other candidates contesting the seat. In short, the electorate seemed unconcerned with a candidate's gender and went about voting in its usual way unaffected by this factor. In one regard this represents a significant change from the inter-war period. Then, continuing with a woman candidate rather than replacing her with a man was a considerable liability. Initial acceptance of women candidates differs little from what it was between the wars, but the electorate no longer seems to penalise a persistent woman for being 'pushy'. To this extent women have made political gains in Britain.

The opportunity structure for women candidates

The analysis turns now to the second main focal point–the way in which the local political elite has treated women aspiring to a career in Parliament. A woman's chances of being elected to Parliament turn not only on her ability to evoke a favourable response from the electorate, but also upon her ability to convince a local party selection committee to adopt her for a winnable seat. On this front women are worse off than they were half a century ago. In the seven post-war elections being analysed there were a total of 381 Parliamentary 'openings', that is seats vacant at the time of the election plus those where the sitting Member was not seeking re-election. In only 3% of these cases–only ten instances–was a woman adopted as a candidate.[7] While this is better than the 1% for the inter-war period, it hardly constitutes great progress. Only 2% of the non-incumbent female candidatures during the post-war period were for seats being defended by their party–exactly the same percentage as for the inter-war period. Admittedly, women suffered less relative deprivation–only 4% of the non-incumbent male candidatures in the post-war period were for seats being defended by their party, compared to 8% in the inter-war period.

The prospects for most women candidates have declined because they have come to be adopted for seats where their party trails the winner by a larger margin than was the case in the inter-war period. In three of the six inter-war elections the average woman non-incumbent candidate of whatever party had a better chance of winning–was fighting a seat where her party had been closer in the previous election–than did either a Labour or a Conservative woman non-incumbent in even their party's best post-war election...

In five of the seven post-war elections the average Labour woman has been adopted for a consistuency in which her party was not as far behind the winner as was the case for the average Conservative woman. Furthermore, in four instances the margin which the average Labour woman had to overturn to be elected was below 20 percentage points, while for Conservative women this was true only twice. These figures help to confirm the explanation given above for the sizeable number of seats lost by continuing Labour women. They are adopted for seats where a good swing to Labour might just bring them into the Commons, but they have great difficulty in retaining the seat as soon as the pendulum swings back.

Table 2 clearly demonstrates that selection committees are not becoming more receptive to female candidates. Women are adopted primarily in constituencies that men are not much interested in contesting. Furthermore, even those 'opportunities' seem to be granted only grudgingly. In 1979 8%–52–of Labour's candidates were women–the largest number ever. But this was an increase of only one percentage point and ten women over 1950. For that matter, it was only one percentage point and 16 candidates more than in 1931. As for the Conservatives, in 1979 they adopted 31 women–5% of their candidates. This was only two candidates more–the same percentage–as in 1950.

The real growth in female candidature has been for the minor parties. The number of women adopted by parties other than Labour, Liberal or Conservative never exceeded 12 until the 1970s. Then, in the first part of the 1970s a fifth of all women candidates stood for minor parties or as independents. In 1979 the proportion rose to 38%. In 1979 the minor party and independent women (not counting the Liberals' 51 women) totalled 81–nearly as many as the Labour and Conservatives parties combined... How ironic that women presumably did not establish a women's party because their prospects for electoral success would have been so limited and now they must rely upon parties with little chance of winning to provide them with expanded opportunities, such as they are, even to contest a constituency. Had a women's

Table 2: Average Percentage Points by Which a Woman Candidate's Party Trailed the Winning Candidate in the Previous Election

	Conservative % (N)	Labour % (N)	Liberal % (N)*	Not Fought[a]
1951	26.8 (19)	18.8 (27)	35.4 (8)	2
1955	17.2 (16)	17.9 (21)	41.2 (9)	7
1964	18.6 (11)	21.6 (20)	35.8 (17)	7
1966	22.9 (12)	20.8 (13)	31.4 (17)	3
1970	21.8 (18)	17.9 (16)	30.8 (14)	8
1974 Oct	24.4 (22)	20.8 (36)	26.3 (42)	7
1979	27.1 (25)	17.5 (36)	34.2 (50)	1

(a. The number is the total constituencies for each election contested by a Liberal woman in which the party had not offered a candidate in the previous election. No Labour or Conservative woman contested such a constituency in these elections.)

party been founded in the 1920s and spent a generation in the political wilderness, women hardly could be worse off in the furtherance of political careers than they are now.

Receptivity to female candidature

While local party selection committees are reluctant to adopt women candidates, some of them may be more receptive than others... Some differences in receptivity appear in Table 3. The English north, particularly rural areas, and Wales are less likely to adopt women as candidates, while the south, particularly the urban constituencies, do so more frequently.[8] More than 70% of the constituencies in northern England never had a woman candidate, even for a minor party, during the five general elections from 1955 to 1970, while a fifth of the Southern urban seats saw a woman stand in two or more elections. In the south urban and rural constituencies differ little in their receptivity to women candidates. Although urban seats in Scotland are more receptive than rural ones–Scottish burghs in fact are less likely than any other type of seat to have refused constantly to adopt a woman candidate–more interesting is the fact that Scotland as a whole has been less resistant to women candidates than have either England or Wales.

Granted that the types of constituencies do vary in their receptivity, more striking is their clustering around the national

Table 3: Female Candidature by Constituency Type, 1955-70

	None		One		Two or More	
	N	**%**	**N**	**%**	**N**	**%**
London	24	57	9	21	9	21
South English boroughs	79	59	28	21	27	20
North English boroughs	75	66	26	23	12	11
South English counties	79	56	36	26	25	18
North English counties	63	77	12	15	7	9
Wales	24	67	7	19	5	14
Scot burghs	17	53	11	34	4	13
Scot counties	24	62	9	23	6	15
Total	385	62	138	22	95	15

The header spanning "One", "Two or More" columns reads: **Number of General Elections in Which a Woman Candidate Contested the Seat**

average. Although the differences between types of constituencies are in the expected direction, except for northern English county constituencies, they are relatively limited contrasts.

The pattern of female candidature is strikingly similar to that which existed during the inter-war period. The proportions for most types of constituencies differ only slightly between the two periods. And in the inter-war period, as in the period since the war, the north of England, especially the rural areas, tended to be least receptive to women candidates. Thus a social conservatism reluctant to grant women political equality appears to prevail in the north. Equally notable, however, is the evidence that those areas more receptive to women than is the north do not appear to have advanced much from their attitudes a generation earlier. The political status of women appears to be becalmed almost everywhere.

Constituency location is only one factor that could have affected the attitudes of local political elites toward the role of women in politics. Predominant occupation is another possibility. Perhaps social conservatism should be anticipated not so much in rural areas generally as in those where farming is important. Perhaps, also, mining may give to those areas where it is an important occupation more of a male orientation than exists in those areas where camaraderie among men in dangerous work is less common. Therefore, grouping constituencies according to occupational type to ascertain whether this is related to the incidence of women candidature is desirable.

Mitchell and Boehm's classification system was used to create seven constituency types: industrial, residential, farming, mining, mixed residential and industrial, mixed farming and industrial, and mixed (constituencies having three or more types of important occupations, e.g. farming, residential and heavy industry).[9] The distribution of female candidature was related only slightly to these occupational type. For example, 31% of all women candidatures for the Liberals, Conservatives, or Labour in 1950 and 1951 were in industrial constituencies and 34% in 1955 to 1970 were. Both figures correspond almost exactly to the proportion (33%) of the 630 total constituencies which were industrial. Residential constituencies during the entire period and residential/industrial seats during the early 1950s tended to have more than their share of women candidates. Farming areas did not appear to have been very receptive to women candidates in the early 1950s but were not markedly resistant later. All these differences were quite modest and others were inconsequential; the extent to which women were welcome as candidates for Parliament seems unrelated to the occupational composition of a constituency.

The redrawing of constituencies before the February 1974 election precludes using the occupational classification system for the three most recent elections. Instead Webber's socio-economic classification was used to produce six constituency types: residential, growth, inner metropolitan and council housing, stable industrial, agricultural, and mining.[10] Except for a slight underrepresentation of women candidatures in agricultural areas, the pattern of distribution for the three main parties combined virtually mirrored that of all constituencies. The chief contrasts are between the parties.

Women candidates were especially prevalent for Labour in residential constituencies and underrepresented in council housing ones–exactly the reverse of Labour's areas of strength. Similarly, the Conservatives were disproportionately likely to offer women candidates in council housing areas and unlikely to do so in residential areas–again the reverse of their strengths. These patterns further confirm the findings above that the local political elite are reluctant to adopt women as candidates except for constituencies where a party's support is so limited that a man would prefer to stand elsewhere.

The role of women in British politics

Thus the impediment to an expanded role for women in British politics tends to reside in local party candidate selection committees more than in the electorate. While local elites in agricultural areas and northern English rural districts have tended to be somewhat less receptive to the parliamentary aspirations of women, the key factor remains the wide-spread reluctance of selection committees–of whatever main party–to adopt women for desirable constituencies. As a result, when a woman has managed to get elected to the Commons, she has been vulnerable to defeat–especially in the Labour party–even though she has been as effective as a man in retaining support for her party. The irony–for women the frustration–is that parties have little to lose by adopting a woman to contest a constituency and once having offered a woman to the electorate have little reason–especially in the Labour party–for replacing her with a man. This is true because the British electorate for its part is little affected in its voting behaviour by candidate gender.

Since these findings tend to support, rather than challenge, previous work, perhaps the most remarkable discovery to emerge is the stability of behaviour. Not only do no trends in response to female candidates during the post-war period appear, but the continuity with behaviour in the inter-war period is striking. In the earlier period the electorate did seem somewhat hostile to women who persisted in contesting a constituency, whereas now that is no longer true. Aside from that, however, little has altered. Nothing suggests that women are about to make a major breakthrough in British politics; no areas of opportunity for advance can be identified. British politics appears to have been insulated from the last third of a century of social change in relations between sexes and in the nature of the family... The evidence of this study is that local political elites will continue to constrain the political role of women despite the electorate's lack of sexual prejudice.

Notes

1 J. Rasmussen, 'The Political Integration of British Women: The Response of a Traditional System to a Newly Emergent Group', *Social Science History,* forthcoming.
2 Although the number of non-incumbent women candidates has been greater in five of the subsequent ten elections, never again have so

many non-incumbent women been elected. The subsequent high was nine in 1970 and more typically the number has been six or fewer.

3   In 1970 the number doubled over the previous election to reach 21, to be followed by 30, 32, and 81 in the next three elections.

4   From this point on unless otherwise indicated the analysis deals with only Conservative, Labour and Liberal women candidates in the elections of 1951, 1959, 1964, 1966, 1970, October 1974 and 1979.

5   The idea here is somewhat analogous to the Nuffield Studies' swing measure, except that it compares a particular candidate to the winner in that constituency rather than seeking to measure the electoral movement between the two nationally dominant parties. In calculating changes in ground the total change is considered regardless of whether a portion of this figure is of one sign and the rest of it the other. For example, if in the first election party A wins 60% and party B 40% of the vote and in the next election they get 45% and 55% respectively, then party A has lost 30 percentage points of ground–the 20 percentage points by which it had won previously plus the 10 percentage points by which it now trails the winner. If the candidate in question has not won the seat, then the calculation is made on the basis of the percentage point gap between that candidate and the winning party regardless of the number, if any, of intervening parties in the order of finish. If the candidate has won the seat, then the relevant gap is the margin over the second place candidate. For example, if in the first election the results are: A 40%, B 30%, C 25%, and D 5% and in the next election A 45%, D 35% and B 20%, then D, which had been 35 percentage points behind the winner and now is only 10, has gained ground of 25 percentage points; B has lost ground of 15 percentage points; A has not gained any ground despite increasing its share of the vote by 5 percentage points, since in each election its victory margin was the same.

6   The Liberals provided only two instances – a woman replacement losing a seat in 1970 and a continuing woman losing a seat in 1951.

7   The Conservatives awarded women these 'plums' five times, Labour four times and the Liberals once.

8   The categories used are those of *The Times* House of Commons guides. The figures in Table 5 include all women candidates, not just those for Conservatives, Labour and Liberal.

9   B. R. Mitchell and K. Boehm, *British Parliamentary Election Results 1950-64* (Cambridge University Press, 1966).

10 R. Webber, *Parliamentary Constituencies: A Socio-Economic Classification* (Office of Population Censuses and Surveys, 1978).

Part Three

Activists, parties and pressure groups

Introduction

In a competitive political system, political parties and pressure groups play a central part in the process of political recruitment and policy – making. Our first two extracts focus on the issue of who is recruited to top political offices in Britain. The UK is a long – established liberal democracy and was the world's first industrial society. Yet political leadership, as several studies have demonstrated, has rarely reflected either formal democracy or our social structure. Historically the UK has been led by 'traditional' elites with close links to old aristocratic institutions. Only the rise of the Labour Party seemed to challenge that pattern, and evidence from the 1960s suggested that Labour's ability to recruit leaders from the wider population was declining. Burch and Moran's (3.1) paper brings up to date the evidence about the social characteristics of MPs and ministers. It presents a picture of both continuity and change, arguing that traditional elites are in a continuing decline and that the Labour Party continues to be a major means for recruiting individuals of working class origins into leadership positions.

Studies of political recruitment have been dominated by an interest in the social and educational characteristics of leaders. The great merit of King's paper (3.2) is that it examines neglected, but vital, questions about the career patterns and skills of politicians. King establishes that in the last generation important changes have taken place, involving the rise of individuals committed to politics as a lifelong career. This change has affected the kinds of occupations pursued before entry to politics, the age at which individuals enter Parliament and the duration of their careers once office is achieved.

The next five selections look in more detail at aspects of the main political parties in Britain. The Conservative Party has dominated modern British politics, and Margaret Thatcher has dominated the modern Conservative Party. Her ascendancy has not just been personal. The debate about 'Thatcherism' as a political philosophy — whether it is indeed a philosophy, and if so, what are its features — has been a preoccupation of political debate and academic enquiry for over a decade. The extracts by Leach (3.3) and by Bulpitt (3.4) address the question of the novelty of Thatcherism and conclude that its novelty has been overstated. The value of Leach's paper lies in the way it sets the recent philo – sophical and policy changes in the Conservative Party into the wider debate about the content of Conservative and Liberal social theories. Bulpitt complements this by presenting Thatcherism against the background of the Conservative Party's preoccupa-tions — with achieving electoral success, and with the problems of governing which follow from electoral victory.

The distinctive feature of the Labour Party in British politics is that it is a successful Parliamentary party joined uneasily to an ex-tra – Parliamentary political and industrial movement: the consis-tuency associations, affiliated societies and trade unions. That is why the vast literature on the Labour Party is preoccupied with questions about the authority of the Parliamentary leadership, es-pecially its authority over the movement outside Parliament. The Party has always experienced difficulties in resolving primary questions — about, for instance, the sources of legitimate authori-ty in the Labour movement and the balance of power to be struck between different sections of the movement. The merit of Druck-er's (3.5) paper is that it succinctly charts the practice of Parliamentary authority from the 1940s to the 1980s.

There have been times in the 1980s when it seemed likely that Labour's place as the Conservatives' chief opponents would be usurped, notably by the Alliance of the Liberals and Social Demo-crats. The extract from Bogdanor (3.6) examines the prospects and problems of this Alliance. Döring's paper (3.7) examines the most potentially significant group of new activists enticed into party politics in recent years. It is an important corrective to media caricatures of the social characteristics and attitudes of the active members of the Social Democratic Party.

The study of pressure groups in recent years has been dominated by two themes; by the argument that there are systematic inequalities in the pressure group system, and by the view that there is a trend towards 'corporatism' in relations between groups and government. Marsh and Locksley's paper (3.8) reflects the first of these themes, arguing that the power of business in Britain's market economy lies crucially in a control over economic decisions conferred by the workings of the market system. Martin's paper (3.9) adopts a very different track. He outlines the 'corporatist' literature which in recent years has provided a conventional wisdom in interpreting pressure groups, and subjects it to fierce examination.

3.1 *Martin Burch and Michael Moran*

The changing political elite

From 'The changing British political elite',
Parliamentary Affairs, Vol. 38, No. 1, 1985, pp. 1 – 15.

The recruitment of political leadership in Britain has been marked
by contradictory forces. On the one hand, powerful democratic influences have long been at work. As the first industrial nation, Britain developed large and confident middle and working classes
who soon made their mark in the political arena. On the other
hand, a tradition of deference, and a politically astute upper class,
ensured that aristocratic influence persisted into the age of mass
parties and a democratic franchise. Over twenty years ago Guttsman documented the glacially slow erosion of aristocratic pro-
minence and the rise of 'new men'. Since then, examination of the
social structure of the elite in Parliament and in Cabinet has been
spasmodic.[1] In the meantime, great social and political changes
have taken place. The culture of deference has weakened. Determined efforts have been made to promote upward social mobility.
Economic growth has created mass affluence and, until recently,
full employment. This is a fitting moment to examine how far the
slow broadening of the elite documented by Guttsman has continued or how far, alternatively, social changes and policy reforms
have produced more radical developments...

Two very different interpretations of the changing shape of elite
recruitment have dominated post – war discussions of the subject
in Britain. The first, most commonly voiced by left – wing radicals
and by some social scientists, is usually labelled 'closure' theory.[2]
This asserts that, whatever the opportunities for upward social
mobility in society at large, at the very top powerful social
mechanisms close off access to elite positions, reserving leadership
posts for a small minority disproportionately drawn from families
of those already enjoying privilege. On this view, elites in Britain
are largely self – recruiting. Little impact is to be expected from
social change or policy reform.

By contrast, the official ideology of some of the most powerful institutions in Britain denies the experience of 'closure'. On this second view, elite recruitment has become increasingly merito-cratic. Consequently, access to elite positions is open to indivi-duals of ability from a wide range of social backgrounds. There also exists a less optimistic interpretation of the working of merito-cracy, best called the 'convergence' view.[3] According to this ac-count, the increasing emphasis on meritocratic criteria is making the parliamentary leaderships of both major parties more alike. Politics is being dominated by individuals who are 'professionals' in a double sense: in the sense that they have a life – long commit-ment to a specialist career in politics, and in the sense that they are drawn from the professional middle classes, and have acquired the conventional marks of merit by success in formal education. In the process of convergence, social groups at the extremes are being excluded from leadership: those of aristocratic backgrounds are being squeezed out of the Conservative Party, those of working class background from the top of the Labour Party.

We now turn to the evidence. As we shall show, the complex evolution during the post – war years of that crucial part of the political elite represented by MPs and Cabinet ministers does not fit any single interpretation.

Members of parliament

Evidence about the characteristics of Labour and Conservative MPs, 1945 – 83, is summarised in Tables 1 – 4. (We have ignored the other small parties.) For the period up to October 1974 we draw on data produced by Mellors,[4] and for the 1979 and 1983 Parliaments we use material extracted from a number of standard directories. Since Mellors exhaustively examines the 1945 – 74 period, we focus chiefly on the last decade, using his evidence to provide a standard by which to measure the extent of recent change.

We have organised the data into two sets of two tables—one for Conservative and one for Labour MPs. Tables 1 and 3 reproduce data on the characteristics of all major party MPs elected in each parliament since 1945. The characteristics of the intake of new MPs at each election are reproduced in Tables 2 and 4. Analysing these two cohorts gives a particularly sensitive measure of the direction of change in the parties...

The Conservative Party

Between 1945 and October 1974 the Conservative benches were remarkably stable in their social composition. The most striking sign of stability was revealed by the extent to which Conservative MPs were predominantly drawn from public school and, to a slightly lesser extent, Oxford and Cambridge (shorthand: Oxbridge). As Table 1 shows, in percentage terms, the public school element remained in the mid to upper seventies for most of the period, while Oxbridge graduates ranged between 50% and 57% of all MPs. There is also evidence of a marginal increase in the public school and Oxbridge proportions in the years the party lost elections—especially 1964, 1966 and February 1974—suggesting that MPs from these backgrounds tended to be concentrated in its safer seats.

Beneath this persistent pattern of public school/Oxbridge domination, some marginal changes were nevertheless taking place. There was a slight drop in the number of old Etonians, a trend clearest among new MPs from 1966 onwards. This perhaps also indicated a decline in the aristocratic element within the party. It was paralleled by a small but fairly consistent rise in the proportion of MPs who had been educated at state secondary schools *and* non–Oxbridge universities: the figure rose from 6% of all Conservative MPs in 1950 to nearly 12% in October 1974. Apart from these changes, the most notable alteration lay in the more or less persistent rise in the number of MPs with local government experience, from just over 14% in 1945 to 31% in October 1974. This change is evidently linked to the rise of 'career' politicians in the party recently documented by King.[5]

Throughout the 29 years following the Second World War Conservative MPs thus conformed to a narrow and exclusive pattern of recruitment based on public schools and Oxbridge. The 1979 and 1983 figures, however, show a decisive change from this established pattern. With hindsight, we can now see that some of the changes were germinating as long ago as 1970.

Five main alterations are revealed in Table 1 and more strongly emphasised in Table 2. First, there is a decrease in MPs drawn from an Oxbridge background. In 1979 the overall total for Oxbridge fell below 50% for the first time since 1945, while in 1983 fully 54% of all Conservative MPs were non–Oxbridge. Second, there is a decline in public school recruitment, resulting in a drop to 64% of all MPs in 1983. The full measure of this change is more clearly revealed by figures for new MPs: among this group the public school intake fell to just over 53% in 1979 and to 47% in 1983. Table 2 also reveals a substantial fall in new Conservatives with a public school *and* Oxbridge background, to one quarter of those newly elected in 1983. The third change is an increase in those MPs who were both educated at state secondary schools and who took their first degrees at non – Oxbridge universities: among the new intake in 1983 these were more numerous than those with a traditional 'patrician' public school/Oxbridge background. A fourth change is the continued decline in the number of Old Etonians, to an all – time low in 1983 of just over 12% of all Conservative MPs and 6% of the new recruits. A fifth and final change—in some ways the obverse of Eton's decline—is the rise, especially amongst new MPs, of those with only elementary and secondary education.

These five changes, of which the first three are most important suggest that in terms of educational background the Conservative Party has become more open and less exclusive in its sources of recruitment. The significance of these developments lies in the way they break with a stable pattern maintained throughout the post – war period until 1970 and only marginally altered between then and the end of the decade.

Some features of the 1979 and 1983 intakes nevertheless marked a continued process of evolution rather than a break with the past. The rise in the numbers of MPs with local government experience continued, reaching 38% of all Conservative MPs in 1983 and over half of those newly elected in that year. The trend towards younger newly elected Conservative MPs has also continued: only 46% were over forty years old in 1983, whereas over 60% were over forty in 1966...

In summary, we have identified a marked shift in the social character of the Conservative Party in Parliament. This shift, moreover, is not a product of the possibly transitory Conservative majority in 1983; it reflects deeper and more enduring developments in the party.

The Labour Party
The most important change in the social composition of Labour Members during the three decades after 1945 is well documented, notably by Mellors. It consisted in the decline in the proportion of

manual workers from just over a quarter (in 1945) to less than an eighth in 1974 (Table 3). This went with a fall in the proportion of MPs who had only elementary and secondary education, to less than half the 1945 level, and a marked increase in the proportion of university educated MPs. At the same time there was a fairly steady, though less substantial, rise in the proportion drawn from Oxbridge, while the proportion of MPs educated at state secondary school and non – Oxbridge universities more than doubled. There also occurred a persistent rise in the proportion of MPs drawn from the professions, notably from teaching and lecturing...

The data for 1979 and 1983 suggest a marginal alteration in this pattern. The figures are, however, open to a variety of interpretations, especially because in these two elections the numbers of Labour MPs reached their lowest level since 1935. The figures for all Labour MPs (Table 3) show a rise in the proportion of manual workers within the parliamentary party and, especially in 1983, a clear fall in the Oxbridge and public school contingents. These developments may indicate a return to the party's immediate post – war state, a view which finds some support in the data on new MPs contained in Table 4. Here a word of caution is necessary. In both instances the number of new MPs is very small, at 40 and 34 respectively, so generalisations are difficult. Moreover, as we shall see, in some cases the data on 1979 and 1983 are contradictory.

With this caution in mind, we may note amongst new Labour MPs a marked decrease in the Oxbridge and teacher/lecturer proportions, as well as an increase in the number of manual worker recruits to a level (20%) closer to the pattern up to 1964. There is also a clear rise in the proportion with local government experience, to an all time high of over 64% in 1983. The other figures are less certain, with those with elementary and secondary education only rising to 40% in 1979 then falling back to half that in 1983. There is also a large drop in state secondary non – Oxbridge university recruits in 1983, a fall in public school *and* Oxbridge Members in 1979, and a marked decline in those with professional occupations in 1983. But none of these developments are confirmed over both election intakes.

Overall, the figures for the Labour Party are less clear – cut than are those for the Conservatives. The trend towards an increasingly middle—class, white—collar, professional party does, however, appear to have slowed down in 1979 and by 1983 may even have been reversed. The truth is that it is too early to be certain.

Cabinets

Few people serve in Cabinets: since 1955 only 77 individuals have been Conservative Cabinet ministers, while the total for the Labour Party is only 56. Detailed analysis of such small groups is plainly difficult. Although we will glance at the characteristics of new Cabinet entrants since 1970, most of our discussion focuses on Cabinet membership over the last three decades. Guttsman's earlier work provides an analysis of selected social and educational characteristics of all Cabinet members for the period 1916 – 1955. This data (reproduced in Table 5 alongside our findings for subsequent decades), provides a set of benchmarks for measuring long – term changes in the characteristics of individuals recruited to Cabinets.

Conservative Cabinets

The most striking social feature of the modern Conservative leadership is, of course, the fact that the two most recent Conservative Prime Ministers have been grammar school/Oxford educated meritocrats of modest social origins. It is often said that Mr Heath and Mrs Thatcher are indicative of a more general rise of lower – middle – class meritocrats in the party, and indeed we found some support for this view when examining MPs.

Table 5 allows us to test the accuracy of this belief as it applies to the very top positions. The figures show that, while important long – term social change is indeed happening, the characteristics of the two most recent leaders are not an accurate guide to either the scale or the direction of that wider change. There has been no remarkable advance in Conservative Cabinets by state school educated meritocrats. On the contrary, products of the public schools were actually more common in 1955 – 84 than in 1916 – 55. Nor is there any sign of a significant advance by self – made men from the humblest social backgrounds: the proportion of Cabinet ministers born to working – class families, and the proportion with only an elementary or secondary education, actually fell slightly in the 1955 – 84 period compared with the earlier decades. Neither the state school meritocrat nor the spectacularly self — made man have become more common. There has been one important social change, reflecting a trend already identified by Guttsman, a continuing decline in the proportions of Cabinet ministers drawn from the very highest ranks of society. Table 5 contains two important signs of this development: the fall in the proportion of ministers with aristocratic backgrounds and the decline of the two most socially exclusive public schools, Eton and Harrow, as suppliers of Cabinet personnel.

The advantage of amalgamating all evidence for 1955 – 84 is that it provides numbers large enough to give some confidence when it comes to statistical analysis; the disadvantage is that it may conceal trends within the years in question. We have checked for this possibility by examining new entrants to Cabinet since 1970 (they number 34). In important respects this group shows no great change from the past: over 80% were public school educated and three quarters went to Oxbridge. However, the two changes already noted have persisted: aristocrats continue to fall (only 15% of post – 1970 entrants have such backgrounds); and there has occurred a further sharp fall in the proportions of Etonians and Harrovians to 15%, whereas between 1916 – 1955 the two schools supplied nearly half of all Conservative Cabinet ministers...

The evidence for the Conservative Party may thus be summarised as follows. Long – term change in the social composition of the Conservative leadership is modest. Mr Heath and Mrs Thatcher are atypical, not signs of the rise of meritocrats from humble origins. Change has not, contrary to common belief, made the party leadership more socially diverse. Conservative Cabinets are in one important sense becoming more, not less, homogeneous. The party is not recruiting a larger proportion of humbly born meritocrats into its leadership, but there has been a marked drop in the representation of those drawn from the very apex of the social structure—as shown by the decline in aristocratic numbers, and in those from the most prestigious public schools. Conservative Cabinets, far from becoming more socially diverse, have thus become more homogeneously middle class.

Labour Cabinets

As Table 5 shows, Labour Cabinets before 1955 were very different socially from those of their Conservative opponents: just over half of Labour Cabinet members had only the legal minimum of education; over a half had not been to university; barely more than a quarter had a public school education; and likewise only just over a quarter had been to Oxbridge. Most distinctive of all, 55% had been born the children of working – class parents.

It is commonly asserted that the subsequent history of Labour's parliamentary leadership has involved social embourgeoisement, the domination of Labour Cabinets by middle – class cohorts increasingly resembling those on the Conservative side. The evidence only partly supports this assertion. It is true that if we compare the post – 1955 period with the preceding forty years there is evidence of a growing middle – class contingent. Though Labour Cabinets have remained socially and educationally distinct from those formed by Conservative Prime Ministers, it is nevertheless the case that there has been a sharp rise in the proportion educated to university level, including a marked increase in the Oxbridge contingent. Though not indicated directly in the table, these figures also reflect a changing balance in favour of those who have practised a middle – class profession, at the expense of those who were at some stage of their adult lives manual workers. There is even a discernible rise in the numbers educated at public schools. But these figures do not tell the whole story, for two reasons: they fail to reveal one significant way in which the elitism of Labour Cabinets has actually declined and they exaggerate the extent to which those of working – class backgrounds have been displaced. We deal with each of these points in turn.

As the figures (Table 5) show, early Labour Cabinets contained a significant sprinkling of aristocrats and—not an identical group—Etonians and Harrovians. This was partly due to a lack of faith in native working – class talent among Labour leaders like Ramsay MacDonald. This upper – class group has been in decline and by the 1970s had nearly reached a point of extinction. New entrants to Labour Cabinets after 1970 (admittedly only numbering 19) contained not a single product of Eton or Harrow nor a single aristocrat. The proportion of the 1970s entrants educated at a public school (at just over a fifth) was smaller even than in the period 1916 – 55.

One reason for the decline of the high – born is that the education system began to produce able meritocrats of modest social origins. This phenomenon also explains why the decline of working – class recruits in the upper reaches of the party is less sharp than is commonly believed. As Table 5 shows, when we follow

Guttsman's original practice of identifying working – class background by parental occupation, the shift away from the working class, though marked, still leaves a sizable contingent of working – class origins. There is indeed evidence of some recent reversal even in the identifiable modest trend towards social embourgeoisement: of the 19 fresh Labour Cabinet entrants in 1974 – 9, eight were children of manual workers.

The most striking long term alteration at the top of the Labour Party is not so much in class composition as in mode of social ascent. In the period examined by Guttsman the majority of Labour Cabinet ministers experienced intra – generational social mobility: they entered adult life in the working class, and then rose out of it through a career in the Labour movement. In our period, a substantial number of Cabinet ministers were likewise born to the working class, but rose through education from the working class, capping this success with a political career.

The recruitment patterns in the Conservative and Labour Parties are different. The changes over time experienced in both parties have likewise differed... The Conservative Party is undoubtedly meritocratic by aspiration: it would like to draw its leaders widely from many social groups in order to be led by the most able. The fact that recruitment outcomes defy these meritocratic aspirations argues for the existence of powerful, deeply – rooted mechanisms closing off the top of the Conservative Party to those not born to privilege.

Yet the party is plainly not immune to change. There is occurring a very slow 'flattening' of the social profile of Conservative Cabinets. Among the wider group of Conservative MPs, change in the post – war years has been even more pronounced. It has accelerated dramatically since the end of the 1970s and has revealed a marked decline in public school and Oxbridge dominance...

The future pattern of recruitment at the top of the Labour Party is even less clear. Indeed, it is not all certain whether Labour will continue to occupy a major place in British politics. If its electoral decline continues, then the social characteristics of the party's leaders will cease to be of much interest to anyone other than specialist scholars of the Labour movement.

It seemed until about a decade ago that Labour was succumbing to mechanisms of closure, with a formally meritocratic ideology producing a party dominated at the top by university – educated middle — class professionals. The notion that working — class recruits are being excluded from the top of the party now has to be modified. For the first time in half a century Labour has a leader of impeccable working class origins in Mr Kinnock. This leader, furthermore, illustrates a facet of recruitment too easily neglected. As the university – educated son of a labourer, he typifies the extraordinary number of Labour MPs who are socially mobile, through education, out of the working class. Of all Labour members returned in 1979, for instance, over half were the children of manual workers; and while the same Parliament contained only 19 MPs who had worked as miners, it contained 35 more who were the children of miners.[6] In short, even in the 1970s Labour provided a relatively open channel for those of working – class origins to enter the political elite. We have seen some signs that the party has also arrested the decline in numbers of MPs with adult experience as manual workers. The long – term significance of these developments nevertheless remains unclear. The great defeats of 1979 and 1983, together with their organisational and ideological consequences, plainly altered the party. Even more than in the case of the Conservatives, the future social shape of the Labour leadership in Parliament and Cabinet is not clear. The patterns of the past are reducible to no single theoretical stereotype; the patterns of the future are likely to be similarly complicated.

Notes

1 W. L. Guttsman, *The British Political Elite* (MacGibbon and Kee, 1963); R. W. Johnson, 'The British Political Elite, 1955 – 72', *European Journal of Sociology,* XIV (1973).
2 A. Heath, *Social Mobility* (Fontana, 1981), p. 61.
3 Johnson, loc. cit., pp. 68 – 73.
4 C. Mellors, *The British MP: A Socio – economic Study of the House of Commons* (Saxon House, 1978).
5 A. King, 'The Rise of the Career Politician in Britain—And its Consequences', *British Journal of Political Science,* 11 (1981).
6 Figures for social origins are calculated from A. Roth, *The MPs Chart* (Parliamentary Profiles, 1980), from whence also come the figures for children of miners.

Table 1 Background of All Conservative MPs, 1945 – 83 (%)

	1945	1950	1951	1955	1959	1964	1966	1970	Feb. 1974	Oct. 1974	1979	1983
All Public Schools	83.2	83.1	70.2	79.7	75.8	77.9	78.9	74.2	75.0	74.6	73.0	64.1
Eton	27.1	26.7	23.7	23.1	19.4	22.2	21.8	19.0	18.2	17.0	15.0	12.4
Oxbridge	53.3	54.0	54.3	53.7	50.6	54.3	57.1	51.3	55.7	55.1	49.2	45.7
Public/Oxbridge	50.3	51.9	51.0	51.3	46.5	49.3	51.6	44.7	48.3	47.5	37.4	37.1
Elem/Sec only	3.7	5.3	6.4	7.2	7.9	8.2	5.1	7.5	7.7	7.2	8.2	8.8
State Sec/Univ	7.0	6.0	6.8	6.6	8.2	7.8	9.0	10.0	11.4	11.9	16.2	17.9
All Universities	64.7	64.7	64.6	65.9	60.7	63.8	67.0	63.5	66.9	67.4	68.0	71.7
Local Government	14.1	16.8	16.6	20.7	25.5	27.2	28.9	30.4	32.0	31.0	35.0	38.1
Numbers	213	298	321	344	365	304	253	330	297	277	339	396

Table 2. Background of New Conservative MPs, 1945 – 83 (%)

	1945	1950	1951	1955	1959	1964	1966	1970	Feb. 1974	Oct. 1974	1979	1983
All Public Schools	81.2	76.5	68.7	70.5	73.1	82.9	84.5	67.0	85.6	87.5	53.2	47.0
Eton	26.1	21.4	25.0	20.5	16.3	21.9	15.4	12.1	14.5	–	13.2	6.0
Oxbridge	42.1	46.9	53.1	50.0	45.2	56.3	46.1	40.7	59.7	62.5	36.0	35.0
Public/Oxbridge	43.5	44.9	43.8	47.4	39.4	50.0	46.1	34.1	53.2	62.5	30.4	25.0
Elem/Sec only	6.9	9.8	11.7	10.3	5.7	3.1	7.6	11.1	1.6	12.5	16.0	12.0
State Sec/Univ	2.7	8.8	11.7	7.7	9.6	9.3	–	13.3	11.2	–	22.6	30.0
All Universities	50.8	61.3	56.3	66.3	53.8	70.4	62.0	57.2	72.6	75.0	73.2	72.0
Local Government	10.8	22.5	22.1	35.9	36.5	34.4	38.7	32.5	27.4	25.0	41.2	52.0
Numbers	72	102	34	77	104	64	13	90	62	8	75	100

Activists, parties and pressure groups

Table 3. Background of All Labour MPs, 1945 – 83 (%)

	1945	1950	1951	1955	1959	1964	1966	1970	Feb. 1974	Oct. 1974	1979	1983
All Public Schools	19.4	22.2	23.4	23.5	24.6	24.0	22.8	19.4	15.7	16.4	17.0	13.4
Oxbridge	14.5	15.4	16.8	16.4	17.2	17.7	19.3	20.4	19.3	20.8	20.4	14.4
Public/Oxbridge	10.4	14.5	13.7	13.1	12.9	12.9	12.7	12.8	9.7	10.4	11.2	9.1
State Sec/Univ	18.7	18.6	18.8	18.6	20.3	24.6	29.8	35.0	39.0	40.3	37.1	38.2
Elem/Sec. only	52.4	49.2	36.9	59.9	47.2	39.4	35.5	31.0	26.5	24.4	28.9	21.5
All Universities	34.2	37.7	38.7	38.2	39.5	43.9	48.5	51.2	53.0	55.7	57.0	54.1
Manual Workers	27.6	27.6	26.2	25.3	21.1	18.4	16.6	13.2	12.3	12.0	19.8	15.3
Teachers/Lecturers	12.1	13.9	14.8	14.3	14.9	16.5	20.1	20.9	25.8	28.1	24.2	25.8
Local Government	43.5	41.4	40.8	40.8	39.3	42.9	43.7	41.3	46.6	46.4	37.6	47.8
Numbers	393	315	295	277	258	317	363	287	301	319	269	209

Table 4. Background of New Labour MPs, 1945 – 83 (%)

	1945	1950	1951	1955	1959	1964	1966	1970	Feb. 1974	Oct. 1974	1979	1983
All Public Schools	21.5	27.4	13.3	15.4	11.9	19.8	15.3	12.5	6.5	18.2	18.0	22.5
Oxbridge	17.7	19.4	13.3	7.7	4.8	17.9	23.6	18.8	15.2	22.7	5.0	11.8
Public/Oxbridge	12.2	16.1	6.7	7.7	2.4	11.3	8.3	9.4	6.5	9.1	2.5	11.8
State Sec./Univ.	19.4	19.4	26.7	26.9	26.2	29.2	48.6	43.7	41.3	50.0	52.5	38.2
Elem./Sec.	51.9	38.7	46.6	50.0	59.5	32.3	22.2	23.4	26.0	13.6	40.0	20.6
All Universities	37.6	43.6	40.0	34.6	31.0	45.3	63.9	56.2	47.8	72.7	52.5	55.9
Manual Workers	19.7	17.6	20.0	19.2	23.8	18.9	12.5	6.2	19.6	4.6	20.0	20.6
Teachers/Lecturers	13.3	17.7	20.0	23.1	9.5	18.9	34.7	29.7	19.9	50.0	15.0	17.6
Local Government	42.2	45.2	40.0	53.0	54.7	51.9	43.1	39.1	56.5	45.4	62.5	64.7
Numbers	227	62	15	24	42	105	72	64	46	22	40	34

Table 5. Background of Cabinet Ministers (%)

	1916 – 1955		1955 – 1984	
	Conservative	Labour	Conservative	Labour
All Public Schools	76.5	26.1	87.1	32.1
Eton/Harrow	45.9	7.6	36.3	3.5
Oxbridge	63.2	27.6	72.8	42.8
Elem./Sec. only	4.0	50.7	2.5	37.5
All Universities	71.4	44.6	81.6	62.5
Aristocrat	31.6	6.1	18.1	1.8
Middle – Class	65.3	38.4	74.0	44.6
Working – Class	3.0	55.3	2.6	41.0
No Data	–	–	4.0	12.6
Number	98	65	77	56

Sources for Tables
Tables 1 to 5: 1945 – 74 figures calculated from Mellors, *The British MP;*
1979 and 1983 figures are from standard directories— *Times Guides to the*
House of Commons, Who's Who, BBC Election Guides, Dod's
Parliamentary Companion. Table 6: 1916 – 55 figures are from Guttsman,
The British Political Elite; 1955 – 84 figures are from *Who's Who, Who*
Was Who, Roth, *The MP's Chart,* and selected biographies and autobio-
graphies.

3.2   *Anthony King*

The rise of the career politician

From 'The rise of the career politician in Britain — and its consequences',
British Journal of Political Science, Vol. 11, 1981, pp. 249-85.

... The argument of this paper is that in the 1980s career politicians
are almost the only politicians left in the upper echelons of British
politics and government. Career politicians have always been
more numerous at this level than non-career politicians; career
politicians are not a new breed. The claim here is merely that,
whereas career politicians once shared the top posts with an ad-
mixture of non-career politicians, they do so no longer — or at
least not to anything like the same degree.

The feeling is certainly widespread among long-time observers
of the British political scene that some sort of subtle shift in the
personnel and attitudes of members of Parliament has taken
place. For example, James Margach, a political correspondent for
half a century from the mid-1920s to the mid-1970s, commented
frequently on the growing 'rootlessness', as he saw it, of modern
politics. He attributed the change to 'the increasing demands of
ever more professionalism in politics.[1] Similarly, Jo Grimond, the
former Liberal leader, noted in his memoirs that the traditional
role of MPs was as 'representative citizens sharing the troubles of
their constituents'. During the 1960s, however, many MPs began
to redefine their role; they sought to become 'an amalgam of civil
servant and researcher with a dash of welfare officer thrown in.'
Grimond commented:

More and more MPs looked on it... as a full-time job. More and
more MPs, and this was particularly apparent in the Labour Party,
wanted to be members of the Government. Even before they
could achieve that, they wanted to be in touch with government
policies. They were by nature insiders not critics. The number of
teachers and lecturers among the Labour Party had swollen. They

were keen readers of blue books and writers of monographs. The
great research industry had invaded the House of Commons.[2]

These are the sorts of ways in which career politicians could be
expected to behave.

Grimond referred in the passage just quoted to the occupational
backgrounds of the younger generation of MPs; but of course one
has to be very careful about drawing inferences from MPs' social
backgrounds to their career orientations. Most of the rich and
aristocratic members of the Conservative party in the House of
Commons before 1939 — the 'knights of the shires' — probably
regarded politics as something of a sideline, the station to which it
fell to the lot of an English gentleman to be called; but some of
them undoubtedly were career politicians in the sense in which the
term is being used here. Similarly, most trade unionists on the pre-
war Labour benches probably did not think of themselves as
career politicians; but some of them must have done. To this day,
to know that an MP is a teacher or journalist is not to know anything for sure about his attitude towards politics as a way of life.

All that can be said is that, if a growing proportion of members
of Parliament have pursued, or are still pursuing, occupations of a
kind that facilitate the pursuit of politics as a serious career, then it
at least stands to reason that the number of MPs with a deep commitment to politics will also have increased. Either people will
have entered a specific occupation in the belief that it would assist
them in making a career in politics, or else, having entered the occupation for some other reason, they will have discovered at some
later stage that politics is a natural and attractive next step. In the
famous words of Woodrow Wilson, 'The profession I chose was
politics; the profession I entered was the law. I entered the one
because I thought it would lead to the other.'[3] The law is indeed
such a politics-facilitating occupation. So are broadcasting, journalism, authorship, public relations, school teaching and university and college lecturing. They all offer a wide range of contacts,
flexible patterns of work, long holidays, abundant opportunities
for leave and a chance to practise politically-relevant skills such as
writing and public speaking. Moreover, for people in these professions politics is thought to be a suitable activity, not one that con-
travenes professional norms.

Against this background, the figures in Table 1 are suggestive.
The percentage of barristers and solicitors in the House of Commons has remained fairly constant since the mid-1930s and shows

Table 1 Percentages of Conservative and Labour MPs in Politics-facilitating Occupations, by Election

	1935*	1945	1950	1951	1955	1959	1964	1966	1970	Feb. 1974	Oct. 1974	1979*
	(%)	(%)	(%)	(%)	(%)	(%)	(%)	(%)	(%)	(%)	(%)	(%)
Barristers, solicitors	14.0	14.2	17.5	17.0	17.4	18.0	18.0	18.1	17.4	16.4	15.8	15.6
Journalists, authors, publishers, public relations personnel	5.0	7.3	7.4	7.6	7.1	6.7	8.9	9.5	8.9	9.0	8.4	7.2
Lecturers	3.3	4.1	3.8	3.9	2.6	3.2	4.3	7.1	6.3	7.4	9.2	4.4
Schoolteachers	1.2	4.6	3.9	3.9	4.4	3.7	4.8	5.0	5.5	6.5	7.2	7.7
'Communicators' (i.e. sum of above three categories)	9.5	16.0	15.1	15.4	14.1	13.6	18.0	21.6	20.7	22.9	24.8	19.3
N	(585)	(613)	(612)	(615)	(620)	(623)	(621)	(618)	(620)	(598)	(596)	(608)

Note that the figures in these two columns are not strictly comparable with the others, having been derived from different sources. In particular, the decline in the percentage of journalists and authors in the right-hand column is probably an artifact of the different coding categories used.

Sources: The data in the 1935 column are taken from *Who's Who , Who Was Who, Dod's Parliamentary Companion* (various volumes) and *The Times Guide to the House of Commons 1935*. The data in the 1979 column are taken from David Butler and Dennis Kavanagh, *The British General Election of 1979* (London: Macmillan, 1980), Table 4, p. 287. All of the other data are recalculated from Colin Mellors. *The British MP: A Socioeconomic Study of the House of Commons* (Farnborough, Hants.: Saxon House, 1978), Table 5.2, pp. 62-6.

no marked tendency to either increase or decline. Moreover, contrary to widespread belief, the proportion of university and college lecturers among MPs is not enormously greater in the early 1980s than it was before the Second World War; the percentage of lecturers rose sharply at the time of the Labour victories in 1966 and 1974 but then fell back equally sharply in 1979.[4] The same is not true, however, of the two other occupational categories covered by the table: journalists, authors and public relations personnel, and schoolteachers. The incidence of both groups among members of Parliament is significantly higher today than it was in the 1930s; the percentage of schoolteachers, in particular, has increased more than sixfold, from 1.2 per cent in 1935 to 7.7 per cent in 1979.

One way of taking the measure of the over-all changes that have taken place is to group together the three occupations that depend to a high degree on the exercise of verbal skills: journalism, lecturing and schoolteaching. This is done in the fifth row of Table 1. As can be seen, there has been a gradual tendency for the numbers of such professional users of words to increase over the years. Following the 1935 general election, scarcely one member of Parliament in ten fell into this broad category of 'communicators'; following the 1979 election, nearly one in five did so. It is just possible that the shift in the balance between lawyers and these other kinds of communicators is significant. The barrister or solicitor is trained to argue the case, any case, that is put before him. He is meant to be professionally neutral — a 'hired gun', as it were. Journalists and teachers, by contrast, are in the business of self-expression. What matters to them are *their* thoughts and *their* words...

Another way, equally indirect but also suggestive, of gauging whether career politicians are more numerous than they used to be is to look at the early stages of MPs' and cabinet ministers' careers — at how old they were when they first entered the House of Commons, and at how many unsuccessful attempts they made to get into Parliament before they were finally elected.

It seems reasonable to hypothesize that men and women committed to a political career are most likely to be found in the group of MPs first elected to the House of Commons in their 30s or early 40s. To be sure, those first returned while still in their 20s will probably include a certain number of career politicians (the lucky ones, those who have succeeded in launching their careers early); but this group is also likely to include a number of young people who are in politics more as a consequence of family tradition than out of any strong personal conviction. In the past, it was not uncommon for the lord of the manor's son to be selected for the safe family seat almost as soon as he came down from Eton or Oxford. At the other end of the age range, the group of MPs first elected at the age of 50 or over seems unlikely to contain a large proportion of career politicians. All but the most compulsive politicos are likely to have given up by then, and in practice most of the over-

50s elected to the House of Commons for the first time are retired trade-union officials and other local Labour worthies despatched to Westminster more as reward for past services than in any great hope of services to come:[5]

Table 2 Age of Entry of New Conservative and Labour MPs into the House of Commons, in Percentages, by Election

First elected aged	Pre-1945 (%)	1945 (%)	1950 (%)	1951 (%)	1955 (%)	1959 (%)	1964 (%)	1966 (%)	1970 (%)	Feb. 1974 (%)	Oct. 1974 (%)	1979 (%)
21-29	13.8	4.3	1.2	6.1	5.9	7.5	2.4	8.2	4.5	2.8	13.3	4.7
30-39	34.7	31.4	37.8	36.7	32.7	32.9	40.2	45.9	42.2	47.2	40.0	55.8
40-49	33.7	37.8	39.0	38.8	38.6	41.8	40.2	34.1	40.9	38.0	40.0	27.1
50-59	14.1	17.4	20.1	14.3	21.8	16.4	16.6	8.2	12.3	10.2	6.7	10.9
60+	3.7	9.0	1.8	4.1	1.0	1.4	0.6	3.5	0.0	1.9	0.0	1.6
N	(326)	(299)	(164)	(47)	(101)	(146)	(169)	(85)	(154)	(108)	(30)	(129)

Sources: Recalculated from Mellors, *The British MP,* Table 3.3, pp. 31-2, except for the 1979 data which are taken from *The Times Guide to the House of Commons, May 1979.*

If this line of reasoning is accepted as broadly correct, then Table 2 makes fascinating reading. It summarizes the ages of first entry into Parliament of all those who served in the House of Commons between the end of the Second World War and 1974. Some of those who served after the 1945 general election had first been elected at some time before it; hence the column headed 'Pre-1945'. Three points stand out from the table. The first is the sharp decline, which occurred immediately after the war, in the number of MPs being returned to Parliament for the first time while they were still under the age of 30. (The high proportion in October 1974 is almost certainly a fluke, the result of the very small number of new members elected at that time.) It seems that the old Tory squirearchy has declined and with it the pre-war platoons of very young (and therefore very inexperienced) Tory members.[6] Secondly, and more important in the present context, fewer and fewer MPs are arriving in the House of Commons for the first time at the age of 50 or more. The slump in their numbers after about 1955 is quite striking. Whereas in the early 1950s, something like one in five new MPs was over the age of 50, the proportion in more recent years has been more like one in ten.

Thirdly, it follows from the previous two points, and emerges clearly from the table, that gradually increasing proportions of new MPs are being elected in their 30s and 40s. Since 1964, the 30-49 age group has accounted at every election for 80 per cent or more of newly-elected members. In addition, the balance has gradually shifted against those in their 40s and in favour of those in their 30s. If the relevant data were to hand, they would probably show that a disproportionate number of those elected for the first time in their 40s are in their early 40s. None of this proves conclusively that the incidence of career politicians has increased, but it is certainly consistent with such a hypothesis.

The same trend has also manifested itself among cabinet ministers. For the purposes of Table 3, the peacetime cabinets of the period since 1935 have been divided into eight groups. Several of the eight correspond straightforwardly to governments, such as

Table 3: Ages at which Cabinet Ministers First Entered House of Commons, in Percentages*

First elected aged	1935-1940 (%)	1945-1951 (%)	1951-1957 (%)	1957-1964 (%)	1964-1970 (%)	1970-1974 (%)	1974-1979 (%)	1979- (%)
21-29	32.5	6.3	36.0	23.5	11.4	9.1	18.2	9.5
30-34	20.0	15.6	24.0	26.4	37.1	50.0	45.5	47.6
35-39	20.0	34.4	20.0	35.3	34.3	31.8	15.2	42.9
40-44	15.0	28.1	8.0	5.9	8.6	0.0	21.2	0.0
45-49	2.5	6.3	8.0	8.8	2.9	4.6	0.0	0.0
50+	10.0	9.4	4.0	0.0	5.7	4.5	0.0	0.0
N	(40)	(32)	(25)	(34)	(35)	(22)	(33)	(21)

Members of the House of Lords who never sat in the House of Commons have been excluded. Members of the House of Lords who once sat in the House of Commons have been included.
Sources: Who's Who, Who Was Who, Dod's Parliamentary Companion, The Times Guide to the House of Commons.

the post-war Attlee government, the first Wilson government and so on; but for obvious reasons of convenience the pre-war National governments of Baldwin and Chamberlain have been merged, and so have the Conservative Churchill-Eden and Macmillan-Home governments of the period 1951-64 and the more recent end-to-end Labour governments of Wilson and Callaghan between 1974 and 1979. The table speaks for itself. The

number of cabinet ministers first elected to the House of Commons in their 20s has declined sharply. The number first elected in
their 30s has risen from 40 per cent in the late 1930s to more than
90 per cent in the 1980s. The number first elected in their 40s has
tended to dwindle; almost no cabinet ministers nowadays are first
elected in their 50s or 60s. One might infer, although still very ten-
tatively at this stage, that the proportion of cabinet ministers who
are career politicians has risen steadily over the past third of a century.

Let us approach the problem from another direction. We mentioned earlier unsuccessful attempts to enter the House of
Commons, and the number of rebuffs that an aspiring politician
was prepared to endure before finally being returned to the House
might seem on the face of it a good indicator of the depth of his
commitment to politics as a way of life. In fact, the true picture is
more complicated than this. The fates of would-be members of
Parliament are determined as much by voters and by local constituency organizations as by the candidates themselves. If more and
more candidates are having to stand more and more often before
finally being elected to the House, that may reflect as much on the
mores of constituency selection committees as on the individual
politicians who appear before them. In fact, there is every reason
to think that, whereas before the war local Conservative and
Labour selection committees in safe or winnable seats were
prepared to select individuals they liked irrespective of their
previous electoral experience, such bodies since at least the 1950s
have preferred to go for candidates who have already been 'blood-
ed' in electoral contests elsewhere. Nowadays the aspiring
member of Parliament is expected to stand for one or more marginal seats, or seats that are safe for the other side, before finally
being adopted for a seat that is safe for his own party.[7] Even so,
the fact that so many people who eventually become MPs have
been prepared to run this obstacle race says much for their determination.

Table 4 sets out the percentages of MPs in each Parliament
since 1945 who have either won at their first attempt — in other
words, fought no unsuccessful contests before entering the House
— or else fought unsuccessfully one or more times. The table, as
can be seen, is a social scientist's dream. It contains forty-four
cells. The entries in three pairs of adjacent cells are identical.
Otherwise the entries in all but three of the cells in the table point

Table 4: Percentages of MPs Who Contested Seats Unsuccessfully Before Their First Election to the House of Commons, by Election

Previous contests	1945 (%)	1950 (%)	1951 (%)	1955 (%)	1959 (%)	1964 (%)	1966 (%)	1970 (%)	Feb. 1974 (%)	Oct. 1974 (%)	1979 (%)
Nil	80.1	76.3	73.2	66.6	61.0	57.6	53.9	49.8	45.3	41.9	41.8
1	11.4	16.0	18.4	19.8	22.8	24.6	26.4	26.9	30.8	32.6	30.6
2	5.4	5.4	6.2	9.8	12.7	13.4	15.2	16.8	17.4	18.3	20.4
3+	2.9	1.8	2.3	3.5	3.5	4.3	4.5	6.5	6.5	7.2	7.1
N	(613)	(612)	(615)	(620)	(623)	(621)	(618)	(620)	(598)	(596)	(607)

Sources: Recalculated from Mellors. *The British MP*, Table 2.4, pp. 20-2, except for the 1979 data which are taken from *The Times Guide to the House of Commons, May 1979.*

Table 5: Percentages of Cabinet Ministers Who Contested Seats Unsuccessfully Before Their First Election to the House of Commons*

Previous contests	1935-1940 (%)	1945-1951 (%)	1951-1957 (%)	1957-1964 (%)	1964-1970 (%)	1970-1974 (%)	1974-1979 (%)	1979- (%)
Nil	52.5	48.5	61.5	58.8	62.1	45.5	39.4	38.1
1	27.5	33.3	38.4	35.3	24.3	27.3	36.4	33.3
2	15.0	15.2	0.0	5.9	13.5	22.7	12.1	28.6
3+	5.0	3.0	0.0	0.0	0.0	4.6	12.1	0.0
N	(40)	(32)	(25)	(34)	(35)	(22)	(33)	(21)

*Members of the House of Lords who never sat in the House of Commons have been excluded. Members of the House of Lords who once sat in the House of Commons have been included.
Sources: Who's Who, Who Was Who, Dod's Parliamentary Companion, The Times Guide to the House of Commons.

in the expected direction. At every general election since 1945, the proportion of members elected at the first attempt has declined: the proportion of members having to fight two, three, four or even more times has increased. The figures are not quite as spectacular as they look, because the special circumstances of the 1945 election brought in an unusually large number of first-time winners; but they nevertheless bespeak a substantial change in the career structure of British politics.[8] The number of MPs determined to make their way in politics has always been large; it would appear to have been growing even larger. If the bulk of the politicians in the bottom two rows of the table are not career politicians in the sense in which the term is being used in this paper, they are certainly behaving very strangely.

Table 5 sets out the same information for cabinet ministers. It covers a somewhat longer period, from 1935 until 1979; the various cabinets have been divided, as before, into eight groups. The cell entries in Table 5 are not nearly as striking or consistent as the cell entries in Table 4; it would be surprising if they were, since the numbers are much smaller and since, in connection with cabinet ministers, so much depends on the judgements, possibly idiosyncratic, of individual Prime Ministers. Nevertheless, the pattern in Table 5 is much the same as in Table 4. The proportion of cabinet ministers who have had to fight more than one election before entering Parliament has increased noticeably in recent years. The fact that the change does not begin to manifest itself until the 1970s simply reflects the fact that almost all cabinet ministers in practice serve for a considerable period of years in the House of Commons before achieving cabinet rank.[9] It is worth noting that fully one-third of the members of Margaret Thatcher's cabinet — including the Prime Minister herself — fought unsuccessfully once before being elected to Parliament; and more than one-quarter were forced to fight two unsuccessful contests. The modern cabinet minister is made of stern political stuff.

Finally, we have already looked at how politicians' careers begin; we should look now at how, barring electoral disaster, they end — that is, at the pattern of voluntary retirements from the House of Commons. The argument here is straightforward. Career politicians will want to stay in politics. They will therefore want to stay in the House of Commons. Accordingly, they will defer their retirement from the House of Commons for as long as possible, at least until they reach a suitable retiring age (unless of course they are defeated in an election or are denied renomination). Thus, if the incidence of career politicians has in fact increased, we should expect the age at which members retire from the House of Commons (as distinct from not being re-elected) to have increased also. Fewer members than in the past should be leaving the House before they reach the age of 60; almost none should be retiring in their 30s or 40s.

And this, too, turns out to be the case. Indeed the cell entries in Table 6 are almost as spectacular as those in Table 4. The table

Table 6: Age of Retirements from the House of Commons, in
Percentages, by Election

Members retiring at the age of	1951 (%)	1955 (%)	1959 (%)	1964 (%)	1966 (%)	1970 (%)	Feb. 1974 (%)	Oct. 1974 (%)	1979 (%)
60 +	37.9	51.4	63.5	72.9	78.4	74.4	71.0	49.9	72.9
50-59	24.1	35.1	19.1	11.9	16.2	14.1	20.1	35.7	18.6
49 or less	37.9	13.5	17.5	15.3	5.4	11.5	8.7	21.4	8.5
N	(29)	(37)	(62)	(59)	(37)	(78)	(69)	(14)	(59)

* In connection with almost every election, it proved impossible to
ascertain the ages of between one and five members. These MPs have
been excluded from the table.
Sources: Who's Who, Who Was Who, Dod's Parliamentary Companion, The Times Guide to the House of Commons.

sets out the ages at which MPs have retired from the House of
Commons at each of the nine general elections since 1951. The top
and bottom rows are the important ones. They do not require a
great deal of interpretation. As can be seen, the proportion of
MPs retiring at the age of 60 or more has increased considerably
over the years; more than 70 per cent of the members retiring at
every election since 1964 have been aged 60 or over (except in October 1974 when, because the election followed the previous election by only a few months, only a handful of members, fourteen
altogether, retired). Likewise, the number of MPs leaving the
House of Commons voluntarily before the age of 50 has declined
steadily. In 1979, the ratio of late to early retirers was as high as
eight to one. Old soldiers never die; old career politicians hang on
for as long as they can.[10]

From everything that has been said so far, there seems reason to
believe that there are more career politicians among members of
Parliament than there used to be, and reason to suspect that there
are more career politicians among cabinet ministers than there used to be...

Notes

1   James Margach, *The Anatomy of Power: An Enquiry into the
    Personality of Leadership* London: W. H. Allen, 1979), p. 70.
2   Jo Grimond, *Memoirs* (London: Heinemann, 1979), p. 166-7.
3   Eulau and Sprague, *Lawyers in Politics,* P. 1. It goes without saying

that, if certain other occupations can open doors to careers in politics, the converse is also true; a successful career in politics (or even a not very successful one) can lead to upward mobility in other fields. Richard Marsh is a good case in point. Sometimes politicians deliberately set out to use politics as a means of self-advancement; Barber in *The Lawmakers* (Chap. 4) labels the state legislators who follow this route 'the Advertisers'. That mobility in politics and mobility in other fields may affect each other is suggested by Heinz Eulau and David Koff in 'Occupational Mobility and Political Career', *Western Political Quarterly,* XV (1962), 507-21.

4 The reason is obvious: almost all of the lecturer-MPs were (and are) Labour; see Colin Mellors, *The British MP: A Socio-economic Study of the House of Commons* (Farnborough, Hants.: Saxon House, 1978), Table 5.2, pp. 64-6. With regard to a large number of the variables discussed in this section of the paper, the differences between the two parties are substantial. If they are not emphasized, it is because the paper seeks to draw attention to something that the parties have in common rather than to ways in which they differ; in most cases, details of the differences can be found in the relevant tables of Mellors' *The British MP.* Some additional data on the changes in the occupational structure of the House of Commons that took place immediately after the Second World War can be found in J. F. S. Ross, *Parliamentary Representation,* 2nd edn. (London: Eyre and Spottiswoode, 1948), Chaps. 7-8, and J. F. S. Ross, *Elections and Electors: Studies in Democratic Representation* (London: Eyre and Spottiswoode, 1955), Chap. 26.

5 Labour MPs are much more likely than Conservative MPs to be elected for the first time when they are over 50. See Mellors. *The British MP,* Tables 3.1, 3.2 and 3.3, pp. 29-32. See also Austin Ranney, *Pathways to Parliament: Candidate Selection in Britain* (Madison, Wis.: University of Wisconsin Press, 1965), pp. 198-200, and Michael Rush, *The Selection of Parliamentary Candidates* (London: Nelson, 1969), pp. 72-3, 208-9 and 221.

6 Of the Conservative members who served in Parliament after 1945 but who had first been elected before 1945, nearly 20 per cent entered the House before they were 30 (Mellors, *The British MP,* Table 3.3, p. 31). Allowances have to be made for the fact that in 1945 no general election had been held for ten years and a disproportionate number of the holdover MPs were bound to have been elected young. Even so, the proportion is high.

7 See Ranney, *Pathways to Parliament,* Chaps. 4 and 7, and Rush, *Selection of Parliamentary Candidates,* Chaps. 3 and 8.

8 Because there had been no general election for a decade, 1945 brought in a substantial number of members who would almost certainly have fought a seat had an election been held in the usual way in 1939 or 1940. Labour's landslide victory also brought in an unusually large number of Labour members without previous electoral experience. Of the 74 new Conservative members in 1945, 73 had never fought before. Of the 244 new Labour members in 1945, 192 had

never fought before. See Mellors, *The British MP,* Table 2.5, p. 22.

9   The high proportions of first-time winners in the cabinets of the 1950s and 1960s reflect the high proportion of Conservative first-time winners in 1945 and 1950 and the high proportion of Labour first-time winners in 1945. See Mellors, *The British MP.* Table 2.5, p. 22. The relatively large proportion of cabinet ministers between 1935 and 1940 who had had to fight three or more times before being elected for the first time probably reflects the electoral turbulence of the 1920s.

10   Table 6 omits one group who should be included and includes another group who should be omitted. On the one hand, it takes no account of MPs who retire between general elections, thus forcing by-elections; on the other, it includes some members who have not really retired voluntarily but who have been denied renomination by their constituency party or association and then decided not to seek re-election. For a partial list of the latter, see Butler and Sloman, *British Political Facts 1900-1979.* p. 221. It is very doubtful whether, if these two groups were allowed for in the table, the over-all pattern of findings would be significantly, if at all, different. The choice of 60 as, in some sense, a 'natural' retiring age for MPs reflects the fact that, since parliamentary can be reckoned to last for four or five years, an MP who does not retire in his early 60s is in effect committing himself, if he has a safe seat, to staying on till his late 60s.

3.3　Robert Leach

What is Thatcherism?

From 'Thatcherism, Liberalism, and Tory collectivism', *Politics,* Vol. 3, No. 1, 1983, pp. 9-14

In a recent newspaper interview Milton Friedman claimed, 'Margaret Thatcher is not in terms of beliefs a Tory. She is a nineteenth century Liberal.' *(Observer,* 26/9/82.) It has become almost an accepted truth that Mrs Thatcher's brand of Conservatism marks a sharp break from the Tory tradition, and has more in common with a nineteenth-century Liberalism, that is historically the antithesis of Toryism. The main elements of Liberalism and Toryism are too well known to require restating. Most relevant here is that Tory thinking was less hostile to state power than Liberalism. R. A. Butler once asserted, 'A good Tory has never been in history afraid of the use of the state.' (Commons debate, 10/3/1947.) 'Paternalism' is a term frequently linked with Toryism, and some writers have talked of 'Tory collectivism' (Beer, 1969; Greenleaf, 1973) while one recent judgement concluded, 'The mainstream of Conservatism has always been collectivist and paternalist in basis.' (Bennett, 1977.) It is from this Tory collectivism that Mrs Thatcher is alleged to have departed. It will be argued here that while her leadership has involved a shift in emphasis in the Conservative party, both her Liberalism and the collectivist tradition she is supposed to have abandoned are exaggerated.

Mrs. Thatcher's Liberalism

In a series of speeches made before she became Prime Minister, Mrs Thatcher set out her views in forthright terms. She argued that Government must limit its activities. The state had attempted to do too much and had intervened in areas where it had no business. In place of state action, she extolled the Victorian values of self-reliance coupled with private charity (Thatcher, 1977, pp. 107-11). Collectivism was singled out for attack, but she suggested, 'the tide is beginning to turn against collectivism' (Thatcher, 1977, p. 93). Elsewhere she referred scathingly to 'bourgeois guilt' (Thatcher, 1977, p. 4), a phrase widely interpreted as a criticism of Tory paternalism as much as of socialism.

The impression that Mrs Thatcher's own words reflect the language and values of nineteenth century Liberalism rather than what is often understood as Toryism is apparently confirmed by examining her sources. She cites remarkably few celebrated Tories. Instead she draws on Adam Smith — 'I urge you to read him' she told one audience in her best didactic manner — and two modern writers who both acknowledge a strong debt to Adam Smith; Friedman and Hayek. Four separate works of Hayek are cited in the generally sparse notes to her speeches (Thatcher, 1977, pp. 26, 66, 72, 91, 114). Significantly Friedman describes himself as a Liberal of the nineteenth-century variety (Friedman, 1962), while Hayek calls himself a Liberal or Whig, and explicitly condemns Conservatism (Hayek, 1960, 1975).

The apparent source of Mrs Thatcher's inspiration has troubled both critics and admirers within the Conservative Party. Sir Ian Gilmour, for example, carefully distinguishes Conservatism from Liberalism, and singles out Hayek for special criticism (Gilmour, 1978). A major theme of William Waldegrave's book is an attack on neo-Liberalism in the Conservative Party, and a reassertion of a Conservative tradition involving the acceptance of state power (Waldegrave, 1978). Considerable reservations concerning Mrs. Thatcher's Liberal rhetoric are also expressed by several generally sympathetic contributors to a volume of 'Conservative Essays' (Cowling, 1978). The point is made most trenchantly by Peregrine Worsthorne, who refers dismissively to 'Some libertarian mishmash drawn from the writings of Adam Smith, John Stuart Mill, and the warmed up milk of nineteenth century liberalism' (Cowling, 1978, p. 149).

Thus what has come to be described as 'Thatcherism' is not surprisingly identified with nineteenth-century Liberalism, and seen as involving a radical shift from the tradition of Tory collectivism. It may be suggested, however, that there are respectable antecedents for Mrs. Thatcher's Liberalism within the Conservative Party, and that her Liberalism is in any case distinctly partial.

It is often suggested that Liberal ideas were absorbed into the

Conservative Party as a consequence of successive secessions from
the Liberal Party (Beer, 1969) or because of a change in the composition of the Conservative Party itself (Ramsden, 1978, pp.
98-9, 360-2), but Greenleaf has traced what he has described as a 'libertarian tradition' in Conservatism right back to Burke (Greenleaf,
1973). Commenting on famine in Ireland, Burke argued, 'To provide for us in our necessities is not in the power of government ...
The labouring people are only poor because they are numerous ...
Patience, labour, sobriety, frugality, and religion should be
recommended to them. All the rest is downright fraud' (Burke,
1795).

Perhaps this only indicates that labels are misleading. Burke, an
active Whig politician during his lifetime, is widely considered the
father of Conservatism, and yet his economic ideas may be regarded as pure Adam Smith, who in turn is generally associated with
nineteenth-century Liberalism, although his own politics might be
considered Tory. Hayek distinguishes between two Liberal traditions. The one that he clearly prefers includes Hume and Burke
who are usually claimed for Conservatism, and he is scathingly
critical of the 'constructivist rationalism' of the alternative liberal
tradition, which he associated with Voltaire, Rousseau, and the
English Utilitarians (Hayek, 1975).

Hayek's Liberalism is thus distinctly partial, and excludes many
figures who are usually regarded as quintessential Liberals. The
same can be said of Mrs Thatcher. There are many nineteenth-
century Liberals that she does not resemble, and many aspects of
Liberalism which she has not absorbed. Liberalism involved rather
more than a belief in free markets and limited government.
Although Mrs Thatcher quotes Adam Smith frequently with approval, one is hard put to it to find references in her speeches to
Bentham, or John Stuart Mill, or Bright. Bentham's approach to
government was fiercely rationalist, and hostile to traditional institutions and usages — the very antithesis of the Conservative approach. Mill's extreme individualism on matters of private tastes
and morals has not been generally approved by Conservatives, and
it might be noticed in passing that Mrs Thatcher has not been con-
spicuously 'liberal' on issues such as abortion, homosexual law
reform, or censorship. Bright's belief in free trade was part of a
genuinely internationalist outlook: he was an eloquent critic of the
Crimean War. This serves as a reminder that the Whig-Liberal tradition was not just suspicious of the strong state at home, but

generally critical of high defence spending and military ventures overseas.

Against this background Mrs Thatcher's Liberalism' seems somewhat limited — extending to the economic sphere only. In other respects she shares the general Conservative predilection for tradition and authority. As one admirer, T. E. Utley, claims, 'She speaks the language of liberty, not of libertariansim. She is an instinctive and wholly English Conservative. Her belief in individual freedom is firmly set in the context of respect for institutions and tradition' (Cowling, 1978, p. 50).

Tory collectivism

However qualified, Mrs. Thatcher's Liberalism might still seem to involve a major departure from Tory collectivism. It depends on what is meant by 'collectivism'. The word is used in various senses, and few who write about collectivism in connection with the Conservative Party bother to define it. It is sometimes used in opposition to 'individualism' to include anyone who holds a vaguely organic theory of society. In this sense, but not in others, Burke might be held to be a collectivist. Sometimes 'collectivism' is used to describe advocacy of a command economy, or socialism (Thatcher, p. 93). Alternatively, any extension of state power, not just intervention in the economic or social sphere, might be regarded as collectivism. Gilmour quotes Dicey, and carefully describes Neville Chamberlain's policies as 'collectivist ... rather than socialist' (Gilmour, 1978, p. 36). In the broad sense, collectivist policies need not be 'progressive' (perhaps tough penal or immigration measures spring to mind here). However, 'Tory collectivism' tends to be associated with paternalism and state initiated social reform of a benevolent nature.

Paternalism is rightly regarded as an important element in Conservatism, but it is wrongly inferred that paternalism necessarily involves state intervention. For Burke, Coleridge or Disraeli it was primarily the church or the aristocracy rather than the state which should show a paternalist care for the poor'. The characteristic Conservative line, in theory at least, is that rights entail obligations, and the enjoyment of property carries with it social responsibilities. Tories, while generally avoiding the extreme individualism associated with classical Liberalism, have tended to prefer assistance for the less fortunate from social agencies such as the family, the church, or voluntary organisations, rather than from a state bureaucracy. Disraeli's own attitude to the state was ambivalent. He once described 'the elevation of the condition of the people' as the third 'great object' of the Tory party, (speech to the National Union 1872, reprinted Buck, 1975, pp. 70-1), but it has been shown that the social reforms passed during his administration were more ad hoc responses to pressing problems than the expression of a coherent political philosophy (Blake, 1966; Smith, 1967). Lord Blake has recently claimed, 'His policies have been much misinterpreted, not least by those who unplausibly regard him as an ancestor of the welfare state — a sort of arch wet' *(Guardian,* 4/10/82). Elsewhere Blake observes, 'He had a genuine hatred of centralization, bureaucracy, and every manifestation of the Benthamite state' (Blake 1966, p. 282). In this context, Mrs Thatcher appears more the heir rather than the betrayer of the Disraelian tradition.

Beer has constructed a persuasive picture of a Conservatism involving a willing acceptance of the state, by linking Disraelian Conservatism with what he calls the 'reassertion of state power' of the inter-war years and the 'new Conservatism' of the post-war period. Beer's interpretation of Conservatism rests, however, on an almost wilful emphasis on some periods and individuals, and a neglect of others, notably Salisbury, who he does not even mention by name, and whose period of dominance he dismisses as a period of 'Conservative inertia' (Beer, 1969, pp. 271ff.). Moreover, Beer's treatment of the periods he does describe in more detail is rather one-sided.

Some policies deliberately pursued by Tories in the inter-war years might fairly be described as collectivist — notably protection and some welfare policies. Other outcomes which might be tagged 'collectivist' such as the stimulation of investment, and managed exchange rates, were the accidental consequence of trying and failing, to pursue orthodox financial and economic policies. The immediate response of the National Government to the economic crisis was to call for public expenditure cuts, and attack the profligate spending of Local Authorities, an approach to recession which has a familiar ring (Taylor, 1965, Ch. 10).

There is more substance to the 'collectivism' of the post-war generation of political leaders. The Industrial Charter of 1947 did mark a significant change in direction, and of course Conservative governments between 1951 and 1964 accepted the managed economy and the commitment to full employment policies. They continued, and in certain directions, expanded the welfare state, and even did not attempt to reverse the bulk of Labour's nationalisation programme. The establishment of the NEDC towards the end of the period apparently signified the conversion of the Conservative Party to economic planning, and certainly involved an extension of the corporatism whose origins have been traced by some commentators to earlier in the century (Middlemas, 1979).

All this scarcely requires restatement, yet even in this period there remained a commitment to the rhetoric and policies of competition, the free market, and private enterprise. The Conservatives were re-elected on the slogan 'Set the people Free', and accelerated the process of dismantling rationing and controls begun by Labour. The return of steel and road haulage to private enterprise involved more 'privatisation' than Mrs Thatcher has yet achieved, and the denationalisation of other industries was scarcely economically or politically feasible. A commitment to competition and private enterprise largely inspired the establishment of commercial television, which subsequently paved the way for commercial radio. The Restrictive Practices Act, 1956, and the abolition of resale price maintenance in 1964 were part of an attempt to make competition work. The removal of controls on land, and the Rent Act of 1957 can clearly be related to a market philosophy. While some of these measures might be characterised as interventionist, or even, on one definition collectivist, they were inspired more by a market than a collectivist approach.

Tory economic and social welfare policies have not generally been inspired by any consistent, coherent, political philosophy, and certainly not by a collectivist philosophy, although some individual Conservatives have had a strong commitment to policies which might be considered collectivist. Tory economic intervention and social reform has largely involved a continuation and sometimes an extension of policies initiated by Liberal and Labour governments. The one major exception, protection in the 1930s, although undoubtedly collectivist, is not what most commentators appear to mean by the term 'Tory collectivism'.

Moreover, the motives for Tory acceptance of much welfare policy may be questioned. Beer makes a significant observation concerning 'Tory inertia' in the late nineteenth-century (Beer, p. 272):

That the Conservatives did not choose to act is most readily explained on simple electoral grounds. In imperialism ... the party had found a cause with a mighty appeal to the voter. Indeed, only from the election of 1886 ... did the party win those majorities of the popular vote which had eluded even Disraeli. Social reform one might infer, was a theme Conservatives could be induced forcefully to support only when defeat left them no other way of winning power.

Similarly, it might be argued that it was the 1945 election defeat which provided a major impetus towards the acceptance of the welfare state. This is not to deny the sincerity of leading Conservative advocates of reform, but it does explain why the bulk of the party was induced to accept change (Gamble, 1974). Throughout the fifties it was commonly assumed that a commitment to full employment and additional welfare benefits was necessary to win elections. It could be argued that what has changed now is not the Conservative party but the economic situation, and the assumptions about electoral behaviour within which parties operate.

Thatcherism: a radical departure from traditional conservatism?

Emphasis on Mrs Thatcher's 'Liberalism' and her supposed departure from a tradition of 'Tory collectivism' obscures the fact that in certain respects she believes in a strong state. Utley is clearly outlining a Thatcherite agenda when he argues

The state must be strong in defending itself against foreign attack, enforcing the rule of law and recovering and strengthening a sense of national identity. It must, however, forswear the pretension to meddle incessantly in the economic and commercial activities of its subjects. (Cowling, 1978, p. 51)

What this means in concrete terms is what Utley calls 'realistic penal policies' and 'fortifying the state against terrorism', as well as having no truck with devolution. It also has clear implications for defence and foreign policy. Mrs. Thatcher's government has in practice substantially followed this agenda.

Commentators operating within a very different political perspective have reached essentially similar conclusions about the nature of Thatcherism. According to Gamble,

The state is to be rolled back in some areas and rolled forward in others ... The real innovation of Thatcherism is the way it has linked traditional Conservative concern with the basis of authority in social institutions and the importance of internal order and external security, with a new emphasis upon free market exchange and the principles of the market order.

(Marxism Today, November 1980)

The only part of this analysis which seems questionable is the degree of novelty attributed to Thatcherism. As Gamble himself points out elsewhere (Gamble, 1974, pp. 115ff.) Powellism involves a similar mixture, while Heath initially placed an equally strong emphasis on the free market. Moreover, the pedigree can be traced back much further, through Bonar Law and Salisbury, right back to Burke.

Nor should it be simply assumed that non-intervention, or reduced intervention, in the economic sphere, necessarily implies a weaker state. British governments have not attempted the kind of economic intervention which would require determined state action backed by powerful sanctions. In practice, governments have attempted to influence the major macro-economic variables, and have flirted with indicative planning. This approach has necessitated securing the cooperation of powerful groups within society, which arguably has involved some abdication of government power (Middlemas, 1979). Mrs Thatcher's preference for market forces has enabled her to eschew the tripartism or corporatism of her immediate predecessors. She does not have to strike bargains with powerful barons.

There are good grounds for concluding then, that while Thatcherism in some respects involves less government intervention in the economy and society, paradoxically it requires a strong state. In other respects (penal policy, immigration, defence and foreign policy) Thatcherism is more interventionist, and the term 'right wing collectivism' might even be employed. While there are certainly important differences in emphasis from some previous Conservative administrations, largely perhaps a consequence of the altered economic environment, Thatcherism does not involve a radical departure from the English Conservative tradition.

References

Beer, S. H. (1969), *Modern British Politics* (London: Faber & Faber, 2nd ed.).

Bennett, R. J. (1977), 'The Conservative tradition of thought: a right-wing phenomenon?' in Nugent N. and King R., *The British Right* (Farnborough: Saxon House).

Blake, R. (1966), *Disraeli* (London: Eyre and Spottiswoode).

Buck, P. W. (1975), *How Conservatives Think* (Harmondsworth: Penguin).

Cowling, M. (ed.) (1978), *Conservative Essays* (London: Cassell).

Friedman, M. and R. (1962), *Capitalism and Freedom* (University of Chicago Press).

Gamble, A. (1974), *The Conservative Nation* (London: Routledge & Kegan Paul).

Gilmour, I. (1978), *Inside Right* (London: Quartet Books, 2nd ed.).

Greenleaf, W. H. (1973), 'The character of modern British Conservatism' in Benewick, R., Berki, R. N., and Parekh, B. (eds.), *Knowledge and Belief in Politics* (London: George Allen & Unwin).

Hayek, F. A., (1960), *The Constitution of Liberty* (London: Routledge & Kegan Paul).

Hayek, F. A. (1975), 'The principles of a Liberal social order' in Crespigny, A. and Cronin, J., *Ideologies of Politics* (Cape Town: Oxford University Press).

Middlemas, K. (1979), *Politics in Industrial Society* (London: André Deutsch).

Ramsden, J. (1978), *The Age of Balfour and Baldwin 1902-1940* (London: Longman).

Smith, P. (1967), *Disraelian Conservatism and Social Reform* (London: Routlege & Kegan Paul).

Taylor, A. J. P., (1965), *English History 1914-1945* (Oxford University Press).

Thatcher, M. (1977), *Let Our Children Grow Tall* (London: CPS).

Waldegrave, W., (1978), *The Binding of Leviathan* (London: Hamish Hamilton).

3.4   Jim Bulpitt

Thatcherism as statecraft

From 'The discipline of the new democracy: Mrs Thatcher's domestic statecraft', *Political Studies*, Vol. XXXIV, No. 1, 1985, pp. 19-39.

Most interpretations of the Thatcher Governments are partisan in character. The three major intellectual cultures of modern British politics–Thatcherite, centre opinion and Marxist–have all produced interpretations which differ in ways which are fairly obvious and to be expected. The interesting point, however, is that they share so many common themes: all are concerned to explain something called 'Thatcherism'; all believe that this phenomenon represents a radical break with past Conservative practice and, more generally, with the post-war Keynesian consensus; all hold that ideas or doctrines, especially monetarism, have had an important influence on key government policies and have contributed to the overall coherence of the Government's operations; and, finally, all stress the consistency of purpose and policy of the first Thatcher Administration–there were no 'U-turns'.

Two qualifications to this picture of thematic (if not substantive) unity must be noted. The first concerns the Marxists and their camp followers. It is true that they accept the four themes outlined above. It is also true that the old ritualistic incantations concerning the links between the Conservative Party, capitalism and the ruling class are still heard. But 'Thatcherism' (along with the wholly superior Continental Marxist theorizing) has had a beneficial intellectual impact on most contemporary British Marxists. What appears to fascinate them is the politics of Thatcherism, the methods which have brought success to the present-day Conservative Party, and the possibilities and dangers for the left in that success. As Andrew Gamble has put it. 'A government that thinks strategically is rare in British politics.'[1] To date two specific and seemingly related Marxist theses have emerged to explain the strategy of Thatcherism, namely those of 'authoritarian populism' and 'the free economy in the strong state'.[2]

The second qualification concerns the existence of what can be called the sceptics' interpretation of the Thatcher Governments. Argued by people with diverse political views, this holds to one major alternative theme, namely that most accounts of these governments overstress their radical character and their consistent, even coherent, purpose.[3] Specifically, it is suggested that the first Thatcher Government did not break the post-war Keynesian consensus (the Callaghan–Healey Administration did that) and monetarism is far too grand a word to describe the succession of mistakes, 'cock-ups' and expedients which have characterized policy implementation since 1979. Rhetoric, says this school, must always be separated from actions where the Thatcher Governments are concerned... Any attempt to generalize about the combined operations of a group of politicians in office will involve drawing coherence out of a mass of complex, often *ad hoc,* even conflicting, activities. It follows that: any such discourse will be concerned with 'essentially contested" matters; and the best that can be aimed for is to isolate the 'main bias' of those concerned and hope that this does not exclude so much that it renders generalizations redundant.[4]

A major problem concerns what it is that needs to be explained. Do we seek to generalize about the operations of a particular government or governments, or some perceived ideological phenomenon called, in this instance, 'Thatcherism' or the 'New Right'? The approach adopted here rejects these two perspectives in favour of something which is historically more permanent and interesting, namely the Conservative Party. In other words, it is the Conservative Party operating, temporarily, under Mrs Thatcher's leadership which is the principal concern of this article. This sort of approach requires an appropriate historical perspective. The party's contemporary operations (in the present context, 1975-1983) must be related to its past practices. The difficulty here, of course, is that how the party's past is perceived and the selection of its most appropriate past, will be contested matters.

How do we identify the principal bias of the present Conservative leadership and assess its connections with past party operations? The crucial question is surely this: In what ways has the Conservative Party sought to gain office, govern satisfactorily and retain office within the British structure of politics? Once posed, this question serves to highlight the curious nature of many popular contemporary descriptions of the party, namely that it is a party dominated by an ideology (monetarism), the client of special (capitalist) interests, or one concerned primarily with policy consistency (no 'U-turns'). It cannot be denied that these characteristics are present. But they are not, and never have been, the party's main bias. That lies elsewhere–in its statecraft.

What is statecraft? The crude answer is that it is the art of winning elections and achieving some necessary degree of governing competence in office. It is not synonymous with, though it may be related to, pragmatism or expediency. It is concerned primarily to resolve the electoral and governing problems facing a party at any particular time. As a result it is concerned as much with the 'how'as the 'what' of politics. The matter may become clearer if we detail some of the major dimensions of statecraft.

1. *Party management*. This is a continuous problem for party leaders, both in and out of office. It involves them in a series of sometimes difficult relations with the various components of the party: parliamentary back-benchers, party bureaucracy, constituency associations and support pressure groups. Most leaders will aim for a quiescent set of party relations. But in certain periods, especially those following an election defeat after a traumatic term of government, leaders may have to adopt a more positive posture. In such circumstances the state of the party may have a considerable influence on leadership activity.

2. *A winning electoral strategy*. On the one hand this involves the manufacturing of a policy package and image capable of being sold successfully to the electorate. But it also involves finding a programme which will unite the party and stimulate members' belief that the party can not only (with luck) win an election but also govern reasonably effectively. At times of incoherence in the party system it may also involve a stance towards a governing coalition in a 'hung' parliament.

3. *Political argument hegemony*. This concerns a party achieving an easy predominance in the élite debate regarding political problems, policies and the general stance of government. Political argument is a much cruder and more comprehensive concept than ideology or theory. It refers more to a winning rhetoric in a variety of locations, winning because either the framework of the party's arguments becomes generally acceptable, or because its solutions to a particularly important political problem seem more plausible

than its opponents'. This hegemony may be achieved both in and out of office. The extent to which it contributes to a party's overall success is not clear. It may be an attribute which party élites require mostly for their own self-confidence and party management.

4. *A governing competence*. Government is about policies, both domestic and external. That is the prevailing orthodoxy. But it is clear that government is not just about policies, it is also about competence–and that is related, amongst other things, to policy choice or selection. Of course, the orthodox stance has a ready response to this: policy choice stems from ideology, citizen or special interest pressure, or problems as they emerge. In many ways, however, the important point is not which policies a government positively adopts, but rather which it rejects or avoids. Now this may be the result of ideological preference, but it may equally well be connected to problems of implementation.[5] Parties in office will not normally pursue policies which they believe they will be unable to implement effectively, either because the opposition is so strong or because they cannot trust those supposed to execute these policies. Again, the domestic and external policy stances of government may be difficult to separate: governments may use their external successes and problems to bolster their domestic operations. Thus a governing competence will be primarily a function of policy implementation, and the relationship between external problems and forces and the domestic scene.

5. *Another winning electoral strategy* A number of points emerge from this list. First, it is presented in the form of a statecraft *cycle,* that is to say the starting point is the party in opposition, and 'end game' is the party winning another election after a period in office, when the cycle begins once again. The specific items on the list, however, are not in any strict sequential order. As noted, party management and hegemony in political argument can be achieved (and lost) at any point in the cycle. Secondly, a party can be assessed in terms of how many of these statecraft dimensions it achieves successfully. It should be noted that they are more comprehensive, but less 'onerous', than the conditions of party government put forward by Richard Rose.[6] Thirdly, what a party does in terms of these various dimensions may not be coherent. There is no reason why the electoral strategy and political argument dimensions should 'fit' its operations under the governing competence category, and the last may be regarded, quite rightly, as of more significance than any of the others...

The Conservative Party and the new democracy

Three aspects of the Conservative Party's history in the 1960s and 1970s need examination: the emergence of a structure of politics perceived by most members of the party to be highly unfavourable to its future electoral and office-holding prospects; the relevance of monetarism; and the reformulation of Conservative statecraft following Mrs Thatcher's accession to the party leadership.

The new democracy

Mrs Thatcher became leader of the Conservative Party in February 1975. To put it mildly, the choice was a surprising one and can be taken as an indication that 'things' were seriously wrong.[7] What then, was wrong, or perceived to be wrong, in the party? Two obvious answers are that the party had lost four out of the last five general elections and, in addition, had suffered embarrassing defeats by the National Union of Mineworkers (NUM) in 1972 and 1974. But the mid-1970s Conservative malaise went deeper. A more plausible response would be that the party's traditional nightmare had reappeared on the scene: since the early 1960s a series of changes in the structure of British politics had occurred which, in combination, seemingly condemned the party to a rôle of permanent and ineffective opposition, with an electoral base limited to southern England. In short, a New Democracy had emerged with malign implications for the Conservative Party. How had this situation developed? Briefly, the following stages in the story require attention.

After the early 1960s, élite culture in Britain was increasingly dominated by a remodernization ethic–the need to update society, the economy and politics to confront new challenges from the outside world. On the external front remodernization involved entry into the European Community. On the domestic front it meant an 'official mind' tuned to the precepts of a post-, or pseudo-Keynesian economic strategy, emphasizing the need for economic growth and addicted to a more promotional and interventionist stance by governments than previously. Pulling demand and exchange-rate levers in the Treasury and the Bank of England was no longer thought to be enough. The Macmillan Government was the first to develop policies which reflected this remodernization culture, but Wilsonian rhetoric concerning the benefits to be gained from the 'white heat of the technological revolution' effectively won the battle for political argument hegemony in this period. Labour also reaped the first electoral rewards in 1964 and 1966. The upshot of all this in terms of a governing competence was, by 1970, ambiguous: the old, insulated, relatively autonomous centre had declined, but the fashionable concern for neocorporatist arrangements had not advanced much in practice.

From the beginning some groups in the Conservative Party had been unhappy with the policies which accompanied this post-Keynesian economic strategy. By the mid 1960s many more had concluded that, whatever the doctrinal considerations, this was not a statecraft game which the Conservatives could hope to win. The response, under Mr Heath's leadership, was to drop the domestic dimensions of Macmillanism and argue that remodernization could be achieved only by lessening government intervention, in particular by dropping incomes policies. In short, after 1965 the Conservative Party appeared to reject the new post-Keynesian consensus. This was the message of the 'Quiet Revolution' and it was good enough to provide a winning electoral strategy in 1970.[8]

The Heath Government's experience in office is crucial for understanding the contemporary Conservative Party. The paradox of that Administration was that although Heath went along with Conservative opposition to the post-Keynesian strategy, he was in fact no part of that anti-culture. A technocrat, his real aim was to make Britain more efficient via a series of specific policies–entry into the European Community, industrial relations and taxation reforms. This meant that at the heart of the 'Quiet Revolution' there was a gaping hole–the Government possessed no serious macro view of the economy. It had only the policies just mentioned plus opposition to compulsory incomes controls. Consequently, when the crunch came in 1972 and 1973, with increasing unemployment and inflation, the Government merely took up the macro strategies already on the political agenda, namely a Keynesian demand boost plus an attempt to construct neo-corporatist arrangements to support the new incomes policies. In the circumstances of the time, specifically world inflation, the advent of floating exchange rates, and the Labour movement's reluctance to conclude any permanent neo-corporatist deal with the Conservative Government (no matter how much was on offer), it is not surprising that many party members believed these policies would inevitably come to grief. The oil crisis in the autumn of 1973 and the NUM's later industrial action merely confirmed these fears.

Thus, the Conservative Party's prospects in the winter of 1974 looked extremely grim. What mattered was not so much that it had recently lost two elections, but that, since the early 1960s, the political world appeared to have been turned upside down in ways completely unfavourable to the party. Specifically, its experience in office appeared to indicate that no future Conservative Government, on its own, could hope to run an incomes policy. Yet the prevailing economic orthodoxy still argued that incomes policies were necessary to combat inflation and sustain employment. Mr Wilson, of course, could claim that Labour's Social Contract allowed it to do just that. As a result, the Conservatives were not only losing the battle for political argument hegemony, but also appeared to have no prospect of achieving a future governing competence. In these circumstances, problems of party management were bound to emerge, especially given Mr Heath's cavalier approach to this matter while in office. Hence by the winter of 1974 many Conservatives found Mr Wilson's claim that Labour was now the natural party of government only too plausible. In a statecraft context the Heath-led Conservative Party represented a total failure on all dimensions.

Monetarism
How important was monetarism to the Conservative Party in the late 1970s? At first glance the arguments in stressing its rôle in the party's policy reformulations after 1975 appear strong. Monetarism, for instance, is often perceived as a wide-ranging coherent economic theory having close connections with right-wing political doctrines. More specifically, we have already noted the propensity to emphasize the necessity for monetary policy in the upper reaches of the party in the 1950s–a tradition that continued to be articulated by Powell and the Institute of Economic Affairs (IEA) during the 1960s and early 1970s.[9] Again, by the mid-1970s important sections of the British economic community, particularly financial journalists, had become converted to monetarist perspectives. All these trends were given an added boost by the policies of the IMF during the 1976 sterling crisis and the conversion of Dennis Healey to a form of 'technical monetarism', or , as one commentator has labelled it, 'monetarily constrained Keynesianism'.[10] On the other hand, the dangers of drawing a direct line between economic theory and political practice–'ideologism'–have already been noted. And within the Conservative Par-

ty in this period there were very few adherents to the monetarist cause, although those that did exist, for example, Sir Keith Joseph, were undoubtedly influential. Equally relevant, is the fact that by the mid-1970s monetarism was no longer a coherent theory. At least five different economic schools–the Gradualists, the Austrians, the New Classical Macroeconomists, the International Monetarists, and the Supplysiders–possessed some 'monetarist' themes. But in other respects, such as their basic theoretical components and their policy prescriptions, they differed considerably.[11]

In these circumstances the key question would appear to be: what was there about monetarism in the mid-1970s which could be understood and appreciated by all sections of the Conservative Party–Wets, Dries and the 'Silent Majority'?

At root monetarism was, and in many ways still is, a modest little economic theory.[12] In its early forms, that is as the quantity theory of money or, more generally, monetary policy (the word 'monetarism' was not coined until about 1968), it merely stated that there was a systematic relationship between the supply of money and the price level. It has never claimed that there is any direct relationship between the supply of money and 'real' economic variables, such as output, employment and productivity. Again, in its early days those who supported the quantity theory of money were largely concerned to remove decisions about the money supply from the political arena and place them in the hands of those (for example, bankers) who would operate according to the non-discretionary automatic rules. These two themes were the basis of all early 'monetarist' thinking. But from them could be drawn two further inferences: first, that the supply of money, if little else, was controllable by governments or other agencies, and secondly, that trade union wage demands did not determine the price level, although they might influence employment levels. Friedman, in his early guise of 'the economists' economist, followed this traditional monetary theory.

From the late 1960s this modest little theory was politicized and made more relevant to policy-makers by a number of forces. It was politicized by Friedman with his constant stressing of capitalist freedoms and the virtuous equilibrium of market forces. Similar results stemmed from his concept of 'the natural rate of unemployment'.[13] The development after the early 1970s of the new classical macroeconomics with its 'rational expectations'

hypothesis also radicalized monetarist theory, as did the renewed
interest in Hayek's writings.[14] But what really changed was its
relevance. Where monetarist theory scored in the mid-1970s was
in its apparent ability to provide more plausible answers than traditional Keynesian theory to questions concerning the causes of inflation and how to combat it in the new régime of floating
exchange rates.[15] In the general context of British politics at the
time this was of tremendous importance. Popular or 'vulgar'
perceptions of monetarist thinking could run as follows. Monetarism provided a method of defeating the most important
economic problem, inflation. It suggested this could be done by
manipulating one economic variable–the money supply. Governments could control money supply because its major component
was government spending itself, or specifically the amount of that
expenditure not covered by tax income, namely the Public Sector
Borrowing Requirement (PSBR). Inflation could therefore be controlled by governments acting on their own, without having to
resort to incomes policies which involved them in difficult and
dangerous bargaining with unions and employers. Governments
which adopted monetarism rediscovered the benefits of automatic
rules or pilots to manage the economy. In this sense economic
management was depoliticized: the 'euthanasia of politics' could
occur once more. Of course, all this may be regarded as pretty
low-level economic argument.[16] But it serves to highlight a
neglected face of the subject. Monetarism can be regarded simply
as an economic theory or a policy framework. It can also be linked
to right-wing ideas, even ideology.[17] But above all, from the point
of view of politicians, especially those in trouble, it seemed to offer in the mid-1970s a superb (or lethal) piece of statecraft. On this
basis two interesting paradoxes emerge. First, 'monetarism' began
life as a technique for taking certain decisions out of politics; it
matured as a device for giving politicians a certain autonomy from
other groups. Secondly, in statecraft terms there is precious little
difference between monetarism and the politics of Keynes' demand management.

The reconstruction of Conservative statecraft, 1975-1979
Whatever Mrs Thatcher's doctrinal inclinations (and those of Sir
Keith Joseph) the discipline of the mid-1970s New Democracy determined that only one escape route was possible for the Conservative Party. Once the new leadership had rejected a coalition

strategy, the dictates of party management, political argument, electoral success, and above all, the necessity to find a future governing competence, ensured that a link would be made with the statecraft of monetarism. Only this would resolve the Conservative's 'Edessa complex'-the necessity to withdraw from territory impossible to defend.[18] In other words, only monetarism offered some prospect of governing effectively, some prospect of attacking inflation without an incomes policy and, therefore, without the consequent perceived necessity to make deals with the unions (and business). It followed that only monetarism as statecraft provided any opportunity to rebuild that relative autonomy of the centre seemingly lost for ever during the Heath Government. The prospect of that goal also yielded benefits for the other dimensions of statecraft. On that simple but brutal fact the whole party could unite. The Wets, who liked to suggest they had alternative policies, possessed no alternative statecraft. Moreover, in so far as monetarism after 1975 was associated in the Conservative mind with 'arm's length', anti-corporatist government, then it seemed likely to offer that degree of reciprocal autonomy for political and governmental agencies outside the centre, which had been such a marked characteristic of the old Dual Polity prior to the 1960s. In this sense the statecraft developed by the Conservative Party in opposition must be viewed less as a radical break with the past and more as an attempt to reconstruct it.

It would be convenient to suggest that the above account represents the whole story for the Conservative Party between 1975 and 1979. But matters were not so simple. To begin with, the party's leaders-above all Mrs Thatcher-were so concerned to win the political argument battle that they talked about many other things. Mrs Thatcher's topics ranged from Adam Smith to Solzhenitsyn, from East Germany to the 'swamping' of British culture, from the need to reduce government to the necessity to exert more authority. This 'moral force' monetarism often threatened to obscure the more simple and important statecraft message. Secondly, the party remained divided, despite the moderate tone of the early policy documents. Labour's 'technical monetarism' forced Mrs Thatcher to adopt more extreme positions which increasingly frightened the Wets. There were specific divisions over industrial relations, incomes policies, devolution and the European Community. Thirdly, the implementation of the centre autonomy statecraft remained ambiguous right up to, and including, the 1979 election manifesto. Arm's length government was promised, but so too were public expenditure cuts. The nature of these cuts, and how the party would confront opposition to them, was left unclear. A similar ambiguity pervaded supply-side policies, apart, that is, from tax cuts. Above all, the party leadership continued to believe that the money supply was controllable and that 'monetarism in one country' was both possible and desirable. The degree of thought, as opposed to rhetoric, which was given to these matters does not appear to have been very great. Finally, the biggest boost to the Conservatives' progress came from the 'winter of discontent', which not only dented Labour's claim to a special relationship with the unions, but put a further nail in the coffin of incomes policies or norms. After this the Labour Government needed the summer of 1979 to recuperate, but the Scottish devolution referendum result and its defeat, by one vote on the related confidence motion, ensured that fortune continued to smile on the Conservative Party. In the last resort statecraft requires luck as well as good management.

The first Thatcher Administration: government by apprentices

The principle aim of those who took office in May 1979 was to achieve a governing competence, through a reconstruction of that traditional centre autonomy enjoyed by British governments prior to the 1960s. It would not be true to say that all else was 'embellishment and detail', but the search for some 'relative autonomy' was the 'principal bias'. If it achieved nothing else the new Government was determined on that, if only because it was thought to be such an essential component of the next electoral strategy. This unheroic objective was not, of course, something which could be easily articulated in public. The conditions of élite political argument in Britain demand a more exciting, more doctrinally-oriented rhetoric and the first Thatcher Administration obliged with its 'moral force' monetarism: its constant stress on the benefits to be gained from a revival of the free market, individual initiative, rolling back the frontiers of the state, public expenditure cuts, and above all, the defeat of inflation. This was not mere talk. In varying degrees most Conservative politicians were committed to all these objectives and not only because they would bolster the relative autonomy statecraft. But when it came to the crunch they were always secondary, or instrumental, to the statecraft. The first Thatcher Administration was designed primarily as an experiment in government survival rather than in economic or political theory.

The initial strategy, pursued in 1979 and 1980, had two components, one involving macro-economic policy, the other involving the Government's relations with powerful domestic political institutions.

On the external economic front the most significant move was the abolition of exchange controls, probably the single decision with the most important consequences taken by this administration. This must be placed in the context of the Government's early belief that the external value of the pound should be left to international market forces to determine, a manoeuvre which, it was thought, would effectively remove this difficult matter from the list of its responsibilities. At the same time, it was also designed to offset some of the 'benefits' of a petro-currency, as well as, perhaps, making life extremely difficult for any future Labour administration. On the domestic front, the Government was committed to managing the economy and defeating inflation without an incomes policy by reducing the money supply, reducing the PSBR, and enforcing cash limits on, and cuts in, public expenditure. On the supply side pride of place in this early stage was given to tax cuts and changing the relative displacement of direct and indirect taxation. After some initial hesitation the macro objectives were combined into that 1980 package labelled the Medium Term Financial Strategy (MTFS). It is worth stressing, given the subsequent emphasis placed on the MTFS, that it was not a consensus item on the early agenda. The Treasury team was divided on the issue.[19] With hindsight, it can be seen that the MTFS exercise was important for what it did not try to predict–namely employment and output.

Although macro-economic policy was formulated in, and carried out from, the centre, it would inevitably affect other institutions. We have seen that before 1979 the Conservative leadership believed that this problem could be tackled by a reconstruction of the old Dual Polity. A reciprocal relative autonomy would be granted to local authorities, nationalized industries, employers and unions, such that they would be allowed to work out their own salvation within the broad macro-economic framework described above. And in the beginning that was how the first Thatcher Adminstration tried to operate. An examination of developments in this early period reveals four common themes in the Government's strategy: the 'hiving-off' of responsibilities (including controls) from the centre; the 'peripheralization' of the problems stemming from the macro-economy policies; attempts to increase the influence of local citizens, consumers, and union members over their respective institutions; and some *ad hoc* (though significant) changes in the rules governing the centre's relations with those institutions, changes always in favour of the centre. It is especially important to note that, where local authorities were concerned, the Thatcher Administration did not initially accept that more specific and direct controls over local budgets were required, despite that fact that such ideas were prevalent in both the Treasury and the Department of the Environment in the late 1970s.[20]

This double strategy to reconstruct a Conservative governing competence was associated with two other items of statecraft in this period. One was the considerable emphasis put in political argument on the benefits soon to be gained from this broad economic approach, which the Government was pleased to call monetarism. The other was that the Wets were allowed a preponderance in the Cabinet, although not in those parts of its operations directly concerned with macro-economic policy. Despite Mrs Thatcher's expressed views before the May 1979 election, concerning the kind of Cabinet best suited to a conviction politican, it is clear that the Cabinet formed after the election did not reflect those convictions.

For a variety of reasons the first phase in the Thatcher Government's operations did not last long. By the end of 1980 most of the practices associated with it had either collapsed or showed signs of collapsing. It was not just that many of the major indicators of economic performance–prices, taxes, public expenditure, money supply and unemployment–continued to rise whilst production went down. These were merely the symptoms of a deeper malaise involving important policy mistakes, the emergence of significant problems not initially perceived or predicted, and difficulties posed by the reciprocal autonomy strategy. The mistakes were related to the inflationary consequences of the Government's 1979 election campaign promise to implement the Clegg Committee reports on public sector pay demands combined with the June 1979 budget decisions to nearly double Value Added Tax levels and, at the same time, cut subsidies to the nationalized industries. The emerging problems concerned the continuing world recession, rising unemployment, the difficulties surrounding the control of, and the best definition of, the money supply and the appropriate attitude to take towards the appreciation of sterling. Finally, the Government increasingly perceived the reciprocal autonomy strategy to be working in ways which allowed important groups and institutions to pursue policies threatening the successful achievement of its macro-economic strategy, and, therefore, the centre's own relative autonomy.

Together these developments enforced some changes in the Government's statecraft. This process was neither very easy nor rapid, and the outcome was a general stance less coherent than in the early period. For the most part the debate on these matters took place in a political climate unfavourable to the Conservatives–falling opinion poll support, public divisions between the Dries and the Wets, and the awkward emergence of the Social Democratic Party (SDP). Moreover, in many ways the process of statecraft reformulation was never completed: once the initial statecraft was dropped the Government, like apprentices, continued to learn on the job. Nevertheless, by the end of the Falklands War the main outlines of the new position were reasonably clear, though by that time matters were often obscured by preparations for the run-in to the next election. The overall result was the reaffirmation of centre autonomy (there was no alternative), but the means to that end had changed and the political arguments employed to bolster it were significantly different from those of the early period. The main features of the story can be briefly summarized as follows.

First, there were some developments in party management. Cabinet changes, especially those of September 1981, ensured that the general preponderance of Wets in it was reduced. Similarly, the replacement of Thorneycroft by Parkinson at Central Office meant that Mrs Thatcher had a more positive supporter in the party bureaucracy than hitherto. Nevertheless, at the national level the Wets were not finally defeated until after the Falklands War and the new régime at Central Office made few attempts to gain more control over constituency parties or local council groups. Within the centre, those immediately connected to Mrs Thatcher increasingly resembled a 17th-century court characterized by a fortress culture. 'Is he one of us?' became the rule which determined the reception of individuals and perhaps some promotions in the senior civil service. This fortress culture was perhaps best explained by the Hoskyns' argument that nothing at the heart of the centre was strong enough to effectively promote policy coordination and planning.[21] Ideas about the development of a Prime Minister's department began to emerge.

Secondly, although after 1980 the Conservatives continued to dominate political argument, the nature of the themes put forward changed significantly. The advent of the promised land was pushed further and further into the future and its features became more ambiguous. By 1983 the Government appeared to be promising nothing more than a future marked by balanced budgets and zero inflation rates. Yet, at the same time, it effectively managed to both 'peripheralize' and externalize responsibilty for its economic failures. The unemployment problem, for example, was offloaded onto the unions, management, the world recession and the Reagan administration. In fact, no previous government had so comprehensively and systematically used its external weaknesses to bolster its domestic position. The rhetoric surrounding and Falklands victory obscured this development. The implication, of course, was the the Government accepted that monetarism in one country was impossible.

Thirdly, by 1983 some important economic policy changes had taken place. The Government reluctantly accepted that the exchange rate could not be left to market forces. Hence its adoption of 'dirty floating': the pound was managed down by changes in interest rates. Supply-side policies gradually assumed more importance since, according to the 'reversal of assignments' argument, it was in this domain that output and employment problems had to be tackled (if not completely resolved).[22] Paradoxically, privatization, which initially had received little emphasis, was the policy eventually given most publicity. Significantly, this was justified as much on grounds of statecraft–reducing the load on the Cabinet and weakening the unions–as by reference to the doctrinal principle of free enterprise.[23] There were also developments in the techniques of money supply controls. The 1982 budget dropped the previous reliance on a single monetary aggregate, sterling M3, and a range of monetary aggregates were employed to assess the position. Moreover, from the middle of 1982 there developed a more relaxed approach to the money supply and public expenditure curbs. Hire purchase controls were abolished and the Government exhorted public institutions to spend, at least on capital account.

A major consequence of these changes was considerable confusion concerning the precise nature of the Government's macro-economic strategy. It is true that the Administration could claim some consistency because of its refusal, notably in the 1981 budget, to formally reflate in the midst of a severe recession and what eventually amounted to over three million unemployed. On the other hand, several trends had emerged which only compounded the general confusion. 'Dirty floating', for example, put the Government under constant pressure from exchange rate developments abroad, notably in Washington. No solution to this little problem was ever devised. Increasingly, the Treasury used the PSBR as its main economic regulator. Perhaps this was because it realized that this was the only variable it could claim to control. Yet the more this Administration relied on the PSBR, the more its macro-economic stance resembled a classic Keynesian counter-inflation policy by fiscal means.[24] Moreover, in 1982 some Government spokesmen were arguing that the failure to reach MTFS money targets did not matter since it had never been designed as a system of monetary control, but rather as a counter-manifesto to the Keynesian emphasis on output and employment. On this view what mattered was not money but the presentational refusal to reflate.[25] So with respect to economic policies it was difficult, by 1983, to find much consistency or coherence of purpose, even less undiluted monetarism.

Finally, after 1980 the Government increasingly dropped its reciprocal autonomy stance towards other institutions in favour of a more interventionist/control strategy. There is no doubt that this abandonment of the reciprocal autonomy stance marked a major break with the old Conservative statecraft and Keynes' politics. But in this period it was obscured by the Government's cautious 'step by step' approach, its refusal to confront any major trade union directly, and its astonishingly casual approach to the 1981 inner city riots.[26] Moreover, initially at least, there appeared to be no general thought behind this development: a mixture of 'presumptuous empiricism' and/or 'panic *ad hocism'* seemed to pervade many of the Government's actions. By the summer of 1982, however, a more coherent line appeared to have developed and the 1983 manifesto commitments to more radical changes for local government, the unions and nationalized industries seemingly reflected this.

End-game for this statecraft exercise was the overwhelming
Conservative victory, at least in terms of seats, at the general election of 1983. The strategy developed after the dark days of 1974-
75 appeared to have worked better than anyone at the time ever
dared imagine. But the election victory was, of course, assisted by
a divided opposition, the electoral system, and the Falklands 'fal-
lout'.[27] It is true that the Conservatives had won the battle for
political argument hegemony and manufactured a party unity. But
we should not forget that the governing competence had been sustained only by a U-turn regarding the means to centre autonomy
and considerable confusion regarding the nature of the macro-
economic strategy.

Conclusions

Interpretations of the first Thatcher Government can be divided
crudely into two groups, those which divine some grand purpose
and consistency in its operations, and those sceptical of any such
conclusion. The former are concerned primarily with ideas and
ideology, the latter with the specific policies initiated. It is clear
that if the primary analytical target is policy, then it is difficult not
to register agreement with Riddell's view that: 'Both opponents
and supporters of the Thatcher Administration have created more
of a pattern from disconnected events and policies than is war-
ranted.[28] This article is prepared to grant that Government a kind
of consistency and a kind of purpose. It finds these characteristics,
however, not in its ideas or ideology, but in the realm of party
statecraft. It also argues, again in statecraft terms, that there is a
greater similarity between the Conservative party led by Mrs Thatcher and its predecessor under Churchill and Macmillan than is
often suggested.

The art of statecraft is to understand and work with the limitations placed on élite activity by the many changing structural constraints arising from within and without the polity. A
distinguishing feature of the Conservative Party since the late 19th
century is that, for most of the time, it has taken greater cog-
nizance of these constraints than its opponents. Perhaps this is
because it has always rejected the idea (foisted on it by its academic opponents) that it is the natural party of government in Britain. The Conservative Party leadership between 1975 and 1983
prudently reasserted that tradition. As a result the story told here

can be best ragarded as a case study of a successful élite operation
in damage control...

Notes

1 A. Gamble, 'The Rise of the Resolute Right', *New Socialist,*
   January-February, 1983.
2 Linked respectively with Stuart Hall and Andrew Gamble. See S.
   Hall and M. Jacques (eds), *The Politics of Thatcherism* (London,
   Lawrence & Wishart, 1983). For an attack on the 'authoritarian
   populism' thesis see the very good article by B. Jessop, K. Bonnett,
   S. Bromley and T. Ling, 'Authoritarian Populism, Two nations and
   Thatcherism', *New Left Review,* 147 (September/October 1984), 32-
   60.
3 See, for example, P. Riddell, *The Thatcher Government* (Oxford,
   Martin Robertson, 1983), pp. 15-20, S. Brittan, *The Role and Limits
   of Government* (London, Temple Smith, 1983), Ch. 11 and S. Beer,
   Britain Against Itself (London, Faber, 1982), pp. 214-18.
4 A method used to great effect by K. Middlemas in his *Politics in In-
   dustrial Society* (London, Deutsh, 1979).
5 Implementation analysis is now a major growth area in policy case
   studies. The *locus classicus,* as they say, is J. Pressman's and A.
   Wildavsky's *Implementation* (Berkeley, University of California
   Press, 1973). See also E. Bardach, *The Implementation Game: What
   Happens After a Bill Becomes Law* (London, MIT Press, 1977) and
   B. Hjern, 'Implementation Research: the Link Gone Missing',
   Journal of Public Policy, 1982.
6 R. Rose, *The Problem of Party Government* (Harmondsworth,
   Penguin, 1976), p. 375.
7 For a good brief account of this episode see N. Wapshot and G.
   Brock, *Thatcher* (London, Futura, 1983), Ch. 7. On the basis of the
   available evidence constituency party opinion appears to have
   favoured Heath. In my own party a group on the Executive Council
   forced an advisory vote on the leadership contest, against the wishes
   of the Chairman and the MP (who happened to be present). The
   Council voted 60:30 in favour of Heath. Typically, after that event,
   no-one presumed to ask the then MP how he had actually voted in
   the leadership election which took place shortly afterwards.
8 The 'Quiet Revolution' theme was first deployed after the 1970
   election, at the Conservative Party Conference in October of that
   year. For the immediate background to Heath's speech which coined
   the phrase see D. Hurd, *An End to Promises* (London, Collins,
   1979), pp. 76-8.
9 Holmes has argued that monetarism had little presence during the
   Heath Government's term of office. See M. Holmes, *Political
   Pressure and Economic Policy: British Government 1970-1974*
   (London, Butterworth, 1982), pp. 56, 68, 73 and 83. For an opposing
   view see T. Congdon, *Monetarism* (London, Centre for Policy

Studies, 1978), Ch. 1. This is a difficult issue to resolve. My own view is that monetarism, as economic theory, was certainly present in this period, but the Heath Government (and most other politicians) chose to ignore it.

10   J. Fforde, 'Setting monetary objectives', *Bank of England Quarterly Bulletin* (June 1983), p. 204.

11   For a somewhat different list of 'monetarist' schools see J. Burton, 'The Varieties of Monetarism and their Policy Implications', *The Three Banks Review* (1982). The difference between the 'traditional' monetarists and the new classical macroeconomic theorists are well brought out in A. Klamer, *The New Classical Macroeconomics* (Brighton, Wheatsheaf, 1985). For the later convergence between monetarist and contemporary Keynesian strategies see D. Cobham, 'Popular Political Strategies for the UK Economy', *The Three Banks Review* (1984).

12   The best short accounts are: T. Congdon, *Monetarism;* J. Trevithick, *Inflation* (Harmondsworth, Penguin Books, 1977) Ch. 5; D. Heald, *Public Expenditure* (Oxford, Martin Robertson, 1983), Ch. 3; and J. Tobin, 'The Monetarist Counter-Revolution Today: an Appraisal', *The Economic Journal* (1981). See also N. Bosanquet, *After the New Right* (London, Heinemann, 1983), Part 1 and H. Simons, *'Rules Versus Authorities in Monetary Policy',* in AEA *Readings in Monetary Theory* (London, George Allen & Unwin, 1952).

13   Friedman first expounded this idea in his 1967 Presidential address to the American Economics Association. See M. Friedman, 'The Role of Monetary Policy', *The American Economic Review,* 1 (1968). In general terms, however, this article makes only modest claims for monetary policy. It was this difference between Friedman's relatively cautious economic theorizing and his enthusiastic support for capitalism which led Sam Brittan to object to his politicization of monetarism. See Brittan's open letter to Friedman in *The Financial Times* (6 December 1976).

14   On the rational expectations hypothesis see Klamer, *The New Classical Macroeconomics.* On Hayek see Bosanquet *After the New Right,* Ch. 2.

15   For the relationship between monetary policy and exchange rate regimes see Congdon, *Monetarism,* p. 50, Fforde, 'Setting Monetary Objectives', and R. Ball and T. Burns, 'The Inflation Mechanism in Britain', *The American Economic Review* (1976), p. 470.

16   Though a reading of David Laidler's recent description of monetarist theory in this period suggests that the gap between 'high theory' and vulgar perceptions was not all that great. See D. Laidler, 'Monetary Policy in Britain: Successes and Shortcoming', *Oxford Review of Economic Policy,* 1 (1985), 35-43.

17   For some of the different dimensions of monetarism see B. Griffiths, *Monetarism and Morality* (London, Centre for Policy Studies, 1985).

18   The County of Edessa was one of the states set up by the Crusaders early in the 12th century. In contemporary language it was a 'front-line' statelet, impossible to defend, and was soon recapturd by the

Muslims.
19   W. Keegan, *Mrs Thatcher's Economic Experiment* (London, Allen Lane, 1984), pp. 141-2.
20   J. Bulpitt, *Territory and Power in the United Kingdom* (Manchester University Press, 1983), Ch. 7.
21   Sir John Hoskyns, 'Conservatism is Not Enough', *Political Quarterly* (1984).
22   For one version of this argument see the Fifth Mais Lecture by Nigel Lawson, *The British Experiment* (London, Treasury Press Release, 103/84).
23   On the statecraft of privatization see M. Rutherford, 'Missed Chances', *The Financial Times* (2 Feb. 1980) and Mrs Thatcher's interview in *The Times* (5 May 1983).
24   Professor Branson commenting on the paper by W. Buiter and M. Miller, 'Changing the Rules: Economic Consequences of the Thatcher Regime', *Brookings Papers on Economic Activity,* 2 (1983), p. 376.
25   J. Fforde, 'Setting Monetary Objectives', p. 207,.
26   On the Government's race policies see J. Bulpitt, 'Continuity, Autonomy and Peripheralisation: the Anatomy of the Centre's Race Statecraft in Britain, *Government and Policy,* 2 (1985), 129-47.
27   There is some controversy concerning the impact of the Falklands War on the 1983 election. See W. Miller, 'There Was No Alternative: the British General Election on 1983', *Parliamentary Affairs,* 4 (1983), 364-84.
28   Riddell, *The Thatcher Government,* p. 16.

3.5 *Henry Drucker*

Changes in the Labour Party leadership

From 'Changes in the Labour Party leadership',
Parliamentary Affairs, Vol. 34, 1981, pp. 369 – 91.

It is to Robert Michels' compelling book *Political Parties* (1915) that we must turn first for a statement of the role and importance of party leadership. The essential position we find there is clear and categorical: "It is organisation which gives birth to the domination of the elected over the electors, of the mandatories over the mandators, of the delegates over the delegators. Who says organisation, says oligarchy."[1] Michels notes that socialists often cherish a belief that a new elite will keep faith with democracy better than existing leaders. Michels does allow that a constant struggle will occur within socialist parties on this question. Each new generation of activists will endeavour to democratise their party. He even allows that the struggle will have healthy consequences for 'their indefatigable labour improves the soil and secures for them a comparative well being'[2] although they can never uncover the democratic treasure they seek. Michels' conception of party oligarchy is well known. The corollary, that struggle between the leadership and each generation of militant activists creates healthy checks on the leadership, is less well known but equally relevant to the present difficulties in the Labour Party.

R. T. McKenzie's *British Political Parties* (1955) is the best known and most influential application of these ideas about the role of party leadership to the main British parties. In addition to addressing himself to Michels—especially to Michels' suspicion that in right – wing parties there was less tension between parliamentary and party leaders—McKenzie also set out to test the prophecies of the late 19th – century French political scientist M. Ostrogorski. Ostrogorski expounded the conservative fear that a political machine, which alone could organise the newly enfran –

chised masses, would quickly come to dominate the people they happened to send to parliament. These MPs, he feared, would become accountable to the rank and file or the caucus leaders of that rank and file outside Parliament.

McKenzie noted that the Labour Party's prejudices were the reverse of Ostrogorski's. Its members were proud to agree with Clement Attlee's claim that the Labour Party Conference 'lays down the policy of the Party and *issues instructions* which must be carried out by the Executive, the affiliated organizations and its representatives in Parliament and on local authorities... The Labour Party Conference is in fact a parliament of the movement'.[3] In McKenzie's words: 'Labour writers appear to imply that no political party has any right to call itself democratic unless its parliamentary leaders are effectively controlled by the mass membership of the party; and they argue that on this test the Conservatives fall down lamentably'.[4] McKenzie believed that Labour's rhetoric was twice misleading. Labour was little different from the Conservative Party, and both were, and must be, dominated by their parliamentary leadership.

The necessity of parliamentary dominance derived, on McKenzie's reading, from the constitution. The role of the extra – parliamentary organs of the parties was rather like the role of Bagehot's monarch: they had the right 'to be consulted, to encourage and to warn'.[5] Labour, by accepting the conventions with respect to the Prime Minister and cabinet government, had ensured that power would be concentrated in the hands of the Parliamentary Labour Party (PLP) and its leaders. McKenzie believed that Labour would have ceased even pretending to itself that the party outside parliament, mainly the National Executive Committee (NEC) and the Annual Conference (AC)—ruled, had it only been in office longer.

As is often the case with British government texts, *British Political Parties* related two incidents in which this tradition of parliamentary dominance was unsuccessfully challenged, as if the decisions made then had the force of judicial precedents. The incidents occurred during and immediately after the 1945 general election. Clement Attlee had been Deputy Prime Minister in the wartime coalition government. He had achieved this position by being the leader of the second largest parliamentary party (Labour) when the 1940 government was formed. He had been elected by the PLP alone but was like his predecessors, known as the Leader of the Labour Party. As leader of the PLP he sat *ex officio* as a member of the party's NEC and gave the 'Parliamentary Report' at each annual conference. His post was distinct from that of party chairman, who was elected annually by the NEC. In practice that post rotated and was allocated according to the well tried Labour principle of 'Buggins' turn'. In 1945 Buggins was Harold Laski.

During the election of 1945 Attlee and his deputy, Ernest Bevin, were invited by Churchill to attend the Potsdam Conference which had been scheduled for the day after polling (there was to be a three — week lapse before the announcement of the vote to allow the forces' vote to be added in each constituency to the civilian ballot). Laski issued a statement which asserted that Attlee would attend the conference 'as an observer only'. His presence was not taken as a sign of party approval, that could be granted by the NEC only. Attlee repudiated Laski's statement telling him that 'a period of silence on your part would be welcome'. Churchill deliberately took up Laski's statement in order to raise an election scare that a future Labour government would be subject to orders from the NEC. Attlee simply denied that the NEC had the power to challenge the actions and conduct of a Labour Prime Minister. That denial settled the issue in 1945. According to McKenzie the denial was correct constitutional doctrine and therefore settled the issue forever: no one could dictate to the PLP and its leader.

A second incident which occurred a few days later is of less concern to McKenzie, but of no less significance to the main participants and to us. Attlee was the leader of the PLP of 1944. After the election there was a new, much larger, PLP. If it met it might elect someone other than Attlee. Laski, amongst others, worked for this end. He wanted Morrison to be leader and hence Prime Minister. Churchill realised what was afoot and went to the Palace to resign before the PLP could meet. The King had no choice but to call on Attlee, the leader of the second largest party (the newly elected parliament having not yet gathered). Attlee accepted without consulting the (old or new) PLP. Two days later the new PLP had no choice when it met but to elect the Prime Minister as its leader.

The import of the constitution it would seem was then (a) that no outside body such as the NEC could dictate to the PLP, but (b) the leader of the PLP and a Conservative Prime Minister acting in concert could.

McKenzie's book owes its authority to the thorough and systematic way it marshalls its evidence, the importance of its subject and, not least, to the interests and individuals its thesis served. *British Political Parties* was published in the midst of the first great row within the post – war Labour Party over the respective roles of the PLP, the NEC, annual conference and the leader. *Tribune* newspaper, founded in 1937, became the focus of a Bevanite group which was challenging the Gaitskell leadership. Backed by *Tribune*, the Bevanites built up a considerable power base in the Constituency Labour Parties (CLPs), which, in the manner marked out by Michels four decades previously, tried to make the leadership more accountable to the party.

Then, as ever, the battle was partly between groups within the party, the majority of the PLP on one side , the majority of the CLPs often on the other. It was partly an ideological battle, the Tribunites claimed to be left – real socialists or democratic socialists as they call themselves. The Gaitskellites claimed to be loyal to the parliamentary leadership and more to the centre (few in the Labour Party admit to being on its right unless they are about to jump ship). They came to call themselves the social democrats. The battle was also partly about personality and career: both Bevan and Gaitskell wanted to succeed the elderly Attlee. After the 1955 election Gaitskell fulfilled his ambition. The PLP elected him leader over Morrison and Bevan.

McKenzie's thesis provided support for the Gaitskellite position. It went further than Michels—whose emphasis on the power of oligarchy was entirely consistent with control of the PLP by the NEC with or without the support of the party secretariat (known for its then headquarters as Transport House). McKenzie asserted that control of the party inevitably and rightly rested with the leadership of the PLP. Yet, in supporting the Gaitskellites' ideology, he underplayed the importance to them of the harmony which had existed between successive parliamentary leaders and the leaders of the largest trade unions. If opposition to the PLP and its leadership was to be successfully mounted, some, or all, of the major trade unions would need to be wooed from their traditional support for the PLP leadership. Both the annual conference and election to the NEC were (and are) dominated by the largest unions. On most major issues (German rearmament was the only important exception) the leadership could count in the late forties and early fifties on its 'praetorian guard'—the leaders of the six largest unions, who in 1948 had between them 3,029,000 of the 5,444,000 total conference vote. So strong indeed was the trade – union – backed PLP leadership at annual conference that Attlee, in particular, never had cause to challenge the militant doctrine of conference sovereignty. The Bevanites never challenged it either, though they chafed terribly under the power of the trade union leaders which was then employed so thoroughly against them.

Gradually, fitfully at first, the Gaitskellite position was undermined. Ascendency within the constituency section of NEC was gained by the Bevanites in 1952 when they succeeded in replacing three ex – ministers with three of their own supporters. These three joined other Tribunites in the seven – place constituency section (the trade unions have 12 places and also dominate the 5 – place women's section). But the greatest defeat for the parliamentary leadership came from mistaken initiatives of their own. Indeed, given the preponderant position enjoyed by Gaitskell and his allies, it was only by their own error that they could have been beaten. The major break came in the wake of the 1959 general election defeat. Labour had counted on the hitherto regular swing of the pendulum to return to office after the successive Tory victories of 1951 and 1955. In the event, the Suez debacle of 1956 notwithstanding, the Conservatives were returned with an increased majority. Thrown by this unexpected reverse, Gaitskell asked the 1959 special conference to water down Clause 4— the most sacred text in Labour's testament. The party refused, and while the decision was so overwhelming that the issue was never taken to the vote, the leader had been defeated by the extra – parliamentary party.

The following year Gaitskell was defeated again, this time on a card vote, over defence policy. The CND – led revulsion against Britain's nuclear deterrent was at its peak and was encouraged by *Tribune*. It became clear well before conference that a unilateralist resolution would pass. As Lewis Minkin has pointed out in *The Labour Party Conference*,[6] Gaitskell could have adopted a number of courses, each of which had been employed since 1931 by his predecessors when the party looked certain to adopt a policy the leader abhorred. He could have neutered it behind the scenes in negotiations with the leaders of the large unions; he could have accepted an adverse decision, saying nothing in public about it (the next election was four years away) until he could reverse it; he could have resigned; he could have carried out the policy. Instead, in an unprecedented act, he chose to 'fight, fight, fight again to save the party I love' and to get the decision reversed. The reversal was accomplished a year later, that is, at the first possible opportunity.

Gaitskell's action was honourable and victorious. But its implications for the leadership of the party were profound. Here, for the first time, a leader of the party chose to advertise his alienation from it. Here was a leader who fought his party. A gap had been publicly opened between the leader of the parliamentary party and the supposedly sovereign annual conference. In an attempt to reorientate his party and make it again a potential government, Gaitskell deliberately confronted his activists. It was part of his attempt in C. A. R. Crosland's words to effect radical changes 'in the party's class image, its basic doctrine, its organisation and its internal distribution of power'. Specifically it was part of a campaign to assert the authority and autonomy of the PLP and to devalue the conference. Gaitskell was fighting to regain ground for the PLP which McKenzie had argued was rightly theirs. The victory over the unilateralists which Gaitskell gained in 1961 was only a preliminary skirmish in the larger war he had declared. The main issue had become and remains the autonomy of the PLP.

If the autonomy of the PLP is to be sustained against the party it needs to be secured in three places. First and foremost, the PLP must elect its own leader. If the rest of the party chooses the leader or is able to force the PLP to accept even one of their own number (say Mr Benn) against the will of the PLP majority, the autonomy of the PLP cannot be sustained. Such a leader would have his power base outside the PLP and would be the outsiders' man. The simplest way to ensure that the PLP chooses it own leader is to have an election in which only Labour MPs have votes. But this is not a sufficient condition of autonomy since the MPs might, in some circumstances, be delegates for outside bodies such as their sponsoring unions, their CLPs or the NEC. On the other hand, PLP autonomy does not require that only MPs have votes. Votes might by given to outside groups who would willingly follow the PLP's lead. Many unions, for example, might willingly endorse the PLP's choice of a new leader provided only that that choice could be made clear to them in advance. Choice of the PLP leader might also not secure the autonomy of the PLP if there was also a different party official (say, the Chairman of the NEC) with the authority to challenge the PLP's leader.

In addition to choosing its own leader, the autonomy of the PLP requires that no outside body be able to dictate policy to the PLP. Given Labour's deeply entrenched manifestoism—its belief that a government has a democratic responsibility to enact its election manifesto—the battleground here is who writes the manifesto. In theory, resolutions which pass annual conference with majorities of more than two – thirds have to be included in the next election manifesto. But such resolutions can be changed almost beyond recognition by manifesto authors. Promises, too, can be devalued if the manifesto becomes no more than a shopping list. This is a special problem when such a list becomes very long—as recent manifestos have tended to be. Traditionally the major parties have kept their manifestos secret until they are produced at the beginning of the election campaign. This tradition is justified by the apparent need to keep the other parties ignorant of their contents. Secrecy limits the potential number of authors: preferably to one. This requirement plays into the hands of the leader. But Labour's desire to portray itself as a democratic party and the feeling of many activists—*pace* Michels—that previous Labour governments have taken their manifesto commitments lightly have led to repeated attempts by CLPs to have a larger say for the NEC in the writing of the manifesto.

Thirdly, PLP autonomy is incompatible with CLP control over MPs. CLPs select Labour candidates. If they could easily choose not to reselect them, MPs would soon lose their autonomy. Behind each request to vote for or against a measure would lie the implied threat of loss of support at the next election.

So far we have been discussing the autonomy of the PLP without considering its internal organisation. R. T. McKenzie's thesis, and his citation of Churchill's resignation in 1945, ought to alert us to the fact that this oversight may be unfortunate. An autonomous PLP is not identical with a democratic PLP. 'Autonomy' may be, for much of its history has been, an opening for elite domination of the PLP by its own leadership. Deference to the wishes of the leader can be induced in MPs by hopes of preferment, the discipline of the whips, and the doctrine of the collective responsibilty of ministers. The McKenzie/Gaitskellite argument for PLP autonomy is less attractive when these factors operate.

Increasingly since 1959 the Gaitskellites have defended the

autonomy of the PLP which, as we have seen, needs protection from the CLPs, the annual conference and the NEC. We have also seen that the Bevanite offensive against the Gaitskellites was originally successful in the CLP section of the NEC. It is easy to exaggerate the number or importance of the clashes between the Gaitskellites and the Bevanites and their heirs. The recent revival of the struggle notwithstanding, their conflict was dormant for much of the sixties and early seventies. Nevertheless, it is important to note that the early association between the trade union 'praetorian guard' and the Gaitskellites was never buffed into an article of ideological faith. On the contrary, even in 1959 when the trade union leaders were still normally allies of the Gaitskellites, Douglas Jay, one of the most consistent and rigorous of Gaitskell's allies, suggested changes in the constitution of the party which would have weakened the unions.[7] For all that they depended on trade union block votes, the Gaitskellites were always wary of the weight of the trade unions in the party and latterly have come to fear that power and to argue against it. It would be an error to see social democracy as the Labour Party without the eccentric CLPs; rather the Gaitskellites wanted a party with weakened CLPs and trade unions as well. Some have even urged the Labour Party to end the formal tie with the trade unions altogether. Certainly few of the threats to PLP autonomy which the social democrats fear could long survive without strong trade union support.

Given that some of the defenders of PLP autonomy wish to weaken, if not extinguish, their party's tie with both the CLPs and the trade unions, one might wonder what they see as their political base. Their answer is the electorate: or at any rate, actual and potential Labour voters. Theirs is a view of the role of MPs and the PLP which has its roots in the pre – socialist 19th century view of representative government on the one hand, and mid – 20th century psephology on the other. John Stuart Mill's *Considerations on Representative Government* (1861) is the best statement of their theoretical position: Mill argued for a parliament of intelligent MPs responsive to the wishes of an educated electorate but guided by their own conscience. Mark Abrams and Richard Rose's *Must Labour Lose* (1960) provided psephological backing for their position. Abrams and Rose came near to answering their question affirmatively. Only by jettisoning its baggage of backward looking socialist commitments could Labour, they argued from extensive survey evidence, win another election.

Thus the social democrats' strategy was not so much democratic as parliamentarian. They sought a power base in the people while reducing the role of the middle men—the party members—almost to insignificance. Their strategy was congruent with the arguments of Michels and R. T. McKenzie and they sought to avoid the traps foreseen by Ostrogorski. Within the ranks of party activists this strategy was seen as elitist. Certainly, it was alien to the letter of the Labour Party constitution. But it was to take more than twenty years' hard work by the social democrats' enemies, some amendments to the constitution, and many important changes in society completely outside their control, to turn the Labour Party round and make the leadership of party conform more closely to the letter of the party's constitution.

Since the publication of the social democrats' bible, C. A. R. Crosland's *The Future of Socialism* (1956), many of the social changes Crosland predicted have occurred. These changes have not, however, produced the changes in the Labour Party he hoped for. On the contrary, they have tended to pull in the other direction: rather than making for a radical modern populist Labour Party with stronger parliamentary leadership and weakened ties with the major trade unions, Labour has become yet more closely tied to the largest unions, more the plaything of its decreasingly numerous but increasingly leftish local activists, more disputatious and at the same time less popular with the electorate. All of these trends have tended to undermine the position of leader, whoever he may be and however he is chosen.

The old working class which threw up the 'praetorian guard' so useful to Attlee has not reproduced itself. Between 1960 and 1980 the number of people in manufacturing jobs in Britain fell from 8.2 million to just over 6.3 million. In the same period employment in services, particularly public services grew equally dramatically. In 1961 573,000 people were employed in education and 608,000 in medicine: by 1978 the figures were respectively 933,000 and 942,000. A movement dedicated to ending the drudgery of manual labour has no need to fear such changes, but a Labour Party leadership bolstered by declining trade unions in declining industries could not be so sanguine. In 1948 the six largest unions could be counted on to support the leadership. They were, in order of importance: The Transport and General Workers (TGWU), the Mineworkers (NUM), the Engineers (AUEW), General and Municipal Workers (GMWU), Shopworkers

(USDAW) and Railwaymen (NUR). By 1980 the Mineworkers had dropped to sixth place and the Railwaymen to tenth. In third place was NUPE, the National Union of Public Employees.. White collar unions which had joined and/or increased their power within the party were ASTMS (11th largest), APEX (12th) and COHSE (17th).

But the position of party leader has been weakened not only by a change in union affiliations, but also by the decreased ability of many union leaders to deliver their delegations. Some of the largest, like the TGWU are no longer subject to autocratic internal rule. Others, like the Engineers (AUEW), find it difficult to make up their minds on crucial issues. In many cases such loosened control is an expression of increased democracy within the unions and, behind that, of a more critical and independent stance by branches and regions. These changes register a maturing trade union movement: but that is small comfort to a party leader looking for support.

If the large unions are no longer the building blocks of the party leader's power, this is also partly the result of widespread struggles within the unions between union officials and groups of shop stewards. During the seventies it seemed that a rising tide of anarchic dissent was melting the sand castles of party and union leaders' defences and for some officials the problem was compounded by the unpopular decisions of Labour governments. Years of incomes restraint and declining standards of living for their members gave potent weapons to dissident members so that some union leaders sought to distance themselves from party leaders in order to protect themselves.

The most dramatic emblem of this problem was the move of the TGWU from the party's right to its left where it was joined by NUPE and, for a time, by the AUEW. While not many unions were to become so dependably opposed to the parliamentary leadership as the TGWU after Frank Cousins' election as its leader in 1956, its move, the anti–leader position of ASTMS, the leftward move of the NUM, meant that no overall or secure control of party conference could be held or even established by anyone. Since no one now has overall control of conference, a development unforseen by Michels and his elitist followers has arisen: immobililty. The party is not dominated by its managers or its leader or the unions, neither is it dominated by its activists. No one person or group of people or collection of organisations is in a position to dominate it at all.

In view of the Tribunite domination of CLP places on the NEC, it might be thought that changes here could hardly worsen a non – Tribunite leader's position; but this is not so. Reliable figures of individual memberships are impossible to obtain. But it is universally admitted that membership has dropped appreciably from its peak in 1952 (when it was officially 1,000,000). The drop has been particularly steep in Labour's safe inner – city constituencies where some commentators guess that 50 members may be the norm. Not surprisingly, given the drop in people engaged in manual occupations and the rise in public service employment, the proportion of the remaining members who come from the latter occupations seem to be rising: sometimes substantially so. Much as Michels anticipated, these new members are often more ideologically strident than the people they replaced and tend to be well to the left of the PLP. CLPs dominated by the small groups of militants who can now—in the party's enervation—take them over, are more likely to select leftwingers as MPs and to be suspicious of existing MPs and the PLP as a whole. These changes have further compounded the leader's problems.

It is tempting to look for underlying social and economic explanations for political changes, especially when these changes occur over a period of years. To the underlying movements already mentioned one must add a personal factor: the character of Harold Wilson. Wilson was leader of the party for a considerable period—from February 1963 to April 1976. If the method of election of his successor in 1976 resembled Wilson's own in 1963, perhaps that was because Wilson chose his moment well and because forces gathering during his period in office had not yet marshalled themselves as they were to do toward the end of James Callaghan's term. There is injustice in this for Wilson as leader was cynical about and contemptuous of his party. Rather than fight adverse conference decisions, he simply ignored them. During his period as leader annual conference and then the NEC came almost into open war with the party leadership and the PLP. Callaghan, on the other hand, tried (ultimately unsuccessfully) to heal the breaches Wilson had opened. In many ways Wilson personified the aloof, irresponsible (to the party) leader, cut off from activist opinion.

The difficulties of Labour's leaders have also been intensified by changes in the party system. From the middle forties to the middle seventies Britain had a strong two – party system. This system reinforced the authority of the leaders of the major parties. Each was either Prime Minister—with all the patronage and authority of that office—or PM – in – waiting. Each either had a firm parliamentary majority behind him or could hope to have one after the next election. Even if he were merely leader of the Opposition, the leader of the Labour Party had enormous authority. The major television and radio programmes and the newspapers would seek his comment on every major public event and his comments were given precedence over everyone else's, save the Prime Minister's. But by the middle seventies this system was losing its hold both on the electorate and on MPs. As a result, there were increasing numbers of minor party MPs in the House and even members of major parties were willing to ignore the whips: and often on important votes.

For most of his three years in office James Callaghan ruled without a parliamentary majority. That he was able to do so was a measure of his skill in holding together his parliamentary colleagues; and if he often snubbed opinion outside the PLP, one reason was the more immediate imperative of holding together his MPs. But the consequences of the rise of minor parties were felt most keenly by the leaders of the major parties when in opposition. Mrs Thatcher did not establish authority over the minor parties until Labour was exhausted and demoralised in April 1979. Callaghan in opposition never recovered from his general election defeat. When the number of parties increases, the authority of leader of the Opposition wanes. He must share the stage with the leaders of the other opposition parties; his backbenchers are less often recognised on the floor of the House of Commons by the Speaker who has a long list of party spokemen to call; his MPs may think of breaking away to form their own new parties; he is less credible as the next Prime Minister.

All these changes—in the unions, the party and the party system—reinforced one another during Mr Callaghan's term as Labour's leader. In the end, in 1980, he was effectively forced from office, the first Labour leader to be so treated since 1935 and the first ever who had been Prime Minister.

Notes

1 *Political Parties: A Sociological Study of the Oligarchical Tendencies of Modern Democracy* (New York edition, 1959), p. 401.

2 *Op. cit.,* p. 405.
3 *British Political Parties: The Distribution of Power Within the Con servative and Labour Parties* (2nd edition), p. 10.
4 *Op. cit.,* p. 11.
5 *Op. cit.,* p. 636.
6 *The Labour Party Conference:* A Study in the Politics of Intra – Party Democracy (Manchester University Press, 1980).
7 *Change and Fortune: A Political Record* (London, 1980), pp. 274 – 5.

3.6 *Vernon Bogdanor*

The Liberal Party and the Alliance

From 'Conclusion: the Liberal Party, the Alliance and the future' in V. Bogdanor (ed.), *Liberal Party Politics,* Clarendon Press, Oxford 1983, pp. 275 – 85.

Two central features of the modern Liberal Party emerge with striking clarity... The first is the remarkable continuity of doctrine and ideas which the Party displays. Parties are, of course, far more than repositories of opinion; they are also vehicles for the advancement of social interests. Yet it remains true that the sort of elector who would find the ideas of the Liberal Party sympathetic during the time of Gladstone or Asquith would also be inclined to support the Liberal Party or the SDP today. The main themes – constitutional and political reform, decentralization of power, economic and social reform, internationalism – have hardly changed, although their priorities at different times have legitimately varied.

But the second theme which emerges is that the Liberal Party exists in a political and electoral environment which is alien to it. Primarily, of course, it is the electoral system which conditions the life of the Liberal Party today. We need only compare the influence of the Liberals with that of the Free Democrats in Germany to appreciate this point. In 1980, the Free Democrats secured 10.6 per cent of the vote in West Germany; while in 1979, the Liberals gained 13.8 per cent of the vote in the British general election. In post – war elections, the FDP has never secured more than 12.8 per cent of the vote; while in the two election of 1974, the Liberals gained 19.3 per cent and 18.3 per cent of the vote respectively. Yet, whereas the FDP has been able to participate as a coalition partner in West German governments since the founding of the Federal Republic, except for the years 1956 – 61 and 1966 – 9, the Liberal Party has not participated in goverment since the war, and its prospects of political influence depend upon the accident of one of the other parties not gaining an overall majority of seats. In addition, the electoral system has denied the Liberal Party representation in the European Parliament, although in the European elections of 1979 it gained one – eighth of the vote, more than was secured by some Continental Liberal parties which obtained representation.

Yet this is not the only way in which the Liberal Party is adversely affected by the electoral system. For, while the Liberal vote is distributed fairly evenly across the country, this is not reflected in its representation in Parliament. Its MPs will come from constituencies where there has been a lucky by – election, or a successful breakthrough in a particular locality. They are therefore almost bound to be unrepresentative. Since the Party has no safe seats, moreover, it cannot easily attract able Liberals into standing for Parliament; while the curious geographical pattern of its representation makes it difficult for the Party to mount a national electoral campaign which concentrates upon the same issues throughout the country. It is understandable, then, that proportional representation should lie at the forefront of Liberal priorities. For electoral reform would entirely transform the position of the Party, making it either a quasi – permanent coalition partner as with the FDP; or, such is the depth of disillusionment with the two major parties, a party of government in conjunction with the Social Democrats.

Nevertheless, the future role of the Liberal Party is still unclear. If the Alliance fails, it may remain nothing more than a receptacle of temporary protest votes, a civically – minded alternative to abstention. In the past, the Party has often relied less on the merits of its policies than upon the unpopularity of the other two Parties. Lemieux has shown how much of the Liberal vote in February 1974 resulted from 'negative issue protest'.[1] Voters supported the Liberals not because they agreed with their policies, of which they had only a hazy understanding, but because they disapproved of the policies of the party they had previously supported. Often, therefore, their support for the Liberals had little to do with liberalism. Disllusioned Conservatives supported the Party because they opposed Edward Heath's decision to take Britain into the Common Market; while erstwhile Labour voters came to support the Liberals because they regarded Labour's policies on immigration and race relations as too permissive!

Because so much of its vote has been a negative one, Liberals have found it difficult to project their identity to the public at large. Nor does such a basis of support seem secure enough to enable the Liberals to become a responsible party of government.

Alternatively, the Liberals could remain simply a pressure groups for ideas, a party for members of what Ralf Dahrendorf has called the 'thoughtful minority'.[2] It would be the Party for those unwilling to adhere to any single overriding affiliation whether that affiliation is perceived in either class or ideological terms. Dahrendorf believes that since modern society necessarily involves increasingly complex social affiliations, the size of this minority is bound to increase. However, such a conception of the Party's role would also condemn it to minority status for a considerable period of time.

The Liberal Party could again become what it was between the years 1926 and 1929, an intellectual think – tank, what Keynes called 'an almost perfect tabernacle for independent thought which shall at the same time be not too independent but in touch with realities of politics and of political life'.[3] As a popularizer of ideas and issues, the Liberals would draw attention to problems which the major parties ignored. This would enable the Party to exert an influence upon policy even if it was not in government; as with the Progressives in the United States in the 1920s, who although electorally unsuccessful, prefigured many of the central features of Franklin Roosevelt's New Deal.

Many Liberals, however, would argue that such a role would not be sufficient to secure the spread of Liberal ideas. For the two major parties would be too dominated by vested interests and ideological blinkers to preceive their relevance. That, they would suggest, was the fate of Keynesian ideas on unemployment in the 1920s. Because the Liberal Party lacked political leverage, these ideas were not accepted by the Labour or Conservative Parties. For the same reason, Britain failed to join the Common Market in the 1950s when she might have been able to negotiate more favourable terms, and failed to adopt non – sectarian policies of economic modernization during the 1960s and 1970s. For Liberal policies to succeed, therefore, the Liberal Party must be stronger.

A third role which the Liberal Party might play would be that of the FDP in West Germany, a corrective to the absolute philosophies of the two major parties. It would become the party of balance and compromise. Whether such a role is possible does not, of course, depend upon the Liberal Party alone. Under the plurality electoral system, it depends upon the chance of whether the

other parties need Liberal help in the Commons, as between
February and October 1974, and in the years 1977 – 8. But with
proportional representation the position of the Liberals as a corrective force will be guaranteed, as it is in West Germany.

Yet such a role also holds dangers for Liberals. It could make it
difficult for the Party to preserve its identity. The Liberal Party is
accustomed to see itself as a radical force; and Roy Jenkins, the
leader of the SDP, called in his Dimbleby Lecture of 1979 for the
development of a new 'radical centre', perhaps a contradiction in
terms. For the radicalism of the Liberal Party is hardly part of the
middle ground of British politics... The Liberal Party is a Party of
radical individualists. Liberal voters, for the most part, are not.
Liberal radicalism has concentrated upon policies such as reform
of the abortion and homosexuality laws, and an attack upon what
the party regards as restrictive immigration policies...

Roy Jenkins has been associated with many of these issues. He
was Home Secretary when David Steel piloted his private
member's bill legalizing abortion through the Commons in 1967;
and he has been responsible for race – relations legislation designed to prevent discrimination against ethnic minorities. Such concerns are those of a minority. albeit a courageous one. Would they
survive the transition of the Liberal Party from a party of ideas to
a party of government?

The Liberal Party – and the SDP – have to confront a basic
dilemma. Faced with the reality of Mrs Thatcher's radicalism and
the possibility of Mr Benn's radicalism is there scope within the
British political system for a third form of radicalism, as espoused
by the Alliance? Or is the Alliance in reality a conservative force
seeking to recreate the Butskellite consensus which the other parties have abandoned? Is the Alliance a radical formation; or a centrist one? It cannot be both.

The Social Democratic Party was formed as a breakaway from
the Labour Party. Two of the three leaders who broke away –
David Owen and Shirley Williams – sought a realigment on the
Left, replacing Labour by a party modelled on the German SPD.
The new party would be of the Left, but it would be revisionist, dis-
claiming Clause 4 and the commitment to wholesale nationalisation, and rejecting trade – union affiliation. This realignment on
the Left could come about either in alliance with the Liberal Party, or through the Social Democrats acting on their own. The first
alternative, the Grimondite one, involves replacing Labour by a

united Social Democrat – Liberal Party. It would signify the coming together of two different but closely related streams of thought – the Liberal and the Social Democrat which, as Peter Clarke shows, were torn apart after the First World War.

Yet, the problem which Grimond never succeeded in resolving remains. How can a realignment on the Left be secured with the votes of the discontented Right, and the aid of a Party which is a receptacle for temporarily discontented Conservatives? It is for this reason that David Owen sees co – operation with the Liberals as purely temporary, until proportional representation is achieved. When that happens, the two parties should go their separate ways. Yet this does not resolve the problem. For the electoral profile of the SDP is far closer to that of the Liberals than to Labour. And the SDP is seen by the electorate as a party of the centre rather than a party of the Left.

It would appear natural, then, to imagine the SDP working together with the Liberals not as a new Left – wing party, but as a central bloc seeking a pivotal role in British politics.

The Alliance, of course, offers the Liberal Party the possibility of another role, that of a party of government. If that happens, it would have to become a more homogeneous and disciplined party paying proper deference to its leaders who would have to gain ministerial credibility. A transformation of this kind would be more difficult for the Liberals than for the SDP. For the leaders of the SDP are men and women of government, while most of those who have joined the Liberal Party have been aware that they are joining a slighty anarchic party far from the seat of power. The Liberals, therefore, could be faced with strong tensions between its parliamentary leadership and its extra – parliamentary activists. It is understandable perhaps if many of the latter fear electoral success more than failure.

Whether the Alliance succeeds in breaking the two – party system depends upon whether it can convert the dissatisfaction with the Labour and Conservative Parties into stable and permanent electoral support. At first sight, opportunites for doing so would appear to be very great. The public's increasing disillusionment with the managerial incompetence and extremist rhetoric of the two major parties has created a climate of electoral volatility in which a new political formation can hope to gain support. For the paradox is that, as the rhetoric of party divisions has widened, so ironically the class basis of voting behaviour has eroded, and social attitudes have converged. Such a situation offers considerable possibilities, though not only for the Liberal Party. It also allows Mrs Thatcher to hope for a realignment of attitudes along a radical populist and authoritarian basis; and Mr Benn to hope that the grievances of the unemployed, the aspirations of youth, and the sectional interests of workers in the public sector can be combined in a new socialist coalition.

But the Liberal Party – as an already established political organization, yet in no way responsible for the country's growing political and economic difficulties – might seem ideally placed to take advantage of the crisis. Centrist and catch – all in its appeal, it seems to offer to the electorate a return to conditions of stabilty together with a programme of economic modernization capable of reversing the long years of economic decline. 'The Alliance', as Andrew Gamble has argued, 'is proclaiming that it alone is the truly classless party, the party that puts nation before class, the party that is moderate and pragmatic in pursuit of the common good, and which has no association with any sectional interest'.[4]

The Alliance, however has plainly not yet succeeded in converting temporary support to a permanent sense of identification. This does not mean that it will prove unable to do so. For political parties can themselves influence social trends creating new political alignments as they do so. They are, to some extent at least, masters of their fate. The 1980s may well prove a decade when the whole structure of British politics undergoes a seismic change. The Liberal Party faces an opportunity such as it has not enjoyed for over sixty years; and one unlikely to recur.

Notes

1 P. H. Lemieux: 'Political Issues and Liberal Support in the February 1974 British General Election' in *Political Studies,* 1977.
2 Ralf Dahrendorf: 'Liberalismus' in Peter von Juling (ed.): *Was heisst heute Liberal?* (Hamburg, 1978), p. 29.
3 John Maynard Keynes: *Collected Writings,* Vol. xix (Cambridge, 1981), p. 733. Letter to J. L. Garvin, 9 February 1928.
4 Andrew Gamble: 'The Rise and Rise of the SDP' in *Marxism Today,* March 1982, p. 8.

3.7 *Herbert Döring*

Characteristics of Social Democratic activists

From 'Who are the Social Democrats?', *New Society,* 8 September 1983, pp. 351-3.

Over the last few years, the Social Democrats' success – though fluctuating – has been remarkable. One of their less dramatic and yet astounding achievements has been the fact they have attracted not only a fee-paying membership of some 60,000 credit-card-carrying members and party supporters, but also a great many activists.

Are they just Labour turncoats? If not, then this build-up of an active membership is even more surprising, because it runs counter to a general trend. Britain in the 1970s was characterised not only by a weakened party identification (as shown by the British Election Study at the University of Essex), but also by a steep decline in individual party membership in the Labour Party and, to a lesser degree, in the Conservatives. In Britain, as elsewhere in western democracies, there is an inclination to favour new ways of political expression, other than those provided by political parties.

How was a breakaway parliamentary party of traditional MPs at the top able to attract at the grassroots a sizeable number of 'new' recruits? The present analysis is based on a survey of the Council for Social Democracy, the SDP's elected 'parliament' which has meetings at least three times a year. (At party conferences only the council members have the right to vote.) So it is concerned with the middle-ranking party elite, the layer between leadership and ordinary members. What makes these 'middlemen' of the SDP sacrifice time and money to participate in party politics? Does their presence signify a new trend in British politics?

Their social characteristics and political opinions are revealed by a detailed questionaire distributed to the 421 council members of registered area parties at the first meeting of the Council for Social Democracy in Great Yarmouth in October 1982: 260 council members (or 62 per cent) responded. Explicit comparisons can be made with previous studies of Liberal, Labour and Conservative party conferences carried out in 1978 and 1979 by Ian Gordon of Kingston Polytechnic and Paul Whiteley of Bristol University.

The council is elected for a period of two years to discuss and decide upon SDP policies. But its different constitutional status does not mean it can't be compared with other British party conferences. Admittedly, the strains of time and money involved in sitting several times a year, and paying expenses out of your own pocket, mean that council members consist chiefly of intellectual people, interested in discussion, and sufficiently affluent or in a job position enabling them to take time off. But, as table 1 shows, the proportion of office holders within the party is even higher than among conference delegates of other British parties, matched only by the Conservative sample.

Table 1 Do you at present hold office within the party?

	Liberal %	Labour %	Tory %	SDP %
no	34	28	12	12
yes	66	72	88	88

If the outlook of the council is disproportionately academic, it only reflects a feature characteristic of SDP membership at large, as shown by an Opinion Research Centre poll for *Weekend World* in November 1981.

The crucial question, on the answer to which all further analysis hinges, is whether council members have overwhelmingly been previous members of the Labour Party. The answer is a resounding No. Of our respondents, over half had not been a member of another party; and only a third had broken with the ranks of Labour.

Those who had not belonged to another party were asked whether they had nevertheless previously considered themselves to be close to one. These 142 council members split: 64 Labour, 11 Conservative, two 'other', and 33 close to no particular party. Even if you lump together all Labour sympathisers, whether former party members or not, the sum total is no more than 58 per cent. This rebuts the conventional wisdom-disseminated, for example, in a recent booklet by the Conservative Research Department-which contends that the SDP mainly attracted malcontents from the Labour Party.

What holds for the middle-ranking party elite is even more true for the average party member. This has been shown not only by the nationwide *Weekend World* survey, but also by a University of Newcastle survey among local SDP members. In the Newcastle study an overwhelming 78 per cent, and in the *Weekend World* poll 67 per cent, were newcomers to party politics.

A homogeneous identity

Even those SDP council members who were previously in the Labour Party are, in terms of their social characteristics and political opinions, distinctly un-Labourish in outlook, and close to the other council members with different origins. Our research shows that a homogeneous identity emerges.

The tables give the results of a comparison of our SDP study with previous surveys of Liberal, Labour and Conservative Party conference delegates.

Table 2: Age

	Liberal %	Labour %	Tory %	SDP %
under 35	41	29	24	25
35-60	47	55	58	66
over 60	13	15	17	9

Table 3: Sex

	Liberal %	Labour %	Tory %	SDP %
male	76	86	76	72
female	24	14	24	27

On age (table 2) and sex (table 3) only slight differences emerge between the four parties. The Liberals are, on average, the youngest. The slightly greater share of women among the SDP council delegates mainly reflects the endeavour, embedded in the party's constitution, to give women parity. This provision worked exclusively in favour of the political novices. The previously

Labour members are as male as ever. Overall, the SDP reproduced the dominantly male and middle class feature of all party activists everywhere.

Table 4: School last attended

	Liberal	Labour	Tory	SDP
	%	%	%	%
elementary	2	23	5	1
secondary modern	8	19	9	6
comprehensive	6	5	6	7
grammar	43	27	37	53
public/private	26	5	28	20
other	15	22	15	12

One striking difference from other parties is educational background. The SDP is a party run by the intelligentsia (table 4). More precisely, it is run by that group within the best-educated people in Britain who, with the expansion of the educational system in the 1950s and 1960s, went to grammar schools (53 per cent of all SDP delegates) and then on to some form of higher education.

A staggering 85 per cent of our respondents said they went to an institution of higher education. The proportion of respondents being educated beyond 18 was 65 per cent–compared with 53 per cent of Liberal, 25 per cent of Labour, and 27 per cent of Conservative conference delegates.

The SDP council members are mainly in the middle of their lives. More than half were born during the decade and a half stretching from 1934 to 1949. They were too young to be affected by the Great Depression and they gained their political beliefs when they were adolescents in the boom years of Britain's postwar prosperity (between, say, 1951 and 1966).

This educational background is matched by the jobs of council delegates. The occupational profile is dominated by supervisory white-collar jobs (29 per cent of respondents), teachers (19 per cent) and the professions (15 per cent). There is a dearth of people from commerce (8 per cent), heavy industry (2 per cent) and banking and insurance (3 per cent); and only 1 per cent can be classified as businessmen.

About 45 per cent were employed in the public sector, and 42 per cent in the private sector. One in ten were unemployed. This may underline the SDP's educational profile: it may be explained by the shrinking job opportunities for graduates in Britain today.

It is important to note that this picture of the SDP council–the activists–does not hold for the party voters. As Ivor Crewe's analysis of the 1983 general election showed, the Alliance drew support evenly across the class spectrum. There is no evidence that if drew disproportionately from the 'middling' strata.

The Social Democrats are, in terms of education, closer to the Liberals than the other two major parties. But it does not follow that they share the enthusiasm for 'voluntarism' and community politics, so typical of the Liberal rank and file. Voluntary organisations other than political parties, such as Shelter, have mushroomed since the 1960s, as individual membership in the established parties has declined. But Social Democrats are not enthusiasts for them. Fewer council members than their equivalents in other parties were members of voluntary organisations, other than those related to their occupation (table 5).

Table 5: Are you a member of any other voluntary organisation (other than party-related or occupational)?

	Liberal %	Labour %	Tory %	SDP %
no		35	31	48
yes	21 79	64	69	52

When asked which of several activities occupied them most, SDP delegates scored remarkably low on 'participation in voluntary associations and public advisory bodies (for example, parent-teacher)' or 'contributing to the services that your party offers potential and actual supporters (counselling, professional training and so on).' This supports the view that tensions between Liberal and Social Democrat activists are rooted not so much in passing tactical skirmishes as in a different concept of what party politics ought to be about.

Two other findings serve to round off this profile of SDP middle-level activists.

First, when asked 'What were the economic conditions of your family when you were growing up?', the respondents rather unexpectedly said (in striking contrast to Liberal, Conservative and even Labour activists) that they had *not* been very well-off (table 6).

Table 6: What were the economic conditions of your family when you were growing up?

	Liberal	Labour	Tory	SDP
	%	%	%	%
relatively good	73	49	84	34
relatively poor	28	51	16	66

Admittedly, 23 per cent of their fathers had been in blue-collar jobs, and another 23 per cent had fathers in white-collar jobs at a clerical level. But given that, altogether, 42 per cent of fathers had been professional people (15 per cent), white-collar supervisory staff (22 per cent) and teachers (5 per cent), there must be a strong element of subjective judgment, probably due to upward social mobility, in assessing childhood living standards as not good.

The second finding is that this feeling of individual deprivation in childhood, and subsequent rise on the social ladder, is coupled with a strong collective feeling of deprivation in Britain, as compared with other western European nations. This question was not put in previous comparable Liberal, Labour and Conservative surveys. But it does allow a tentative comparison of the SDP middle ranks with the population at large, because the wording of a 1974 British Election Study survey question was, fortunately, replicated in a national survey commissioned by NEW SOCIETY TY in 1979. As table 7 shows, the SDP's critical attitude towards

Table 7: Compared with other European countries, do you think British industry is well run, badly run or is it about average? Or: is Britain well governed, badly governed or about average?

	British Election Study Oct 1974	New Society survey 1979	Council for Social Democracy 1982
	%	%	%
industry			
well	18	—	2
badly	27	—	70
average	48	—	24
don't know	7	—	4
government			
well	33	26	14
badly	11	16	27
average	52	55	54
don't know	4	3	4

NB: The 1979 New Society survey did not include the industry question

British industry and, to a lesser extent, British government is so divergent from the population at large that it cannot possibly be attributed to different samples and changing times. It must be central to the party's view of the world.

To what extent, then, is the SDP activist a new kind of political animal in Britain?

The SDP has carved out, to man the middle ranks of the party, a sizeable segment of an academically-trained stratum which was vastly increased by expanding educational facilities in the 1950s and 1960s. Most of the Council for Social Democracy members had not previously bothered to organise themselves to become active in party politics. They were mainly interested in politics as *voters*.

Rather more often than not, these SDP activists do not think of themselves as belonging to a particular class (No: 53 per cent; Yes: 46 per cent). Even those who came from the ranks of the Labour Party, and who opt slightly more for a class choice, correctly classify themselves as upper middle (20 per cent) or middle class (60 per cent), and much less often as lower middle (10 per cent) or working class (10 per cent).

This self-assessment of the upwardly socially mobile SDP activists stands in striking contrast to Labour Party activists who also originated from this rising meritocracy. Radical middle class Labour activists tend to over-identify with the working class, in spite of their well-to-do white-collar occupations, as was shown in the Whiteley and Gordon survey of the Labour Party conference in 1978.

The growing stratum of intellectuals in Britain has split at least three ways. One strand became radical Labour activists. Another became Liberal participatory amateurs. Neither of these accords with the ideals of an SDP activist. This new third group concerned themselves neither with party politics, nor with voluntary organisations other than professional ones. They became sophisticated free riders with a 'Butskellist' Labour leaning, and benefited from the working of the two-party system. It was only after the two-party system was felt to have broken down-hampering, as they perceived it, both their professional, individual chances as well as the national interest–that they felt the need to become active to redress the balance.

These sophisticated free riders, now organised in the SDP, *are* a new bread in British party politics.

The influence of business

From 'Capital: the neglected face of power?' in David Marsh (ed.), *Pressure Politics,* Junction Books, London 1983, pp. 21-52.

... [Most] studies of interest groups concentrate upon their direct influence on policy. If one uses such an approach there is no doubt that the influence of capital is limited. In addition, at this level the manufacturing sphere appears better organised and more influential than the banking sphere.

Grant and Marsh present an analysis of the CBI, the most visible and obvious representative of industrial capital during the first decade of its life (1965-74), although a number of subsequent articles have updated this analysis. These authors conclude fairly decisively that, 'the CBI has little direct influence over the policy pursued by government.... The CBI's influence is greatest over the details of legislation rather than over policy itself.'[1] While this conclusion still appears broadly true, two important qualifications must be made. First, some of the detailed concessions obtained by the CBI can be important. So when in November 1974 Dennis Healey in his budget eased price controls and made changes in corporation tax, largely as a result of CBI pressure, this injected in excess of £1,500 million into the manufacturing sector. Secondly, there is no doubt that as the CBI became a more overtly political organisation after 1974, its political influence increased. In particular, as Coates shows, its leadership of the opposition to the Majority Report of the Bullock Committee on Industrial Democracy was one of the key factors in its rejection by the government,[2] a point we shall return to at length later.

We have rather less material on the direct influence of City interest groups on policy-making, although it is generally suggested that the City has less direct effect. For this reason Sargent's study of the UK Banking Act of 1979 is revealing.[3] Sargent shows that while both the CLCB and the BBA agreed with the government that legislation was needed to control the activities of banks, neither was consulted before the White Paper on 'The Licensing and Supervision of Deposit-taking Institutions' was published in August 1976. The White Paper proposed legislation to establish a system of supervision for the banks and a deposit protection scheme. In fact, many of the White Paper's provisions were accepted by the BBA and the CLCB, but they objected to proposals to exempt building societies, trustees saving banks and the National Giro bank from these provisions. The two organisations made representations to that effect to both the Bank of England and the Treasury. However, the BBA found difficulty in finding, or indeed creating, a consensus among its members; in particular, a clear division emerged between the interests of its larger and smaller members and this weakened the impact of its representations.

When the Bill was published it comprised three parts. Part One, which dealt with the granting of licences to recognised deposit and banking institutions, and Part Three, which controlled advertising for deposits, received universal support. In contrast, Part Two, which outlined the details of a deposit protection scheme, was opposed by all the banks, who objected to both the basis of contributions to the deposit protection funds and the fact that they were not to be represented on the proposed deposit protection board. Although the BBA and CLCB made continued representations to obtain changes, as Sargent shows, they were largely unsuccessful. The CLCB did achieve some amendments to the Consumer Credit Act which was included in the final legislative package, but most of the changes were minor and uncontentious. Certainly this case indicates the relative weakness of City interest groups.

Overall it is not easy to distinguish between the direct and indirect influence of capital, or between the influence of the manufacturing and the banking sectors. Certainly on occasion the interest groups representing one or both sectors successfully and directly, influence Government policy. However, often the influence is less direct stemming either from the structural position in the economy which capital enjoys, or from the fact that the interests of capital underpin the ideological background against which policies are made. Nevertheless, it is our contention that the structural and ideological influence of capital are related and reflected in policy decisions. As such, we shall look at one crucial area, industrial policy, where the direct and indirect influence of industrial and banking capital is evident.

Industrial policy: The industrial democracy debate
The discussion within the Labour Party of industrial democracy was reopened in the late 1960s largely as a result of the efforts of Jack Jones, and became one of the policy changes endorsed by the Trade-Union–Labour Party Liaison Committee. Calls for such a change were subsequently incorporated into the Labour Programme of 1973 and both the 1974 Labour Party manifestos. When the Labour Government came to power it established the Bullock Committee as a first step to honouring these commitments. In its evidence to Bullock, and in its subsequent reaction to the Report, the CBI backed voluntary schemes for employee participation which they hoped to see negotiated on a company by company basis. They strongly opposed any attempt to create worker directors. The voluntary schemes envisaged by the CBI should be allowed to develop slowly with representatives drawn from all the workforce rather than made up of trade union representatives. In contrast, the TUC wanted the immediate creation of worker directors on a single board with recognised unions enjoying equal representation to that of the shareholders.

When the Bullock Committee reported it was clear that the unions had won the first round. The independent, largely academic members of the Committee had supported the unionists and together they produced a Majority Report which very much reflected the trade union position. In fact, the Majority Report advocated that a single board of directors should be established using a $2x$ plus y formula – that is, there should be equal representation by worker directors and shareholder nominees, and a smaller group of independent directors. Large companies would have to establish such a board if the idea was supported by the majority of their employees. The worker directors would be selected or elected from a joint representative committee of all interested unions. In direct opposition, the Minority Report signed by the industrialists on the Committee advocated participation below board level with a requirement that such machinery be established within four years. Companies would be able to enter into voluntary arrangements to create worker directors, but only on a supervisory board. Such directors would be chosen by, and from, the whole work force and should not be merely trade union representatives.

work force and should not be merely trade union representatives.

The reaction of both the CBI and business and the TUC to the Report was predictable. The CBI completely rejected the majority recommendations which they saw as likely to undermine the autonomy and power of mangement. In order to substantiate their position they argued that workers' representation on boards would lead to inefficiency, as a result of a decline in the confidentiality essential in a competitive system, and a growing reluctance by investors to invest. Speaking to *The Times* in February, Lord Watkinson, the CBI President, reaffirmed the CBI's position and indeed threatened the withdrawal of the CBI's cooperation with government if they went ahead with the Bullock Committee's recommendations:

If in spite of this, the Government decides to go ahead with legislation based on the Bullock majority report it will not only be introducing highly divisive legislation, it will also be showing complete disregard for the efficient management of our major companies on which the economic future of the country depends.[4]

The TUC by contrast welcomed the Report, although a number of influential unions rejected it, among them the NUM, EETPU, AUEW and NUGM, fearing that trade union incorporation into management would emasculate them when it came to collective bargaining.

The Labour government's response was also unsurprising. It needed the support of industry and especially the City for its economic policy and was obviously worried about their reaction. In addition, the Cabinet was clearly split. Edmund Dell, the minister responsible for this area, advocated a gradual approach, which took account of industries' criticisms while Albert Booth, the Secretary of State for Employment, took a more pro-Bullock line. As a result the government procrastinated and established a committee under Shirley Williams to look at all the proposals and consider the objections. The Government did not produce a White Paper until April 1978.

The proposals in the White Paper were far more moderate than those of Bullock. The emphasis was upon the need to develop a voluntary two-tier board, with workers represented upon a supervisory board with limited powers. The key difference between the White Paper and the Bullock proposals, then, was that the former stressed the role to be played by management in initiating changes to the structure and allowed for the gradual development of participation under the surveillance of management. Any worker directors would be elected by the workforce as a whole rather than being drawn from among union representatives. Finally, of course, even this proposal was not proceeded with and in the Queen's Speech of 1978 the government professed itself still willing to discuss the proposals more fully.

The fact that some trade unions opposed the Bullock Report's version of industrial democracy, and that the Liberal Party – the government's saviours through the Lib–Lab pact after March 1977 — opposed certain of its elements, helped to prevent the introduction of legislation. Nevertheless, it is clear that as Coates says, 'The push to industrial democracy petered out in the face of sustained opposition ... from the political spokesman of private capital.' It is evident that the CBI exerted considerable direct pressure and exercised significant influence. At the same time, however, the government was always conscious of the need to retain cooperation, if not support, particularly from the financial sector, for its economic policy. This was a less direct, if more crucial constraint, which established the background against which more direct representations were successful.

Industrial policy: the 1975 Industry Act
A very similar pattern emerges if we examine the passage of the 1975 Industry Act. In opposition, the Industrial Policy subcommittee of the National Executive Committee (NEC) of the Labour Party established a Public Enterprise working group to examine proposals to create a State Holding Company (a National Enterprise Board). The work of the committee was underpinned by the ideas of Stuart Holland, then a lecturer at Sussex University but since 1979 a left-wing Labour MP. The policy document produced by that Committee, and subsequently approved after considerable debate and dispute in the IPSC, had two major radical elements. A NEB was to be established which would control the equity in the top 25 industrial companies, 1 major bank and 2 major insurance companies, which it was planned to nationalise. In addition, all large companies were to be required to negotiate planning agreements with government concerning their plans for investment, employment, trade, etc. In other words, these proposals, if enacted, would have significantly changed the nature of the British economic system, dramatically increasing the size of the public

sector and restricting the autonomy of management in the private sector. The subsequent history of this proposal is revealing.

The proposal was enshrined in an opposition Green Paper entitled 'The National Enterprise Board', published in April 1973. The document was subsequently considered by the NEC and included in the draft policy programme which was presented to the 1973 Conference. At the NEC meeting the so-called '25 companies clause' was the only one voted upon but Dennis Healey's proposal to have it deleted was defeated. In fact this particular clause was to prove the first casualty. Although Holland's ideas were endorsed by the Conference, opposition was mounting among the PLP leadership and particularly from the Prime Minister, Harold Wilson. Indeed, Wilson made his own view clear in the Conference debate,

My own view on the twenty-five companies proposal has been stated. I am against it, the Parliamentary Committee is against it. I will leave it with these words, that the Parliamentary Committee charged by the Constitution with the duty of sitting down with the Executive to select, from the Programme adopted by Conference the items for including into the election Manifesto, entirely reserves its full constitutional rights on this matter, and there could be nothing more comradely than that.[5]

Here Wilson got his way, for the Party manifesto published in January 1974 contained no specific reference to the takeover of 25 companies and only promised, 'we shall create a powerful NEB with the structure and functions set out in Labour's Programme of 1973'.[6]

The process of emasculation has begun, but it was to speed up after the election of a Labour government. The initial moves seemed to suggest that radical legislation might result because Tony Benn and Eric Heffer, both strong supporters of the proposal, were appointed to the top two positions in the Department of Industry. They immediately coopted Stuart Holland onto a drafting committee established to produce a White Paper. However, the situation changed rapidly. The major problem was that industry, particularly the CBI, and the City strongly opposed the proposals. This opposition soon began to influence and then shape government thinking. Almost at once the Treasury produced a minute in which it argued that the NEB would inevitably be inflationary and too expensive to operate given the need to reduce public expenditure.[7] In response to this unrest Wilson took direct control of the Cabinet's Public Enterprise Committee which was to consider the Industry Bill. At the same time the Chancellor obviously felt the need to attempt to reduce the CBI's fears when he told them; 'the Government has no intentions of destroying the private sector or encouraging its decay'.[8] In similar vein at the Socialist International Conference in June, Wilson argued, 'confidence demands that a clear frontier must be defined between what is public and what is private industry'.[9]

Despite this, the CBI and the City were not reassured and Aims of Industry announced in July that it planned to spend up to £1½ million on a pre-election campaign with the theme: 'Say No to State Control'. It was against this background that Benn's draft proposals were first circulated among, and then considered by, the Cabinet. Wilson's statement after that Cabinet meeting amply reflects the reasons for the modifications in policy which were made:

The Cabinet have now agreed on the programme; I took charge of this operation several weeks ago, chaired all the meetings and the Cabinet on Friday accepted the draft which a small group of us put before it ... Above all, it meets my demand that it is clear and removed a great deal of uncertainty for business which has been created by public debate.[10]

The White Paper, entitled 'The Regeneration of British Industry', finally appeared on 15 August, reportedly after some 25 redrafts.[11] It was called by *The Economist* 'a toned down electioneering version of earlier works[12] and was certainly much less radical than the early proposals. These were two main differences between the White Paper and the original Green Paper. First, the NEB was no longer to hold equity in the top 25 companies but rather was to take over the government's current holding (for example in British Leyland) and also to hold equity in those companies assisted by government grants.[13] In other words, it would operate in much the same way as did the old Industrial Reorganisation Corporation. Secondly, the planning agreements, while still wide ranging, were to be voluntary not compulsory and thus inevitably linked to the provision of government grants. Despite these changes, however, there was a new wave of protests from the Engineering Employers Federation, the Aims of Industry, the Institute of Directors and the CBI.[14]

When the Bill was published at the end of January 1975 it broadly followed the content of the White Paper but with one major
change. Whereas the Regeneration of British Industry had
devoted four pages to planning agreements, the bill dealt with
them in one clause which guaranteed that firms voluntarily entering such agreements would not suffer a cut in their regional development grants.[15] In addition the NEB was given a limited initial
finance of £700 million while the Secretary of State retained
powers tightly to control the Board's investment decisions.[16]
These changes had been worked out in the Cabinet's Public Enterprise Committee and were thus strongly opposed by the parties'
left-wing MPs and union leaders.[17] Wilson's main aim
throughout, however, was to preserve the confidence of the City
and industry. Indeed, when he spoke at the CBI's annual dinner
he made it clear that industrial policy would remain under his personal direction and he would be making all the appointments to
the Board of the NEB.[18] Almost as if he felt the need to reempha-
sise his position, while the Bill was in Standing Committee, Wilson
moved Benn to the Department of Energy and replaced him with
Eric Varley, a man with similar views on industrial policy to his
own. The situation took on an almost comical aspect when Eric
Heffer, who had resigned over the Common Market issue, led a
number of left-wing Labour MPs who opposed the now
emasculated Bill in Committee and on Report.[19]

There is little doubt then that the Bill was emasculated as it went
through the policy-making process, but what does this tell us about
the power of capital? Certainly we have seen that both the CBI
and the City made direct representations opposing the proposals at
all stages. Perhaps more significantly, however, the Prime
Minister and the Chancellor consistently stressed the need to retain the confidence of both industry and the City. Indeed the preservation of confidence at a time when the pound was in trouble
on the foreign exchanges was perhaps the major aim of the
government. This appears to be another example of the other
faces of power at work — the interests of capital shaped government policy not merely, or perhaps even mainly, because of the
direct representations by its agents but because their interests were
identified with the national interest. As Coates says, the industrial
policy changes were 'part of the Government's increasing concern
to reassure private industry about its commitment to a healthy
private sector, and about its willingness to sub-ordinate its social

programme to the gaining of greater industrial production'.[20]

Industrial versus banking capital

Our evidence would suggest, then, that the power of capital is rarely simply direct, but more often is a structural power which is sometimes reflected in government decisions. We have, however, avoided one major discussion in the literature, the relative power of the banking and industrial sectors. Much of the Marxist literature in particular emphasises the power of the banking sector and indeed sees the dominance of that sector in Britain as a major characteristic and cause of the British economic crisis. Longstreth, for example, points particularly to the defence of sterling by governments of both parties in the 1960s, even when this policy severely restricted the government's opportunity to promote economic growth. In Longstreth's view, 'Maintaining the exchange rate was ... the top priority in deference to the City and its international support in the IMF and the United States.[21] Jessop develops this point even more strongly. He argues that the defence of sterling was against the interests of industrial capital:

The policies intended to maintain the position of sterling discouraged and distorted industrial investment through high interest rates ..., restriction on investment outside the sterling area ... and recurrent bouts of deflation to restrain internal demand and 'free' resources for export production.[22]

The argument thus has three elements. First, the interests of the banking and industrial sectors are seen as significantly different with the banking sector, in particular, preferring high interest and exchange rates while the industrial sector favours low interest rates. Secondly, the banking sector is seen as dominating British economic policy, exercising this influence through the close links between the Bank of England and the Treasury. Consequently the state policies are seen as consistently favouring banking as against industrial capital.

This position has some force but does not appear totally convincing. As we have seen, while there is not a fusion between the two sectors, there is little doubt that their contacts and presumably therefore their interests are becoming closer. At the same time, as Moran points out, the industrial sector in general, and the CBI in particular, supported the defence of sterling in the 1960s despite the fact that in Longstreth and Jessop's terms this was against their real interest. Of course it might be argued that industrial capital was not aware of its true interests because of the dominance of what Thompson calls the 'consolidationalist ideology' of the financial sector. At present, however, we have insufficient evidence on the role of banking capital to answer this question. Certainly the financial sector's influence appears indirect rather than direct but the rapid expansion in the activities of trade associations in this area indicates both that the City is no longer confident that the Bank of England represents their interest and that they see the need for stronger *direct* representation.

In conclusion

There is no doubt that the interest groups representing both fractions of capital have grown in importance and have become more overtly political in the last decade. This has resulted largely from the increased level of government intervention first in the industrial sector and more recently in the financial sector. Despite this, however, it would appear misguided to suggest that the formal contacts between capital and government, through interest groups, provide the key to capital's influence over government. Interest groups representing both sectors of capital consistently make representations to government but the effect of these representations has less to do with strength of the arguments than with the consequences of consistently opposing capital's interest. Governments, regardless of their ideology or policy commitments, are constrained by the imperatives of the economic system. We have attempted to show in the industrial policy field how such constraints are reflected in the day-to-day decisions taken by the government, a point which appears to us to have been amply demonstrated in Coates's excellent study of the 1974-9 Labour government.

None of this should be taken to mean that capital has simple, consistent and coherent interests which are always inevitably and directly reflected in the decisions taken by government. It is clear, as we can see elsewhere in this book, that other interest groups can exercise important constraints on government. Nevertheless our review suggests that Lindblom's analysis has a great deal of force. Capital is different from other interests because it exercises power or influence in two ways — directly through interest groups and structurally because of the crucial role boards and managers exercise over the production, investment and employment decisions which shape the economic and political environment within which government makes policy. Capital is not the first among equals: its power is qualitatively as well as quantitatively different.

Notes

1   W. Grant and D. Marsh, *The CBI* (London: Hodder and Stoughton, 1977) p. 214.
2   D. Coates, *Labour in Power* (London: Longman, 1980), pp. 86-146.
3   J. Sargent, 'The effect of legislation and pressure group development: a case study of the British Bankers' Association' (mimeo, London School of Economics, 1980).
4   *The Times*, 8 February 1978.
5   For Wilson's full views see *The Labour Party Annual Conference Report* (1973), pp. 160-70.
6   *Let's Work Together: Labour's Way Out of the Crisis* (London: The Labour Party, 1973), p. 6.
7   Details of the 'Treasury Minute', in *The Times,* 17 June 1974.
8   Healey speech reported in *The Times,* 15 May 1974.
9   Wilson speech reported in *The Times,* 1 July 1974.
10 *The Times,* 5 August 1974.
11 'The Regeneration of British Industry', Cmnd. 5710 (London: HMSO, 1974).
12 *The Economist,* 17 August 1974, p. 73.
13 'The Regeneration of British Industry', paras. 8 and 23.
14 *The Times,* 29 August 1974, 6 and 20 September 1974.
15 Industry Bill, 1975 (London: HMSO, January 1975), para. 21.
16 *Ibid.,* paras. 8 and 10.
17 *The Times,* 8 March 1975.
18 *The Times,* 21 May 1975.
19 See D. Liston, 'The Industry Act (1975) — a personal critique', *Poly Law Review* (1976), pp. 42-8.
20 D. Coates, *Labour in Power,* p. 34.
21 F. Longstreth, 'The city, industry and the state', in C. Crouch (ed.), *State and Economy in Contemporary Capitalism* (London. Croom Helm, 1979), pp. 157-90, (quotation p. 183).
22 R. Jessop, 'The transformation of the state in postwar Britain', in R. Scase (ed.), *The State in Western Europe* (London: Croom Helm, 1980 (quotation p. 32).

3.9 *Ross Martin*

A pluralist critique of corporatism

From *'Pluralism and the new corporatism'*, *Political Studies,* Vol. XXXI, No.1, 1983, pp.86 – 101.

The term 'corporatism' has long enjoyed a certain popularity. The literature in which it figures ranges in bias across the political spectrum.[1] Although employed mostly with either a prescriptive or a pejorative intent, there is a corner of the literature in which the term has purportedly been used for more strictly analytical purposes. It has been taken narrowly by some writers, mainly American, to mean the political influence of business corporations.[2] Others have applied it more broadly with reference to organised interest groups in general and their formalized involvement in government decision – making processes. This is the way 'corporatism' has been used by such writers on British politics as Andrew Shonfield, Harry Eckstein and Samuel Beer[3] —loosely, without troubling to define it closely, and without making any large claims for its heuristic capacity.

Since the early 1970s, however, the term has been credited with great analytic power in a growing body of writing. There appear to have been two main inspirations of this line of thought, at least in the English – speaking world: a brief article by R. E. Pahl and J. T. Winkler, first published in 1974 in England; and a longer, more scholarly study by Philippe Schmitter, which appeared the same year in an American journal.[4] Schmitter's study has had the greater influence among those who seem to think of themselves as new corporatists.[5]

Like their predecessors in the analytic tradition, the new corporatists are primarily concerned with the relations between government and organized groups. But, unlike their predecessors, they are obsessed with terminology and tend to adopt a somewhat proprietorial attitude towards 'corporatism' itself.

Schmitter set the tone in his seminal article. He confesses that he once 'tended to define corporatism exclusively in relation to authoritarian rule'. but now wants to 'rescue the concept ... from various usages of it which have crept into the literature and which seem ... to do more to dissipate or to disguise than to enhance its utility',[6] This heavily Platonist conception of a pure idea of 'corporatism', the true nature of which has been disfigured by misuse, pervades the new corporatist writings. Thus Cawson, too, is intent on 'rescue'; while Panitch refers to the 'essence' of the 'corporatist paradigm' and scolds those writers (both those he cites as examples being pre – Schmitter) who have 'carelessly characterized virtually any and all intimate interest group – state relations which have become accepted as legitimate in the political culture as corporatist'.[7]

The principal task the new corporatists set themselves, as a result, is to delineate the boundaries of corporatism. The general sense of the term has given them no great trouble. But problems have arisen from their need to distinguish two sub – types, one associated with liberal democratic regimes and one with other regimes. Schmitter entitled these 'societal corporatism' and 'state corporatism', respectively, but Lehmbruch's 'liberal corporatism' and 'authoritarian corporatism' fasten more plainly on the point of the distinction drawn by Schmitter and others.[8]

Liberal corporatism is the focus for the new corporatists. It is, as Lehmbruch puts it,[9] that form of corporatism which remains 'embedded in a system of liberal constitutional democracy, comprising institutional rules such as freedom of association'; and in which interest groups both 'enter voluntarily' into appropriate relationships with government and, in principle, are 'free to terminate' such involvement. The new corporatists are generally agreed, also, that the kind of group – government relations which liberal corporatism entails are radically different from those characteristic of 'pluralism'. Schmitter accordingly depicts liberal corporatism as

an attractive alternative to the pluralist model, suggesting not only a different institutional configuration in the relation between specialised interest associations and the political process, but also a different way of conceptualizing the role and importance of the state.[10]

Schmitter also forsees 'the decay of pluralism and its gradual displacement by societal [liberal] corporation'.[11] Otherwise, liberal corporatism is seen as co – existing with pluralism in the same political system. Thus Lehmbruch writes of the 'corporatist subsystem', enclosing interest groups 'included in the corporatist pattern', while other groups remain 'largely confined to the classical pluralist "pressure politics" '.[12] Cawson similarly distinguishes a ' "corporatist sector" of the political system from a ' "pluralist sector" ', and others follow suit.[13] In addition, as Panitch emphasizes, the relationships characterizing the corporatist sector typically exhibit a 'high degree of instability'; and when they break down, as they are liable to, a reversion to pluralist relationship is the outcome.[14]

The new corporatists' conception of liberal corporatism is substantially uniform so long as its definition is limited to context (constitutional form of the political system), obligation (voluntary group involvement with government)[15] and the distinction from pluralism. However, the divergencies emerge as soon as one casts around for the further defining elements that are required if the conception is to fulfil the new corporatists' ambitions.[16] These additional defining elements comprise the topic of the first section of this paper...[17]

1. The new corporatists' conception of liberal corporatism

A reading of the new corporatists' published writings suggests two things about their conception of liberal corporatism. The first is that in addition to the factors of context, obligation, and dissimilarity from pluralism, there are four defining elements which emerge fairly clearly from the literature. The second is that there is a further defining element which *ought* to emerge from the literature, but does not do so.

Defining elements
1. *Inter – group co – operation*. Lehmbruch may not have been the first to make the point explicitly, but he makes it most sharply. 'The distinguishing trait of liberal corporatism is a high degree of collaboration among ... groups'.[18] By collaboration he means, at one level, the existence of bargaining relationships between major interest groups; and, at another level, 'bargaining between government and the 'cartel' of organized groups'.[19]
    2. *Economic policy*. Corporatist inter – group collaboration is 'most conspicuous in economic policy – formation' and, above all,

in incomes policy which constitutes ' a core domain of liberal corporatism'.[20] Liberal corporatism, as Panitch depicts it, thus centres on 'national economic planning and incomes policy
programmes', the latter comprising 'the frontispiece of corporatist
development'; while 'corporatist structures' typically take the
form of 'economic planning and incomes policy bodies'.[21]

3. *Capital and labour.* It is 'the collaboration of 'capital' and
'labour' in a corporatist scheme' which consitutes the 'central
feature' of liberal corporatism.[22] In other words, trade unions and
employers' organization are 'the core constituent elements, alongside the state, of corporatist political structure', and bargain about
economics issues, both among themselves and with government.[23]

4. *Administration.* Inter – group collaboration and
group – government collaboration are concerned not only with the
formulation of policy but also with its administration. Liberal corporatism, following Cawson, is thus a 'method... of economic administration', entailing group assumption of 'responsibility for
delegated. enforcement of government policy'.[24] It is, moreover,
an organised group's enforcement of government policy in relation to its own members which the new corporatists have particularly in mind; and it is to this that their rather cumberstone term
'intermediation' primarily refers.

The missing element
A working definition of liberal corporatism obviously requires at
least one element in addition to the four specified above—and that
is a conception of the state's role. One of the virtues of 'corporatism', Schmitter claims, is that it provides 'a different way of
conceptualizing the role...of the state'.[25] Yet the views of the new
corporatists on this point run the gamut.

At one extreme, there is Pahl and Winkler's depiction of the
state as controller. 'The essence of corporatism...is *private* ownership and *state control*...over all the major aspects of business decision making', with the consequence that (to use their somewhat
flashy phrase) liberal corporatism is merely 'fascism with a human
face'.[26] At the other extreme, there is Nedelman and Meier's
perception of a weak, manipulated state that 'would only play the
role of an executor of the solutions made by the associational organizations', the latter thus being 'expected to dominate state policies'.[27]

Between the extremes, Schmitter leans towards Pahl and

Winkler. He neglects to deal directly with the point, but the defini-
tional distinction he draws between 'societal' (liberal) and 'state'
authoritarian) corporatism entails, it seems, only a marginally
qualified version of the state control postulated in his general
definition of corporatism,[28] although the nature and extent of the
qualifications are admittedly obscure. What is not at all obscure is
the fact that control, as an attribute of the liberal corporate state,
is emphasized by Schmitter in a way that it is not by Lehmbruch.

For Lehmbruch, the state's role is not that of a controller, but of
a bargainer.[29] Cawson appears to hover between Schmitter and
Lehmbruch: the liberal corporatist state is controller in that it
'directs the activities of predominantly privately – owned industry', but it does so 'in partnership' with major interest
groups—which implies Lehmbruch's bargaining role.[30] Crouch's
position seems much the same. There is the implication of a fluid
situation falling between 'full corporatism' (in which union
'priorities [are] determined by government and employers', and
the unions themselves are 'controlled from above and outside')
and 'bargained corporatism' in which the state participates as a
'bargaining partner',[31]

Panitch, for his part, does not deal directly with the issue in an
early paper, and apparently perceives no difference between
Schmitter and Lehmbruch in this respect—with the implied result
that he accepts both versions.[32] In a later paper, however, he
clearly moves towards Schmitter's position when he postulates 'an
element of state control over the groups whereby their autonomy
is limited'.[33] Panitch's falterings are symptomatic of the new corporatists' uncertainly, as a group, about the state's role under
liberal corporatism. Indeed, given the obvious importance of the
question, it is astonishing how often it is either ignored or given
only passing attention in their writings.

II. The new corporatists' conception of pluralism

The new corporatists are not well disposed towards pluralism.
They spill a good deal of ink decrying it, in one way or another,
but very little explaining what they take the term to mean. They
do, however, devote much more attention to the definition of
liberal corporatism, which obviously shares with pluralism at least
the factors of context (a liberal democratic political system) and of
obligation (the basically voluntary nature of group – government

relationships). Where the two are seen, or appear to be seen, as differing is in relation to the other four defining elements specified above as emerging from the new corporatist literature. These defining elements thus implicitly contribute—if initially in negative terms—to an approximate definition of pluralism as well.

The implication is clear enough in the case of 'economic policy'. although not specifically touched on by the new corporatists themselves. It is that pluralist relationships are concerned with issues extending beyond economic matters: in other words, an unlimited policy range.

In the case of 'administration', the implication is that under pluralism interest groups are confined to a purely advisory role in relation to the administration of policy. Cawson hints a confirmation of this interpretation when he remarks that the corporatist state – group relationship involves 'both interest articulation (the classic pressure group role) and the responsibility for delegated enforcement of government policy'.[34]

In the case of 'inter – group co – operation', the implication for the pluralist model is at least an absence both of inter – group collaboration and of formal tripartite negotiations. Cawson, however, takes the point further when he writes of 'the *competitive* role of interest groups' under pluralism.[35]

Finally, there is 'capital and labour' as a defining element of liberal corporatism. This implies a pluralist model in which government deals with organized groups other than trade unions and employers' associations: that is to say, an unlimited range of politically involved groups. Schmitter seems to deny this implication when he comments that 'pluralist labels' are attached to some political systems 'for no better reason than the mere existence of a multitude of organized interests.[36] Nevertheless, in the same article, the numerical factor is the first criterion specified in ideal – type definitions of corporatism and pluralism—'a limited number' of groups in the former case and 'an unspecified number' in the latter.[37] The point is confirmed by Ralph Miliband (who, though no new corporatist, has evidently influenced their notion of pluralism) when he defines pluralist political systems precisely in terms of the fact that 'they permit and even encourage a multitude of groups.. to organize openly and freely'.[38]

There is, of course, one major aspect of pluralism that cannot be discovered by this method of negative definition. The role of the pluralist state is unascertainable in this way because the new corporatists lack a common view of the state's role under liberal corporatism. Yet, paradoxically, the role of the state is the one characteristic of pluralism about which the new corporatists are both reasonably explicit and, apparently, in substantial agreement. They assume, to put it shortly, a state that is 'the passive recipient of group pressures'.[39] The trouble is that this amounts to a caricature of mainstream contemporary pluralist thought.

The 'concept of pluralism', Bernard Crick once remarked, 'is ambiguous and contentious'.[40] All the more so because for many years there has been no school of self – professed 'pluralists' expressly committed to staking out pluralism's claim as a theory of politics.[41] The concept has thus been the subject of a variety of intepretations.[42] The new corporatists, however, seem oblivious of this. Their vision is effectively confined to one version of pluralism known otherwise as 'group theory' and indentified with Arthur Bentley, David Truman and Earl Latham.[43] Cawson cites these three as the leading exponents of the 'doctrine of pluralist democracy'; and elsewhere 'the Bentley – Truman approach' is described as having 'defined the dominant [pluralist] orthodoxy since the 1950s'.[44]

Indentifying group theory as coterminous with analytical pluralism is not uncommon among anti – pluralists.[45] For the new corporatists, such an identification has one supreme advantage. Group theory, especially as expounded by Latham, does in fact depict the state as playing a passive role.

The legislature referees the group struggle, ratifies the victories of successful coalitions and records the terms of surrenders, compromises and conquests in the form of statutes.[46]

That sentence was first published in 1952. It has been claimed to typify the pluralist position of the later 1970s: 'There are many conventional statements of the group pluralist conception of the political process, but Latham's ... is probably as......representative as any'.[47] That claim, at best, is mistaken; at worst, it is a gambit in the oldest of all academic games (Plato was a pastmaster)—creating a straw man.

Group theory enjoyed a brief vogue among political scientists, mainly American, in the 1950s and early 1960s,[48] During this time it was the subject of a spirited literary controversy in which many of its critics were quite evidently not at all unsympathetic to other versions of the pluralist persuasion.[49] The bibliographies of the new corporatists acknowledge the work of the major group theorists and their anti – pluralist critics, but totally neglect the writings of their pluralist critics.

Group theory is commonly misinterpreted as a theory about political pressure groups in liberal democracies. It was much more than that. It had pretensions to being a truly general theory of politics.[50] and thus applicable to all and any political systems—unlike the 'pluralism' which the new corporatists have in mind. On the other hand, so far as group theory can be said to have had any issue, that, it is true, takes the form of pressure group studies which are probably the core of analytical pluralism both before and since group theory's brief heyday. But these studies, heavily empirical as they are for most part, are a far cry from the grandeur of group theory. Their authors have effectively shared the basis of a common theoretical position in so far as their analytical concerns imply an assumption that the interplay of organized groups and government is a critical element in the politics of liberal democratic regimes.[51] But their explicit theoretical concerns have usually extended no further than conceptual problems of quite immediate empirical relevance. Nevertheless, it is clear enough from their work that few, if any, could accept the version of pluralism expounded by anti – pluralists (including the new corporatists) in terms of group theory. In particular, they display little or no sympathy for the notion of a passive or neutral state that merely registers group pressures. Mostly, this conclusion has to be drawn as a matter of implication (such as an unstated assumption reflected in the approach to case – study, or an obvious inference to be drawn from an empirical account had the appropriate question been thought worth asking). But some pluralist writers have been explicit on the point.

For example, as early as the mid – fifties when the group theory comet was at its zenith, Samuel Beer, in an influential account of British pressure groups, bluntly rejected the idea of 'an inert government'.[52] In 1963, when the comet was all but spent, the authors of another particularly influential study made the same point in a different way, with reference to the United States: 'The people supposed to make decisions, officeholders, often really do make decisions'.[53] A general survey of American pressure groups, published a year later, was purportedly 'guided by what is generally referred to as group theory', but nevertheless disavowed 'the false realism which describes governmental decision makers as passive pawns being pushed and shoved about according to the whims and fancies of 'powerful pressure groups'.[54] A similar British survey noted in 1968 that 'there is little evidence to suggest...that the function of government is merely to 'register' decisions which are made by pressure groups'.[55] Writing in the following year, the authors of one study were clear that, 'in its relations with pressure groups...government is not condemned to a purely passive role';[56] and the author of another advanced the same proposition in a more elaborate form.[57] Moreover, even before the first of the new corporatists took up the mantle in 1974, there were pluralists who considered that group theory in general was more of an historical curiosity than anything else. Some thought it was dying, in that

the group – focused conception of pressure politics has lost something of the éclat it enjoyed when sketched in simplistic terms of unilateral, group – to – legislator orientation ... 'the Senator is far from a passive puppet manipulated from afar.' Lobbying now emerges as a matter of bargaining, a two – way flow of influence.[58]

Others thought it was long dead:

It has been the misfortune of 'group theory' ... to have been out of fashion with most political scientists for a considerable period. Various attempts to revive it have found little support [59]

And later still, when the new corporatists were in full cry, another writer criticized the 'conventional wisdom' among pluralists because, he claimed, it under – played ('minimizes') the influence of pressure groups[60]—a point predicating a conception of the state's role that was virtually the opposite of the 'passive state' which the new corporatists were then depicting, and have continued to depict,[61] as characteristic of mainstream pluralism.

It is not part of the present argument that pluralists nowadays all hold to a single, clearcut version of the state's role under pluralism which is diametrically opposed to that of the group theorists. My argument is simply that the new corporatists grossly distort matters when they presume to identify contemporary pluralist thought exclusively—or even predominantly—with the notion of a passive state..

Notes

1 See N. Harris, *Competition and the Corporate Society* (London, Methuen, 1972), pp. 65—9.
2 See R. Marris, 'Is the Corporate Economy a Corporate State?', *American Economic Review,* 62 (1972), 103—15; A. S. Miller, 'Legal Foundations of the Corporate State,' *Journal of Economic Issues,* 6 (1972), 59—79.
3 A. Shonfield, *Modern Capitalism* (London, Oxford University Press, 1965), pp. 161 – 3; H. Eckstein, *Pressure Group Politics* (London, Allen & Unwin, 1960), 24; S. Beer, *Modern British Politics* (2nd edn), (London, Faber, 1969), pp. 427 – 8.
4 R. E. Pahl and J. T. Winkler, 'The Coming Corporatism,' *Challenge,* March – April 1975: reprinted from *New Society,* 10 October 1974; P. Schmitter, 'Still the Century of Corporatism?', *Review of Politics,* 36 (1974), 85 – 131.
5 Foremost among these for the purposes of the present article, in ad – dition to Schmitter and Pahl and Winkler, are Alan Cawson, Colin Crouch, Gerhard Lehmbruch and Leo Panitch.
6 Schmitter, 'Still the Century of Corporatism?'. pp. 86, 92n.
7 A. Cawson, 'Pluralism, Corporatism and the Role of the State', *Government and Opposition,* 13 (1978). p. 178; L. Panitch. 'The Development of Corporatism in Liberal Democracies', *Comparative Political Studies,* 10 (1977), p. 65.
8 Schmitter, 'Still the Century of Corporatism?', p. 103; G. Lehmbruch, 'Liberal Corporatism and Party Government', *Comparative Political Studies,* 10 (1977), p. 92.
9 Lehmbruch, 'Liberal Corporatism and Party Government', p. 92. The literature is rich in contrived synonyms including 'pluralist corporatism' (Harris, *Competition and the Corporate Society* p. 18), 'corporate pluralism' (S, Rokkan in R. A. Dahl (ed.), *Political Oppositions in Western Democracies* (New Haven, Yale University Press, 1966), p. 70), 'democratic corporatism' (H. L. Wilensky, *The 'New Corporatism', Centralization and the Welfare State (London, Sage 1976), pp. 23, 45), 'privatist corporatism'* (G. O'Donnell in J. M. Malloy (ed.), *Authoritarianism and Corporatism in Latin America* (Pittsburgh, University of Pittsburgh Press, 1977), p. 48), 'free corporatism' (G. Heckscher, quoted in N. Elvander, 'Interest Groups in Sweden'. *Annals of the American Academy of Political Science,* 413 (1974), p. 43), 'voluntarist corporatism' and 'bargained cor – poratism' (C. Crouch, *Class Conflict and the Industrial Relations Crisis* (London, Heinemann, 1977), pp. 35, 262; and his *The Politics of Industrial Relations* (Manchester, Manchester University Press, 1979), pp. 179, 193), and 'corporate bias' (K. Middlemas, *Politics in Industrial Society* (London, Deutsch, 1979), pp. 20, 374ff.). Similarly, the term 'trapartism', although initially defined by David Marsh and Wyn Grant as designating 'a sub – type of "liberal corporatism" ', is later in the same article used virtually interchangeably with 'liberal corporatism' ('Tripartism:

Reality or Myth?', *Government and Opposition,* 12 (1977), pp. 197, 211), a common enough practice.

10 Schmitter, 'Introduction'. *Comparative Political Studies,* 10 (1977), p. 4.

11 Schmitter, 'Still the Century of Corporatism?'p. 107.

12 Lehmbruch, 'Liberal Corporatism', pp. 96, 122.

13 Cawson, 'Pluralism, Corporatism', p. 196; and pp. 181, 185, 194. See also Panitch, 'Recent Theorizations of Corporatism: Reflections on a Growth Industry'. *British Journal of Sociology,* 31 (1980), p. 173; C. Crouch (ed), *State and Economy in Contem — porary Capitalism* (London, Croom Helm, 1979), pp. 22 – 3; Nedel — man and Meier, 'Theories of Contemporary Corporatism: Static or Dynamic?', *Comparative Political Studies,* 10 (1977), p. 49; C. W. Anderson, 'Political Design and the Representation of Interests', *Comparative Political Studies,* 10 (1977), pp. 129, 136. Schmitter makes much the same point in a footnote: 'Still the Century of Corporatism?', p. 100n.

14 Panitch, 'Development of Corporatism', p. 68. See also Lehmbruch in G. Lehmbruch and P. Schmitter (eds), *Trends Toward Corporatist Intermediation* (London, Sage, 1979), p. 303; Crouch, *Politics of Industrial Relations*, p. 189.

15 Although Schmitter is somewhat ambiguous on the issue of obligation: see 'Still the Century of Corporatism?', pp. 103 – 5.

16 Panitch, for one, is in no doubt about these divergencies: see his 'Recent Theorizations of Corporatism: Reflections on a Growth Industry', pp. 159 – 60, 181 – 2.

17 What is involved, in the upshot, is a quest for something like a composite account of liberal corporatism. Sometimes this means rely ing on majority opinion; and sometimes silence has been taken as consent.

18 Lehmbruch, 'Liberal Corporatism', p. 94; and see his 'Consocia — tional Democracy, Class Conflict and the New Corporatism', in Schmitter and Lehmbruch (eds), *Trends Toward Corporatist In — termediation,* pp. 53 – 4. See also Cawson, 'Pluralism, Corporatism', p. 184; and Panitch. 'Development of Corporatism', pp. 64, 78 and 'Recent Theorizations', pp. 173, 176.

19 Lehmbruch 'Liberal Corporatism', p. 94.

20 Lehmbruch, 'Liberal Corporatism', p.96

21 Panitch, 'Development of Corporatism', pp. 63, 74, and 'Recent Theorizations', p. 174. See also Lehmbruch, 'Liberal Corporatism', pp. 94, 96; and Cawson, 'Pluralism, Corporatism', p. 185.

22 Lehmbruch, 'Liberal Corporatism', p. 96.

23 Panitch, 'Recent Theorizations'. pp. 173 – 4.

24 Cawson, 'Pluralism, Corporatism', pp. 184 – 5.

25 Schmitter, 'Introduction', p. 4. On the other hand, a sym — pathetic outsider has suggested that the role of the liberal cor — poratist state is peculiarly difficult to identify: R. J. Harrison, *Pluralism and Corporatism* (London, Allen & Unwin, 1980), p. 188.

26   Pahl and Winkler, 'The Coming Corporatism', p. 31. See also Winkler, 'Corporatism', *Archives Europeenes de Sociologie*, 17 (1976), pp. 103, 105, 109; and Winkler in R. Skidelsky (ed.), *The End of the Keynesian Era* (London, Macmillan, 1977), pp. 86 – 7.

27   Nedelman and Meier, 'Theories of Contemporary Corporatism: Static or Dynamic?', pp. 48, 57.

28   Schmitter, 'Still the Century of Corporatism?', pp. 93 – 4, 102 – 3; and see also pp. 104 – 5. The point is implied also in terms of his distinction between corporatism and pluralism: see pp. 93 – 4, 96, 127.

29   Lehmbruch, 'Liberal Corporatism', p. 94. Winkler refers to a 'bargaining' phase, but this is preliminary to the expansion of the state's controlling role: see Winkler in R. Scase (ed), *Industrial Society: Class, Clearage and Control* (London, Allen & Unwin, 1977), p. 56.

30   Cawson, 'Pluralism, Corporatism', p. 186 and note.

31   Crouch, *Politics of Industrial Relations,* pp. 131, 179, 189 – 90, 195.

32   Panitch, 'Development of Corporatism', pp. 64 – 5. Although his subsequent reference (p. 67), to the large, important, even deter – mining role that is assigned to the state in the [liberal] corporatist framework', suggests at least an inclination towards Schmitter's view.

33   Panitch, 'Recent Theorizations', p. 173.

34   Cawson, 'Pluralism, Corporatism', p. 184.

35   Cawson, 'Pluralism, Corporatism', p. 184. (Emphasis added). See also Crouch. *State and Economy in Contemporary Capitalism* (London, Croom Helm, 1979), p. 24 and Schmitter, 'Still the Century of Corporatism?' p. 96. The new corporatists, along with other anti – pluralists, seem to overlook the fact that the existence of inter – group competition in some areas does not exclude co – operation between the same groups, in others: see, e.g., R. M. Martin, *TUC: The Growth of a Pressure Group 1868 – 1976* (Oxford University Press, 1980), pp. 349 – 50.

36   Schmitter, 'Still the Century of Corporatism?' p. 100.

37   Schmitter, 'Still the Century of Corporatism?' pp. 93, 96.

38   R. Miliband, *The State in Capitalist Society* (London, Weidenfeld and Nicolson, 1969), p. 146.

39   Anderson, 'Political Design and the Representation of Interests', p. 129. See also Panitch, 'Development of Corporatism', p. 66; Nedelman and Meier, 'Theories of Contemporary Corporatism', p. 40.

40   B. Crick, 'The Strange Death of the American Theory of Consensus', *Political Quarterly,* 43 (1972), p. 57. But for a concise and particularly clear – headed version of contemporary pluralism, both as descrip tion and as ideology, see H. A. Clegg, 'Pluralism in Industrial Rela – tions', *British Journal of Industrial Relations,* 13 (1975), pp. 309 – 16.

41   Instead, the term became 'almost exclusively the property of scholars who employ it as a weapon of attack': R. E. Wolfinger, *The Politics of Progress* (Englewood Cliffs, New Jersey, Prentice – Hall,

1974), p. 10.

42 For some idea of the range, see D. Nicholls, *Three Varieties of Pluralism* (London, Macmillan, 1974), espec. pp. 1 – 4.

43 A. Bentley, *The Process of Government* (Cambridge, Mass., Har – vard University Press, 1967), originally published in 1908; D. Tru – man, *The Governmental Process* (New York, Knopf, 1951); E. Latham, 'The Group Basis of Politics: Notes for a Theory', *American Political Science Review,* 46 (1952).

44 Cawson, 'Pluralism, Corporatism', pp. 182 – 3, Anderson, 'Political Design', p. 128. See also Panitch, 'Recent Theorizations', p. 179.

45 See. e.g., H. S. Kariel. *The Decline of American Pluralism* (Stan – ford, Stanford University Press, 1961), pp. 130 – 2; and Miliband. *The State in Capitalist Society*, p. 147. Even Mancur Olson, a cooler critic, falls in with this (in both editions—1965 and 1971—of his book) despite a hint on p. 118 that the category of 'analytical pluralists' is rather wider in scope: *The Logic of Collective Action* (cambridge, Mass., Harvard University Press, 1971), pp. 125 – 31.

46 Latham, 'Group Basis of Politics', p. 390.

47 Anderson. 'Political Design', p. 138.

48 It 'lost its credability soon after it was hailed as the long awaited general theory of politics': Harmon Ziegler in R. Scott (ed), *Interest Groups and Public Policy* (Melbourne, Macmillan 1980).

49 They included, among others: B Crick, *The American Science of Politics* (London, Routledge, 1958), Ch. 7; P. H. Odegard. 'A Group Basis of Politics: A New Name for an Old Myth'. *Western Political Quarterly,* 11 (1958): S Rothman, 'Systematic Political Theory: Observations on the Group Approach', *American Political Science Review,* 54 (1960): J. LaPalombara, 'The Utility and Limitations of Interest Group Theory in Non – American Field Situations', *Journal of Politics,* 22 (1960); three articles by R. E. Dowling M. Q. Hale and R. T Golembiewski under the general title of 'Bentley Revisited', *American Political Science Review* 54 (1960); R. C. Macridis, 'Interest Groups in Comparative Analysis, *Journal of Politics,* 23 (1961); R. S. Parker, "Group Analysis" and Scientism in Political Studies', *Political Studies,* 9 (1961); H Eckstein, 'Group Theory and the Comparative Study of Pressure Groups' in Eckstein and Apter (eds), *Comparative Politics: A Reader* (New York, Free Press, 1963), pp. 389 – 97.

50 See Eckstein, *Comparative Politics: A Reader,* pp. 391 – 2 for an in – cisive elaboration of this point, which David Truman himself subse – quently affirmed in his 'Political Group Analysis'. *International Encyclopaedia of the Social Sciences* 12 (1968), 241 – 5.

51 This is a long way from grand theory, to be sure. But I suggest that it is enough to blunt, perhaps even to rebut, Richard Hyman's charge that pluralism has no 'clearly identifiable core of belief, theory or principle': 'Pluralism, Procedural Consensus and Collective Bar – gaining', *British Journal of Industrial Relations,* 16 (1978), p. 28.

52 S. Beer, 'Pressure Groups and Parties in Britain', *American Political Science Review,* 50 (1956), p. 23.

53 R. A. Bauer, I. de Sola Pool and L. A. Dexter, *American Business and Public Policy* (Chicago, Aldine – Atherton, 1963), p. 487; see also 2nd edn (1972), p. 487. The 'passive state' thesis, it should be noted, was distinctly more plausible in relation to a political system like the American which, in contrast to the British, involved a federal – cum – presidential system of government, a bureaucracy more susceptible to spoils – of – office appointments and, in parti – cular, a legislature lacking strong party disicipline.

54 Harmon Ziegler, *Interest Groups in American Society* (Englewood Cliffs, New Jersey, Prentice Hall, 1964), pp. iii – iz.

55 S. A. Walkland, *The Legislative Process in Great Britain* (London, Allen & Unwin, 1968), p. 36.

56 G. C. Moodie and G. Studdert – Kennedy, *Opinions, Publics and Pressure Groups* (London, Allen & Unwin, 1970), p. 73.

57 See Graham Wootton, *Interest Groups* (Englewood Cliffs, New Jersey, Prentice – Hall, 1970), pp. 96 – 102.

58 N. Meller in M. Haas and H. S. Kariel (eds), *Approaches to the Study of Political Science* (Scranton, Penn., Chandler, 1970), p. 248. Thus Kariel and Miliband were arguably kicking an already very dead horse when they levelled the 'passive state' charge against the pluralist mainstream at the end of the 1960s: see H. S. Kariel. 'Pluralism', *International Encyclopaedia of the Social Sciences* 12 (1968), p. 168; and Miliband, *The State in Capitalist Society*, p. 82.

59 R. Kimber and J. J. Richardson (eds), *Pressure Groups in Britain* (London, Dent, 1974), p. 3.

60 M. T Hayes. 'The Semi – Sovereign Pressure Groups: A Critique of Current Theory and an Alternative Theory', *Journal of Politics*, 40 (1978), p. 134.

61 Thus: 'The pluralist tradition has, by – and – large, remained true to its historical... passive conception of the state.' P. C. Schmitter and W. Streeck, *The Organization of Business Interests: A Research Design to Study the Associative Action of Business in the Advanced Industrial Societies of Western Europe* (Berlin, International Institute of Management, 1981), p. 83.

Part Four

Central political organisations

Introduction

Until comparatively recently the study of the institutions of government in the UK pictured the system as stable, powerful and efficient. Parliament, it was believed, was tightly controlled by the Executive: and the Executive in turn, centred on the Cabinet, was cohesive and decisive. The UK was widely viewed as a model of effective government. Like so much else in the study of British politics, this picture has been changed in recent years. One of the most dramatic alterations has concerned the behaviour of MPs. Once a by-word for discipline and obedience, they have, since the early 1970s, shown a preference for more open dissent. The most influential chronicler of this change has been Philip Norton. In Reading 4.1 he continues his work, tracing patterns of dissent into the 1980s, and identifying the evolution of those patterns in an era of large Parliamentary majorities.

Disenchantment with the quality of UK government has grown because, with greater scrutiny of its operations, more has become known about the working atmosphere of Whitehall. Clive Ponting was a senior Civil Servant in the Ministry of Defence who was unsuccessfully prosecuted for 'leaking' to a back-bench MP official documents concerning the sinking of the cruiser *Belgrano* in the Falklands War. Following his acquittal, he resigned and produced a book highly critical of the workings of central government. Reading 4.2 is from this work. Ponting's book repeated many familiar criticisms of the supposed shortcomings of Whitehall — its secrecy, amateurism and elitism. But perhaps its most valuable feature is the picture it conveys, from someone recently inside the machine, of the everyday experience of work in government: the fierce pressure of time on ministers, the range of jobs performed by Civil Servants at different parts of the career ladder, and the way they ascend that ladder. Our extract concentrates on these areas.

One of the most important debates among both practitioners and academics interested in central government has concerned the survival capacity of the Cabinet. After the publication of Walter Bagehot's classic, *The English Constitution* in 1867, the Cabinet became acknowledged as the most important institution in the machine — so important, indeed, that 'Cabinet Government' was a common characterisation of the UK system of government. But Bagehot's account referred to a period when government had a minimal role, when parties were comparatively unimportant, when the franchise was restricted and when the Cabinet itself worked in an informal way. Modern debate has centred on how far the Cabinet has been able to maintain influence and effectiveness in a world of big government, mass democratic politics, a powerful Civil Service and an extensive system of Cabinet Committees. Peter Hennessy's paper (4.3) is a valuable contribution to this debate because it compares the experience of Cabinet Government at two critical periods, the late 1940s and the early 1980s, under two great reforming administrations, those of Attlee and of Thatcher.

The Thatcher Administration came to power in 1979 dedicated to cutting the size of the Civil Service and to increasing the efficiency of what remained. Its degree of success in these two aims has been the subject of much argument, but of the Thatcher Government's substantial impact on the Service there can be no doubt. During the 1980s a wide series of issues previously considered routine and administrative — issues concerning pay, staffing levels and organisation — have become fiercely political. Reading 4.4 by Fry examines the process by which this has happened.

One of the most remarkable features of British Government in recent years has been the transformation of law enforcement into a major political issue. The law was once thought of as something above and beyond politics. Judges were assumed to be the neutral interpreters of the law, and the police were pictured as the servants of detailed statutes which allowed little discretion. But in areas of social life ranging from the workplace to the street corner this view has now been widely challenged. The content of law, and the way it is applied, are now widely seen as political acts — and as political acts serving some interests at the expense of others. In debates among academics and practitioners this change of view was deeply influenced by Griffiths *The Politics of the Judiciary,* which argued that the views and judgements offered from the bench were systematically influenced by the social experience of the elite of the legal profession. Reading 4.5 is drawn from the edition of Griffiths' work which brings his argument up to date to the 1980s.

John Alderson (4.6) had a long career as a policeman, culminating in a spell as a Chief Constable. He is therefore ideally placed to give a sketch of the changing organisation of policing, and of the factors causing that change. Both he and Griffith suggest that in the field of-law and order, as is the case with other central institutions, the established ways of understanding and perceiving activity are rapidly altering.

4.1   *Philip Norton*

The pattern of backbench dissent

From 'Behavioural changes: backbench independence in the 1980s' in P. Norton (ed.), *Parliament in the 1980s,* Basil Blackwell, Oxford 1985, pp. 22-47.

Prior to 1970, various generalizations could be made about backbench behaviour in the House of Commons. The two most significant and observable concerning voting behaviour were: (a) MPs rarely if ever voted against their own side, and (b) on those rare occasions when government backbenchers did vote against their own side, they never did so in numbers sufficient to deny the government a majority. Cohesion was a much commented upon feature of parliamentary life. In his seminal work *Modern British Politics,* Samuel Beer referred to the 'Prussian discipline' of MPs. Day after day, he declared, MPs 'trooped into the division lobbies at the signals of their Whips and in the service of the authoritative decisions of their parlimentary parties.'[1] Party cohesion had increased 'until in recent decades it was so close to 100 per cent that there was no longer any point in measuring it'.[2] Such assertions were easily borne out by the empirical data. Indeed, so great was party cohesion on the Conservative side of the House that there were actually two sessions in the 1950s when not one Conservative MP cast a dissenting vote against the advice of the party whips. On those occasions in other sessions when some cross-voting did take place, it had no appreciable impact upon government. Not once between 1945 and 1970 was a government defeated because of its own supporters voting in the Opposition lobby. Throughout the post-war period up to 1970, Government appeared to have little to worry about in terms of dissent by its own backbenchers in the Commons' division lobbies. It could take its majority for granted.

So much for the period from 1945 to 1970. After 1970, backbench behaviour in the Commons' division lobbies changed dramatically. The generalizations descriptive of pre-1970 behaviour ceased to be applicable. Members of Parliament proved willing to vote against their own side and to do so on occasion with serious effect. So much so that by the early 1980s, Beer — who fifteen years earlier had been lamenting the regimented discipline of Members — was able to write in glowing terms of the rise of back-bench independence. There was, he declared, an abrupt and radical discontinuity in the behaviour of MPs, dating from 1970 onwards.[3] Indeed, such were the changes taking place that Beer felt justified in referring to 'the rise of Parliament'.[4] According to another American observer, John Schwarz, the changes were such as to provide the House with a new role in policy-making.[5] Clearly, the House of Commons was a much changed body from that which had existed in earlier days.

To what extent, then, was there a change in backbench be-haviour in the 1970s and to what extent has that change been con-tinued in the 1980s? Just as importantly, what explains such a change, and what effect, if any, has it had? Has the House ac-quired a new role in policy-making or has the effect of greater backbench independence been a marginal one in terms of the ac-tivities of government? For some critics, the events of recent years have been of no great import. To some students of Parliament, they have been limited but significant, a useful guide to what the House of Commons could and should achieve in its relationship with that part of it which forms the government.

The incidence of backbench dissent

That there was a change in backbench behaviour in the years after 1970 is easily demonstrated. However, that change has not been uniform. There are three distinct periods in the post-1970 era of backbench independence. The first is that of 1970 to 1979, encom-passing three Parliaments (those of 1970-4, 1974 and 1974-9). The second is that of the Parliament of 1979 to 1983. The third is that of the present Parliament returned in June 1983. Though there is a linkage between the three periods, each has its own distinguishing characteristics.

The Parliaments of the 1970s
The three Parliaments of the 1970s were distinctive because of the extent to which MPs proved willing to vote against their own side in the Commons' division lobbies and to do so with serious effect.

The increase in intra-party dissent in the division lobbies is demonstrated by the data in Table 1. Whereas few divisions in the pre-1970 Parliaments had witnessed cross-voting, dissenting votes

Table 1: Divisions witnessing dissenting votes, 1945-1979

Parliament (number of sessions in parenthesis)	Number of divisions witnessing dissenting votes			Number of divisions witnessing dissenting votes expressed as a percentage of all divisions
	Total	Lab.a	Con.a	
1945-50 (4)	87	79	27	7
1950-1 (2)	6	5	2	2.5
1951-5 (4)	25	17	11	3
1955-9 (4)	19	10	12	2
1959-64 (5)	137	26	120	13.5
1964-6 (2)	2	1	1	0.5
1966-70 (4)	124	109	41	9.5
1970-4 (4)	221	34b	204	20
1974 (1)	25	8	21	23
1974-9 (5)	423	309	240	28

aAs one division may witness dissenting votes by Labour *and* Conservative Members, the Labour and Conservative figures do not necessarily add up to the totals on the left.
bExcluding the Labour backbench 'ginger group' votes of February–March 1971.

Source P. Norton, *Dissension in the House of Commons 1974-1979* (Oxford: Oxford University Press, 1980), p. 248.

in the Parliaments of 1970 onwards were far from uncommon. In the Parliament of 1970-4, Conservative backbenchers proved willing to vote against their leaders not only on more occasions but in greater numbers than before. The same was true, only more so, of Labour backbenchers in the years from 1974 to 1979. The size of Labour dissenting lobbies in the post-war period is given in Table 2. As it reveals, there were 44 divisions in the 1974-9 Parliament in which 50 or more Labour MPs voted against their own side. The incidence of cross-voting in the Parliament increased until, in the final session, almost one in two of every division witnessed dissenting votes cast by one or more Labour Members.[6] The 1970s, in short, witnessed an upsurge in cross-voting in the House of Commons' division lobbies. The change was of such a magnitude as to

Table 2: Size of dissenting Labour lobbies, 1945-1979 (number of divisions in which Labour dissenters entered official Conservative lobby given in parenthesis)

Number of Labour dissenting voters	Number of divisions									
	1945-50	1950-1	1951-5	1955-9	1959-64	1964-6	1966-70	1970-4	1974	1974-9a
1 only	16 (14)	1 (0)	1 (1)	2 (0)	12 (7)	1 (1)	18 (13)	13 (7)	1 (1)	53 (32)
2-9	27 (15)	2 (1)	5 (0)	6 (1)	8 (0)	0 (0)	16 (4)	6 (2)	0 (0)	87 (41)
10-19	17 (4)	1 (0)	3 (0)	0 (0)	1 (0)	0 (0)	44 (1)b	5 (1)	1 (0)	49 (14)
20-9	5 (1)	0 (0)	2 (0)	0 (0)	4 (0)	0 (0)	10 (1)	1 (0)	1 (0)	31 (4)
30-9	9 (1)	1 (0)	2 (0)	1 (0)	0 (0)	0 (0)	10 (0)	3 (0)	2 (0)	20 (0)
40-9	4 (0)	0 (0)	1 (0)	0 (0)	1 (0)	0 (0)	5 (0)	3 (0)	2 (0)	25 (1)
50 or more	1 (0)	0 (0)	3 (0)	1 (0)	0 (0)	0 (0)	6 (0)	3 (1)c	1 (0)	44 (3)
Total	79	5	17	10	26	1	109	34	8	309

aIn addition, in this Parliament Labour dissenters joined with a sufficient number of unwhipped Conservative Members to impose government defeats on six occasions.
bLabour Members voting against government during passage of Parliament (No.2) Bill not included as voting in official Conservative lobby (Opposition whips not being applied in the divisions).
cVote on the principal of entry into the EEC when Labour dissenters entered unwhipped Conservative lobby.

Source: P. Norton, Dissension in the House of Commons 1974-1979 (Oxford: Oxford University Press, 1980), p. 439.

make invalid the generalization previously drawn as to the cohesion of MPs. The point was well summarized by Leon Epstein. 'It was clear', he observed,

That in the 1970s both Conservative and Labour MPs voted more independently, and more consequently so, than their predecessors of the 1950s. The change need not have been overwhelming in order to be important ... We can also appreciate that the decline in parliamentary party cohesion might, like that of the electoral capacity of the major parties, be reversible. But, at least for the 1970s, we must say that the British party model itself substantially changed. A cohesive party as well as a majority party became less certain.[7]

Not only were Members of Parliament prepared to vote against their own side on more occasions and in greater numbers, they were prepared also to do so with greater effect. For the first time in the twentieth century, government backbenchers demonstrated their willingness to enter an Opposition lobby and purposely deny the government a majority. Significantly, the defeats began in the Parliament of 1970-4 in which the Heath government had a clear overall majority. Conservative MPs voted with the Opposition in sufficient numbers to deny the government a majority on six occasions. Three of the six defeats took place on three-line whips, the most important taking place on the immigration rules in November 1972.[8] (On that occasion, the government went down to defeat with a majority of 35 against it, a total of 56 Conservative MPs having cross-voted or abstained). The number of defeats was to be added to significantly in the next two Parliaments.

In the short Parliament of March to October 1974, the minority Labour government was vulnerable to defeat as a result of opposition parties combining against it. After some initial reluctance, opposition parties did prove willing to defeat the government in the division lobbies, doing so on 17 occasions.[9] In the Parliament returned in October 1974, the Labour government was open to defeat as a result of some of its own backbenchers voting against it and as a result (after April 1976 when it lost its overall majority in the House) of opposition parties combining against it. In that Parliament, the government suffered a total of 42 defeats, 23 of them because Labour MPs voted in the Opposition lobby and 19 because opposition parties joined forces against it (see Table 3). Thus, in the seven-year period from April 1972 (when the defeats began) to April 1979, there was a total of 65 government defeats in the House of Commons' division lobbies. For a similar number of defeats in a seven-year period, one has to go back to the 1860s.

Table 3: Government defeats in the Commons' division lobbies, 1970-1979

Number of defeats

Parliament	Caused by intra-party dissent by government backbenchers	Caused by opposition parties combining against a minority government	Total
1970-4	6	0	6
1974	0	17	17
1974-9	23	19	42
Total	29	36	65

Many of the defeats took place on important issues, the more so as the decade progressed. In the 1974-9 Parliament, the government lost its most important constitutional measure, the Scotland and Wales Bill, following defeat on the guillotine motion for the Bill. The two subsequent Bills, the Scotland Bill and the Wales Bill, were subject to radical amendment as a result of backbench dissent. The provision that in a referendum 40 per cent of eligible voters had to vote 'Yes' (otherwise a motion for the repeal of the measure was to be tabled) was inserted in each Bill against the wishes of the government.[10] Another amendment, to exclude the Orkney and Shetland islands from the provisions of the Scotland Bill if a majority of islanders voted 'No' in a referendum, was carried against the government by a majority of 86 votes, 50 Labour Members voting with Conservative and Liberal MPs to ensure its acceptance. The government also suffered the effective wrecking of the Dock Work Regulation Bill as a result of backbench dissent, as well as a change in the basic rate of income tax as a result of a defeat on the 1978 Finance Bill. The government likewise suffered defeats on motions covering its economic policy, Expenditure White Papers and the devaluation of the green pound before its final and definitive defeat on a vote of confidence on 28 March 1979.

Nor were these defeats in the division lobbies the only defeats to be suffered by the government. Throughout the decade, a large number of defeats were inflicted in standing committees. The Heath government of 1970-4 suffered 24 such defeats (more than the combined number to have occurred in the preceding three Parliaments);[11] the Parliament of 1974 witnessed the same number of defeats (24), while in the first four sessions of the 1974-9 Parliament there were approximately a hundred such defeats (97 up to April 1978).[12] These included the so-called Rooker/Wise amendments to the 1977 Finance Bill, which raised the levels of income tax allowances and partially indexed them against inflation. Most of the defeats imposed in standing committee were accepted, wholly or in part, by the Labour government.[13]

A combination of backbench dissent on the floor of the House and in standing committees, at least that which resulted in government defeats, and opposition parties combining against a minority government ensured that a significant proportion of government measures were modified against the government's wishes. Indeed, according to John Schwarz's analysis, more than half the govern-

ment Bills considered in the 1975-6 session were altered as a result
of division-lobby or standing-committee defeats. In the remaining
sessions, the proportion of Bills altered ranged from 22 per cent to
45 per cent.[14] The extent of the changes in the Parliament, argued
Schwarz, was such as to justify the claim that the House of Commons had acquired a new role in policy-making.

The 1979-83 Parliament
Towards the end of the 1970s, the experience of dissent and, more
especially, of government defeats induced a change of attitude
towards government on the part of many MPs. Many Members
began to take a degree of voting independence for granted.[15] They
shed their old deferential attitude towards government in favour
of a more participant one.[16] They wanted to be more involved and
to have some effect on government measures.

This changed attitude on the part of many Members was to be
carried into the new Parliament returned in 1979. It was reflected
in Members' continued willingness to dissent from the line taken
by their leaders. In this Parliament, though, there were two
aspects to the dissent. One was the continued expression of dissent
in the division lobbies. The other was the significance of the threat
of dissent. Despite the return of a government with a clear overall
majority and an Opposition that was facing difficulties in maintaining cohesion within its own ranks, the government had to con-
tend on occasion with the possibility of defeat. The factors
peculiar to the 1974-9 Parliament (a minute and then a non-
existent parliamentary majority) were no longer present, but the
dissent expressed by government backbenchers, and its effect, was
at least on a par with that of the Parliament of 1970-4. There was
no reversion to the pre-1970 position of cohesion and guaranteed
government majorities.

Let us consider the two aspects of dissent in the Parliament.
Throughout the four sessions, there were instances of cross-voting
by Conservative backbenchers. Any expectation on the part of
government and Opposition whips that they were in for a quiet
Parliament was dispelled within the first two months of the opening session. Before the House had recessed for the summer, one in
three of all divisions was witnessing dissenting votes cast by one or
more Conservative or Labour backbenchers, the dissenters often
forcing the divisions themselves.[17] The most significant occasions
of Conservative dissent in the Parliament, by vote or abstention,

tion, are given in Table 4. As that table shows, there were at least 16 occasions when ten or more Conservative MPs either voted against their own side or abstained from voting. On four occasions, the number of dissenters exceeded 40. An examination not only of the numbers involved but also of the government response to the dissent suggests the importance of those occasions. Nonetheless, the number of divisions involved is a very small one, minute in relation to the total number of divisions held in the Parliament (just over 1 per cent of the total). Furthermore, despite the numbers of dissenters involved, on only one occasion did Conservative MPs enter an opposition lobby in sufficient numbers to inflict a defeat on the government (in December 1982 on the immigration rules). Not surprisingly, therefore, some observers have been inclined to dismiss intra-party dissent in the Parliament as of little significance.[18]

More significant, and somewhat overlooked by some students of Parliament, was the threat of defeat. Voting against one's own side in the division lobbies, it should be remembered, constitutes essentially an admission of failure, failure at an earlier stage to persuade one's own leaders not to persist with the measure of motion under debate. If a dissenter is alone in his dissent, or is joined by like-minded Members insufficient in number to threaten the government's majority, then cross-voting may merely serve to confirm that failure. It is at the discretion of government whether or not it chooses to ignore that dissent. What was significant about the 1979 Parliament was that backbenchers proved effective in influencing government *prior* to issues being taken to the division lobbies. Ian Gilmour once observed that 'concord and peace may signify backbench influence, not dull obedience.'[19] The truth of this was borne out to some extent by the experience of this Parliament. Various measures were introduced by a government which did not enjoy the wholehearted support of the parliamentary party. On occasion the number of backbenchers who made it clear to the whips that they were prepared to vote against the government was such as to threaten the government's majority. Rather than run the risk of such defeat, the government conceded the dissenters' point, either wholly or in part. Hence there was little or no dissent in the division lobbies: there was no need for it.

Instances of such pre-lobby dissent are, in one sense, more significant than cross-voting in the division lobbies (at least that which does not entail government defeats) but are, by their

Table 4: Main occasions of Conservative dissidence in the Commons' division lobbies, 1979-1983

Date	Issue	No. of Conservative MPs dissenting (by vote or abstention)	Comment
11.6.79	Kiribati Bill	15	No effect on Bill
4.12.79	Immigration rules	19	Proposals withdrawn/rules relaxed
11.2.80	Charges for rural school transport	20	Provision withdrawn
23.4.80	Amendment to Employment Bill (on closed shop reform)	42	Backbench proposal incorporated in 1982 Employment Act
5.6.80	Opposition motion calling (in effect) for repeal of so-called 'sus' law	6	Government accepted need for change in law
16.3.81	Increase in petrol duty	28	Increase halved (from 20p to 10p)
7.7.81	Reductions in defence expenditure for naval dockyards	11	No effect
12.11.81	Referendum requirement for local rate increases	18	Proposal abandoned
8.12.81	Public expenditure reductions	14	No immediate tangible effect
9.12.81	Increased weight allowance for heavy lorries	11	Review of Armitage recommendations undertaken
Feb-July 82	5% abatement in real value of unemployment benefit	41a	See below
17.6.82	Opposition motion attacking EEC and European Union	9	No effect
23.6.82	Provision for Northern Ireland Assembly	14	No effect
11.11.82	Immigration rules revision	52	Review of immigration quotas undertaken
22.11.82	Abatement in unemployment benefit and abatement in child benefit	25	Abatement restored in March 1983 Budget
25.11.82	Increased weight allowance for heavy lorries	23	No immediate effect
15.12.82	Immigration rules	51	Government defeat. Some tightening of immigration register
15.2.83	Immigration rules	15	No effect

Figures for numbers of dissenters are usually minimum figures, given that they seek to include abstentions.

a More than one division involved.

Source: M. Shah, 'Revolts and Retreats: Division Lobby Dissent within the Parliamentary Conservative Party, November 1979-March 1983', unpublished undergraduate dissertation, Essex University Department of Government, 1983; supplemented by author's research of *House of Commons Debates (Hansard)*.

nature, less observable. Known instances in the Parliament encompassed two occasions when the government withdrew Bills, a
Local Government Finance Bill and the Iran (Temporary Provisions) Bill. In the latter case, a special meeting of senior ministers
was called when a Labour MP obtained an emergency debate to
discuss the government's plans to introduce the measure. According to *The Times,* as many as 100 Conservative MPs were prepared
to vote with the Opposition.[20] The chief whip reported to the
meeting that the government faced defeat and the decision was
taken to withdraw the measure.[21] In the former case, backbenchers made it clear that they would not accept the provisions for
limiting supplementary rates levied by local authorities. The Environment Secretary offered six alternative schemes. None proved
acceptable and so the decision was taken to abandon the Bill.[22]
Other proposals withdrawn under threat of defeat included
charges for eye tests, reductions in the BBC's external services, a
three-stage payrise for MPs (Members opposed the staggered element of the proposal), 'hotel' charges for patients in NHS hospi-
tals, and, in practice, transport charges for school travel in rural
areas.[23] Furthermore, the threat of dissent and, more generally,
anticipation of likely dissent helped create the broad limits within
which the government operated its economic policy. The disquiet
prevalent among a section of the parliamentary Conservative party was one of the influences on the Chancellor of the Exchequer in
shaping his 1982 Budget. 'Sir Geoffrey Howe', declared *The
Economist,* 'may be the first Tory chancellor who, in forming his
budget, must take into account his chances of getting it through
the House of Commons.'[24] (Twenty-six MPs had earlier written to
the chief whip demanding a change of policy; 14 had abstained on
the Chancellor's mini-Budget proposals of 2 December the
previous year.) In a radio interview early in 1982, the Prime
Minister also conceded that she had not been tougher on public
spending because of anticipated parliamentary reaction. 'I would
like to be tougher on public spending. But I have to do what I
think we can get through Parliament.'[25] Though Parliament was
only one (and not necessarily the most important) of many influences upon government, it was a more significant one than in
pre-1970 days; and in many ways the influence it was exerting was
more subtle (and consequently less observable, certainly less quan-
tifiable) than in the preceding Parliaments of the 1970s.

1983: 'The frustration Parliament'?
The position changed significantly in the Parliament returned in
June 1983, the result primarily of an overwhelming Conservative
presence in the House. The government enjoyed a majority over
all other parties of 144. Shortly before the general election, the
then Foreign Secretary, Francis Pym, had expressed the view that
a large majority would not be a desirable thing. Subsequently,
after being relegated to the backbenches, he was to write: 'to put it
bluntly, I was right.'[26] Government, he believed, was not capable
of being kept in check by a 'tiresome' House of Commons if the
House itself was saturated with government supporters.[27] There
was the danger also that, with so many Conservative MPs, service
in the House for many would prove unrewarding and frustrating,
unable to have much impact on government. This view was given
some credence by the Speaker when, addressing journalists, he
referred to it as the 'frustration Parliament'.

How valid, then, are these observations? What effect, if any,
has the House had upon government? Clearly, the effect of a large
government majority — the largest since 1945 — has had a significant limiting effect. The government stands little chance of being
defeated in the division lobbies in heavily whipped votes. Whereas
in the preceding Parliament the threat of cross-voting by 20 or 30
Conservative MPs would have put the government's majority in
jeopardy, it would require 70 to 80 Conservative MPs to threaten
to cross-vote to achieve a similar result in the present Parliament.
The government is thus largely in a position where many believe it
can safely ignore its parliamentary critics, be they on the opposition side of the House or its own. To some extent, this is correct;
but not wholly, and it is not borne out completely by the evidence
of the first session of the Parliament.

A large government majority is assumed to facilitate or rather
not to deter backbench critics of the government in casting dissenting votes, because they know that by so voting they can make a
point without jeopardizing the government's majority. This
assumption was partially borne out by the data on division-lobby
dissent in the first session. Indeed, in its occurrence it was more
extensive than that experienced in the other two post-war Parliaments with large government majorities (1945-50 and 1959-64), being on a par rather with the incidence of dissent in the preceding
Parliaments of the 1970s (Table 5; compare with Table 1). The
spirit of independence instilled in the 1970s carried over into this

Parliament. On the Conservative side of the House, 137 backbenchers cast a total of 416 dissenting votes against the government. The main occasions of dissent are listed in Table 6. None threatened the government's majority. (In one division on the Rates Bill, the government's majority fell to 21, though there was no cross-voting by Conservative Members.)[28] The extent of the dissent was nonetheless distinctive for the first *session* of the new Parliament.

Table 5: Divisions witnessing dissenting votes: June 1983 to summer recess 1984

Number of divisions witnessing dissenting votes			Number of divisions witnessing dissenting votes expressed as a percentage of all division
Total	Lab[a]	Con.[a]	
115	54	62	25[b]

[a]As one division may witness dissenting votes cast by Conservative *and* Labour Members, the Lab. and Con. figures do not necessarily add up to the total on the left.
[b]When expressed solely as a percentage of all whipped divisions, the figure increases to 28 per cent.

It was distinctive also for another reason. Despite its extent, it was remarkable that there was not more of it. On a variety of issues, the number of Conservative MPs opposed to the government's proposals was known to be greater than the number actually voting against; examples would include the Rates Bill, housing benefits and the rate support grant for England.[29] In the case of the rate support grant, for instance, at least 20 Conservatives were known originally to be opposed to it; yet in the division only three voted against.[30] On many issues, a majority of dissenters contented themselves with (at most) abstaining from voting. Why? Because the government, though knowing it was not going to be defeated, was prepared to make concessions to avoid the embarrassing display of public, large-scale dissent. The approach adopted was summarized by one journal thus: 'To avoid an open revolt, the chief whip, Mr John Wakeham, would normally seek a negotiated deal between the rebels and the relevant minister before an issue reached the floor of the House. This happened with housing benefit... as it did with the proposed withholding of Britain's EEC budget contribution;'[31] More often, it recorded,

Table 6: Main occasions of Conservative dissidence in the Commons' division lobbies, 1983/4 session

Date	Issue	Number of Conservative MPs voting against government (Number of abstainers, where known, given in parenthesis)
1.12.83	Opposition amendment 'that the own resources of the European Community should not be increased'	6 (17)
17.1.84	Rates Bill: Second Reading	12 (20/30)
17.1.84	Rates Bill: motion to commit to Committee of the Whole House	20
19.1.84	Opposition motion urging government to reconsider changes in housing benefits	3 (5/10)
23.1.84	Rate Support Grant for England 1984/5	3 (c.10)
27/28.3.84	Rates Bill: various amendments	14
28.3.84	Rates Bill: Third Reading	9 (10/20)
2.4.84	Trade Union Bill: amendment to require 'contracting in' for paying political levy	43
11.4.84	Local Government (Interim Provisions) Bill: Second Reading	19 (10/20)
2.5.84	Health and Social Security Bill: amendment re safeguards in dispensing of glasses by non-registered opticians	10
9/10.5.84	Local Government (Interim Provisions) Bill: various amendments	22
14.5.84	Police and Criminal Evidence Bill: amendment to provide that police officers had to be in uniform to arrest under the 1956 Sexual Offences Act	7
6.6.84	Agricultural Holdings Bill: new clause (waiver of contract)	5 (1+)
13.6.84	Matrimonial and Family Proceedings Bill: amendment to allow solicitors to appear in family court proceedings	5
24.7.84	Trade Union Bill: various amendments	37

Sources: House of Commons Debates (Hansard) for data on cross-voting; national press for reports of abstentions.

such negotiation did not have the desired effect. Nonetheless, on a number of significant occasions, concession by government served to reduce the scale of dissent.

In the instance of housing benefits, the Social Services Secretary announced in the House that he was prepared to consider modifying his own proposals if they looked like having a harsh effect on some households;[32] he was also reported to have given some privately expressed assurances to the backbench dissenters.[33] Concessions were also forthcoming on the Rates Bill and EC milk-production regulations. On the Rates Bill, the Environment Secretary announced that the Bill would be amended to exempt from general rate-capping powers those authorities which had followed government spending guidelines.[34] As one backbench critic declared, 'It goes a long way... to make the Bill much more acceptable.'[35] The government withdrew the EC milk-production regulations it had originally tabled, substituting instead regulations that were somewhat more satisfactory to dairy farmers and backbench critics.[36] Ministers also moved to make conciliatory gestures in anticipation of dissent on other issues, including the Police and Criminal Evidence Bill and the rate support grant.[37] Anticipated disquiet on the backbenches also affected Cabinet discussion on a number of issues, including a Treasury proposal for a freeze on capital spending by local authorities. It was resisted by Environment Secretary Patrick Jenkin. 'Mr Jenkin has been given ample warning in recent weeks that a freeze would encounter the deepest hostility from Conservative as well as Labour councils as well as from Tory backbench MPs... Many of Mr Jenkin's ministerial colleagues at last night's meeting share his belief that the Government would be foolhardy to alienate them further.'[38]

Thus on occasion backbenchers were able to persuade government to make concessions, in some instances concessions of some substance. In so doing, they lacked the clout that flows from being able to threaten the government's majority in the lobbies. But they were aided by developments elsewhere — in the 'other place'. Government appears to have been influenced by the occasional axis developed between dissident Conservative MPs and the Upper House... The government could confidently seek to reverse Lords' amendments if it had a united parliamentary party behind it. If it did not, seeking a reversal could produce not a defeat but further serious embarrassment, exploited by both the Opposition and dissident backbenchers alike. Hence, in many respects, for government the 'opposition' that caused it most concern was not the official Opposition but instead the combined opposition of Lords and dissident backbenchers.

Relative to preceding Parliaments, MPs were able to wring fewer concessions out of government than they would likely have wished. Nonetheless they were able to have some, however limited, impact upon government deliberations (the Prime Minister, as one occasional dissident put it, 'remained a good listener'),[39] and the more independent spirit generated in the 1970s was still apparent. Indeed, this independent spirit was marked on those issues which are by tradition considered House of Commons matters and on those considered issues of conscience. On the selection of the Speaker, Members made it clear that they were unwilling to support the Member preferred by the Prime Minister, making sure that the appointment went instead to Bernard Weatherill (an MP, for some reason, out of favour with the Prime Minister). On the issue of MPs' pay, Members failed in one division to go along with government advice (in the division, government whips acting as tellers, the vote went against government advice by 233 votes to 160).[40] And in a series of divisions on capital punishment, a conscience issue, a majority of Members voted consistently against its reintroduction, despite both the Prime Minister and the Home Secretary voting for it.[41]

There were clearly significant differences between the Parliaments in the three periods identified. However, there was one generalization that was no longer appropriate to any of them. At the beginning, two generalizations appropriate to pre-1970 Parliaments were identified: MPs rarely voted against their own side, and when they did so they did not deny the government a majority. This latter generalization (not defeating the government) was not borne out by the Parliaments of the 1970s and that of 1979-83, but would seem applicable again to the present Parliament. The first generalization, however, applies to none of the Parliaments covered. Expressed in sheer behavioural terms (that is, ignoring the impact or otherwise of suchn behaviour), Members of Parliament have proved significantly more willing since 1970 to vote against their own party in the division lobbies. As one MP expressed it, by the late 1970s Members were taking a degree of voting independence for granted.[42] The change is relative — cohesion remains a feature of the division lobbies — but it is significant...

Conclusion

The House of Commons, in its behaviour, has changed a great deal since 1970. Members of Parliament have proved significantly more willing to vote against their own side. They have also proved willing, for most of this period, to do so in such numbers as to threaten or remove the government's majority on a number of occasions. Cohesion remains a feature of parliamentary voting, but it is not the cohesion of the pre-1970 era. Party leaders can no longer take their parliamentary parties for granted. Relative to preceding Parliaments (i.e. pre-1970) MPs have become more independent in their voting behaviour, an independence which has been maintained in the present Parliament returned in 1983. By indulging in such behaviour, Members have served to dispel a number of assumptions previously held about the House of Commons, they have served to make the House a more significant policy-*influencing* body (though the extent of that influence has varied from Parliament to Parliament, depending upon MPs' willingness and ability to deny the government a majority in the division lobbies), and they have served to generate parliamentary structures for subjecting government to more regular and sustained scrutiny. Though the House has not achieved anything approaching the policy-making role ascribed to it by some observers, to write — as Beer does — of 'the rise of Parliament' in the 1970s is probably not inappropriate. What one is now witnessing is a period of consolidation. The government's large majority in the House provides a barrier to the House exerting greater or as much policy influence as it did in the 1970s; but the select committees created by the House in 1979 are now in established operation and, according to some of their members, operating more smoothly and with at least as much effect as in the first Parliament of their existence. Thus the behavioural changes of recent years are important both for the effect they had at the time and for their long-term implications. Because of them, the House of Commons is unlikely to revert to being quite the same animal that it was in the decades prior to 1970.

Notes

1 S. H. Beer, *Modern British Politics* (London: Faber, 1969 edition), pp. 350-1.
2 Ibid.

3   S. H. Beer, *Britain Against Itself* (London: Faber, 1982), p. 181.
4   Ibid. Beer uses the phrase as the heading for the section on Parliament.
5   J. E. Schwarz, 'Exploring a New Role in Policy-making: The British House of Commons in the 1970s', *American Political Science Review,* 74 (1), March 1980, pp. 23-37.
6   P. Norton, *Dissension in the House of Commons 1974-1979* (Oxford: Oxford University Press, 1980), p. 437.
7   L. D. Epstein, 'What Happened to the British Party Model?' *American Political Science Review,* 74 (1), 1980, pp. 19-20.
8   See P. Norton, 'Intra-party Dissent in the House of Commons: A Case Study. The Immigration Rules 1972', *Parliamentary Affairs,* 29 (4), 1976, pp. 404-20.
9   See Norton, *Dissension in the House of Commons 1974-1979,* p. 491.
10 See ibid., pp. 310-12, 327-9 and 345-6.
11 P. Norton, 'Dissent in Committee: Intra-party Dissent in Commons' Standing Committees 1959-74', *The Parliamentarian,* 57 (1), 1976, table 1, p. 18.
12 Schwarz, 'Exploring a New Role in Policy-making', table 3, p. 27.
13 Ibid., pp. 27-8.
14 Ibid., table 3, p. 27.
15 Note the comments of G. Cunningham MP, book review, *The Parliamentarian,* 61, 1980, pp. 192-3.
16 Beer, *Britain Against Itself,* p.190.
17 Of 82 divisions held prior to the summer recess, 60 were whipped on the government side. In 19 divisions, backbenchers forced the vote. In eight of these, Conservative backbenchers were to be found voting against the government.
18 As, for example, in D. Judge (ed.), *The Politics of Parliamentary Reform* (London: Heinemann, 1983), pp. 188-9.
19 I. Gilmour, *The Body Politic* (London: Hutchinson, revised edition 1971), p. 269.
20 *The Times,* 20 May 1980.
21 BBC Radio 4 Programme, 'Today', 20 May 1980.
22 *The Economist,* 19 December 1981.
23 The proposal had encountered cross-voting when it first went through the Commons and had then been defeated in the Lords (see chapter 5). Conservative opposition to the proposal increased (influenced by constituency pressure) and it appeared that the government might not be able to muster a Commons' majority to reverse the Lords' amendment. It was therefore decided not to try to overturn the Lords' decision.
24 *The Economist,* 16 January 1982.
25 Quoted in *The Times,* 11 January 1982.
26 F. Pym, *The Politics of Consent* (London: Hamish Hamilton, 1984), p. 78.
27 Ibid.
28 On 26 June 1984. *HC Deb.* 62, cols 859-62.
29 See *Financial Times,* 29, March 1984; *Daily Telegraph,* 24 January

1984; and *Financial Times,* 20 January 1984.

30 *Daily Telegraph,* 24 January 1984.
31 *The Economist,* 4 August 1984, p. 22.
32 *HC Deb,* 52, cols 465, 471.
33 *Daily Telegraph,* 20 January 1984.
34 *HC Deb,* 57, cols 326-7.
35 *HC Deb,* 57, col. 328.
36 The new regulations allowed for more production by farmers who had entered into commitments before 2 April 1984 and who were unable to obtain sufficient quotas to sustain their businesses. *The Times,* 12 July 1984.
37 On the Police and Criminal Evidence Bill, Home Office ministers sought to reduce support for a Liberal amendment — requiring police officers making arrests under the 1956 Sexual Offences Act to be in uniform — by announcing a tightening of Metropolitan Police rules to ensure that plainclothes officers were not used as *agents provocateurs.* (There was pressure from many Members for such an announcement following an incident in a Soho gay theatre involving the arrest of a Conservative MP by a plainclothes officer. See *Daily Telegraph,* 15 May 1984). More generally, backbench opinion and anticipated reaction had had an influence in the revision of the Bill, following the loss of the original Bill with the calling of the 1983 general election: Home Secretary Leon Brittan QC, MP to author in interview.
38 *The Times,* 11 July 1984.
39 Robin Maxwell-Hyslop MP addressing students from Hull University, House of Commons, 7 March 1984.
40 *HC Deb.* 46, Cols 344-6.
41 *HC Deb.* 45, cols 972-96.
42 G. Cunningham MP; see above note 15.

Life in Whitehall

From *Whitehall: Tragedy and Farce,* Hamish Hamilton, London 1985, pp. 40–93.

Ministerial life

Whitehall takes over a Minister and assumes that all his time is available for public business. The working day is long, crammed full of meetings and visits, and then in the evening there are receptions and dinners followed by more work from the ubiquitous red boxes, full of paper from the Private Office. Social life is built around the job and the few politicians who want a separate life in the evenings have to fight very hard to get it. The routine is ideal for workaholics and insomniacs, as Joel Barnet dicovered to his dismay:

I soon found that good health, and an ability to manage on little sleep – I am fortunate in only needing five or six hours – were invaluable assets .. Even with that amount of time spent working, it was often extremely difficult to read the papers adequately to brief myself for the host of meetings I had to attend ... the sheer weight of work gives one little time to sit back and just think about the way the job should be done.[1]

This is no new phenomenon and only a few Ministers are able to avoid this fierce pace of work, as Hugh Gaitskell observed in 1949:

I must say the technique of modern Government becomes almost intolerably difficult. On the one hand, the key Ministers are hopelessly overworked. Stafford [Cripps, Chancellor of the Exchequer] spends his time dashing between Paris, Brussels and London ...The PM [Atlee] is perhaps so successful because he is content to let others do the work. I noticed that he was at Lords on Saturday morning and Wimbledon on Saturday afternoon, and went down to Chequers for the weekend. Poor Stafford spent most of his weekend in bed writing his latest paper in a state of complete exhaustion.[2]

Mrs Thatcher is not like Clem Attlee and certainly tries to personally direct the whole of Whitehall and prides herself on her machismo style of regularly working to the small hours of the morning and needing very little sleep.

It is instructive to look at a short period, chosen at random, in the life of one Minister – Barbara Castle – to see the strain under which they operate. On Monday, 25 March, 1974, after a weekend spent working on official papers in her red boxes, she was able to get up late and leave her country cottage for a 10.30 meeting with officials in the DHSS to discuss expenditure negotations with the Treasury. At 11.30 it was time for the Cabinet meeting to hear the details of the Budget. Lunchtime was spent eating sandwiches during a meeting with officials. At 3 pm she had to go to the House of Commons to make a major statement. This lasted till 4.30 pm and in the next two hours she worked in her room at the House of Commons and had more meetings with officials and junior Ministers. Before a reception and dinner at Lancaster House she was able to visit the dying Dick Crossman. At 9.30 pm it was back to the Commons to go through more papers, with a vote at 11.30 pm. She arrived home at midnight and worked till 1 am, but when another red box was delivered in the early hours she gave up and went to bed. The rest of the week was no better. On Tuesday she not surprisingly fell asleep in the Commons during the Budget speech, before attending a political dinner and returning to work at the Commons till the early hours. On Wednesday she was up at 6 am to tackle more boxes of papers. The day was taken up with meetings and speeches and she got to bed at 1 am. Up again at 6 am on Thursday, she had to attend a Cabinet meeting, make a statement in the Commons and appear on TV. She then went home to rewrite a speech for the next day but gave up and wrote in her diary, 'By then I just didn't care what happened and headed for bed.'[3]

[Civil Service life]

Joining the Civil Service
What sort of life faces the young graduates who have successfully passed through the Civil Service selection processs? The first discovery is that they have not joined the 'Civil Service' – they join a Department. And this Department will be their career. They will be initiated into its values and view of the world. Some may have

one posting to another department, usually the Treasury or the Cabinet Office to 'broaden' their experience slightly, but they will spend the bulk of their life in one area. They will meet people from other departments at meetings or on the occasional course at the Civil Service College, but they will be judged on their performance in the Department and promoted by the people at the top of their Department. Whitehall is itself a limited and closed world, and many civil servants only see a very small and fairly self – contained part of this world. The young graduate can express a preference but will be given little information or choice about the department he is allocated, and will just have to make the best of it. The chances of getting a transfer are small.

The young graduate will, as an administration trainee (or AT), usually work with a young Principal in his early thirties. Apart from a small number of short courses at the Civil Service College, all his training will be given 'on the job' (and this will often mean being given a lot of odd jobs to do). Such an approach reflects the great feature of the British Civil Service. Administration is not thought of as something that can be taught – it is something that is learnt by doing a job and by observing others. In the 1950s one senior Civil Servant tried to sum up 'the Spirit of British Admininstration'. He caught the mood brilliantly and the philosophy he set out still applies today. Administrators were, he said: 'intelligent amateurs who form their judgements on the basis of experience rather than as a result of a prescribed course of theoretical training'.

Indeed some administrators who went abroad were naturally 'shocked to discover that many countries were administered by men who read books about public administration. Such people were committing the crime of learning from books something one just does'.[4] The young AT will also be introduced at an early stage in the initiation process to another fundamental aspect of the Civil Service. He will learn that his essential contribution to the work of government is to be 'administration'. This does not require, indeed positively militates against, gaining specialised knowledge about a particular area. An administrator must be able to pick up any job quickly – his skill comes not from knowing anything about the job he is doing but by knowing how the departmental machine and the wider Whitehall machinery work. He must be capable of making the machinery work as smoothly as possible. He must know how to process paper, write the correct sort of brief or committee paper, and how to achieve a compromise between competing interests. The exact nature of that compromise matters far less than the fact that various groups have agreed and the well – oiled machine can continue. In order to get this sort of experience the young AT will be moved to a new job every six to eight months. Although, later in his career, this movement will slow down to about once every two years, the basic principle remains unchanged.

After two years the successful AT will become a Higher Executive Officer (Development) (HEO(D)). His jobs will bear little relation to the relatively tedious jobs of the normal HEO but the title was introduced in the 1970s to give a facade of equality. The HEO (D) is marked out for rapid promotion. There will be a job in a Minister's private office or with the Permanent Secretary. The HEO (D) does not make any great contribution, and his responsibility is limited. These jobs are educational. They are designed to show the young administrator life at the top of Whitehall so that the accepted ways of operating are passed on and the right values are learned at an early stage. After a year or so comes promotion to Principal and the first real job.

Moving up the ladder

A Principal in a Whitehall job usually runs a small section of about half a dozen people, often less. He concentrates on a small area of policy and provides the first drafts of important papers, answers to Parliamentary questions, etc. He may have responsibility for a limited area of work and send papers direct to a Minister's office. But normally his work and role in policy – making is fairly circumscribed. This is still, to some extent, a learning grade. The senior Civil Service sometimes likes to encourage a degree of radical thinking at this level. It is often useful to be able to show Ministers that the Civil Service is capable of major policy re – thinks which then enables the senior people to show how difficult it would be to implement this sort of proposal. Also it can be tactically advantageous to let loose some radical thoughts about policies in other departments as part of the internal Whitehall battle.

The newly – promoted Principal usually starts in a relatively straightforward job but performance here matters in order to get the right second job which is of vital career importance. Very early on the Principal will be aware of the career treadmill of the Civil Service and the importance of the annual report. As he spends only about two years in each job, the first annual report is vitally important since it is the major influence on the choice of the next job. Although the choice of job is usually made at the last moment by the senior staff involved, the most important factor is their perception of the young Civil Servant. Does he look like a candidate for the best jobs, is he a 'high – flier' – the ultimate accolade in the Civil Service?

After the second job – and by now the Principal is probably in his early thirties – the important age of thirty – five is rapidly approaching. This is the earliest age for promotion to Assistant Secretary and three jobs is the usual minimum before this can happen. So it is vital to keep changing jobs every two years to get enough experience. Depth of experience is not important – width is the crucial factor. The last job as a Principal can be as Private Secretary to a senior Minister. To get such a job is virtually a guarantee of promotion at the end and is a sign of somebody marked out for the top.

Elevation to Assistant Secretary is the single biggest step up the promotion ladder and marks a major change in status. A Principal often has to share an office, relies on the typing pool and photocopying pool to get work done, whereas an Assistant Secretary has his own much larger office (with a fitted carpet and regulation issue hat – stand) together with a secretary who sits in the outer office, does all his typing and photocopying, makes phone calls and the coffee and tea.

An Assistant Secretary is definetely part of the senior management of the department. Normally they have two or three Principals working for them and a total staff of about twenty. The job is essentially one of linking together the area where the basic work is undertaken and the higher world of policy – making. Some work, such as the answers to Parliamentary Questions, has to be cleared at this level before it is passed to the Ministers, and on many other occasions an Assistant Secretary will send papers direct to the Minister. The career pattern is much the same as that for a Principal. The ambitious Assistant Secretary will be looking to do three or at the most four jobs each lasting about two years before promotion to Under – Secretary in his early forties. Again, breadth of experience and not depth of knowledge is the most important factor.

Choosing the top Civil Servants

It is worth pausing at this stage in our climb up the Civil Service
ladder to examine how the top Civil Servants are chosen. In all
departments, promotions to Principal are determined by the
system of annual reports together with a promotion board which
interviews and selects successful candidates. Some departments
have promotion boards to Assistant Secretary, most do not. Above
Assistant Secretary there are no annual reports, no selection
boards, everything is decided by the personal assessment of those
at the top of the department.

What qualities are required in the top Civil Servant? The standard annual report form makes fascinating reading and contains as
many highly subjective elements as the Civil Service selection procedure – indeed many of the qualities to be judged are exactly the
same. After a brief description of the job the form requires the
person to be marked by their immediate superior on a scale from 1
to 6, 'exceptionally effective' to 'definitely not up to the duties'.
These extreme marks are hardly ever used and indeed most marks
are graded 2 and 3, 'more than generally effective' and 'generally
effective'. In other words most people are marked as better than
average! In 1983 this reached such a point inside the Ministry of
Defence than an official reminder was circulated to all staff saying
that more realistic marking was required.

The next section of the annual report is the largest and in it a
number of qualities have to be marked on a six – point scale from
A to F. Thus for 'foresight' A means 'anticipates problems and develops solutions in advance' and F means 'handles problems only
after they arise'. Apart from 'foresight' all the classic Civil Service
virtues reappear, – penetration, judgement, expression on paper,
oral expression, relations with others, acceptance of reponsibility,
reliability under pressure, drive and determination. One of the
most enlightening is the marking of judgement. A is gained for
'his/her proposals or decisions are consistently sound'. To be
'sound' is the highest of all the Civil Service virtues, to able to
judge what those up the chain will find acceptable is the greatest of
all gifts. This makes you a team player, a person who can be
trusted. To be regarded as 'unsound' is the most damning epithet
in the Civil Service.

Two sections on training needs and the type of job to be given
next follow. Both are usually treated as unimportant. Training is

not taken seriously and everybody knows that the next job is decided not on the basis of the report but by those in charge of the department. Then comes a section on promotability with a three – point scale, well fitted, fitted and not fitted. Next there is an important section on long – term potential and then a 'short and vivid pen – picture'. A final section is completed by a second person normally two grades above the individual being reported on. He also provides a short picture and is supposed to hold an interview or 'Job Appraisal Review' (JAR) to discuss the year's performance and how this can be improved in the year ahead. The idea of the JAR was part of the post – Fulton proposals to improve Civil Service management. In practice a JAR often does not happen, or if it does it is only perfunctory.

Even though the Civil Service has this elaborate reporting system most of the judgements and reasons for promotion or non – promotion depend on the personal views or idiosyncracies of those at the top of the department and their opinions of those under them. One of the great delights of the Permanent Secretary and his head of personnel is to sit late at night over a whisky moving people around the department. It is after all one of the few areas where they have almost total power.

The top of the Civil Service

Below Permanent Secretary the two most senior grades are Deputy Secretary and Under – Secretary. But it is very difficult to define what they actually do. They are always both represented in the management chain, they both chair committees, sit on inter – departmental committees and attend meetings with Ministers. In some way they usually allocate the work between them but their exact responsibilities are never really defined and distinguished. In some large departments the Principal Finance Officer and Principal Establishment Officer are both Deputy Secretaries, in others, they are Under – Secretaries. The result is that there tends to be administrative confusion at this level with too much copying of paper and people doing each other's jobs. Much of the emphasis is not on executive responsibility but on co – ordination.

The bulk of Under – Secretaries are promoted from Assistant Secretary between the ages of forty – three and forty – eight, though a third will be promoted in their fifties and will probably go no further. The real 'high – flyers', the people who will become Permanent Secretary, make Under – Secretary before forty – three. Most Deputy Secretaries reach the grade aged between forty – nine and fifty – one. The top two grades of the Civil Service are therefore composed of people between fifty and sixty who emerge from an exhausting series of high pressure jobs, who have been assessed as good team – players and who, by the time they reach the top, have lost what little, if any, reforming zeal they might have had. They are simply content to operate the machine as it is.

The training of those at the top, so far as it exists, is incredibly introverted. They will have been in the Civil Service since their early twenties and apart from the odd job, entirely in one department. At present just two of the current eighty or so Permanent and Deputy Secretaries have had any experience at all outside the Civil Service. The Civil Service ensures that there is no way of joining aged about forty or forty – five with outside experience in management, finance or any other specialist skill. Only three out of the eighty did not join as fast stream graduates and have instead worked their way up through the promotion structure from the bottom. Eighty per cent of them went to Oxbridge and a third to public schools. Over a third belong to one of the recognised London clubs.

In view of this very narrow experience what happens at the top if the Civil Service structure is even more extraordinary. After a career spent almost entirely inside one department a Permanent Secretary is often expected to take over and run a completely new department for the last few years of his career. Seven of the current twenty Permanent Secretaries have never served before in the departments of which they are heads. This is Civil Service amateurism with a vengeance. It is a perfect illustration of the view that specialist knowledge of a subject is a handicap and that a top civil servant is really an expert in the peculiar art of 'administration' or oiling the wheels of the Whitehall machine.

'Amateurism'

The word that has caused the greatest offence to the top Civil Service was the basis of the Fulton critique – 'amateur'. The senior ranks of the Civil Service believe strongly that they are professionals – professionals in the art of government. But this means knowledge of how Ministers really operate; and this as we have already seen is a seedy and cynical world. The mandarins can only justify themselves on the basis that there is a separate function of operating the Whitehall machine in which knowledge detracts from so - called professional objectivity and is therefore positively harmful.

This is a bogus claim invented and sustained with great determination to provide a justification for the adminstrative class. It is encapsulated in the views of Sir Warren Fisher, Head of the Civil Service, to the Royal Commission on the Civil Service in 1930:

Let us guard ourselves against the idea that the Permanent Head of a department should be an expert: he should not be anything of the kind. Instead he should be a man of such breadth of experience that he will soon find himself picking out the essential points; and remember, there is a great deal to be said for a fresh eye.[5]

Another senior civil servant described the work of the mandarin administrator as follows:

[He] knows the construction of the whole machine, the position of his own and other departments as wheels of the machine and their relations to the other wheels, and the general principles of operation which must be observed if the machine is to work smoothly. Finally, and perhaps most important of all ... it is the business of the high official to know the men who for the time being are, like himself important parts of the central and controlling mechanism.[6]

In other words the mandarins can be left to get on with oiling the wheels of government, confident in their arrogance that they can master any problem however complex or specialised and come to sound judgements, perhaps with help of other 'good chaps' they happen to know.

This 'amateurism' has left an appalling catalogue of failure in Whitehall. At times its effects verge on the ludicrous as the following examples illustrate:

1. In 1976 the Head of the central Management Services Department for the whole of Whitehall had had no previous experience of management services work,[7]
2. Two out of the last three heads of the division in the Ministry of Defence responsible for the control of the £18 billion a year Defence Budget had had no previous experience of budgetary or financial work.
3. The Department of Education Planning Unit investigating the future needs of education in the UK contained no sociologist,

no economist and no educational expert.[8]

4. Apart from some accountants in the Ministry of Defence's section responsible for internal audit (the examination of accounting procedures) Whitehall had no professionally qualified auditors to control expenditure of nearly £140 billion a year.[9]

5. In 1983 the Deputy Secretary, Under-Secretary, Assistant Secretary and Principal in the Ministry of Defence responsible for controlling the £18 billion a year Defence Budget and conducting all negotiations with the Treasury were all classicists who had read Greats at Oxford.

6. Until the early 1980s the Controller and Auditor General responsible to Parliament for auditing all government expenditure was always an ex-Permanent Secretary with no training in accountancy.

7. The trading activities of the Crown Agents, that were to cost the public £200 million in the mid-1970s, was controlled by one lowly-qualified accountant (before 1964 there were no professional staff) and until 1968 the accounts were kept on odd pieces of paper in the office and the basic device of double-entry book-keeping, known for over six hundred years, was not used.[10]

8. One of the newly appointed Directors of the Ministry of Defence's Information Technology Unit responsible for introducing new technology has never worked with computers before.[11]

Life in the Civil Service

Much of the life of the Civil Service is physically squalid. The staff are poorly accommodated in badly decorated buildings, with inadequate typing and photocopying facilities, and surrounded by petty regulations. In the Ministry of Defence until the early 1970s the 'modern' invention of the roller towel was unknown and an old lady with a trolley used to come round once a week distributing new towels and pieces of cheap gritty soap. The canteens are all too often depressing places tucked away in the basement, generally justifying their nickname of the 'Greasy Spoon'.

But much of the work even at the top of the Civil Service is equally depressing. The amount of personal responsibility is very limited. An individual rarely takes a decision on his own partly because as the work gets divided up into smaller and smaller units the degree of overlaps increases. The job of a senior civil servant is not to take decisions but to consult others, to co – ordinate views, to produce pieces of paper which are agreed by everybody. The invention of the photocopying machine has reinforced this tendency with a vengeance. Now everybody who has even the slightest interest in any aspect of a subject will receive a copy of a paper and will in turn send copies of his comments, often only of marginal interest, to everybody else. So the mountain of paper accumulates.

The watchword is caution and the avoidance of failure. This system does however have one great advantage for the participants. It makes it very difficult to allocate responsibility to an individual when something goes wrong. But, even if it were possible, the ethos of the Civil Service is against openly allocating blame. That is contrary to the rules of the club, although the club does, of course, have discreet ways of dealing with the individual who it is decided should take the blame, as Sir Ian Bancroft, former Head of the Civil Service, explained:

If the advice was, as I assume it must have been, honestly given on the facts available...I don't think I myself would want to see a large label hung round that man's neck for the rest of his career, saying he gave the wrong advice on a particular subject. It will be apparent to his peers that he had given the wrong advice, and the grapevine in the Civil Service...is a fairly powerful one.[11]

The work of the top Civil Service is always conducted in unfailingly polite terms. No instructions are ever issued, instead they are couched in terms like 'I should be grateful if ...' The idea that Whitehall is just one big game is reflected in the language used. Civil Service prose is scattered with cricketing terms such as 'straight bat', 'googly', and comments on a draft are normally required by 'close of play'. One Deputy Secretary sitting in a departmental promotion board once described a young administrator as 'not Test standard; but a good county player'. He was promoted. Other sporting analogies are slightly less common, though 'par for the course' and 'own goal' are quite popular. Latin phrases occur fairly regularly, though the excessive use of French is limited to the Foreign Office where the tradition of elegant dispatches find – ing the *mot juste* to describe the *démarche* dies hard.

The Civil Service is a job for life. Unless performance is catastrophically bad nobody is sacked. In 1983 just 0.1% of the non – industrial Civil Service were retired early. The numbers in

senior grades are even lower. Each department usually has a quota
of jobs where people who are well over the top can be posted and
where it is hoped they will do little damage to the work of the
department. But the pay is the same, the job undemanding and life
is pleasant.

The Civil Service has gradually become more ossified. In 1920
Sir Warren Fisher was made Head of the Civil Service at the age of
forty, and a few years later Sir Horace Wilson was Permanent
Secretary at the Ministry of Labour at the age of thirty – nine. It is
now rare for anybody to be made a Permanent Secretary below
fifty. Promotion times have become slower. Before 1945 the majority of Assistant Secretaries took less than fourteen years to
reach that grade. Now 83% take more than fifteen years. Similarly
before 1945 22% of Under – Secretaries had taken less than nine-
teen years to reach the grade. Now only 6% do so. Promotion is a
matter of slowly working up the ladder, waiting your turn, with the
pace depending on the rate of retirement. The modern Civil Service sees this as a positive virtue, as Sir Ian Bancroft said:

> Of course one's got to have some general pattern, otherwise the
> able characters, not absolute fliers but the able characters, who
> ought to be able to expect a reasonable career in the Service
> would constantly get overtaken by the young fliers.[12]

The result is predictable. The safe , unimaginative people, those
lacking originality and new ways of looking at things, move steadily up the ladder. The idea that somebody young and brilliant could
be promoted out of turn is anathema, as Barbara Castle found out
in 1974 when she discussed with Sir Douglas Allen (then Head of
the Civil Service) who might replace Sir Philip Rogers as her Permanent Secretary at DHSS. Castle suggested one or two names of
younger people she had known in the Department of Employment. Allen at first reacted favourably. 'Then he had second
thoughts and wonders whether the older people in my department
might not resent being put under someone so young'.[13]

Notes

1 Joel Barnett, *Inside the Treasury* (London, 1982), pp. 16 – 19
2 P. M. Williams (ed.), *The Diary of Hugh Gaitskell 1945 – 56*
   (London, 1983), p. 117 (28 June 1949).
3 B. Castle, *The Castle Diaries, 1974 – 76* (London, 1984), pp. 49 – 50.
4 C. H. Sisson, *The Spirit of British Administration* (London, 1957).

5 Royal Commission on the Civil Service (1929–31), *Cmnd 3909,* *HMSO, London.*

6 H. E. Dale, *The Higher Civil Service of Great Britain* (London, 1941).

7 *Eleventh Report from the Expenditure Committee. The Civil Service* HC 535, Session 1976–7, Vol. III–I, Q.92, p. 74.

8 *Ibid.,* Vol. II–II, p. 483.

9 *Ibid.,* Vol, II–II, p. 626: Evidence by the Head of the Government Accountancy Service.

10 *Tribunal of Enquiry into the Crown Agents Affair,* HL 364, 1982.

11 H. Young and A. Sloman, *No Minister* (London 1982), p. 70.

12 *Ibid.*

13 *Castle Diaries, 1974–76,* pp. 198–3 (21 October 1974).

4.3 *Peter Hennessy*

The quality of Cabinet government

From 'The quality of Cabinet government in Great Britain', *Policy Studies,* Vol. 6, No. 2, October 1985, pp. 17-25 and 34-9.

... In the 1970s, as a Whitehall journalist with a historical background and an interest in political science, I found myself reading the Cabinet papers of the Attlee administration as each new batch was declassified and comparing the performance of the Labour governments of 1945-51 with those of Wilson 1974-76 and Callaghan 1976-79 which I was engaged in reporting. Wilson in particular did not shine in comparison. I was sufficiently impressed by the performance of 'the diminutive, monosyllabic former solicitor from Stanmore'[1] to co-author a study of his Cabinet Committee structure.

Nothing has happened in the interim to alter substantially the conclusion of *Mr Attlee's Engine Room* that:

> Perhaps the virtue most appreciated, with over 30 years of hindsight, is his sheer effectiveness. Late 1940s Britain like early 1980s Britain felt itself strapped for cash. Yet Attlee's Whitehall achieved things, substantial things, on very little money ... One way and another, Attlee looks better with every passing year — a kind of benevolent public school master, whose sense of duty and justice raised him above the sectional partisanship to class or party.[2]

The study's thesis was that Attlee built on the Whitehall machine constructed in World War II and used it to implement the Labour Party's reform programme. Lord Hunt of Tanworth, at the time a young official in the Dominions Office and later Cabinet Secretary under Heath, Wilson, Callaghan and Thatcher, offered a similar interpretation in his 1983 survey of what had happened to Cabinet government since Lloyd George and Hankey invented it in its modern form. Speaking of the machinery of government implications of Beveridge, Keynesian economics and Labour's programme of public ownership, he said:

The field of government activity and interest extended rapidly, and the size of the Cabinet with it; and at the same time Ministers found — particularly with an economy weakened by the war — that these new problems were both more complex and inter-related than they had perhaps expected. How then could one get the necessary co-ordination at ministerial level and make a reality of collective discussion and responsibility?

The answer was to develop the system of Cabinet Committees to reduce the load on the Cabinet by settling minor matters and, in other cases, sharpening up the issues for decision. Indeed it has been argued that 1945 to 1951 was government by committee — hundreds of them — rather than Government by Cabinet. The system worked remarkably smoothly.[3]

New material, both archival and interpretative, requires those judgements to be modified to some degree. First, internal Cabinet Office files suggest that Mr Attlee's engine room was not quite as clean a machine as I had portrayed it. In fact, within a year of the formation of the Labour Government, senior officials in the Cabinet Office, Treasury and Board of Trade had become seriously alarmed by the cumbersome nature of the organisation supporting the Attlee cabinet, the proliferation of committees and the prolix and indecisive performance of some ministers. Attlee took their concern seriously and a review of Cabinet machinery was commissioned which took place in the summer and autumn of 1946.

The initial impetus for the rethink came not from the officials but from Sir Stafford Cripps in the summer of 1946. Cripps, at that time President of the Board of Trade, had long had a penchant for machinery of government matters and had been active as a Minister in the wartime coalition on reconstruction committees established to consider the issue.[4] The beginning of the story is recorded in a minute exchanged between the two dominant figures in postwar Whitehall, Sir Edward Bridges, Head of the Civil Service and Permanent Secretary to the Treasury, and Sir Norman Brook, Secretary of the Cabinet. On July 5, 1946, Bridges wrote to Brook:

I happened to see Sir John Woods (Permanent Secretary to the Board of Trade) tonight and he told me that Sir Stafford Cripps had been reading the minutes of Cabinet committees during his absence (in India where he hab been for nearly four months trying to reach a settlement which would lead to independence) and had been depressed by the amount of time and energy taken up in the Ministerial Committees with the discussion of quite minor matters which individual Ministers ought to settle in their discretion. He asked whether anything could be done about this.[5]

Bridges reckoned that in every new administration, Ministers had a tendency in their first year 'to bring matters to the committees which with greater experience they would settle themselves'. Shortage of supplies was also forcing more decisions to be taken centrally. But he thought Attlee ought to consider the problem 'and send a little note to his colleagues or address some remarks to them in Cabinet about the working of the committee system'.[6]

Lower down the hierarchy and, apparently, quite independently of his seniors, the young William Armstrong (who was to head the Treasury in the 1960s and the Civil Service in the 1970s), as Brook's private secretary, was trying to make sense of the proliferation of committees, some of which had been inherited from the coalition and some created by the new government. There is a note of despair in his minute of July 19, 1946 to Alexander Johnston, under secretary in Herbert Morrison's Lord President's Office, about the contents of the Cabinet Committee Book, the Cabinet Office's instrument for tracking the growth of its machine:

Another point which has given me some concern is that the present book is supposed to be a directory of Cabinet Committees. So far as I know there is no definition of what constitutes a Cabinet Committee and, as the practice has grown, I believe there may be among the 70-odd Committees in the book some with less title to be treated as Cabinet Committees than some of the 700-odd interdepartmental committees of which we have no detailed information at all.

'The point is of some importance since a number of rules of procedure are growing to be applicable to Cabinet Committees and we ought to know where there is a real, useful distinction or whether it is merely the pragmatical difference that some are serviced by the Cabinet Office and some are not. If there is anything in the distinction I believe that the term Cabinet Committee ought to be kept for Mininsterial committees and perhaps for committees of officials directly subordinate to a ministerial committee; but I am far from certain that the distinction is worth making.'[7]

Back at the stratospheric level of government, Bridges pursued the problem of the performance of the Cabinet system with Attlee and recorded a note of the conversation which took place in Number Ten on July 26, 1946:

In a talk with the Prime Minister this morning he asked whether I thought too much time of Ministers was taken up by Committees and whether there were too many Committees. I said I thought a great deal of time was taken up with Committees. The [Parliamentary] recess would be a suitable moment for having an overhaul of the committee system and seeing whether any could be reduced. It might also be appropriate for him [the Prime Minister] to issue instructions to the Chairmen of Committees to see that time is not wasted in the discussion of irrelevant matters.

The Prime Minister also asked whether I thought that Ministers brought matters unnecessarily to the Cabinet. I said I thought there was a tendency to do this.[8]

Armstrong, meanwhile, was struggling doggedly to create some sort of classification system, a Domesday Book in miniature, for the Cabinet Committees. On July 23, 1946, he minuted W.S. Murrie, Brook's deputy, that:

I am attracted to the idea of a printed Directory of Committees in a number of parts:

I Standing Ministerial
II Ad Hoc Ministerial

III Standing Official
IV Ad Hoc Official

I should also be prepared to include in the appropriate sections, committees which, though not Cabinet Committees, in fact perform closely similar functions.[9]

At this stage the Bridges-Brook review of Cabinet procedure and the Armstrong exercise on committees came together. The need for a more efficient Cabinet machine was discussed in Number Ten on September 4 at a meeting between Attlee and Hugh Dalton, Chancellor of the Exchequer.[10] Attlee saw Bridges the following day. The Prime Minister told the Head of the Civil Service what he wanted as the ingredients of reform:

(1) When the Government was newly formed it was perhaps natural for many matters to be discussed in Ministerial Committees which, with growing experience, should now be settled by the individual ministers concern-

ed. Alternatively, if there are differences between Ministers, these can often be resolved by a meeting of two or three Ministers, if need be under the chairmanship of a Minister-without-Portfolio.

(2) Papers for Committees must be short and must contain a concise summary of the proposals put forward for consideration. It is the responsibility of all Ministers to see that papers are drawn up on these lines.

(3) Ministers when they come to Committees should assume that other Ministers have read their papers and time should not be spent on an oral regurgitation of what already appears in writing in the paper.

(4) Fewer papers should be taken at very short notice before there has been time for the Departments to comment on them.[11]

Brook proceeded to turn Attlee's proposals into the more statuesque prose of the standard Cabinet paper. Armstrong urged Brook to persuade Attlee to announce simultaneously the abolition of a number of Cabinet committees. Brook ruled this out: 'I do not, however, favour this suggestion — we could not adopt it without undertaking a review of the Cabinet Committee organisation and that always takes a substantial time, as so many Ministers and others have to be consulted. Nor do I think that there are at the moment Committees which cause unnecessary work.'[12]

Brook clearly thought this anti-committee mania was getting out of hand and minuted Bridges to this effect:

I should rather like to have an opportunity of putting to the Prime Minister some of the arguments *in favour* [Brook's italics] of handling business through Cabinet Committees. I suspect that at the moment he sees all the disadvantages and none of the advantages of committee work. I should like, in particular, to explain that if, as he himself desires, the size of the Cabinet is to be restricted, [it was 20-strong, more than twice the size of Churchill's War Cabinet which oscillated between five and nine,[13]] the Committee structure affords a useful means of preserving the collective responsibility of Ministers as a whole.

Another point which should not be overlooked is that Committee papers are read by a good many Ministers who do not attend the meetings, and these papers are often the only means they have of keeping themselves abreast of developments in policy.[14]

Bridges agreed. It is not clear which of the pair put these points to Attlee. But somebody did. The ploy worked. The Cabinet paper circulated on September 26, 1946, was in the Prime Minister's name but was imbued with the Cabinet Secretary's philosophy. In addition to classic injunctions such as 'I look for a marked reduction in the number of problems put forward for discussion in Ministerial Committees' in the terse Major Attlee style, the paper contains a passage which is pure Brook:

The Cabinet Committee system has a valuable part to play in the central machinery of government, both in relieving the pressure on the Cabinet itself and in helping to give practical effect to the principle of collective responsibility at times when the Cabinet does not include all Ministers in charge of Departments.[15]

Attlee's 1946 directive did not solve some of the more important machinery of government problems of his administration. It needed a sterling crisis and the ministerial reshuffle caused by Morrison's demotion as economic overlord after the convertibility crisis of August 1947, and the second ministerial reshuffle triggered by Dalton's resignation the following November, before the Cabinet machine adapted itself adequately to tackle the fundamental problem confronting the Government with the creation of the Economic Policy Committee. Under Attlee's chairmanship EPC became the most important Cabinet Committee in the system, where all the big economic issues — domestic and overseas — were handled.[16] Armstrong, by this time back in the Treasury, had the belated satisfaction of witnessing a modest committee cull.[17]

These internal Office organisation files in the CAB 21 series at the PRO do not seem to have been used by previous commentators on British Cabinet government. They are an important source for two reasons: they indicate that the overload problem has been a constant since World War II and is not a feature of the Sixties, Seventies and Eighties; and that even what has come to be regarded as the most efficiently run administration since 1945 had serious difficulties in the handling of business.

Recent material also illuminates another intractable problem — the quality of the pool of talent from which ministers are chosen — something no amount of reboring the Cabinet machine can remedy. Sir Alec Cairncross, a former Chief Economic Adviser to the Treasury, in his highly regarded new book, *Years of Recovery,* heaps praise on the Attlee governments at the end of his study: 'Whether one tries to look forward from 1945 or backwards from forty years later, those years appear in retrospect, and rightly so, as years when the government knew where it wanted to go and led the country with an understanding of what was at stake.'[18] Yet even he concedes:

... the economic problems encountered by the government were not, as a rule, those which it had expected. Equally, the solutions to the problems were rarely of the government's devising. There were exceptions, as when Bevin grasped at what became the Marshall Plan. But more commonly ministers were the reluctant pupils of their officials. On one economic issue after another — the American Loan, the coal crisis, the dollar problem, devaluation, the European Payments Union — they were slow to grasp the true options of policy and had great difficulty in reaching sensible conclusions.[19]

Hugh Gaitskell, an economics don and wartime civil servant, elected to Parliament in 1945, who enjoyed a rapid rise up the hierarchy from backbencher to Chancellor of the Exchequer in six years, illustrates with his diary entry for October 14, 1947 (when he was Minister of Fuel and Power) just how little impact Attlee's directive of a year before had had on the performance of individuals:

Sometimes Cabinet meetings horrify me because of the amount of rubbish talked by some Ministers who come there after reading briefs which they do not understand. I do not know how this can be avoided except perhaps by getting more things settled at the official level, and when they cannot be settled there having the issues presented plainly to ministers.

Also, I believe the Cabinet is too large. A smaller Cabinet, mostly of non-Departmental ministers, would really be able to listen and understand more easily and hear the others arguing the matter out.[20]

But it was Sir Norman Brook who identified what to 1980s eyes is the most startling of the missing links in the Cabinet process of the late Forties — the lack of any systematic attempt to review long term public expenditure trends and the future spending implications of current policies. In a file graphically labelled 'Cabinet Procedure. Memorandum on classes of business not regarded as appropriate for Cabinet discussion' is a minute from Brook to Bridges dated April 21, 1950, two months after Labour had been returned to power with a slim majority of six and two months before the Korean War stimulated a huge increase in defence spending. Brook wrote:

It is curious that in modern times the Cabinet, though it has always insisted on considering particular proposals for developments of policy and their cost, has never thought it necessary to review the development of expenditure under the Civil Estimates as a whole.

It is remarkable that the present Government have never reflected upon the great increase in public expenditure, and the substantial change in its pattern, which has come about during the past five years in consequence of their policies in the field of the social services.[21]

Brook added that his analysis confirmed the importance of the proposal to submit twice yearly forecasts to the Cabinet on the trend of future spending, He urged that a review procedure should be devised to assist ministers to ponder 'its distribution between the various services'. Very little seems to have come of the initiative until the Treasury created something along these lines for the Conservative Chancellor, R.A. Butler, some five years later.

By the time Labour left office in October 1951, its Cabinet machine — what might be called the Attlee-Brook model — was enormous. It consisted of 148 Standing Committees and 313 Ad Hoc Committees...

Conviction Cabinet, 1979-85

It must be a convicton government. As Prime Minister I could not waste time having any internal arguments.
Mrs Margaret Thatcher, February 1979.[22]

She cannot see an institution without hitting it with her handbag.
Julian Critchley, MP on Mrs Thatcher, 1982.[23]

I take your point about frankness! That's what Cabinets are for, and lively discussions usually lead to good decisions.
Mrs Thatcher to Mr James Prior, August 1984.[24]

Whatever views political scientists may hold of Mrs Thatcher, they owe her a great deal. Her style, her methods and her personality have enabled her to work a miracle in one area of national life at least. She has done the impossible and made the study of public administration interesting! As for Cabinet government, the stress upon it had not gone unnoticed outside Whitehall even before Mrs Thatcher took her famous handbag to it. The corrosive effect on governments of managing decline had obliged political scientists to reformulate the old examination standby, complete with standard quote from Walter Bagehot, about which bits of the system were 'dignified' and which 'efficient'. In the Sixties the debate hovered around the matter of whether Cabinet had joined Monarch in the dignified bit, leaving Prime Ministerial power holding sway over the efficient.[25] By the turn of the decade, it was more to the point to wonder if any particle was efficient. Full circle came at a meeting of officers of the Political Studies Association and Fleet Street political correspondents in the Royal Commonwealth Society on December 5, 1984 when Peregrine Worsthorne, commentator for *The Sunday Telegraph,* declared that 'these days the only efficient part of the British constitution is the Monarchy'.[26]

Consistency cannot be expected of politicians. But how can one reconcile Mrs Thatcher's declaration of the age of conviction government some four months before entering No 10 and her effusive endorsement of frankness and lively discussion in the Cabinet Room in her letter accepting the resignation of Jim Prior? Her hymn to frankness caused a great deal of harmless pleasure to those Thatcher-watchers with ringside seats in Whitehall; though it struck her former Cabinet colleague, David Howell, 'with some foreboding because I feel that the word "lively" discussion is a code word for "argument" and I don't regard high-pitched argument as the best means of reaching decisions.'[27]

At first glance the verbal contrast between the iron cabinets of 1979 and the frankness cabinets of 1984 would imply that experience of government changed Mrs Thatcher from a no-argument conviction leader into a classic practitioner of Cabinet government encouraging free-ranging, collective discussion. The evidence suggests that this is not so. Take first the raw statistics of Cabinet business; compared to the Attlee-Churchill era, with Cabinet papers per year in the four hundreds, the total is well down. The CP (84) series, as it will be classified in the Cabinet Office's Confidential Library, reached to between 60 and 70 papers last year, or about one sixth of the flow of the early fifties. Could it be that the business is being done in Cabinet Committee? As we have seen, Attlee accumulated 148 standing and 313 ad hoc groups in $6\frac{1}{4}$ years and Churchill 137 and 109 respectively in $3\frac{1}{2}$. The figures for Eden, Macmillan and Home remain a complete mystery and one which the current Cabinet Secretary refuses to resolve. Thanks to Mrs Castle's Diary, we have some intelligence on Wilson Mark 1. Elected in October 1964, he had by early 1969 (i.e. after $4\frac{1}{4}$ years) reached his 236th ad hoc group. The Heath era is another unknown. Wilson Mark II, between March 1974 and March 1976, ran up to somewhere around 120 ad hoc committees.[28] According to his *The Governance of Britain,* he had settled down to one Cabinet meeting a week when Parliament was sitting.[29] Allowing for Parliamentary recesses and the occasional crisis necessitating more frequent gatherings, he was probably somewhere around 45 Cabinet meetings a year, about half the frequency of the busier periods of the Attlee and Churchill administrations. Callaghan in the two years between April 1976 and April 1979 commissioned about 160 ad hoc committees, a similar growth rate to Attlee.[30] Judged by the Cabinet Committee criterion, Mrs Thatcher has done exceedingly well. She has about 30 standing committees and 115 ad hocs in just over six years.[31] So Cabinet *and* Cabinet Committee discussion is down.

Does that indicate that the load has diminished in parallel? Has Britain against the odds re-entered a period of small government? In philosophical terms the answer is 'yes'; in practical terms 'no'. The reason has been stated frequently by Sir John Hoskyns. In the short-run, disengaging from state activity is just as difficult and time consuming as getting into it — if not more so. Privatisation, like nationalisation, imposes a stiff workload and absorbs a great deal of Parliamentary time.

So, where is the business being done? A fair amount is conducted by ministerial correspondence, a perfectly acceptable method in constitutional terms. The Franks Report on the Falklands gives an indication of just how much this goes on. One reason, for example, why the Falklands issue figured so infrequently on the agenda of the Cabinet's Oversea and Defence Committee before the Argentine invasion of April 1982 is that Lord Carrington, then Foreign and Commonwealth Secretary, disliked bringing FCO business before committee meetings of his colleagues.[32] Another swathe of high-level business is tackled by Mrs Thatcher in ad hoc groups which fall outside Sir Robert Armstrong's Cabinet Committee Book. The 'Economic Seminar' was her first and most important. Such bodies reflect the PM's preferred method of working. She uses them both for quick fixes, such as the rapid climbdown on increased parental contributions to student fees in December 1984, and for handling medium-term matters, like the outcome of the joint DOE-Treasury Efficiency Unit review of the urban programme earlier that year.[33]

The pattern varies but is often along these lines. Mrs Thatcher will ask a particular Cabinet colleague to prepare a paper on a particular issue just for her, not for the Cabinet or a Cabinet committee. This explains why the tally of Cabinet Papers is so low. The Minister is summoned to Number Ten with his back-up team. He sits across the table from Mrs Thatcher and her team which can be a blend of people from the Downing Street Private Office, the Policy Unit, the Cabinet Office and one or two personal advisers. She then, in the words of one insider, proceeds to 'act as judge and jury in her own cause'.[34] It is this practice more than anything else which causes those on the inside to speak of 'a devaluation of Cabinet government' and her 'presidential style'.[35]

The build up of leaks and stories create a cumulative impression of an overmighty premiership. Here are three scenes from Cabinet and neo-Cabinet (those unofficial groups) life in 1984.

* Senior civil servants called to a 'judge and jury' session have their own four-minute warning system. If asked by your secretary of state to speak to the departmental paper, you have four minutes to explain it, however complicated the subject matter, to present the choices and to add a touch of heterodoxy. Beyond that point, unless her interest is awakened, Mrs Thatcher's eyes glaze over. To continue is to jeopardise future promotion.[36]

* It is January 1984. The place is Number Ten. The forum is the Cabinet's Overseas and Defence Committee. The subject is the possibility of an attempt to normalise relations with Argentina, not the sovereignty of the Falklands which is the Great Unmentionable of mid-Eighties Whitehall. Sir Geoffrey Howe is four minutes into the Foreign Office paper on the need to open exploratory talks with the Alfonsin Government. Mrs Thatcher cuts in 'Geoffrey, I know what you're going to recommend. And the answer is "No!" ' End of item — Nobody argues with the boss.[37] One permanent secretary has called her 'the most commanding prime minister in recent memory'.[38]

* Seasoned Cabinet Minister walks into the Commons Tea Room late on a Thursday morning. 'What are you doing here?' asks a Tory backbencher. 'I thought you'd still be in Cabinet'. 'Cabinet?' replied the Minister. 'Oh, we

don't have those any more. We have a lecture by Madam.
Its government-by-Cabinet-Committee now. Half the
decisions I read about in the newspaper.'[39]

But has Mrs Thatcher really handbagged the British Cabinet
system into a shape that is no longer recognisable? Is she on the
way to becoming a President within a Monarchy? In some weeks
and on some issues, the answer would appear to be 'yes'. But the
obituaries are premature. For a start, her style is not collegiate.
But to call it 'presidential' is to exaggerate.

Senior officials in a position to judge recent holders of prime
ministerial office reckon Cabinet government is largely intact.
They point to a range of issues where Mrs Thatcher's personal in-
stincts are constrained by the knowledge of what Cabinet will not
take, for example on Northern Ireland, the closed shop, public expenditure, the National Health Service, student loans, rates and
the BBC.[40] And, in the period of her greatest trauma — the invasion and retaking of the Falklands — Cabinet government was
restored. As one Cabinet Minister who was not a member of the
'War Cabinet' put it, 'She had to carry us on every major decision.
That Task Force would never have sailed without Cabinet approval.'[41] And yet, the system is not performing as it should. It
may be that overload has obliged successive prime ministers to
modify the conventions — Wilson with his Inner Cabinets, Callaghan with his 'Economic Seminar', with Mrs Thatcher being the
most overt and energetic about it.

One experienced figure reckons the Thatcher method is more
efficient than the traditional, collective model and asks: 'Does it
matter that temporarily we don't have Cabinet government, that
we have presidential government? Does it matter in Parliament
that the Minister is the monkey? The number of Cabinet Committee meetings is not necessarily an index of efficiency. We have a
form of presidential government in which she operates like a
sovereign in her court.'[42]

Sufficient people think such manipulation of the Cabinet conventions does matter. Many experienced figures reckon that, Mrs
Thatcher apart, the system has been crumbling for years and that
the present Prime Minister had done no more than to recognise
this and to act unilaterally in attempting her preferred solution.

Notes

1 Peter Hennessy and Andrew Arends, *Mr Attlee's Engine Room: Cabinet Committee Structure and the Labour governments, 1945-51.* Strathclyde Papers on Government and Politics No. 26, 1983.
2 *Ibid.,* pp. 2-3.
3 Hunt, 'Cabinet Strategy and Management'.
4 See J.. M. Lee *Reviewing the Machinery of Government 1942 — 1952, An Essay on the Anderson Committee and its successors,* 1977, available from Professor J. M. Lee, Department of Politics, University of Bristol.
5 Public Record Office CAB 21/1701, 'Organisation of Cabinet Committees, 1946-47', Bridges to Brook, July 5, 1946.
6 *Ibid.*
7 PRO CAB 21/1703, 'Cabinet Committee Book', Armstrong to Johnston, July 10, 1946.
8 PRO CAB 21/1701.
9 PRO CAB 21/1703.
10 *Ibid.*
11 *Ibid.,* Bridges to Brook, September 5, 1946.
12 *Ibid.*
13 Alec Cairncross, *Years of Recovery: British Economic Policy, 1945-51,* Methuen, 1985, p. 49.
14 PRO CAB 21/1701. Brook to Bridges, September 13, 1946.
15 PRO CAB 21/170. CP (46) 357. Cabinet Committees. Note by the Prime Minister. Spetember 26, 1946.
16 PRO CAB 21/1702. CP (47) 280. Attlee informs the Cabinet of the new Committee arrangements. For the pre-EPC weakness see Cairncross, *Years of Recovery,* Chapter Three.
17 PRO CAB 21/1702. Brook's Note of a conversation with Attlee which took place on September 11, 1947. In CP (47) 280 Attlee informs Ministers of the abolition of 14 Cabinet Committees.
18 Cairncross, *Years of Recovery,* p. 509.
19 *Ibid,* p. 20.
20 Philip M. Williams (editor), *The Diary of Hugh Gaitskell, 1945-1956,* Cape, 1983, p. 36
21 PRO CAB 21/1626.
22 Interview with Kenneth Harris, *The Observer,* February 25, 1979.
23 *The Times,* June 21, 1982.
24 The PM's reply to Mr Prior's resignation letter was reported in *The Times* on September 1, 1984.
25 The most accessible method for becoming familiar with the 1960s debate is to read the protagonists — John Mackintosh, Richard Crossman and George Jones — in Anthony King (Editor) *The British Prime Minister,* Macmillan, 1969.
26 The author was present.
27 Howell, 'The Demanding Mistresses'.
28 Private information.
29 Private information.

30   Wilson, *The Governance of Britain,* p. 85.
31   Private information.
32   Private information. For an excellent survey of Mrs Thatcher's Cabinet Committee structure and for a comparison with other western nations see Brian Hogwood and Tom Mackie, 'The United Kingdom: Decision Sifting in a Secret Garden' in Hogwood and Mackie (editors), *Unlocking the Cabinet: Cabinet Stucture in Perspective,* Sage, 1985.
33-42   Private information.

4.4 *Geoffrey Fry*

The Thatcher Government and
The Civil Service

From 'The development of the Thatcher Government's grand strategy for
the Civil Service: a public policy perspective', *Public Administration,* Vol.
62, Autumn 1984, pp. 325-35.

... That the Thatcher Government saw the higher civil service as a
potential opponent was not as unreasonable a position as some
observers chose to portray it. The service had got above its station.
Sir Antony Part, for instance, revealed in 1980 that

the Civil Service always hopes that it's influencing Ministers towards the
common ground. Now that's not to say influencing them towards some
piece of ground which the Civil Service has itself constructed; it is the
Civil Service trying to have a sense of what can succeed for Britain, and
trying to exercise its influence on Ministers to try to see that they do cap-
ture the common ground with their ideas, from whatever origin they start
(Jessel 1980, 775).

This 'common ground' was not 'the centre' because that was 'literally
half-way between the two poles, while the common ground is the ground
on which, or to which the majority of people can be persuaded to move.
You have to remember that in recent times neither of the main political
parties has been elected by a majority of the electorate (ibid)'.
   Unlike the higher civil service, though, these political parties did present themselves to the electorate, and, under the electoral system, the
party which won the most seats could expect to have the authority to form
the Government, and to have the opportunity to implement its programme. That the civil service has the right to guide Governments
towards 'the common ground' seems questionable. What is this common
ground to consist of? In the days of the Keynesian consensus the agenda
could be fairly easily established but its collaspe had led to the radicaliza

zation of British politics. Sir John Hoskyns, at one time an adviser to Mrs Thatcher, was right when he said that the civil service has no legitimate role in acting as constitutional ballast. If polarization is a fact of political life then seeking the common ground is not an a-political position.[1] There is survey evidence that, in general, Conservative policy attitudes commanded wide support outside the ranks of Tory voters in 1979.[2] If there was a common ground, the Conservative Government elected then seemed to be occupying much of it.

Yet there was discord between that Government and some of its leading officials. In the central area of economic policy the Thatcher Government did not accept what Sir William Armstrong had called the Treasury's neo-Keynesian framework of economic thinking (*The Times* 15.11.76). When the Government sought to reconsider its financial commitments in the area of social provision a series of leaks of confidential documents occurred. Indeed, at times, the Labour Party's 1983 election campaign relied heavily on such material. After the Conservative victory, Sir Robert Armstrong, the Head of the Home Civil Service, in a letter to all 40 permanent secretaries which was itself leaked, wrote that higher civil servants must have been the main source of the leaks which could only have been deliberately perpetrated with the object of embarrassing the Tory Government. Sir Robert said that such behaviour displayed a corrupt sense of values: those civil servants who could not act loyally towards the Government of the day should resign (*Guardian* 31.8.83). Only those with a taste for casuistry could easily quarrel with that position. Civil service affection for the Keynesian consensus — the common ground in disguise — was not necessarily disinterested. The scale of machinery needed to sustain that consensus provided higher civil servants with generous opportunities for advancement and for interesting work — 'fine tuning' the economy and so forth. Cutting back on the role of the state, as the Heath Government had been initially committed to do, and at which the Thatcher Government has made a more sustained effort, threatens those arrangements. Thus far, at least, the Thatcher Government has shown no inclination to implement radical proposals of the type made by Sir John Hoskyns for a clear-out of the higher civil service and its displacement by politically appointed outsiders, preferably from the private sector.[3] Nevertheless, the unprecedented Bancroft dismissal, the chopping back of the career hierarchy, and the even tual extension of the MINIS approach — of which more later — were clear indications of the Thatcher Government's determination to assert political control over the service in its quest for greater efficiency in support of sound money policies.

Assault on the pay and promotion system

The Thatcher Government inherited a heavily unionized civil service, one in which the non-industrial element had grown during the Keynesian era, in which the Civil Service Department had its own central personnel department presiding over arrangements whereby civil servants, while normally enjoying security of tenure, in principle had their salary scales primarily based on 'fair comparisons' with outside pay, together with index-linked pensions. With inflation rampant and with unemployment rising too, and in a political context in which 'where will the money come from?' was once again a pertinent question to ask, what were seen as the service's cosy pay and promotion system and privileges were bound to be targets for an 'economizing' Government. The Scott Inquiry of 1980-81 into the value of pensions failed to supply the Conservative Government with the condemnation of index-linked pensions which it must have hoped for.[4] However, this was one of the few setbacks which the Thatcher Government experienced in a campaign which witnessed the ending of the 'fair comparisons' salary system, the defeat of a civil service strike, the demise of the Civil Service Department, and all to the accompaniment of cuts in civil service numbers.

The Conservative Government was better placed than its predecessors to secure a reduction in numbers because, unlike them, it was prepared to envisage reduced functions. As regards the open structure (then defined in terms of under-secretary and above), the Wardale chain of command review, completed in 1981, while recommending that no grade at that level should be abolished and noting that the open structure was already being reduced in size, concluded that 'there are unnecessary posts ... a number of Open Structure posts can be removed and should be' (Wardale 1981, 35). As Table 1 shows, there was scope for 'rationalization' of the home civil service in 1979. The growth in the size of the administration group in the 1970s was remarkable; and the expansion that took place, for instance, at senior principal, principal, senipal, senior executive officer, higher executive offi-

Table 1: Civil service staff numbers

Grades/Groups	1.4.70	1.4.79	1.4.82	% Increase 1970-79	% Cut 1979-82
Non-Industrial Civil Service	493000	565815	527970	14.8	6.7
Open Structure	664	823	743	23.9	9.7
Administrative Group	243879	299882	284155	23.0	5.2
Assistant Secretary	1048	1245	1084	18.8	12.9
Senior Principal	502	812	694	61.8	14.5
Principal	3195	4608	4146	40.2	10.0
Senior Executive Officer	5789	8489	7676	46.6	9.5
Higher Executive Officer	16866	25198	23941	49.4	5.0
Executive Officer (inc Local Officer 1)	46305	62479	61538	34.9	1.5
Clerical Officer/Clerical Assistant					
(inc Local Officer 2)	170174	197051	185076	15.8	6.1
Science Group and Related Grades	17970	17284	15784	-3.8	8.7
Deputy Chief Scientific Officer	177	205	191	15.8	6.8
Senior Principal Scientific Officer	579	716	706	23.7	1.4
Principal Scientific Officer	1898	2477	2303	30.5	7.0
Senior Scientific Officer	3485	3734	3421	7.1	8.4
Higher Scientific Officer	4179	4072	3750	-2.6	7.9
Scientific Officer/Asst Scientific Officer	7652	6080	5413	-20.5	11.0
Profession and Technology Group and					
Related Grades	40235	41114	36728	2.2	10.7
Director B (introduced 1.4.72)	—	164	143	—	12.8
Superintending Grades	485	676	628	39.4	7.1
Principal P and T Officer	1956	2515	2359	28.6	6.2
P and T Officer I	4818	5865	5483	21.7	8.5
P and T Officer II	7688	8690	7967	13.0	8.3
P and T Officer III	11533	11836	10477	2.6	11.5
P and T Officer IV	13755	11368	9671	-17.4	14.9

Source: IPCS Bulletin, August 1983, p. 9.

cer and executive officer levels was suggestive of slack standards of staff inspection and of 'grade drift' in the face of successive incomes policies.

The application of such incomes policies had been a factor in the overt radicalization of the civil service union movement, which had staged its first official strike in 1973 in response to the Heath Government's 'interference' in civil service pay determination, and which in 1979 had joined in the public sector disruption that helped to undermine the Callaghan Labour Government. The Thatcher Government did not intend to have an explicit incomes policy, but its application of cash limits had the same effect on a service normally enjoying security of tenure. When the theory of sound money had dominated economic thinking before, civil service salaries had been decided by a 'formula' devised by the Tomlin Royal Commission of 1929-31 which was essentially a compromise with the market (Royal Commission on the Civil Service 1931). This formula had continued to be applied until the Priestley Royal Commission of 1953-55 recommended changed arrangements, which reflected more expansionary times and the contemporary fashion for completely rejecting market economics in favour of fair pay.[5] Under the Priestley formula, civil service pay was primarily based on 'fair comparison' with outside rates, taking into account internal relatives, with provision for compensation for inflation (Royal Commission on the Civil Service 1955, paras 87-32). Special pay machinery was set up for the higher civil service,[6] and the Civil Service Pay Research Unit was established for the main body of civil servants. This Unit assembled the data and excluded ministers from what eventually became an annual pay cycle until near the end when they were presented with the prospective salary bill (Ibid paras 133-185; Civil Service Pay Research Unit Board 1979, 11; Civil Service Department 1981, 28). How governments were going to find the money had not been deemed a problem by the Priestley Commission, making its recommendations at a time when Keynesianism seemed to be going so well: but ministers at least came to see things differently when the economic situation deteriorated later. Incomes policies postponed the payments, a practice which according to the civil service union leader, W. L. Kendall, constituted the 'brutal robbery' of his members (*Red Tape* 1969, 69). But such policies did not affect the entitlement to fair salaries. The Thatcher Government was more concerned with the plight of taxpayers and of its own need to find the money; and, in October 1980, by declining to implement some expensive pay research findings, and thus unilaterally tearing up the civil service pay agreement, that Government dispensed with the Priestley pay system.

The Conservative Government's behaviour led directly to the civil service strike, which began with a 24 hour stoppage on 9 March 1981, and lasted for 21 weeks until 30 July, when the unions were forced to concede defeat. Aside from a further one day stoppage on 1 April, and a half day stoppage on 14 April — both less well observed than that of 9 March — the Strike was prosecuted by selective action. The unions, often led by radicals even in the more amiable days of traditional Whitleyism, seemed to have been anticipating a fight with the Thatcher Government from the election onwards. The establishment of a Council of Civil Service Unions in May 1980 in place of the national staff side appeared to be at least partly motivated by recognition of the need for a stronger central organization should a confrontation occur.[7] When the strike came, the CCSU strategy was to emphasize the disruption of defence establishments (when asked about the danger to Britain's nuclear deterrent, W. L. Kendall replied: I'll be on the end of a phone if anybody wants to ring me up about some great invasion' [*The Bulletin* 1981, 126]), and interference with revenue collection and the gathering of statistics. This was widely said to be a sophisticated strategy, and it certainly seemed well planned. Nevertheless, there were also obvious reasons why, despite the Kendall-style rhetoric, it was the only one available to the CCSU: namely, the lack of support for more sustained, extensive, incisive action from the public, the Trades Union Congress, and, it was feared, probably most union members. At a time of rising unemployment, outside sympathy for civil servants, who had job security and who many might well have regarded as striking for still better pay deals, was always bound to be minimal. The CCSU strikes did interfere with the issue of passports and, for a time, they disrupted airports. Generally, though, the CCSU's approach was aimed at not antagonizing the public, which would certainly have occurred if the unions had gone beyond halting computer operations and had stopped social security payments. The TUC, moreover, ruled out action which would hurt the old, the sick, and the unemployed and, where appropriate, emergency benefit procedures ensured that the payments were made.. In return for this restraint, all that the TUC leadership did was to express general support, and make gestures like declining to cross a picket line to go to an NEDC meeting, and referring the dispute to the International Labour Organization. So, when W. L. Kendall said that the CCSU was going to 'put the boot in' with its programme of selective strikes (*The Times* 10.3.81), that was exactly what the unions did not dare do. While Lord Soames, the Minister responsible for the Civil Service Department, was said to favour compromise, Mrs Thatcher and her immediate allies in the Con-

servative Government proved determined to enforce a surrender
on the part of the civil service unions, and effectively secured one
at the end of July 1981. In the meantime, the Thatcher Government had appointed the Megaw Inquiry into civil service pay in
June, which was given the brief of devising a successor to the
Priestley pay system. In its report, 13 months later, the Megaw
Committee came up with a compromise with the market resembling a modernized Tomlin formula', the 'normal' application of
which was designed to bring a substantial block of public expenditure more consistently within ministerial control (HM Treasury
1982, 90).

While the Megaw Committee had been deliberating, Mrs Thatcher had dismissed Lord Soames, and then in November 1981,
towards the end of the year in which conventional wisdom believed the U turn had come, her Government suddenly struck again at
the service and its unions by abolishing the Civil Service Department. An earlier internal review had stressed the difficulties of
changing the post-Fulton arrangements of a division at the centre
between the Treasury and the Civil Service Department. The
House of Commons' Treasury and Civil Service Committee had
come down against change (Treasury and Civil Service Committee
1981, VII), and in February 1981 a White Paper had recorded the
Government's decision to leave things alone, at least for the immediate future (HMSO 1981, para 2). 'I've never known a
business organisation with two headquarters at opposite ends of
the street. It's crazy', Sir Derek Rayner pronounced (Sunday Telegraph 1.2.81). The Thatcher Government's ambition seemed to be
to make the civil service as much like a business organization as
possible, and the dictates of sound money indicated the desirabili-
ty of ending the division at the centre and formally restoring
Treasury predominance. The CSD's 'pusillanimous' behaviour
during the civil service strike provided the opportunity to kill it
off. Mrs Thatcher — 'Madame Guillotine', according to *The
Times* (13.11.81) — played the part of the CSD's executioner with
some zest:

setting up the Civil Service Department 13 years ago had a number of advantages compared with the situation as it existed before. But it had one
consequence whose disadvantages have become increasingly apparent
over time. It divorced central responsibility for the control of manpower
from responsibility for the control of government expenditure. I judge
that the balance of advantage now lies in favour of consolidating the

CSD's manpower control responsibilities with the central allocation and control of all resources, and to make the Treasury responsible for control over civil service manpower, pay, superannuation, allowances and for the Central Computer and Telecommunications Agency.

She could have added the civil service catering organization too. The staff concerned were transferred to the Treasury, as was the minister of state, who would answer in the House of Commons for the whole range of civil service matters. The Prime Minister emphasized that:

it remains my view that there should not be a total merger of the Treasury and the CSD. The efficiency of the civil service in carrying out its functions and the selection and development of civil servants are as important to the Government as the control of public expenditure. The machinery of government should make special provision for this, since it is a subject in which any Prime Minister is bound to take a close personal interest. I shall therefore continue to be Minister for the Civil Service and to be responsible for the organization, management and overall efficiency of the Home Civil Service and for policy on recruitment, training and other personnel management matters.

The Chancellor of the Duchy of Lancaster was to discharge these responsibilities on a day-to-day basis, and to answer in the House of Lords for the whole range of civil service matters. Mrs Thatcher said that:

the staff involved in these functions will work alongside the Cabinet Office in a new Management and Personnel Office. Sir Robert Armstrong will be Permanent Secretary of this Office and will also continue, as Secretary of the Cabinet, to head the Cabinet Office. He will be assisted on the business of the new office by a second Permanent Secretary.

The administrative changes dated from 16 November 1981 and — the sting in the tail of the announcement — they meant the early retirement of Sir Ian Bancroft and his Second Permanent Secretary at the CSD, Sir John Herbecq. Bancroft was replaced by Sir Robert Armstrong and the Treasury's Sir Douglass Wass as Joint

Heads of the Home Civil Service, (HC 1981), with Armstrong continuing as sole Head on the latter's retirement in April 1983. The Management and Personnel Office was brought within the Cabinet Office in June 1983.

The demise of the CSD predictably outraged the civil service unions. Their Council commented:

So, the CSD has gone. After 13 years of somewhat precarious existence, the CSD has been abolished and its functions distributed between the Treasury and the Cabinet Office. The CSD's last day of operation was, appropriately enough, Friday the 13th ... With it, one must regretfully record, went the last vestiges of the Fulton Report — for ... a return to the pre-Fulton regime is clearly envisaged. Nobody can seriously believe, for example, that the Treasury will be *more* generous on civil service pay. Equally, it is naive to believe that, in the quest for 'greater efficiency' (which really means stepping up the tempo for the galley-slaves) personnel management, as Fulton envisaged it, will get a look in. The possibility of a return to the Dark Ages is indicated, and nobody in the civil service should have any illusions about the implications (*The Bulletin* 1981, 153).

The unions, possibly punch-drunk after their defeat in the civil service strike, credited their opponents with a more coherent programme than was actually being pursued. The civil service's pay and promotion system had been attacked: but the career service had survived and in a form which still made it doubtful that the search for 'greater efficiency' would result in radical change.

The financial management initiative

The Thatcher Government's drive for a more efficient civil service was eventually translated into something resembling a long term strategy, based on the example set by Michael Heseltine when he was Secretary of State for the Environment. Knowledge of private sector management practice, together with his experience as Minister for Aerospace, led Heseltine to introduce into the DOE in 1979 a management information system for ministers (MINIS) which would enable him to be aware of 'who does what, why and what does it cost?' In that Department. His need for such information was understandable, given that in 1981, for instance, he had to deal with no less than 48 under-secretaries. In addition, a Rayner inquiry conducted by an official, Christopher Joubert, devised an organizational structure which divided the DOE into 120 responsibility units or cost centres, each of which had an annual budget to cover running costs, including those for staff. A computerized management information system told managers at all levels how expenditure was going against plan and a central budget unit oversaw the system and was to conduct systematic reviews (on a three yearly cycle covering the whole department) of cost centre budgets. The other departments seemed less impressed with developments in the DOE than bodies like the Treasury and

Civil Service Committee. The MOD, for example, was clear that it preferred its own cost control system which was called ABC (Acquisition, Buffer, Consumption). Its Permanent Under-Secretary, Sir Frank Cooper, told the Committee that in such matters the MOD tended to look at its counterparts in other Western countries and not at Whitehall developments. Heseltine introduced MINIS into the MOD when he became Secretary of State for Defence, and other departments were soon required to follow suit.[8]

The universalization of the MINIS and Joubert systems throughout the main central government departments formed the Thatcher Government's 'grand strategy' for securing an efficient civil service — the financial management initiative (FMI) which was launched in May 1982. The FMI's aim was described as being to promote in each department an organisation and a system in which managers at all levels had:

(a) a clear view of their objectives, and means to assess, and wherever possible measure, outputs or performance in relation to those objectives;
(b) well-defined responsibility for making the best use of their resources, including a critical scrutiny of output and value for money; and
(c) The information (particularly about costs), the training and access to expert advice which they need to exercise their responsibilities effectively (Treasury and Civil Service Committee 1982, 5; 21).

The Minister for the Civil Service, Barney Hayhoe, later stated that the FMI meant a push to greater decentralisation and delegation down the line, which will represent a highly significant change in the culture of the Civil Service ... Recruitment, training, promotion, prospects and practice will all be affected (HC 1982). The MPO's supporting review of personnel work in the civil service — the Cassels Report — was published in July 1983, followed two months later by the publication of the departments' plans for implementing the FMI strategy (HM Treasury 1983, 17).

The recent history of British central government is littered with failed institutional developments and failed attempts to 'rationalize' its procedures — PESC and PAR and PPB.. Why should the FMI succeed? In its favour, when launched, was political commitment, especially at Prime Ministerial level — the application of 'the clout'. Essentially the CSD was supposed to achieve the results now expected from the FMI, but was not able to do so. Richard Wilding, who was personally involved, suggested that:

while finance was the responsibility of the Treasury and management was the responsibility of the CSD, financial management was apt to fall down the crack between the two. The CSD did its best — and not without success — to promote management accounting and internal audit, but mainly in a consulting and advisory mode. It was not until the redistribution of functions in 1981 that the leading responsibility for financial management was clearly located in the Treasury and the machinery needed for a sustained central drive could begin to be properly developed (Wilding 1983, 41).

But even assisted by 'the clout', the prospects for the effectiveness of FMI depend upon ministerial priorities. Not all ministers are as interested in matters of departmental administration as Michael Heseltine seems to be. They are more concerned with policy; and higher civil servants react accordingly. Twenty years after the Plowden Report underlined the importance of managerial responsibilities, Sir Robert Armstrong, the Secretary of the Cabinet, admitted that officials continued to find 'policy work' more glamorous and more interesting than management work' (HC 1982a). A former Permanent Secretary, Sir Kenneth Clucas, crisply spelt out the reality:

To achieve a least-cost deployment of resources may be only one of a number of objectives, and in any particular case, not a top political priority. Other factors such as compatability with the ideology of the government of the day, the attitude of important interest groups, acceptability to government backbenchers, effect on individual geographical areas, are all perfectly proper considerations for Ministers to take into account when deciding for or against any particular step. There will thus frequently be a clash between considerations of efficiency and other political priorities. Indeed it can be said that the more possible it is in any area of work to set an attainable objective, and realistically allocate a budget to it, the further away this is likely to be from current political interest and sensitivity. There may equally be a clash between accountable management and political control. If a civil servant is to be made individually answerable for a particular area of work then if follows that he must be given the power of decision. If the exercise of that power is subject to ministerial or parliamentary direction then the individual ceases to be responsible. There are large areas over which Parliament would be unwilling to surrender control in this way, and this effectively limits the extent to which management principles can be applied (Clucas 1982, 35).

The cost centre approach, if fully applied, would give line managers powers that would threaten what the service's critics believe to be its comfortable world of established pay scales with automatic increments, routine career expectations, and security of tenure. There is little obvious sign of this order of change, however, in the Cassels Report or in the accompanying MPO material about management development in the service in the 1980s. The latter emphasized that 'the Civil Service is a career Service, i.e. its staffing policy is primarily based on recruiting people as they leave the education system and retaining them in the Service until they retire (MPO 1983, 18) — not much sign here of heads rolling if the sums do not add up. Nor is there much indication elsewhere in the material of the considerable investment in post-entry training which the detailed application of the FMI by line managers would require. The civil service has little choice about wearing the currently fashionable clothes, but much the same bodies remain underneath — and, it must be remembered, widely dispersed and still numerous too. More immediately threatening to the middle rank civil servant than the FMI is the Government's intention to extend unified grading down to senior principal (and, eventually, to principal level) (*The Bulletin* 1983, 18). As the Society of Civil and Public Servants recognized (Opinion 1983, 3), this is a 'revolutionary proposal' from the standpoint of those now occupying what used to be the former executive ladder because it makes that ladder more easily accessible to members of specialist groups — and, the union could have added, normally without compensating opportunities on the specialist side for generalists.

The structure required by the FMI bears some resemblance to the use of directorates in French central government and in the European Commission, which may be the eventual path of development. For the present, the Conservative Government's 'grand strategy' for changing the civil service has gone as far as breaking down departments into their constituent parts for the purpose of cost control: It remains a matter for speculation as to whether the Government will go further and break up the home civil service itself.

Notes

1 David Dimbleby in conversation with Sir John Hoskyns, BBC1 television, 7 December 1982.
2 The Conservative hold on 'the common ground' by 1979 was documented by M. Harrop in R. M. Worcester and M. Harrop (eds.) *Political communications* (Allen & Unwin 1982, 9), and B. Sarlvik and I. Crewe *Decade of dealignment* (Cambridge University Press

1983, 119).
3 David Dimbleby in coversation with Sir John Hoskyns, BBC1 television, 7 December 1982; Sir John Hoskyns, Whitehall and Westminster: an outsider's view, *Parliamentary Affairs,* 36, 137 (1983); Hoskyns, 'Strip Down the State Machine and Start Again', *The Times* 16 February 1983; Hoskyns, Conservatism is not enough, *Political Quarterly* 55, 3 (1984).
4 The report of the (Scott) Inquiry into the Value of Pensions (Cmnd. 8147, 1981, 20) evaded the issue by suggesting that the way out of the situation in which in pension terms there were 'two nations' — one indexed and one not — was for everybody to have inflation proofed pensions. Not surprisingly, the Scott Committee was unable to show convincingly how the private sector in general could finance an open ended commitment.
5 G. Williams, The myth of 'fair' wages, *Economic Journal,* 66, 621 (1956). One of the members of the Priestley Commission, Barbara Wootton, wrote a book advocating 'rational pay' (*The Social Foundations of Wages Policy,* Allen & Unwin 1955, 11; 161).
6 Royal Commission on the Civil Service 1955, 356. Initially, the machinery was called the Standing Advisory Committee, established in 1957, which was replaced in 1971 by the Review Body on Top Salaries. That body advises the Prime Minister on the pay of higher civil servants as well as the salaries of the higher judiciary, senior officers of the armed forces, MPs and ministers of the Crown. Until 1980 it made recommendations about the salaries of the chairman and members of the boards of nationalized industries.
7 *Whitley Bulletin* May 1979, 67-68; *Whitley Bulletin* March 1980, 34; *Whitley Bulletin* June 1980, 89; P. D. Jones, The Council of Civil Service Unions, *Management Services in Government* 35, 136-40 (1980)
8 A. Likierman, Management information for ministers: the MINIS system in the Department of the Environment, *Public Administration* 60, 127; G. H. Chipperfield in RIPA *Management information and control in Whitehall* (RIPA 1983, 22); Third Report from the Treasury and Civil Service Committee, *Efficiency and effectiveness in the civil service,* HC 236-I (1981-82), xv; xxviii; xi; HC 236-II (1981-82), 108; 424; q. 1071; HC 236-III (1981-82), 156; *Financial management in government departments* (Cmnd. 9058), 1983, 5.

Civil Service Department 1981. *Civil service pay: factual background memorandum on the non-industrial civil service: submitted to the enquiry into non-industrial civil service pay.* London: HMSO.
Civil Service Pay Research Unit Board, 1979. *Annual report 1979* (incorporating Civil Service Pay Research Unit 1979 annual report). London: HMSO.
Clucas, Sir Kenneth, 1982. Parliament and the civil service, in RIPA *Parliament and the executive. London: RIPA..*
Fry, G. K. 1983. Compromise with the market: the Megaw report on civil service pay 1982, *Public Administration* 61.

HMSO. 1981. *The Future of the Civil Service Department. Government observations on the first report.* House of Commons. 1979. 967. Deb. 5s. c. 1050.

—. 1980. 984. Deb. 5s. c. 1050.

—. 1981. 12. Deb. 6s. c. 658-659.

—. 1982. 38. Deb. 6s. c. 918.

—. 1982a. 236-II (1981-82) q. 1226.

Jessel, D. 1980. Mandarins and ministers, *The Listener,* 11 December.

Management and Personnel Office. 1983. *Civil service management development in the 1980s. London: MPO.*

Oakeshott, M. 1962. Rationalism in politics and other essays. London: Methuen.

Royal Commission on the Civil Service, 1931. (Chairman: Tomlin). *Report of the* ... Cmd. 3909. London: HMSO.

—. 1955. (Chairman: Priestley). *Report of the* .... Cmd. 9613. London : HMSO.

HM Treasury. 1982. (Chairman: Megaw). (Majority) *Report of the inquiry into civil service pay.* Cmnd. 8590. London: HMSO.

—. 1983. *Financial management in government departments. Cmnd. 9058. London: HMSO.*

Treasury and Civil Service Committee. 1981. *The future of the Civil Service Department.* HC. 54. London: HMSO.

—. 1982. *Efficiency and effectiveness in the civil service.* Cmnd. 8616. London: HMSO.

Wardale, Sir Geoffrey, 1981. *Chain of command review: the open structure. Report.* London: Civil Service Department.

Wilding, R. W. L. 1983. Management information and control: the role of the centre, in RIPA *Management information and control.* London: RIPA.

4.5 *J. A. G. Griffith*

The political role of judges

From *The Politics of the Judiciary,* Collins/Fontana, Glasgow
1985, pp. 222 – 35.

...It is common to speak of the judiciary as part of the system of
checks and balances which contains and constrains the power of
the government; or as one of the three principal institutions of the
State, each of which acts to limit the powers of the other two. The
image has a pleasing and mechanistic appearance suggesting some
objective hidden hand which holds the constitution in perpetual
equilibrium. The extent to which the image reflects reality is less
obvious.

If we limit our examination to the working of the three institutions – Parliament, the government, and the judiciary – in their
relationships with each other, then it is clear that each of these
groups influences the way in which the others act. And it is clear,
in particular, that the judiciary may oppose the government to the
extent of declaring its actions invalid or requiring it to pay compensation or even subjecting one of its members or servants to
penalties.

If however we look more broadly and more widely we see that
this judicial activity of opposing governments is a deviance from
the norm, an aberration, which occurs most infrequently and in
very special circumstances. The judiciary is not placed constitu-
tionally in opposition to the government but, in the overwhelming
mass of circumstances, alongside it.

In our society, as in others, political power, the power of
government, is exercised by a relatively small number of people.
Senior ministers are most obvious of that number, as are senior
civil servants, chairmen of nationalized industries, the chairmen
and chief officers of the largest local authorities. Among those
who are not members of State institutions should be added a few

industrialists and, under Labour governments, a few trade union leaders. And the leading members of Her Majesty's Opposition are also, from time to time, a part of the decision – making process at this highest level. The whole group numbers a few hundred people. They represent established authority.

The rest are outside. Some may be influential as advisers. Others may be very important as professional men and women. But they, along with the population at large, remain outside the governing group. Of course there are many organizations which exercise many different kinds of power within their own sphere. In this narrow sense, we live in a pluralist society. But the political power of governing the country is oligarchic, exercised by a few.

The senior judges are undeniably among those few.. The importance of their task, their influence on behaviour, the extent of their powers, the status they enjoy, the extrajudicial uses to which they are put, the circles they move in, the background from which they come, their habits of mind, and the way in which they are regarded by other members of the group confirm beyond question their place within the governing group of established authority. And, like other members of the group, they show themselves alert to protect the social order from threats to its stability or to the existing distribution of political and economic power.

I have said that judges look to what they regard as the interests of the whole society. That, in itself, makes political assumptions of some magnitude. It has long been argued that the concept of the whole society suggests a homogeneity of interest among the different classes within the society which is false. And that this concept is used to persuade the governed that not the government but 'the State' is the highest organization and transcends conflicts in society. It is a short step to say that it is the State which makes the laws, thus enabling those in political power to promote their own interests in the name of the whole abstracted society, Inevitably the judiciary reflects the interests of its own class. Lord Wedderburn has written that 'the eras of judicial "creativity", of new doctrines hostile to trade union interests, have been largely, though not entirely, coterminous with the periods of British social history in which the trade unions have been perceived by middle – class opinions as a threat to the established social order'.[1]

In one analysis, the judiciary is no more than an instrument of the ruling class. Rules are made by the government or, through the common law and statutory interpretation, by the judiciary. These rules are 'the law' and that phrase gives them a supra – political respectability. The rules are what they are because of the nature of the society, because of its cultural and particularly its economic ordering. The government is the political manifestation of the economic forces and the judiciary also subserves those forces. E. P. Thompson summarizes this 'sophisticated, but (ultimately) highly schematic Marxism' which to his surprise, he says, 'seems to spring up in the footsteps of those of us in an older Marxist tradition' in these terms:

From this standpoint the law is, perhaps more clearly than any other cultural or institutional artifact, by definition a part of a 'superstructure' adapting itself to the necessities of an infrastructure of productive forces and productive relations. As such it is clearly an instrument of the *de facto* ruling class: it both defines these rulers' claims upon resources and labour – power – it says what shall be property and what shall be crime – and it mediates class relations with a set of appropriate rules and sanctions, all of which, ultimately, confirm and consolidate class power. Hence the rule of law is only another mask for the rule of a class.[2]

The Marxist view depends on the notion of the State as an organization created by and serving to protect and promote the interests of the ruling class.[3] Law is the will of that State which seems to stand outside and above society. This seeming independence of the State and therefore of law helps to obscure the real power relationships which are determined by the economic relationships between classes, helps to legitimate the exercise of that power, and enables the State and the law to appear neutral.

Their (the capitalists') personal rule must at the same time be constituted as an average rule. Their personal power is based on conditions of life which as they develop are common to many individuals, and the continuance of which they, as ruling individuals, have to maintain against others and, at the same time, maintain that they hold good for all. The expression of this will, which is determined by their common interest, is law.[4]

For my purposes the Marxist brush is here much too broad. Nor can I accept the view of law and of judges as no more than superstructure or as adequately defined by that metaphor.

My thesis is that judges in the United Kingdom cannot be politically neutral because they are placed in positions where they are required to make political choices which are sometimes present to them, and often presented by them, as determinations of

*where the public interest lies; that their interpretation of what is in
the public interest and therefore politically desirable is determined
by the kind of people they are and the position they hold in our
society; that this position is a part of established authority and so is
necessarily conservative and illiberal. From all this flows that view
of the public interest which is shown in judicial attitudes such as
tenderness towards private property and dislike of trade unions,
strong adherence to the maintenance of order, distaste for minority
opinions, demonstrations and protests, indifference to the promotion of better race relations, support of govermental secrecy, concern for the preservation of the moral and social behaviour to
which it is accustomed, and the rest.*

Professor Mancini of the University of Bologna has singled out
'the susceptibility of English judges to be analysed as a politically
cohesive group' – what I have called their homogeneity – as the
factor distinguishing them from judges in Italy, France and Spain.
'What I mean', he says, 'is (a) that English judges seldom make
decisions of a nature to challenge a universally received notion of
public interest; and (b) that when they happen to do it, their decisions are a result of strictly individual options,' He draws a very
sharp contrast: 'the trend towards a more politicized and politically polarized judiciary ... in Italy, France and Spain ... has acquired, or is in the process of acquiring, traits so neat and forcible
as to rise to the dignity of a major national issue'.[5]

One reason for this continental phenomenon is historical and
political: the greater divergence between the right and the left in
Italy and France as compared with Britain, But it is made possible
by the fact that in those countries judges are appointed in their
early or mid – twenties after open competitive examinations. It is
therefore possible for men and women with widely different, and,
at the time of their examination, unknown political opinions to
reach the bench and to remain there, effectively, until retirement.
If they display political attitudes of which their superiors disap-
prove, their promotion may not be speedy. And these superiors
continue to be 'politically cohesive'. But to remove the dissidents
from office is much more difficult. This split between right and
left among the judiciary in those countries is highly significant and
wholly without parallel in Britain.

Indeed, the similarities with the position in Britain are to be
found among the more rigid regimes of Eastern Europe, South
Africa and other countries, capitalist and communist, where the

judiciary is manifestly more at one with established authority. In all these countries judges perform similar functions, reflecting their respective societies.

By this I do not mean that the influence exerted directly on the judiciary by the political arm of the State in those countries is paralleled by a similar direct influence in Britain. No doubt, in the great majority of cases before the courts, the judges in those coutries act independently of the executive and are prepared to invalidate actions by its members. But in the small number of crucial cases where the offences are political the political influence is more obviously direct. And here political offences means offences which may be drawn in broad terms to include conduct deemed detrimental to State interests. Further, I am speaking of the judiciary only and not of the activities of the political police, or of powers to detain without trial. If I were of a radical turn of mind with a leaning towards iconoclasm and a distrust of those in authority, I would (to put it mildly) find more scope and greater continuity for my activities in Britain than in more totalitarian societies.

But the relative responsiveness of the judiciary to political pressure is not an attribute or a function specific to capitalism or to communism. It would be easy to name a score of countries which are undeniably capitalist and where the judges are as strongly under the influence of the political executives as they are in any communist society. That relative responsiveness reflects the extent to which the judges share the aims and values of the political system, and the extent to which they are its enthusiastic supporters.

It is in this sense that I speak of judges in different countries performing similar functions, reflecting their respective societies, and the political power which operates in them.

Again any analysis which places the judiciary in the United Kingdom in a wholly subservient position to the goverment misteads history and mistakes the source and nature of the common law. Those who criticize existing institutions in the United Kingdom need always to remember that, in comparison with most other countries, this country enables its citizens to live in comparative freedom. To what extent is this a consequence of our judicial system and of our judges?

That they play some part is undeniable. They will even, on occasion, enforce the law which forbids arrest without reasonable cause or imprisonment without trial, and support the right of free association or, within its limit, of free speech. The idea of the rule of law is not wholly illusory...

What then is meant by 'the rule of law'? The law rules in this sense: that government and all who exercise power as part of established authority are themselves bound by the existing body of laws unless and until they repeal or reform any of those laws. When a government makes a law under Parliamentary authority it makes a rod for its own back as well as for the backs of others. The Declaration of Rights of 1689 declared illegal the suspending or execution of laws by royal authority without the consent of Parliament; and the power to dispense with laws. The exercise of arbitary power by goverments is contrary to the rule of law and the true mark of the despot is that he can, at his own wish and without restraint, set aside the existing laws in any case. Judges are similarly constrained in their law – making function by the doctrine of precedent.

There is another way in which the powers of goverments are restricted. As Thompson has observed, if laws are to be plausible as legitimating agents they must not be excessively partial or unjust.

So, because the powers of governments in Britain are limited by law (even though governments may make new laws and change existing laws), there is always the possibility that the exercise of power by governments may be challenged; and because judges, however much they share the values and aims of governments, are not governmental servants, the challenge may be successful.

There is a sense, however far it falls short of what is claimed for it, in which those who exercise legalized force in our society must have regard to the existence of a judiciary which may be prepared to condemn them in some circumstances and will be supported in so doing. Nevertheless, in the event of an attempt by a government to exercise arbitrary and extensive powers, curtailing individual liberty, it cannot be forecast how the judges would react. The political circumstances would be crucial and the judiciary would be divided, as Lords Parker and Gardiner were divided over official torture in Northern Ireland. A left – wing attempt would meet with judicial opposition more immediately than a right – wing attempt. And there is little evidence to suggest that the judiciary would be quick to spring to the defence of individual liberty wherever the threat came from.

To whatever extent we seek to define more precisely the function of the judiciary in our society so as to take account of the power of judges to act independently of others, their place as part of the governing group remains unaffected. Nor must we lose sight of two major determinants of the whole. The first is that we in the United Kingdom do live in an increasingly authoritarian society and that this is the outstanding phenomenon of all modern states. I do not mean to belittle the remarkable achievements in authoritarianism of the great systems of government in the past. But modern authoritarianism deals with millions where the tyrants of the past dealt with thousands. And the means of control today are obviously more scientific and much more thorough. It is within such systems that the judges operate; and they operate to help to run these systems. And authoritarianism is always, by its essential nature, conservative and reactionary. It must preserve itself.

Secondly, judges are the product of a class and have the characteristics of that class. Typically coming from middle – class professional families, independent schools, Oxford or Cambridge, they spend twenty to twenty – five years in successful practice at the bar, mostly in London, earning very considerable incomes by the time they reach their forties. This is not the stuff of which reformers are made, still less radicals. There are those who believe that if more grammar or comprehensive schoolboys, graduating at redbrick or new glass universities, became barristers and then judges, the judiciary would be that much less conservative. This is extremely doubtful for two reasons. The years in practice and the middle – aged affluence would remove any aberration in political outlook, if this were necessary. Also, if those changes did not take place, there would be no possibility of their being appointed by the Lord Chancellor, on the advice of the senior judiciary, to the bench. Ability by itself is not enough. Unorthodoxy in political opinion is a certain disqualification for appointment.

Her Majesty's judges are unlikely to be under great illusions about the functioning of political power in the United Kingdom today. And I think we come close to their definition of the public interest and of the interests of the State if we identify their views with those who insist that in any society, but especially societies in the second half of the twentieth century, stability above all is necessary for the health of the people and is the supreme law.

It follows that governments are normally to be supported but not in every case. Governments represent stability and have a very considerable interest in preserving it. The maintenance of authoritarian structures in all public institutions is wholly in the interest of governments. This is true of all governments of all political complexions, capitalist and communist alike. Whenever governments or their agencies are acting to preserve that stability – call it the Queen's peace, or law and order, or the rule of law, or whatever – the judges will lend their support and will not be over concerned if to do so requires the invasion of individual liberty.

When, then, is it justifiable, in the opinion of judges, not to support governmental power? From recent cases, certain generalizations can be drawn. First, none of the decisions which conflict with that power falls within that aspect of the judicial view of the public interest which is concerned to maintain law and order, the pre – eminence of which is wholly preserved. Secondly, the courts seem very willing to intervene when the essence of the plaintiff's case is that he is the victim of an exercise of the political policy of ministers, as in *Laker, Tameside, Padfield* and *Anisminic*. Perhaps this is part of that old common law resentment which judges have against statute law. Perhaps it is all that is left of the former tradition of protecting individual liberty.

All those judicial decisions struck down political decisions taken during the period of Labour governments. But, with the exception of the ministerial decision in *Tameside*, it is doubtful whether the political complexion of the government had much to do with those decisions. Much more significant is that these cases and others reflect the emergence of a period of judicial activism or intervention which began in the early 1960s and has been growing in strength ever since. How far this development has been inspired or assisted by the fact that between 1964 and 1979 Labour governments were in office for all but four years is an open question. Perhaps all that can be said is that Labour governements are more likely than Conservative governments to act in ways which offend the judicial sense of rightness, the judicial view of where the public interest lies.

It is interesting to speculate how far the judges would be willing to push their opposition to the government of the day if convinced that its policies were contrary to the public interest, and how far the government would permit such opposition to continue. Lord Devlin, writing about the *Padfield* decision, wondered, 'whether the courts have moved too far from their base' which, he said, was 'the correction of abuse'. He continued, and here he was also speaking of the *Tameside* decision:

One may also share to some extent the apprehensions of the Civil Service.
All legal history shows that, once the judges get a foothold in the domain
of fact, they move to expand.
Questions of fact become in a mysterious way questions of law. The fence
between error and misconception crumbles with the passage of time. The
civil servant may fear the day when he dare not reach a conclusion without
asking himself whether a judge will think all the deciding factors as relevant as he does. I do not think that the judiciary should be thrust out of
the domain of fact.

Lord Devlin wanted above all to see judicial review 'preserved as a
weapon against arbitrary government and I am conscious that its
efficacy depends upon the good will of Whitehall'. Because of the
power of government to exclude judicial review by statutory provision 'judicial interference with the executive cannot for long very
greatlu exceed what Whitehall will accept':[6] Or, as the Prime
Minister said in 1977 in the House of Commons: 'We should
beware of trying to emboil the judiciary in our affairs, with the
corresponding caveat that the judiciary should be very careful
about embroiling itself in the legislature.'[7] And in *Dupont Steels
Ltd v. Sirs* Lord Scarman said: 'If people and Parliament come to
think that the judicial power is to be confined by nothing other
than the judges's sense of what is right ... confidence in the judicial system will be replaced by fear of it becoming uncertain and
arbitrary in its application. Society will then be ready for Parliament to cut the power of the judges.'
   The ultimate, if partial, subservience of the judiciary to the
government is spelt out clearly in those words. But the phra-
seology seems to me greatly to overstate, by implication, the willingness or the desire of judges to control 'arbitrary' government.
Behind the administrative difficulties which the minister foresaw
in *Tameside,* and the consequent harm to groups of pupils, lay the
principle of comprehensive schooling. There, as in the cases arising out of legislation concerned with housing and planning, trade
unions, and race relations, the judiciary digs its trenches against
what it sees as government not in the public interest. But *Padfield,
Tameside* and *Laker,* thought significant of the modern trend
towards greater judicial intervention, are still untypical. They
represent the judicial desire, not so much to control arbitrariness
as to protect the individual against political policies which are seen
by the judiciary to be contrary to the public interest. This, of
course, is not always possible as Lord Denning reluctantly decided

in *Smith v. Inner London Education Authority* (1978) when some parents sought to prevent the Authority from closing St Marylebone Grammar School as part of the change to comprehensive schooling, 'Search as I may,' said Lord Denning, 'and it is not for want of trying, I cannot find any abuse or misuse of power by the education authority ... It is sad to have to say so, after so much effort has been expended by so many in so good a cause.'[8]

Lord Scarman's plea for the introduction of a Bill of Rights is relevant here.[9] The purposes he has in mind may be wholly admirable being biased largely on the Universal Declaration of Human Rights. But others who have also spoken in favour of such a Bill, whose provisions would be entched and only repealable or declared inapplicable with the approval of special (perhaps two – thirds) majority in Parliament, have amongst other things hoped it would prevent the curtailment of freedom of speech in the Race Relations Acts, the educational policies of the Labour government which denied parental choice, the right of entry of factory and health inspectors, and a tax policy, the effect of which would be (it was claimed) to destroy a substantial proportion of independent business,[10]

The European Convention of Human Rights, also a candidate for entrenchment in our law, after listing a number of desirable purposes, adds provisos to each in terms like:

No restrictions shall be placed on the exercise of these rights other than such as are prescribed by law and are necessary in a democratic society in the interests of national security or public safety, for the prevention of disorder or crime, for the protection of health or morals or for the protection of the rights and freedom of others. This Article shall not prevent the impositions of lawful restrictions on the exercise of these lights by members of the armed forces, of the police or of the administration of the state.

It is difficult to see how the welfare of the individual would be promoted by the enactment of such provisions if they were to be interpreted by the judiciary of today.

Nevertheless, the approach to an examination of the nature of judicial power through a consideration of human rights had, for the British political system in the mid – 1970s, an air of novelty. Liberal thinking among the judiciary has, as we have seem, shown itself only occasionally and then only in minority judgments or dissents. The protection of the public interest in the preservation of a stable society is how the judges see their role.

In other eyes their view of the public interest appears merely as reactionary conservatism. It is not the politics of the extreme right. Its insensitivity is clearly rooted more in unconscious assumptions than in a wish to oppress. But it is demonstrable that on every major social issue which has come before the courts during the last thirty years – concerning industrial relations, political protest, race relations, governmental secrecy, police powers, moral behaviour – the judges have supported the conventional, established, and settled interests. And they have reacted strongly against challenges to those interests. This conservatism does not necessarily follow the day – to – day political policies currently associated with the party of that name. But it is a political philosophy nonetheless.

Many regard the values of the bench and bar in Britain as wholly admirable and the spirit of the common law (as presently expressed) to be a national adornment. The incorruptibility of the English bench and its independence of the government are great virtues. All this is not in issue. When I argue that they regard the interests of the State or the public interest as pre – eminent and that they interpret those interests as meaning that, with very few exceptions, established authority must be upheld and that those exceptions are made only when a more conservative position can be adopted, this does not mean that the judges are acting with impropriety. It means that we live in a highly authoritarian society, fortunate only that we do not live in other societies which are even more authoritarian. We must expect judges, as part of that authority, to act in the interests, as they see them, of the social order.

Notes

1   See *Industrial Law Journal,* June, 1980, p. 78.
2   E. P. Thompson, *Whigs and Hunters* (1975), p. 259.
3   For a useful summary see Maureen Cain, 'The main themes of Marx's and Engels's sociology of law' in 1 *British Journal of Law & Society* 136, to which I am indebted.
4   Marx and Engles, *The German Ideology* (1965 ed.), p. 358, quoted by M. Cain, *op. cit.*
5   G. F. Mancini, 'Politics and the judges – the European perspective' in 43 *Modern Law Review* (1980)1.
6   *The Times,* 27 October 1976.
7   941 HC Deb. col, 909 (15 December 1977) (Mr Callaghan).
8   [1978] 1 A11 ER 411; see also *North Yorkshire County Council* v.

Secretary of State for Education and Science, The Times, 20 October 1978.

9 Sir Leslie Scarman, *English Law, the New Dimension* (1975).

10 See the examples collected by M. Zander, *A Bill of Rights?* (1981).

4.6 *John Alderson*

Police and public order

From 'Police and public order', *Public Administration,*
Vol. 63, winter 1985, pp. 436 – 42.

...As the economy in a developed nation contracts and a new industrial revolution exacts its social price the mood reflects fear and
apprehension. Bigness gives way to smallness in many ways.
Smaller business ventures, smaller bureaucracies, buildings,
schools, communities, tend to reflect the economic contraction,
and the police are no exception.

During the sixties and early seventies the police expanded in
numbers, and technology. Bureaucarcy grew as the number of
police forces decreased from 125 to 43 and their avearage size increased. The largely local, beat patrolling police had been
superseded by remote technological cops. The mood changed
within police forces and amongst police officers. Policing efficiency in terms of quick reponses backed by force of numbers induced
a more cavalier style and the nature of policing changed. By 1981
inner – city riots exploded, not only on the street, but in the minds
of thinking people and police officers alike. Lord Scarman, in a
brilliant analysis and inquiry on the Brixton disorders, highlighted
the dangers inherent in a police approach mainly based on
repressive force applied in deteriorating social conditions (Scarman 1981). The idea that policing policies should be based in part
on consensus meant to Scarman and his supporters the need to establish consultation in neighbourhood communities. The Home
Office was not slow to seize on the point. Memoranda of advice to
police forces stressed the need to establish a better police/public
dialogue, which in turn should influence policing policy. The final
triumph of the 'community school' over the bureaucratic professional model was the inclusion of a clause in the Police and
Criminal Evidence Bill in 1984, laying down a statutory duty upon

police authorities to set up consultative machinery. The question remains however as to whether future stress placed upon policing public order will make it possible for the traditions of local government policing to survive. Barely had the printers' ink dried on the Police and Criminal Evidence Bill than the dispute which broke out in the mining industry in March 1984 plunged the police into a much wider role than had yet been envisaged.

It has always been envisaged that in times of public disorder one police force could call upon another for 'mutual aid'. This happened on a large scale during the 1926 General Strike. It was during the 1970's however that concept grew of a reporting centre at national level, controlled by a chief constable, and co – ordinating the complex and large scale movement of officers and equipment to sites of disorder. It was felt by politicians and senior civil servants that in a time of crisis there should be not doubt that the police would hold the necessary advantage. The Heath Government (1970 – 74) felt that in 1972 the police had failed to withstand the mass flying pickets of the miners and others led by Arthur Scargill. New arrangements for speeding allocation of police reinforcements were set up at national level.

By 1981, the year of the inner city riots, the new system was working well. There were, however, other difficulties. The riot equipment of the police was felt to be inadequate. Perspex shields developed to protect standing police officers from bricks, bottles and stones were too cumbersome for quick moving anti – riot formations. Clothing, offensive equipment and vehicles were also felt to be inadequate. By 1982 most of these defects had been put right and the British police now and for the first time became barely distinguishable from the riot police of continental Europe. They even held some of the more lethal plastic bullets which had proved to be controversial even in Belfast.

The policing of the miners strike of 1984 put the new arrangements through a rigorous test out of which they emerged successfully. Instead of being obliged to seek an early compromise, the Government were able to puruse a policy of attrition and invest heavily in breaking the strike through a drift back to work. The striking miners might be expected, like their forebears in 1926, to be gradually forced to give in through economic and social deprivation, and with effective police protection, go back to work. That the strike did not suceed is primarily due to the capacity of the new policing strategy and tactics, together with the substantial number of miners who have continued to work. A number of important issues for policing have however been raised, including constitutional, strategic, and organizational questions.

Hitherto the police system has rested upon the idea of joint administration by the Home Office and the police authorities or committees of local government. Chief constables are accountable to both, yet solely responsible for law enforcement and policing operations. In the Metropolitan Police District local government plays no part as the Home Secretary is himself the police authority and accountable to Parliament. From time to time conflict has arisen between police authorities and their chief constables. The cause of this conflict is to be found in the vagueness of the wording of the Police Act 1964, and since it can be predicated that this issue will remain a lively one, it may be worth giving it some consideration.

The Police Act of 1964 requires local police authorities to maintain 'an adequate and efficient' police force in their area and to ensure that they do this the Home Secretary has powers of inspection. The annual granting of a certificate of approval ensures that central government's grant – aid will be forthcoming.

The chief constable is required by the same Act to 'direct and control' the police force under his command. For the efficient discharge of this task he is accountable to his police authority. He is the subject of annual inspection by the Home Secretary's inspectors of constabulary. He can only be dismissed on the grounds of inefficiency or gross misconduct. In a conflict with the police authority he may achieve the support of the Home Secretary, or he may not. He may also receive the support of his police authority in a conflict with the Home Office.

There may be times when the chief constable's law enforcement policies are against the wishes of his police authority who have no power to make him alter them. They may call for reports, seek the approval of the Home Secretary to restrain or discipline the chief constable, but they cannot direct him to change, though hopefully in most cases persuasion and compromise bring about agreement. It is in times of great stress however that any system or institution is given its greatest test, and the inner city riots of 1981, rising crime rates, and the mining dispute of 1984/85 have revealed the stress points of the police system. The setting up of the National Reporting Centre to administer the supply of mutual aid between police forces has raised problems of democratic accoun –

tability. Since further outbreaks of public disorder are likely from time to time, the National Reporting Centre is here to stay.

Under the direction of a chief constable the Centre requires all police forces to report the amount of their police resources available for mutual aid. Such resources include those elements trained and equipped for riot control. The chief constable co – ordinating the operation allocates resources, and maintains records, including intelligence, and disseminates relevant information. Should a police authority seek to stop the supply of mutual aid, the Home Secretary can intervene to use his powers under the Police Act to require them to conform. When all this happens the police system for the time being ceases, at least operationally, to be a local one and takes on the characteristics of a national force, a de facto national police. It also raises the important question of democratic accountability.

The chief constable directing the overall plans for resource allocation is accountable neither to local nor to central government. No one, it seems, can or is prepared to take responsibility, save the police themselves.

At local level the chief constable remains accountable to the police authority but whilst the police authority can regulate, with Home Office agreement, the normal strength or size of the local force, they have no say concerning the amount of mutual aid which is requested by their own chief constable and allocated by his colleague controlling the operation of the National Reporting Centre. This position could be improved if a supervising committee were to be appointed for the national operation. It could operate along the following lines.

A national emergency police committee would be activated as soon as the Home Office in consultation with the chief constables had decided to set up the National Reporting (Police) Centre. Such a committee would comprise the Home Secretary or his representative, and representative members of the local police authorities. The chief constable in charge of the National Reporting Centre would be accountable to this committee. The vexed question of who is to pay for the operations could be aired and dealt with at the meetings and the so – called partnership between central and local government for ensuring the police system would be strengthened. This however may not be enough if the state of public disorder were to generate a more ruthless authoritarian government. Such a government may wish to complete the trends towards centralization of police administration which have been quite discernable since the Police Act of 1919.

Addressing the subject of central control of the police the 1962 Royal Commission on the Police commented:

That there is a strong case for bringing the police of this country under complete central control is undeniable. Such a step might well enable the service more effectively to fulfil its purposes and would at the same time put it under effective Parliamentary supervision. (para. 128)

The most excellent dissenting memorandum of Dr. A. L. (later Lord) Goodhart provides further compelling evidence for any government strong enough in Parliament to centralize the police. Nor in the eyes of the Royal Commission of 1962 would the central unification of the British police system adumbrate a 'police state'. When addressing such arguments they said:

British liberty does not depend, and never depended, upon the dispersal of police power. It has never depended upon any particular form of police organization. It depends on the supremacy of Parliament and the rule of law. (para. 135)

The conversion of the existing system into a centrally controlled one would be easy and many chief constables would support it. Some chief constables have long been irked by the role of the local government police authorities, others have the opposite view. (I have also heard police officers in national police forces expressing views hostile to the central bureaucracy which interferes too much with their local discretion).

Hitherto the strength, traditions, and importance of local government has provided a sound basis for the police system. The Royal Commission described the position appertaining in 1962 as follows:

In our opinion the present police system is sound because it is based upon, and reflects, a political idea of immense practical value which has gained wide acceptance in this country, namely the idea of partnership between central and local government in the administration of public services. (para. 142)

The same confidence is not so discernable in 1984. Since 1979 there has been a tightening of the grip of central government over its local counterpart. Education, social and welfare services, housing and even the police services have felt the tug from the centre. The abolition of the recently created Metropolitan Counties and above all the Greater London Council have delivered a severe blow to the pride and morale of local government in some areas of the country. The central operation of the police service during the miners' strike to the exclusion of local government's police authorities only serves to underline the trends. If the trends are to continue Britain can expect to have a police system indistinguishable from its continental counterparts which have been looked down on by the British for at least two hundred years. Hart (1951) records some of the comments made when the 1856 County and Borough Police Act gave the Home Secretary powers to regulate local police affairs by inspection and grant:

It took away the right of self – government and destroyed local institutions which had existed since Alfred; by requiring Chief constables to make annual reports to the Home Secretary as to the state of crime it was no better than the Continental spy system...the proposal to give the Chief Constable control of his men might have originated from an Austrian or Russian nobleman; indeeed it was the most un – English measure ever seen and was more fitted for Naples than for England. (p.33)

The absence of consensus politics in the 1980s marked by the conflict between recalcitrant local authorities and a radical, impregnable, Conservative Government, is likely to ensure that the more sentimental attachment to local government is weaker. It has been said that:

It is only by historical accident that control of the police is vested in local authorities. Clearly the preservation of order is a fundamental duty – if we may so express it – of any state. According to the principles of public administration the police should be under the control of central government. Jennings (1960)

If the creation of a centrally controlled police system were brought about it could take one of two forms. The first, like the French, would be outright and total centralization, with control vested in a minister. The division of the poliice system into regions and divisions would follow with a direct hierarchial chain of command from Whitehall unimpeded by any intermediate or local involvement. This would provide the stronger model for the purpose of an authoritarian central government.

Another model more difficult to manipulate politically, (which after all has been advanced as the main advantage of our present system), is that which has emerged in Japan since 1947.

The Anglo – American system of local police forces was imposed upon the Japanese by the Allies in 1947. A Public Safety Commission was appointed to oversee its democratic development and functioning. The chairman of this body is the Minister of Home Affairs. It was felt by the Japanese that there were defects in the local system similar to those observed in 1962 by the royal commission in Britain. The present system was introduced in 1954 after the Allies had handed over government to the Japanese. It is centrally controlled by the Public Safety Commission, but each designated region of the country has its own Public Safety Commission and a large degree of (though by no means total) autonomy. It works well. But then local government traditions in Japan have not developed the strength and importance of local government in Britain. It should be anticipated that any attempt to centralize control of the police would be met with considerable hostility and resistance, but given the right climate, and fear of continuing public disorder on a wide scale, a determined and strong government could and no doubt would do it. Any such radical constitutional change would be better done however through the device of a royal commission on the police and the setting up of such an inquiry would be better done sooner rather than later.

It is extravagant use of language to refer to Britain at the present time as a 'police state'. Under an authoritarian government however there could perhaps develop a drift into some kind of tightly controlled, i.e. policed society...

References

Hart, J. M. 1951. *The British Police*. London: Allen and Unwin.

Jennings, Sir Ivor. 1960. *Principles of Local Government Law*. London: The University of London Press. *Observer* (1974) 4th August: p.7.

Royal Commission on the Police (1962) para. 128. Cmnd. 1728. London HMSO.

Scarman, Lord. 1981. Report of the Brixton Disorders; 10th – 12th April 1981; Cmnd. 8247, London HMSO.

Royal Commission on the Police (1962) para. 128. Cmnd. 1728. London HMSO.

Scarman, Lord. 1981. Report of the Brixton Disorders; 10th – 12th April 1981; Cmnd. 8247, London HMSO.

Scarman, Lord. 1981. Report of the Brixton Disorders; 10th – 12th
April 1981; Cmnd. 8247, London HMSO.

Part Five

Local political organisations

Introduction

The themes of economic constraint and the growth of partisanship have been reflected in a number of the extracts in this reader. They are also relevant to the analysis of developments at the level of local politics. In recent years many local authorities have become more openly self-assertive, while central government has increasingly attempted to influence, and in some cases direct, the actions of local governments. These trends have raised questions about local autonomy and central predominance and the proper spheres of operation that can be accorded to each tier of government. As local authorities are directly responsible for about thirty per cent of public expenditure and receive about fourty-eight per cent of their income from the national level it is perhaps inevitable that in a period of financial constraint central government will develop an increasing interest in their activities.

This impulsion towards central intervention can be seen to be at least in part a response to the central difficulties facing British policy-makers which are highlighted in the first part of the reader. But the party political complexion of some local authorities has also altered as have the problems faced by authorities in areas of significant economic decline. Increasing demands at the local level, coupled with central government's search for financial control, have shifted the balance and style of the relationship between the two levels of government from one based on consensus to one increasingly based on conflict.

The issues of local autonomy and the increasingly partisan nature of local politics are examined in the pieces contained in this section. Rhodes (Reading 5.1) gives particular attention to changes that have taken place in central—local relations since 1979 and he attempts to evaluate their distinctiveness. He shows that the weakening of local autonomy began under the auspices of public sector financial constraint in the mid-1970s, if not earlier. Hence the innovative and radical nature of the post-1979 Conservative Government's activities is open to question, as its move towards greater intervention in the financial affairs of local government simply carried further forward a trend that had already been developing under the previous Labour Government.

However, the style and manner of the Conservative Government's intervention is distinct. Rhodes shows that there has been a move away from a relationship based on bargaining and mutual involvement in financial decision-making ('incorporation') to one increasingly based on direction by central government. Rhodes examines these changing relationships with particular reference to the activities of the local authority associations — those bodies which liase with central government on behalf of all local authorities.

Rhodes's conclusions about a more directive approach by central government in the financial field are applied to central—local relations in general. He charts the various aspects of the increasingly fraught relationship between centre and locality. He argues that a unilateral style of decision-making on the part of central government has led to an increase in the use of litigation by local authorities and has increased opposition and recalcitrance on the part of some of them. Because of the uncertainties of the relationship and the lack of mutual consultation many authorities have tended to play safe and avoid risk when it comes to planning ahead. As Rhodes shows, one of the unintended outcomes of the move towards a more directive style has been to create a problem when it comes to controlling some local governments which is more difficult than was previously the case. The problems of central—local relations remain in operation, though clearly Rhodes believes that central direction is no long-term alternative to an approach based on the voluntary co-operation of the various parties involved.

Gaining agreement between the two levels of government is made all the more difficult if, in addition to differences in interest, politicians from different parties are in control at each level. The party politicization of local government is examined in the extract by Gyford (Reading 5.2). He shows the major growth of party politics in local government to have taken place in the period since

1945—and this was accompanied by a tendency to bring national issues to predominance at the local level, so that the local dimension became increasingly an appendage of the national party battle. In this sense the local and central worlds of politics developed a greater degree of coherence and contact, so one of the effects of politicisation was to weaken rather than enhance local autonomy. As Gyford points out, this attempt to dragoon local government into the army of national party politics reached its zenith in the 1950s and 60s and it was reflected in the tendency for local voting patterns to follow national trends.

This nationalisation of local politics through the spread of party politics began to show signs of weakening in the 1970s, partly because there were ideological splits within the two major parties themselves. Also the various factions, especially within the Labour Party, gained influence in some local authorities. Additionally, third parties were beginning to make progress at the local level and the pattern of local voting no longer reflected national trends quite so closely. Finally the Conservative Government's attempt to constrain local authority spending brought about a direct conflict on party political lines with some Labour-controlled authorities—increasingly such authorities have seen themselves as fighting for local interests as well as socialist ideas. Gyford also points out that some Conservative-controlled authorities have developed more ideologically right-wing policies and these have sometimes meant that these authorities have pursued policies which are distinct at least in pace and emphasis from those being pursued by the Conservative central government.

Gyford emphasises the growth of ideological politics at the local level and suggests that there has also been a move away from 'closed politics' to a more open politics in which the authority's political links with local economic and social interests have become more important elements in its decision-making. In the end Gyford remains uncertain as to whether the increase in party politics at the local level will create a more vigorous and organized form of local autonomy or a more rigid adherence to national guidelines.

5.1 *R. A. W. Rhodes*

Relations between central and local Government

From 'Continuity and change in British central local relations: the
"Conservative threat" ', *British Journal of Political Science,* Vol. 14,
1984, pp. 261-83.

1. Introduction

Conservative policies have been seen as a grave threat to local
government. They are said to undermine its constitutional foundations and considerable concern has been expressed about the erosion of local autonomy.[1] This paper attempts to evaluate the
distinctiveness of present policies. But in order to assess recent
changes, it is necessary to look to the immediate past and to identify any continuities as well as disjunctions in central government's
policy. A decade is a short time in the life of a polity but, by insist-
ing that current developments be located in even this confined
context, it will become clear that there is, in fact, a large measure
of continuity in the relationship between central and local government. Whether the government has been Conservative or Labour,
the trend has been towards the increased control of the level and
pattern of sub-national expenditure.

The focus of this paper is unusual because it is not confined to
the individual local authority; it examines the role of the *national*
level of *local* government. Although individual local authorities
can and do have direct contact with central departments, communications has been channelled increasingly through the national
representative organizations of the different types of local
authority. The most prominent of these organizations are the local
authority associations, and they have grown in importance since
the reorganization of local government in 1972...

2 Understanding the context of change

The changes in the relationship between central and local government during the 1970s can be characterized as a shift from bargaining through incorporation to direction in the 1980s. The bargaining phase lasted from 1966 until 1973. In these years the national associations of local authorities bargained with central government over the rate of growth in government grant and, over the distribution of the total grant between the various types of local authority. Central government may have been the more powerful actor in these negotiations, being able to determine the timetable and set the broad parameters for the discussion, but the Associations none the less achieved changes at the margin in both the growth rate and the distribution. During this period, there was a growth in public expenditure in general and local expenditure in particular.[2]

The second phase began in 1974 and lasted until 1979. It was characterized by 'strategies of incorporation': that is, central government employed various institutions and processes to involve local government in central decision making, hoping thereby to commit local government to central decisions. A number of distinct developments need to be disentangled.

An important pre-condition of incorporation is that central departments identify the group or groups which can speak (and preferably act) authoritatively for the interest concerned. Central-local relations has a 'game-like' quality, however, with both sides deploying the resources they control to maximize their influence over outcomes and trying to avoid becoming dependent on the other player.[3] This 'game' encompasses a variety of interest. Firstly, there are the differences between central departments, most notably between the Department of the Environment (DoE), the other service departments with specific policy responsibilities corresponding with the functions of local authorities, the Treasury and rival departments with no service administered by local government. Secondly, there are the different interests within local government, most notably the interest of the different types of local authority and variations in the pattern of party control. Finally, there are the diverse interests encompassed by the national local government system or 'the set of organizations and actors which together define the national role and state of opinion in local government as a whole.[4] Strategies of incorporation required a reduction in this range of interests and aggregation is the first distinct strand in the incorporation phase: the centre acted to strengthen the national community of local government or the national organizations representing the multiple interests of local authorities in their interactions with central institutions.

The local authority associations are the most prominent of these bodies and, as their names suggest, each Association represents a particular type of local authority: e.g., the Association of County Councils (ACC), the Association of District Councils (ADC) and the Association of Metropolitan Authorities (AMA). However, it is a mistake to limit the discussion of the national level of local government to the Associations. They have established a series of joint bobies to carry out specific functions and a number of these bodies are of key importance — e.g., the Local Authorities' Conditions of Service Advisory Board (LACSAB) which acts as the chief negotiator for local government in pay negotiations. In addition, a small number of professional societies are extensively involved with the Associations and joint bodies providing information and expertise and acting as supplementary staff (e.g., Society of Local Authority Chief Executives).

The phrase 'national community' draws attention to the set of organizations at the national level. Moreover this set of organizations is best described as a community because they are interdependent. They are closely linked together financially and by the exchange of personnel. Although the Associations are often seen as in perennial conflict, the contact between them, and thier joint activities, are extensive. Moreover, membership is exclusive. It encompasses the elected members and senior officials of local authorities. Other major actors in local government, such as the trade unions, are deliberately excluded — a characteristic which sharply distinguishes the national community from 'policy communities'. Finally, and most important, there are shared interests. The organizations within the national community are not primarily concerned to promote a particular service but to promote local government and local democracy and to protect their particular type of local authority. Underlying these high-blown terms are highly specific issues. There are three policy areas in which the national community is ever prominent: alterations to the structure and functions of local government, negotiations over central grant and decisions on pay increases for local government employees...

The aggregation of interests is not peculiarly a function of the national community. The service interests within local government are aggregated in 'policy communities':

personal relationships between major political and administrative actors — sometimes in conflict often in agreement, but always in
touch and operating within a shared framework. Community is the cohesive and orienting bond underlying any particular issue.[5]

Rhodes extends this definition to organizational networks and
further suggests that such policy communities will not be restricted
in membership to the functionally equivalent departments of the
two levels of government.[6] They will have extensive membership
and encompass the affected professional associations, other
'private' pressure groups, including business and trade-union interests, and quasi-governmental bodies...

The national community and the single function policy communities are key networks within the national local government
system... Local authority actors (both councillors and officers) do
not decide policies for their areas in isolation; instead they often
look to the national community and policy communities for
guidance about what standard of service to provide, for ideas to
imitate or to avoid, for ways of tackling common problems, and
for justifications or philosophies or particular strategies. Some
councils are innovators across a wide field of policy, but they are
rather exceptional. Most councils most of the time follow national
trends in the local government world, or national trends in their
kind of authority facing their kind of general problem under their
kind or political control. Each of them will innovate from time to
time in one issue area or another, adding their own small contribution to the national picture. Many local decisions, however, are
made within the nationally defined parameters of what counts as
good policy which emerge from the multiple contributions of individual local authorities. This important role for the national
community on general issues and for policy communities in individual functions goes a long way to explain their influence with cen-
tal government.

Before 1979, the national community took on the dual role both
of representing members to government and of attempting to
regulate its members on behalf of government. And it adopted this
role with the active encouragement of the centre. Thus, the DoE
issued guidelines on consultation both to the several divisions of
the DoE and to other government departments: refused to consult
individual local authorities: provided funds to reinforce the functions of specific organizations within the national community: and

created new consultative mechanisms with membership restricted to the Associations. Without claiming that these initiatives successfully strengthened the national community, none the less their very existence demonstrates a clear trend in central-local relations. Both central departments and the Associations sought to create a strong, intermediate tier of representation between centre and locality.[7]

The most notable event in the period was the creation of the Consultative Council on Local Government Finance (CCLGF). In tandem with this initiative, local government was promised involvement in the public expenditure survey system (PES), the processes employed by central government to determine future levels of expenditure. The CCLGF is a forum at which ministers of the major spending departments involved with local government meet the political leaders of the Associations. It represents the first time that regular discussions have taken place at the political level and, initially, the Council was seen as an important vehicle for improving mutual understanding. Its purpose is the promotion of:

regular consultation and co-operation between central and local government on major financial and economic issues of common concern, with special emphasis on the deployment of resources both in the long term and the short term. In this way local government can be associated with the process of settling priorities for the whole of the five-year public expenditure period and local government would be consulted at an early stage when individual proposals for new policies directly involving local government are being shaped.

The work of the Council is supported by a range of working groups comprised of central and local officials, including the Grants Working Group which carries out an enormous amount of preparatory work for the grant negotiations. Perhaps most significantly, the Treasury has been directly involved with local government for the first time through its participation in the CCLGF. Previously the DoE had been not only the 'lead' department in grant negotiations but the sole department. Although the DoE had to negotiate with the Treasury about the total amount of grant, and the Secretary of State had to secure Cabinet agreement to the total, contact with local government about the grant was the DoE's exclusive 'turf'. The significance of the Treasury's involvement, and that of the other spending departments, in the CCLGF is perhaps reflected in the caveat to the CCLGF's terms of reference that it 'should not affect the existing relationship between Departments and local government'.[8]

It is important to note that economic context within which the CCLGF was established. Local authority expenditure had grown very rapidly up to 1975/76. With the escalation of world oil prices and the onset of double-figure inflation, the (then) Labour Government faced severe problems in managing the economy. The Government's system for planning and controlling public expenditure seemed to be one the the verge of collapse and the so-called 'cash limit' system was introduced. In short, the CCLGF was part of the response to economic crisis and between 1975/76 and 1978/79 local expenditure was contained... The inception of the CCLGF saw a marked emphasis on the rhetoric of co-operation: on both levels of government joining together to restrain public expenditure and to correct the deficiencies of the national economy.

The CCLGF was not the only means for controlling local expenditure, however: reductions in central grant and the introduction of cash limits were equally important. Thus, grant was reduced from 66.5 per cent to 61 per cent and, although in the early days the Government denied that the function of cash limits was to impose 'hidden' cuts on local government, they have achieved this end from their inception. In deciding on the (reduced) total of grant (in money terms) available to local government, the Government made assumptions about the future rate of inflation. This assumption was invariably less than the actual rate of inflation... The net result was a further decline in the total of local expenditure.

The period 1973-79 saw a number of changes of paramount importance. First, local expenditure had been 're-classified': it was now treated as an integral part of the national public expenditure process and, as such, a legitimate target for Treasury influence in an attempt to manage the national economy. It had not been so treated before. Second, and the CCLGF notwithstanding, the period illustrates the importance of local government's 'responsibility ethic'.[9] At no stage was the national community able to regulate member local authorities: it had no sanctions it could bring to bear on them. Rather, the acceptance of restraint by Conservative controlled local authorities — the result of mid-term swings in the local elections against the government of the day — provides a clear illustration of the importance of voluntary compliance to effective control in British central-local relations. Third, with ever intensifying economic problems, the policy communities were challenged by the Treasury. The period before 1973 can be seen as 'the era of the professional'. Central departments and the professions had a vested interest in the continued expansion of the welfare state: the policy communities were dominant. As the guardian of the purse strings, the Treasury increasingly intervened to restrain and ultimately curtail the expansive proclivities of the spending departments or advocates.[10] Not only was the CCLGF a Treasury initiative but its objectives also including improved co-ordination between central spending departments concerned with local government and not just control of local expenditure. Finally, the national community became more prominent not only for grant negotiations, but also for local pay negotiations. Given the increasing need to control the level of expenditure, given the built-in tendency of central spending departments, the professions and local service departments to promote expenditure, it is not surprising that the second prong in the attack on the advocates was to promote those representative bodies not specifically committed to a single service. Just as the Treasury represented guardianship at the centre, so the national community of local government was an obvious ally in the fight to restrain expenditure: in theory at least their interests encompass local government in its entirety, and they could be expected 'to see the problem in the round'.[11]

In short, the balance of advantage shifted in favour of the generalist national community in an era of financial restraint. Given the role of the policy communities in the growth of the welfare state, this shift of advantage was not insignificant... Has the Conservative Government accentuated many of the pre-existing trends, or has it, as many allege, transformed intergovernmental relations in Britain?

3 The changing pattern since 1979: an era of direction

If one single theme permeates recent developments, it is the search by central government for more effective instruments of *control* (not influence) over the expenditure of local government. Control is not, however, the only development of significance. The government has also sought to restrict the size of the public sector by divesting local government of some of its functions: that is, by *privatization*. Although its 'progress' under this head has been slow, none the less it is a distinctive feature of current Conservative policy. Both control and privatization can be seen as an attack on the public sector, as means for curtailing its role in British society, and certainly local government has railed vigorously against its containment. As relations between the two sides have deteriorated, so there have been marked changes in behaviour. The Secretary of State for the Environment has adopted a *unilateral* style of decision-making and the more normal consultative mode of proceeding has been forsaken. Both sides have shown an increasing willingness to resort to *litigation* to resolve their differences. With changes in political control at the local level, *recalcitrance* has replaced consultation with an increasing number of Labour controlled local authorities demonstrating a willingness to defy the Government's edicts on expenditure. The vast majority of local authorities have adopted *risk avoidance* strategies: that is they have sought ways and means for reducing the uncertainties of the present situation. In short, the consultation so distinctive of the mid-seventies has been replaced by direction and confrontation. Moreover, this confrontation is no longer confined to central and local government. It has also come to typify relations between local authorities and between their national representative organizations. For central government the results of this new style of central-local relations has been a series of *unintended consequences* amongst which the constant changes in the grant system to gain effective control must be numbered the most serious...

(i) Control

The Government employed three means for achieving the reduction in local expenditure. Firstly, the approval of central departments is required for local capital expenditure programmes. In order to reduce capital expenditure the Government simply placed a ceiling on the programmes.[12] This control was most effective and the consequences for some services — e.g. the provision of council houses — were particularly severe, although the previous Labour Government's control of borrowing through loan sanction had the same overall effect. Secondly, it employed cash limits and, again, the Government differed little from the previous Labour administration. Finally, there was the Local Government Planning and Land Act (1980) and this particular piece of legislation has been the chief object of criticism for the defenders of local government.

The 1980 Act introduced the Block Grant. Under this new system, the Secretary of State for the Environment assesses how much a local authority needs to spend: the grant-related expenditure assessment (GREA). He also specifies the rate to be levied for each of the various levels of expenditure. The total grant for an individual local authority is a function of its assessed level of expenditure, the specified rate level and its total rateable value. The key feature of this change is that the Secretary of State can now penalize local authorities which 'over-spend'. Local authorities can still determine the rate to be levied but, if their actual expenditure is greater than the Secretary of State's assessment, then the amount of grant paid will be reduced. For the first time, therefore, central government has direct (rather than indirect) controls over the level of expenditure of the individual local authority.

The 1980 Act was a compendious piece of legislation which introduced changes ranging from the introduction of the new system for the approval of capital expenditure to the removal of some two hundred detailed controls including the Secretary of State's powers for approving the sites and plans for crematoria.[13] Given its scope, some legislative respite might have been anticipated. Unfortunately from the standpoint of local government, the ensuing years were ones of considerable uncertainty. Temporary arrangements for the distribution of grant to local authorities were employed in 1980/81. Even more troublesome was the Secretary of State's decision to change the new system virtually before it had come into being. The Government was concerned that the new system would not deter 'over-spending' local authorities. The threat of reducing grant, indeed actual reductions in grant, did not bring about reductions in the level of expenditure of local authorities. To protect their services, local authorities compensated for the fall in grant by increasing local taxes. The Secretary of State reacted to this development by threatening to place a ceiling on the non-domestic rate (i.e. the property tax on companies) and by requiring local authorities to hold a referendum before levying supplementary rate increases. In other words, if in the course of the year a local authority found that its expenditure exceeded its income, it could increase taxes by issuing a second demand for rates to local residents. Under the 1980 Act, the Secretary of State suggested a guideline tax level to local authorities. Under the proposed legislation, he was taking steps to control directly rate increases. However, this proposal met con

siderable opposition, crucially from the Conservative backbenchers, and the referendum proposal had to be dropped. Undeter-
red, the Secretary of State introduced the Local Government
Finance Act (1982) which abolished supplementary rates. As importantly, the Act gives the Secretary of State the power to reduce
the grant to an individual local authority *in the course of the year* if
he thinks they are 'over-spending'. The 1982 Act provides a vivid
illustration of the determination of the Government to control
both local expenditure *and* local income. Equally, the changes illustrate the elusiveness of this goal. Since 1979 it is possible to
identify seven major changes in the grant system:

(1) the rate support grant system based on needs and resources elements, inherited from the previous government:
(2) the system as under 1 above, but with the 'transitional arrangements' penalities applied in 1980-81;
(3) the block grant system based on grant related expenditure, introduced under the rate support grant settlement for 1981-82;
(4) the block grant system with the holdback penalities based on
volume targets, introduced in June 1981;
(5) the block grant system with holdback penalties based on
volume targets. but with exemptions for authorities meeting
grant related expenditures, introduced in September 1981;
(6) the block grant system with holdback provision related to a
composite target base on GREAs and volume targets, introduced in the rate support grant settlement for 1982-83;
(7) the arrangements which ... followed the abolition of supplementary rates under the Local Government Finance Act,
1982...[14]

(ii) Privatization
The size and scope of the public sector can be reduced not only by
cutting public expenditure but also by returning functions to the
private sector.

The term privatization is widely used to describe any and all attempts to reinforce the market principle. In the local government
context, it covers at least four distinct policies: establishing or rein-
forcing individual rights *vis-à-vis* local authority services; contracting public services out to private companies; charging for local
services; and the withdrawal of the public sector from the provision of a service. It is probably too late to insist that the term be

limited in usage to this last policy and it is used here as an umbrella term.

There are a number of major and minor examples of the several species of privatization. The Housing Act (1980) requires local authorities to sell council houses... The Act contains provisions for central government to take over the task from recalcitrant local authorities. Thus, if a local authority uses administrative delays to frustrate sales, the Secretary of State for the Environment can appoint a Housing Commissioner to administer the scheme, although this power has only been used on one occasion. These provisions for central control are less important, however, than the rationale of the legislation which lies in vesting statutory rights in individuals for the purchase of public assets...

Perhaps the clearest example of the Government's attempts to implement a competitive market philosophy lie in the several measures to increase the role of the private sector in local government services. Thus, the Government has introduced a series of controls over direct works departments with the avowed aim of increasing the role of the private sector in public-sector construction programmes. Similarly, it has established an Audit Commission to stimulate economy and efficiency in local government and it has laid considerable emphasis on the use of private-sector companies. Finally, the Urban Development Grant scheme provides finance for projects jointly prepared by local authorities and the private sector which involve 'significant' private finance. None of these examples, however, can be seen as more than local government dipping its toe in the waters of privatization.

In as far as privatization involves central control and regulation, it is obviously congruent with the changes in the grant system: it serves to reinforce centralization. Conversely, by re-asserting the market principle, such measures could be said to increase decentralization. Either way, privatization has had one important effect on central-local relations: because the effect of all these measures is to reduce the scope of the public sector, it has increased conflict between the two levels of government. Local authorities have been most reluctant to see their services eroded, whether by financial controls or by privatization, and the result has been some marked changes in the behaviour of the participants, changes which can be summarized as unilateralism, litigation, risk avoidance and recalitrance.

(iii) Unilateralism

If it is a truism that Government can coerce local government by legislation, it is equally true that the 'normal' way of proceeding is by consultation and negotiation. The characteristic style of Michael Heseltine when he was Secretary of State can only be described as unilateralist. Thus, the recent proceedings of the CCLGF have been described as follows:

Consultation has ceased since 1979 ... it isn't consultation, it's a forum where they start telling you what you're going to do...

In as far as consultation exists, it is on party-lines: 'They've got a club situation where they all talk in private corners, the Tories almost go to bed with each other they're so close.,[15] It is difficult to avoid the conclusion that prior agreement on the policy is the essential prerequisite of consultation. Certainly, the Secretary of State unilaterally altered the rules of the grant game and the Thatcher Government rejected corporatist-style arrangements in the arena of central-local relations as it did in other areas of policy-making.

(iv) Litigation

The conflict between central and local government has been mirrored in an increase in the importance of litigious behaviour. Recent years have witnessed an almost unprecedented number of key court cases at the instigation of both central and local government... There can perhaps be no clearer indication of the breakdown of 'normal processes' than this resort to the courts to regulate key aspects of the relationship between central and local government. Moreover, it is important to note that this conflict was not limited to central and local government: there are sharp differences between Conservative and Labour controlled authorities in their approach to the control of local expenditure. As a result, legal conflicts also occur between local authorities, as in the case of the Greater London Council (Labour controlled) and the London Borough of Bromley (Conservative controlled).

(v) Risk avoidance

The third feature of current behaviour is the uncertainty created by government policy and the steps taken by local authorities to minimize its effects. The changes to the grant system have already been noted. When, for example, the Government determined the GREAs for individual local authorities and then set local authorities cash limited spending targets below their GREAs, the incompatible nature of these two sets of targets virtually required the prudent local authority to act to minimize the effects of such changes. Even local authorities which had consistently shown restraint in determining their level of expenditure found that they were classified as 'over-spenders' and subject to grant penalties: a situation which arose simply because the Government's targets were arbitrary. Two examples will serve to illustrate the strategy of risk avoidance. Firstly, the Government has continued to seek reductions in current expenditure whilst, more recently encouraging local authorities to increase capital expenditure to revive the construction industry and thus aid the more general recovery of the British economy. Local authorities are showing considerable reluctance to undertake such capital expenditure because any capital project invariably has implications for current expenditure. For example, if you build a home for children, you have to heat, maintain and staff it. All of these items are a charge against current expenditure. Without assurances that grant money will be forthcoming to cover the future costs, local authorities prefer to forgo any increase in their building programmes. Secondly, the continuing uncertainties surrounding central-local relations have bred an attitude of 'never do now what you can leave until later'. Local authorities build up, therefore, contingency funds to cover unexpected developments, delay new projects to avoid incurring expenditure and 'massage' their statistics — 'creative accountancy' — by, for example, reclassifying current expenditure as capital expenditure to avoid 'over-spending'.[16] The net result is that, in total, local government spends less than the Government wants to instead of contributing to increases in inflation — for which it has been frequently criticized — it contributes to the continuing deflation of the British economy...

(vi) Recalcitrance
Another important trend has been the refusal of many local authorities to comply with Government demands. As Michael Heseltine abandoned consultation in favour of unilateralism, so local authorities abandoned co-operation for confrontation. That the response of local authorities to the Government's demands for

cuts has varied is clearly shown by Cooper and Stewart: 'For the last three years ... on average, Labour authorities increased expenditure by about 2 per cent more than the Conservatives. This year the difference has widened ... to 4.5 per cent. The differences are still small between the parties in the shire districts, the gap having been widened through the influence of the GLC and the non-met counties'.[17] Moreover, 49 per cent of Labour authorities were above their effective spending target whilst 51 per cent of Conservative authorities were more than 6 per cent below their targets. Similarly, for 1983/84, Conservative councils plan to spend 0.3 per cent above target whilst Labour councils plan to spend 7.7 per cent over target...[18]

(vii)   Unintended consequences
Assessing the record has become a complex 'numbers game'... Care has to be taken, therefore, in negotiating the maze of local authority expenditure statistics.[19] But cautions to one side, it is clear that Conservative cuts have not been as distinctive as is widely perceived.

Between 1975/76 and 1978/79 local authority expenditure (capital and current) fell, as a percentage of GDP, from 15.5 per cent to 12.8 per cent and, as a percentage of total public-sector expenditure, from 31 per cent to 28 per cent. Duke and Edgell calculate that, over all major programmes, total public expenditure fell by 1.3 per cent. There was, however, considerable variation in the incidence of these cuts. They fell more heavily on local than on central government and some services had an increase in expenditure. For example, social security expenditure increased by some 6 per cent whilst education experienced a cut of 2.4 per cent, environmental services 4 per cent, housing 7.4 per cent and transport 8.1 per cent.[20]

Between 1979/80 and 1982/83, under the Conservatives, total public expenditure rose as a proportion of GDP and central government's expenditure increased sharply. The big spenders were not for the most part local government services. Defence, social security and lending to the nationalized industries were amongst the major beneficiaries. Indeed, some local services declined dramatically, e.g. housing. The Conservative cut substantially the centre's contribution to local services — the proportion of net current local expenditure financed by grant fell from 61 per cent to 56 per cent. Local government manpower fell by 4 per cent in the same period. Most dramatically, local capital expenditure was subject to stringent regulation and it was still lower in *cash* terms in 1983 than in 1979, although it had risen slightly in 1983. And yet, in spite of the 'cuts', local current expenditure *increased* between March 1979 and March 1983 by at least 2 per cent (in volume terms). This figure is, of course, disputed with the Government claiming that the increase is 7 per cent (in cost terms). It is *not* disputed, however, that local current expenditure has increased... As with the previous Labour Government, the bulk of the 'cuts' fell on local government and on capital expenditure whilst, ironically, the Conservatives presided over both an increase in total public expenditure and local current expenditure.

Nothing in this discussion denies that 'cuts' have had a deleterious effect on various local services. Quite obviously, housing expenditure has been decimated. Equally, a discussion limited to resources omits the crucial topic of needs. To the extent that the need for services has increased, and in an economy with mass unemployment such an increase seems more than probable, even growth in public expenditure can represent a reduction in the scale and quality of service provision as a smaller proportion of the target clientele is reached or resources are spread more thinly. The simple point is that, for the 1979-83 Conservative Government, there is a divergence between the rhetoric and the reality of its policy on public expenditure: the 'cuts' were neither unique nor even outstandingly draconian.

The continuous changes to the grant system reflect the Secretary of State's disappointment in the ability of the new grant system to deliver reductions in local expenditure on the desired scale. As Raine has pointed out, the 1980 Act did not have the expected results: the 'over-spenders' had no great incentive to reduce their expenditure because it would have dramatic effects on the services whilst authorities spending below their GREA had an incentive to increase marginally their expenditure.[21] Nor are the continuous adjustments to the grant system to overcome recalcitrance the only unintended consequence arising out of the new style of central-local relations.

Firstly, as noted earlier, capital expenditure has fallen sharply in line with Government plans. However, the tight revenue squeeze on local councils has made them reluctant to use the revenue from capital sales. In addition, the receipts from such sales were far greater than expected. As a result, capital spending has fallen below intended levels.

Secondly, the squeeze on local authority expenditure has increased the cost of service provision in other parts of the public
sector. For example, the process of transferring long-stay patients
out of expensive and often inappropriate national health service
care to local authority social service departments has more or less
halted... But with their existing social service spending badly
squeezed, local authorities are in no mood to accept any new
responsibilities, so that the transfers involved have jammed up,
causing a growing problem for the NHS and Whitehall in funding
much more expensive provision with the health service. The consequence of the DoE's 'success' in curbing council revenue spending thus involves higher spending by the DHSS. Something similar
is happening in the field of housing rents.

Since 1980 the DoE has compelled local councils to raise rents
for council housing in line with rigid national estimates of
'realistic' levels, which in some cases brought about increases of
almost 80 per cent between 1980 and late 1981. By 1982 many
councils were already making a profit on their council housing (so
that council tenants were subsidizing ratepayers). Since around
half of all council house rents are now paid by the DHSS (because
tenants are unemployed or pensioners or on supplementary benefits), much of the rent increases has simply put up the bill facing
another central government department.

The consequences of the new style of central-local relations are
more varied than is widely allowed, and they extend to the national local government system. If the 1970s saw the Government
attempting to incorporate the national community of local government, the 1980s have seen the Government abandon the attempt.
'Guardianship' has remained the dominant theme of the Government but the national community was no longer seen as an ally but
rather as an adversary. Consequently, *both* the national community and the policy communities have been on the defensive for the
past four years. As ever, there are caveats to such a general assessment.

Firstly, individual Associations have been able to wring concessions from the Government provided party affiliation and interest
over-rode the interests of local authorities. The most notable instance of such behaviour was the support of the Association of
County Councils for the Lords' stage of the Local Government
Planning and Land (No. 2) Bill when they agreed to withdraw their

opposition to the Bill — to the acrimonious disappointment of their fellow Associations — in return for a number of essentially detailed amendments to the legislation.

Secondly, the policy communities have been able to mitigate some of the Government's calls for reduced expenditure. The cuts were selective, falling on capital not current expenditure, on local not central departments. The resistance of central departments, and the policy communities, lie at the root of this disparity. Some of the policy communities have been able to mount a rearguard action of consequence: and the dominant strategy can be called 'off-loading to the periphery':

or 'anybody else but us'. It's a process whereby the administrators deciding on the allocation of cuts push the cuts to the periphery, as far away from themselves as possible...[22]

Thirdly, the clampdown on capital expenditure for new council housing looks set to recreate a gross housing shortage in the United Kingdom (i.e. a situation where there are fewer dwellings than there are households) by the mid-1980s.

Finally, the key feature of recent developments is the instability of relationships within the national local government system and between that system and the Government. For the bulk of the post-war period, continuity and common understandings would have been seen as the dominant characteristics. Care must be taken not to overstate the degree of change. The national community of local government still sends representatives to the CCLGF, and it is still prominent in pay negotiations. Consultations on specific service issues continue within the policy communities. But over the past decade both have been challenged by the Government. The ground conquered by the policy communities in the 1950s and 1960s will have to be reconquered in the 1980s. Relationships within the national local government system continue to fluctuate with party, type of authority and service interests in an ever shifting pattern of alliances. For the Government, the overwhelming fact of life is the institutional inertia confronting its policies: that is, any change has to overcome the conservatism of vested interests lodged in the actual structure of government. For the national local government system, it is the recurrent instability coupled with the defence of ideas and policies they considered entrenched and immutable.

4 The 'Conservative threat'

In circumstances where central-local relations are subject to regular changes to counter recalcitrance, it is peculiarly difficult to predict the long-term effects of recent developments. Certainly the Conservative Government has affected significant changes in central-local relations. They have intensified the search for control. In this process, the rules of the game have been changed unilaterally. The Government seeks to impose nationally determined targets on local government. Most significantly, they have moved from control at the aggregate level to control over the expenditure decisions of individual local authorities. But these changes were already marked out by earlier developments. The Labour Government 're-classified' local expenditure as part of the national public expenditure survey, thereby denying that it was, as in the past, a matter for local decision and providing the essential foundations for the Conservatives' innovations. In and of themselves these innovations do not justify the contention that the Conservatives are responsible for the demise of local government. In an era of central direction, local government current expenditure (in volume terms) did increase, not fall as intended. The fortunes of the Government in its attempts both to reduce public expenditure and to restructure the welfare state have clearly been mixed.

The concern with the dangers for local government of Conservative legislation has led to a degree of myopia.[23] Current events are not specific to local government nor peculiar to the present Government. A number of important caveats to the 'Conservative threat' or the 'demise of local government' thesis should be noted.

Firstly, the dominance of national economic management problems in the practice and reform of intergovernmental relations is a feature of the 1970s and not, peculiarly, of the present Conservative Government... Recent developments do not have their roots in a specific Act of Parliament. They are manifestations of longer-term economic trends: a conclusion which bodes ill for the future of local government, suggesting that too much faith should not be placed in the repeal of, for example, the 1980 Act.

Secondly, and in spite of protestations and (ostensibly) policies to the contrary, confusion and ambiguity have remained preeminent characteristics of intergovernmental relations over the past decade. It would require saint-like charity to describe the ever-changing grant system as stable, consistent or predictable. To state the point baldly, the Government appears to have a vested interest in confusion and ambiguity... Any system which clearly specified responsibilities and accountability (however crudely) would, at one and the same time, limit central government's ability to react to short-term economic problems... The most disturbing features of recent trends in intergovernmental relations are *not*, therefore, recent legislative changes but the continuities. Local expenditure has remained a sub-set of national public expenditure decisions. Confusion and ambiguity continue to prevail over clear accountability.

Thirdly, the Government's unilateral decision to change the rules of the grant game is not, in itself, unique... Central-local relations operate in a system characterized by a strong executive tradition and can be no more divorced from the effects of the larger system than any facet of British politics.

Finally, the lesson of recent developments for Whitehall seems to be that its potential to acquire new formal powers of control may not be a stable, long-run substitute for a system better able to secure the voluntary co-operation of local authorities. These are various means to influence local authorities available to the centre, ranging from direction and penalties through incentives and incorporation to persuasion and advice. A somewhat broader mix of means with considerably less emphasis on direction and penalties would seem essential preconditions of a more stable, compliant system.

If the ship of local government is heading towards the rocks, the hand on the rudder is as likely to be Labour as Conservative and the effectiveness of any centralizing policies will be diminished by local recalcitrance and confused by a range of unintended consequence. Central to any understanding of central-local relations is the tension between the interdependence of centre and locality on the one hand and authoritative decision-making by central government of the other. This tension has remained to plague all post-war governments of whatever political complexion...

After four years of direction and control, the Conservatives returned to office facing a choice between intensifying direction and a more conciliatory mix of strategies designed to win compliance. It has chosen to intensify direction. The Government proposes to limit the rate levels of high spending local authorities —

'rate-capping' — and to abolish both the Greater London Council and the metropolitan counties.[24] Local expenditure will be brought under control by regulating the income as well as the expenditure of local councils and by abolishing the worst 'overspender'. Legislation will be enacted during 1984. If the precise form of these proposals remains to be determined, the likely outcome seems all too clear. Developments over the past decade suggest that, when control is the preferred strategy, the outcome will be unintended consequences, recalcitrance, instability, ambiguity and confusion: in short, the *policy mess* that has become the defining characteristics of British central-local relations.

Notes

1 See, for example, J. D. Stewart, G. W. Jones, R. Greenwood and J. W. Raine, 'In Defence of Local Government' (Birmingham: Institute of Local Government Studies, 1981); and T. Burgess and T. Travers, *Ten Billion Pounds: Whitehall's Takeover of the Town Halls* (London: Grant McIntyre, 1980).

2 For more detailed information on local expenditure in this period see C. D. Foster, R. Jackman and M. Perlman, *Local Government Finance in a Unitary State* (London: Allen & Unwin, 1980); R. J. Bennett, *Central Grants to Local Government* (Cambridge: Cambridge University Press, 1982).

3 R. A. W. Rhodes, *Control and Power in Central-Local Government Relations* (Farnborough: Gower, 1981), Chap. 5.

4 Dunleavy, *The Politics of Mass Housing,* p. 105. See also P. Dunleavy, *Urban Political Analysis* (London: Macmillan, 1980), p. 105. For a full discussion of the disparate interests in central-local relations see: P. Dunleavy and R. A. W. Rhodes, 'Beyond Whitehall' in H. M. Drucker, ed., *Developments in British Politics* (London: Macmillan, 1983), pp.106-33.

5 H. Helco and A. Wildavsky, *The Private Government of Public Money* (London: Macmillan, 1974), p. xv. See also A. Wildavsky, The Art and Craft of Policy Analysis (London: Macmillan, 1980), Chap. 3.

6 Rhodes, Control and Power, p. 115.

7 For detailed evidence see Rhodes *et al.,* 'Constraints on the National Community of Local Governments', Chaps. 1 and 2.

8 For a detailed description of the CCLGF see R. A. W. Rhodes, B. Hardy and K. Pudney, ' "Corporate Bias" in Central-Local Relations: A Case Study of the Consultative Council on Local Government Finance' (University of Essex: SSRC Central-Local Relations Project: Discussion Paper No. 1, March 1982).1

9 See C. Bramley and M. Stewart, 'Implementing Public Expenditure Cuts' in S. Barrett and C. Fudge, eds, *Policy and Action* (London: Methuen, 1981), pp. 39-63.

10 A. Wildavsky, *Budgeting: A Comparative Theory of Budgetary Processes* (Boston: Little, Brown, 1975), pp. 7-9

11 See also A. Alexander, *Local Government in Britain since Reorganisation* (London: Allen & Unwin, 1982), Chap. 7.

12 For a more detailed account of all the financial terms used in this section see: N. P. Hepworth, *The Finance of Local Government,* 4th edn (London: Allen & Unwin, 1980).

13 For a compendious summary of Conservative policy on central-local relations between 1979 and 1982 see the speech by Michael Heseltine, Secretary of State for the Environment, at the Annual Conference of the National Housing and Town Planning Council, Brighton, 9 November 1982.

14 G. W. Jones and J. D. Stewart, 'The Layfield Analysis Applied to Central-Local Relations under the Conservative Government', *Local Government Studies,* VIII (1982), 55-6.

15 Rhodes *et al.,* ' "Corporate Bias" in Central-Local Relations', pp. 73-5.

16 For many more examples see E. M. Davies, J. G. Gibson, C. H. Game and J. D. Stewart, *Grant Characteristics and Central-Local Relations* (Report to the Social Science Research Council, July 1983).

17 N. Cooper and J. Stewart, 'Local Authority Budgets 1982/83', *Public Finance and Accountancy,* June 1982, 17-21.

18 P. Smith and J. Stewart, 'Local Authority Spending 1983/84', *Public Finance and Accountancy,* June 1983, 35-9.

19 The major sources for the statistics in this section are the publications of the Chartered Institute of Public Finance and Accountancy, most notably 'Local Government Trends' and 'Financial and General Statistics'.

20 V. Duke and S. Edgell, 'Public Expenditure Cuts in Britain and Local Authority Mediation', paper to the PSA Urban Politics Group. University of Birmingham, December 1981.

21 Stewart, *et al.,* 'In Defence of Local Government', p. 3.

22 B. Donoughue, Senior Policy Adviser to the Prime Minister 1974-79, quoted in H. Young and A. Sloman, *No, Minister: An Inquiry into the Civil Service* (London: BBC Publications, 1982), pp. 33-4.

23 The characterization of recent commentaries is clearly illustrated by the references in fn. 1 and by many of the articles in the local government press. Turning from polemics and journalism, the self-same concerns can be seen in the academic literature. See R. Greewood, 'Pressures from Whitehall' in R. Rose and E. Page, eds, *Fiscal Stress in Cities* (Cambridge: Cambridge University Press, 1982), pp. 44-76; and Greenwood, 'The Politics of Central-Local Relations in England and Wales 1974-81' from which the phrase 'the demise of local government' is taken.

24 See department of the Environment/Welsh Office, *Rates* (London: HMSO, Cmnd 9008, 1983); and Department of the Environment, *Streamlining the Cities* (London: HMSO, Cmnd 9063, 1983).

5.2   *John Gyford*

The politicization of
local government

From M. Loughlin, *et. al.*, *Half a Century of Municipal Decline, George Allen and Unwin, London 1985, pp. 77-97.*

Five stages of politicization

... It is possible to trace within the history of local government a process of gradually increasing politicization during the century and a half after 1835. Politicization involves the growing participation of organized political groupings in such aspects of local government as local elections, the internal organization and workings of councils, the formulation and execution of council policies, and the relations between local and central government and between local government and the public. It is possible to conjecture that there were a number of stages in this process of politicization, though in doing so one runs a considerable risk of over-simplification...

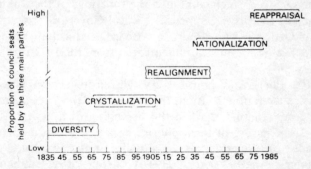

Figure 1 : *Party politics in local government: five conjectural stages.*

The three decades after the 1835 Act was a period of great diversity, if not confusion, with politics in local government assuming a somewhat kaleidoscopic form. A variety of actors in different towns — Whigs, Tories, Liberals, Conservatives, Radicals, Chartists, Improvers, Economizers, Independents, and a bevy of personal cliques and factions — argued over whether to expand, or to economize on, the provision of public services. This political diversity was matched by administrative diversity. There was a bewildering patchwork of functions and areas divided amongst municipal coporations, improvement commissioners, local Boards of Health and Poor Law Guardians ... Thereafter, in the last third of the nineteenth century, with the larger towns leading the way, there came a stage of crystallization. In this period, despite a continued preference by some candidates for the Independent label, local politics gradually solidified into a Conservative-Liberal contest, the pace and style having been set perhaps by the impact of the 'civic gospel' of Joseph Chamberlain's Birmingham Liberalism. This was also a period in which local elections began to be seen as having national implications. Sir John Gorst, the Conservative Party's Principal Agent, began using local election results as indicators of parliamentary results in the 1870s, though Disraeli was not wholly convinced of their relevance (Hanham, 1959, pp. 388-90); and in 1894 the Marquess of Salisbury saw the LCC election as useful practice for the general election that was to follow (Young, 1975, p. 32&. This was also a time when attempts were made to rationalize English local government. The early 1870s in particular were 'something of a watershed' (Fraser, 1979, p. 152). A Local Government Board was set up in 1871, which combined the functions of the Public Health branch of the Privy Council, the Local Government section of the Home Office and the Poor Law Board, and a uniform pattern of public health administration emerged from the 1872 Public Health Act.

After this era of political crystallization, accompanied by administrative rationalization, the creation of the Labour Party early in the new century marked the beginning of a period of realignment. The nature of local politics became transformed as Labour replaced the Liberal Party, gradually at first but with gathering pace during the 1920s and 1930s. This stage of realignment in local politics was followed, in turn, after the Second World War, by one of nationalization, in which local politics became harnessed, partly in aspiration and partly in actuality, to the national fortunes of the major parties, with local government itself becoming an important arm of the postwar welfare state. Finally, in the wake of local government reorganization in the early 1970s, though by no means simply as a result of it, there developed what might be described as a stage of reappraisal in local politics, with the emergence of major debates both between and within the political parties about the role of local government in society.

The nationalisation of party politics in the post-war period

The years after 1945 saw a major escalation of party politics in local government and a concomitant decline in the number of Independent councillors. In the years between 1947 and 1952 the Independents suffered an unbroken series of annual net losses totalling some 1,500 seats in the county and municipal elections. In the following decade they lost a further 340 seats. The spread of party politics was not uniform but occurred largely in the urban areas. By the time of the last local elections before reorganization, in 1972, the Independents had been reduced to holding only one seat in nine in the county and non-county boroughs. Their fate here differed from that in the county councils, where they were able to hold approximately 30 per cent of all seats throughout the eight triennial elections from 1949 to 1970. Thus, the overall position as it developed after 1945 was very much that discovered by the Maud Committee inquiry in 1964-5: three out of four of the boroughs and urban districts were run on a party basis compared with only one-third of the counties and fewer than a quarter of the rural districts (Maud, 1967. pp. 108-9).

The expansion of party politics after 1945 was accompanied by a certain assimilation of local political battles into the national contest between the two major parties, a process later christened the 'nationalization of local politics' (R. W. Johnson, 1972; Young, 1975; Schofield, 1977). An important component of this process was a growing and more systematic involvement with local government on the part of the national leaderships at party headquarters and Westminster. The Conservative Party set up a National Advisory Committee on Local Government in 1944, created its own Central Office Local Government Department in 1946, began to convene annual local government conferences for Conservative councillors in 1947 and launched a monthly journal, *The Council-*

lor, in 1948. On the Labour side, despite an earlier initiative in
1936 in establishing a Local Government Department at Transport
House, the inauguration of a *Newsletter for Labour Groups,* the
setting-up of an NEC local government subcommittee and the initiation of an annual local government conference did not occur
until 1954, 1955 and 1956 respectively.

Meanwhile, however, both parties had seen ways in which local
politics might be played in aid of their national struggle. After
Labour's campaign attempted to link the two levels of politics in
1945, the Conservatives were not long in replying in kind. The
1947 local elections saw substantial Conservative gains, which
Central Office felt laid the foundations of eventual recovery at
parliamentary level after the disaster of 1945. The 1947 gains were
due not to a decline in Labour support (which actually increased in
terms of votes cast) but to an even larger increase in Conservative
votes. The voters, moreover, were responding to a Conservative
campaign that had been waged not only on a 'Town Hall versus
Whitehall' theme of defending local autonomy but also on national issues, such as food shortages, the abolition of the basic
petrol ration and the general 'austerity' which accompanied the
export drive.

The 1950s and 1960s saw repeated attempts to bring local and
national politicians of each party to march in step. The calls for
greater co-ordination did not come solely from the top; from the
bottom, from the councillors, came intermittent pleas for
ministers of each party to bear in mind the electoral and other problems of their respective local colleagues, for example, in the tim-
ing of controversial policy initiatives. The 'marriage' of local and
national politics was perhaps best symbolized by the decision of
Conservative Central Office to exploit the party's massive gains in
the 1967 local elections by taking control of the Association of
Municipal Corporations, which had previously been run on largely
non-political lines. In a concerted campaign, the more numerous
Conservative-controlled boroughs represented on the association
succeeded in capturing all but two of its thirteen committee chair-
manships. The eventual outcome of this coup was the conversion
of the local authority associations, before and after the 1974 reorganization, into political bodies to a previously unknown degree,
with Labour retaliating in kind when electoral circumstances
allowed.

A noticeable feature of the three decades after 1945 was the extent to which local voting patterns seemed to be largely a product of national trends rather than local issues, a phenomenon which had been observed in the nineteenth century but which had declined during the period of realignment. Its re-emergence meant the appearance of marked peaks and troughs in the local electoral cycle, as councillors across the country reaped the reward, or paid the price, of their national party's standing in the voters' esteem. The most marked of these, after Labour's triumphs in 1945, was the Conservative victory of 1968 when the party gained 1,630 seats in the provincial boroughs and urban districts, with Labour losing 1,602. An important consequence of these developments in 1968 was the sweeping from office of many long-entrenched Labour councillors and the undermining of the traditional right-wing Labour leadership on many authorities, thereby opening the way for a new generation of local Labour politicians in the years which followed. The explanation for such electoral events lay in a tendency noted by Butler and Stokes (1975, p. 40): they found that voters in council elections 'voted to an over-whelming degree in line with their expressed [national] party self-image ... well over 90 per cent of our respondents stayed with their generalised ties to the national parties'. In such circumstances local elections were not so much a test of opinion on local issues but more an opportunity to exercise the party machine, a fact which led party organizers to favour annual local elections in particular.

Butler and Stokes' references to the voters' 'generalised ties to the national parties' reminds us that they were studying political behaviour within a stable two-party system wherein each party enjoyed a large block of 'captive' potential voters, whose loyalties were chiefly influenced by factors of family and class, leaving electoral outcomes to be heavily affected by differential abstention and a minority of floating voters. Moreover, the majority of the politicians who operated within this system, whether at the local or national levels, inhabited the same 'assumptive world' (Young and Mills, 1980). They took for granted the permanency of the welfare state and the mixed economy so that their partisan disagreements covered a rather narrow range of opinions. Such an era of stable consensus politics, sustained by a level of economic growth which seemed to provide resources for many otherwise competing demands, was fertile ground for the nationalization of local politics.

Within local government itself political debate tended to revolve around what policies to adopt within the framework of the welfare state, for example around issues such as the 11-plus examination or rent levels rather than around more basic topics, such as the merits of state education or of council housing. There were few serious ideological stresses and strains within either of the parties and little disposition to raise fundamental arguments about the respective roles of local and central government.

In such circumstances, the nationalization of local politics, with its overtones of 'homogenization' (Bristow, 1978) and 'a gradual ironing our of autonomous local characteristics' (R. W. Johnson, 1972, p. 53), can be seen as the particular expression in local government of that bipartisan collectivism which Samuel Beer (1965) identified as being the then distinctive feature of British politics. As such, it is not to be equated with the demotion of local authorities into mere tools of central government, with all power centralized in Whitehall. As recent research has suggested, the central-local relationship has been more complex; councils have had some degree of room for manoeuvre (Rhodes, 1981). The nationalization of local politics rested less on organizational or administrative mechanisms within parties or public authorities and more on the shared assumptions and values of local and national politicians. It represented one aspect of the mid-twentieth century *rapprochement* between the feudal paternalism of Tory Democracy and the Fabian centralism of Social Democracy.

The impact of party on local government in this period became a matter of considerable academic interest. Party was becoming an increasingly pervasive phenomenon, but were there any discernible consequences for local authorities? Observers concluded that parties did fulfill certain functions. They acted as channels of recruitment for council candidates and, arguably, enlarged the pool of potential councillors; they represented different social groups and interests in the community; and they could, through their party groups, give some coherence to the internal workings of councils and their committees (Lee, 1963; Bulpitt, 1967; Wiseman, 1967; G. W. Jones, 1969; Hampton, 1970; Dearlove, 1973). Moreover their expenditure patterns did show some differences, with Labour authorities spending more readily on ameliorative and redistributive services and Conservative authorities doing likewise for nondistributive service such as police and highways (for example, Alt, 1971; Boaden, 1971; Sharpe and Newton, 1984). Although they were often keen to support the expansion of existing services, when it came to initiating new policies local party groups often seemed either unable or unwilling to go very far. In what was perhaps one of the major instances where local authorities undertook new ventures high-rise housing and town centre redevelopment—both Labour and Conservative councils alike, in getting caught up in the spirit of large-scale planning nad modernization, were responding as much, if not more, to pressures from the professional, commercial and industrial sectors and from central government than to pressures from within their own ranks or from their own local party branches (Dunleavy, 1981).

The politics of local government in the three decades after 1945 was thus in most cases closer to what Hill (1972) described as 'administrative politics'. Administrative politics is found where the administrators dominate the decision-making process, yet acknowledge the claims of democratic politics by bargaining, negotiating or consulting with people outside their own organization, and, when necessary, securing legitimacy for their own actions through the use of formal democratic mechanisms. In such circumstances politicians play two roles. They are seen by the administrators as representatives of public opinion in general or of particular interest groups. As such they must be consulted and policies must either be sold to them or constructed so as to avoid giving political offence. Additionally individual politicians may become, in effect, co-opted into the ranks of the administrators, often becoming 'socialized' into the professional ethos of the education officers, or the planners, or the housing managers. As the local government service became, after 1945, increasingly the preserve of graduates and professionals the possibility of less well-qualified part-time and unpaid councillors becoming co-opted or dominated by their officers grew increasingly real. In such circumstances, politicians might certainly scrutinize their officers' policies, and might accept, modify or occasionally reject them; but rarely would they initiate any of their own. This statement is not to suggest that initiatives never occurred, but rather that they rarely originated with the politicians (Green, 1981). Hill speculates, for example, that securely entrenched political control in one-party authorities might merely provide 'the stability necessary for administrators to take bold policy initiatives under the protection of a stagnant political situation' (Hill, 1972, p. 231).

Hill contrasts administrative politics with ideological politics in which 'unified political parties provide specific programmes' (ibid., p. 211). The contesting of elections on a party basis, and the operation of a party group system within the council, does not, of itself, signify the existence of ideological politics since the majority party may content itself merely with legitimizing the policies prepared by the officers rather than with formulating its own. It is the promotion by the party of a set of distinctive policies based on its own ideology which is the particular feature of ideological politics. This latter practice, however, was to become increasingly common in local politics in and after the mid-1970s, with Labour leading the way in the production of often very detailed policy manifestos for the larger authorities (Fudge, 1981; Game and Skelcher, 1983).

Reappraisal

In the years since the 1974 local government reorganization, some changes in local government suggest that another distinctive stage in its political history may be unfolding. One clear trend has been a further escalation in the spread of party politics. By 1983 85 per cent of all councillors in England and Wales were representatives of the Conservative, Labour or Alliance parties. Only in the non-metropolitan districts did the three parties account for less than that proportion, and even there the figure was 80 per cent. In the metropolitan counties and districts and the Greater London area, the proportion was 98.2 per cent. The continuous advance of party since the first elections to the reorganized authorities in 1973 has been sustained as an act of deliberate policy by the parties themselves. It has, however, been taking place under very different political circumstances from those which attended the previous escalation of party conflict after 1945.

Local party politics after 1945 took place inside the confines of a stable two-party system operating within a widespread welfare state consensus, providing a localized version of 'Butskellism'. The most recent phase of local politics has emerged at the same time as a number of developments very different from those of the consensus years. These include: a greater electoral volatility accompanying class dealignment, with public/private sector location, union membership, and, in some localities, ethnicity becoming important factors in voting behaviour; the emergence of a strong third-party challenge to the two major parties; ideological polarization within the Conservative and Labour parties; an emerging debate about the future of the welfare state; and persisting economic difficulties.

These last two developments were of considerable consequence for local authorities, as they created pressures for a major reappraisal of the role of local government. The desire of successive governments to overcome the nation's economic difficulties by curbing public spending made local government the target for measures designed to control all local authority spending, including even that financed from the rates. In addition, local government found itself embroiled not only in arguments about public expenditure but also in a wider debate about the appropriate role of the state. After a generation of widespread acceptance of the welfare state there emerged in the 1970s a growing tendency to question its virtues from a wide variety of points of view. Local government became one of the objects of this questioning.

Local government has thus found itself in a position of some political insecurity since 1974, the object of often sceptical, and sometimes unfriendly, comment. Growing electoral volatility has made far more rapid changes in party control of councils, one consequence of which has been what Hampton (1980, p. 5) describes as 'a decline in the mellowing effects of several years' socialisation of newly elected councillors'. Cut-backs in service whose provision had come to be taken for granted in an earlier period aroused concern amongst those affected, as did the issue of rate levels, and some evidence has emerged suggesting that local elections might now be rather more affected by local factors than in the immediate past (Gyford, 1984, pp. 117-19). Meanwhile, as the parties themselves, even allowing for the switchbacks of electoral fortune, became more deeply entrenched in local government, the two major parties experienced a degree of ideological polarization, with economic individualism emerging as a dominant philosophy on the Conservative right and Marxism on the Labour left. Thus, even local councils remaining nominally under the control of the same party experienced pronounced switches of policy as one party faction gained the upper hand over another. In other cases, the growth in the number of Liberal councillors, from 897 in 1977 to 2,010 in 1984, and the emergence of the Social Democratic Party (SDP), with 302 councillors in 1984, have led to the creation of 'hung' councils with no one party in overall control. Hung councils had in any case been rendered more likely after 1974 by the abolition of aldermen whose six-year term of office had sometimes enabled parties to cling to power even when defeated at the polls. The various changes of control and of direction flowing from this political instability have in turn provided further fuel for arguments about what those in charge of local councils think they are doing, as the 'mellowness' of earlier years has given way to the more vigorous cut and thrust of inter-party and inter-factional contests.

The embattled image of local government has been further sharpened by the way in which the conflicts between central and local government, inherent in the former's attempts to control the latter's expenditure, have been overlain by both inter- and intra-party disputes. Thus, in the debates over the Conservative government's policy on local authority spending after 1979 the government's stand was under constant sniping from some Conservative local politicians (and, indeed, back-bench Conservative MPs) defending the prerogatives of local government; at the same time the Labour Opposition spokesmen came under fire from some Labour councillors for failing to secure a more concerted opposition to the spending cuts amongst Labour-controlled authorities.

These internal party debates have reflected the fact that none of the parties possesses any machinery by which local councillors can be forced to comply with the wishes either of the party at the centre, be it at headquarters or in the House of Commons, or of the party at large convened in annual conference. In the party constitutions there are indeed provisions for making councillors accountable in varying degrees to local party units but none for making them accountable to any wider or superior constituency within the parties. In so far as it expressed itself in harmony between a party's councillors and parliamentarians, the earlier nationalization of local politics was a product of shared values and ideas rather than of formal constitutional mechanisms within the party. The tendency of the parties to appear to work in a unitary fashion in the 1950s and 1960s was a reflection rather than a cause of widespread agreement on the issues of the time. The rebirth of ideology in the 1970s produced strains within both the Conservative and Labour parties. These tensions became particularly evident as local and national politicians of both parties tried to cope with the Conservative legislation on local government after 1979. The divisions which this legislation produced within the two major parties revealed them each to be, in the words of Richard Rose (1980, p.

254), 'a complex set of plural institutions' within which contending views of local government came to be expressed, with radicals of both right and left developing their own distinctive approaches.

These two radical approaches evince certain parallels. Both view local government in the context of its relationship to the economy, the radical right picturing it as an impediment to the fulfilment of the promise of the free market, the radical left seeing it as caught up in the social conflicts generated by capitalism and, thus, as a possible arena for opposing the capitalist system. Both express hostility towards the managerial power of the professional local government officer. From the radical right, Michael Forsyth (1981) deplores 'unnecessary layers of bureaucracy' and 'impersonal, sneering professionals', while from the radical left, Ken Livingstone (1982, pp. 34-5) complains that 'what is easy for the bureaucracy takes precedence over everything else' and that 'we are drifting into a dreadful bureaucratic paternalism'. Both express a concern for greater participation by the public, though one seeks it through individual consumer control in a free market and the other through and expansion of collective decision-making at the grass roots of politics. Both also desire to see local government in some way 'opened up', either to the impact of market forces or to the influence of popular political pressure.

None the less, these two lines of thought are heading in different directions and lead to highly contrasting policies when the Conservative right or the Labour left take control of local authorities. By early 1983 over two dozen Conservative councils had contracted out to private enterprise such services as adoption, community care of the elderly, highway maintenance, legal services, rent collection, street cleaning, pest control and recreation management. By mid-1984, one council — Merton — had privatized street cleaning, refuse collection, school meals, school cleaning and meals for the elderly and was contemplating the transformation of its finance department into a private company. Left-wing councils meanwhile were concentrating on the development of a 'local socialism', embracing such features as decentralization to ward or neighbourhood offices or committees, economic intervention through local enterprise boards, financial support for radical community and minority groups, nuclear-free zones and the mobilization of popular support for local services faced with government-inspired cut-backs (Boddy and Fudge, 1984). Such policies, moreover, were not the creation of local authority officers, as under 'the administrative politics' model. Officers might advise, but these policies represented initiatives stemming from political sources. In addition, the policies were increasingly likely to have been put before the local electorate in the form of detailed manifestos running sometimes into scores of pages and thousands of words. On the Labour side at least, the party outside the council would be likely to see itself as 'guardians of the manifesto', keeping up the pressure on its councillors to ensure that party policy was implemented. In such developments we see the incursion of Hill's 'ideological politics' in which parties 'provide specific programmes' (Hill, 1972, p. 211).

Hill (p. 216) has observed that ideological politics 'puts great strains upon administrators'. It seems likely that the strain may be all the greater if the administrators have been brought up within the tradition of administrative politics. Certainly one development of the past few years has been a questioning in some quarters of the traditional model and role of the non-political local government officer. A number of town planners formed a Radical Institute Group within the Royal Town Planning Institute to promote a more egalitarian approach to managing urban change. Some planners have decided to serve as officers in one authority and as councillors in another. This practice has been by no means confined to that profession alone in recent years, especially since the replacement of county boroughs by two-tier local government in 1974 made it a practical proposition in the major provincial conurbations. Social work too has become increasingly conscious of a political dimension to its work. A measure of this can be seen in a report by the National Institute for Social Work in 1982 which accepted that social workers saw 'links between social policies and the problems clients being' and that it was not their role 'simply to accept things as they are'. 'The "political" element of their work is therefore an integral part of the whole ... We would urge elected members ... to ensure that social workers have channels open to them ... to bring their assessments of the effects of policies forward.'

Other departures from traditional practice have included the appointment of staff who are known to be politically sympathetic to the politics of the majority party and the breaking down of the traditional division of labour between members and officers by involving both of them in research and report-writing. The campaign for NALGO affiliation to the Labour Party, so far unsuccessful, may be seen as a further attempt to break with past practice. A leading pro-affiliation campaigner amongst NALGO members, Derek Hatton, an officer of Knowsley District Council, later emerged as Deputy Leader of the majority Labour group in Liverpool, thereby integrating within his own person the four roles of officer, trade-unionist, party activist and councillor. He was also one of the growing number of assertive full-time councillors who were as much at home in the town or county hall as the officers thanks to the generosity of their employers and/or to the payment of councillors' allowances.

The case of Liverpool also highlights another departure from previous practice in respect of local authority trade-unionsism, namely the attempt to involve the unions more closely in the decision-making processes of the council. Thus, in June 1983 the council agreed that its Personnel Committee should include twelve members of the Joint Shop Stewards Executive Committee as non-voting advisory representatives and that the unions should be represented on all interviewing panels for vacancies and promotions. The Liverpool arrangement was not wholly innovatory. A survey for the Society of Local Authority Chief Executives in 1976 found that Hereford and Worcester, Basildon and Slough made provision for non-voting employee representatives on some committees in addition to the more widespread use of Joint Consultative Committees and a number of other authorities have since followed suit. In addition to participating in such formal arrangements, the trade unions have had an impact on local government through their growing readiness to take industrial action, with the 1970s seeing the first official strikes called by the local government unions on a nation-wide basis. Initially, this increased militancy amongst local government workers reflected reaction to what was seen as central government interference in local authority pay bargaining and in the established patterns of industrial relations and trade union rights; subsequently it also acquired another dimension, that of defending jobs threatened by cut-backs in local government spending (Walsh, 1982).

The role of trade-unionists in local politics is not confined to the stage provided by local government itself. The presence of members and officials of NALGO, NUPE, NATFHE and the NUT on local Labour Party committees whether as union delegates (in the case of NUPE) or as party branch members has grown with the expansion in public sector employment and

unionization and in white-collar activism within the party. Some
observers have noted the possible emergence of a public sector or
public service 'class' of Labour councillors, often quite as well
qualified academically and professionally as the council officers
who serve them, and drawn disproportionately from the ranks of
education, local government, trade unions, public corporations
and publicly funded voluntary and community groups (for example, Lipsey, 1982; Walker, 1983).

The place of voluntary and community groups in local politics
has aroused increasing interest in the wake of major programmes
of funding by some Labour councils. For example, in 1983-4, the
GLC's Grants Subcommittee authorized 184 grants costing nearly
£3 million in addition to grants made by the major committees of
the GLC; the Women's Committee granted £3.14 million to 216
groups in 1983-4 and the Housing Committee £4 million to 280
groups in the same year (GLC, 1984).

It should not, however, be supposed that public sector professions, trade unions and voluntary groups were alone in being
drawn in varying ways into local politics. The Conservative
government was simultaneously introducing legislation making it
obligatory for a local authority to consult industrial and commercial ratepayers about its expenditure plans before it could set its
budget. An even more direct commercial involvement could be
seen amongst those private firms which received the contracts to
carry out local authority services subject to privatization by Conservative councils.

The common theme these developments represent, over and
above the growth of ideological politics, is a move away from a
form of what C. P. Snow called 'closed politics' towards a more
'open politics', in which the authority's political links with elements of the wider economic and social structure became important features of its decision-making. The openness is not however
total, since the political complexion of the council may determine
which elements in the community are affforded more open access
to the authority. Changes in the style of local political leadership
have also taken place, with strong and sometimes rather secretive
leadership being replaced by a more open and democratic system
of decision-making within party groups in which leaders often
become brokers between different factions or interests (G. W.
Jones and Norton, 1979; Elcock, 1981). It is therefore not surprising that a major body of academic research after the mid-1970s

focused not simply on the local authority itself and its inner workings but also on the place of the authority, and indeed of local government itself, in its wider setting. Studies of urban social theory, of local political economy and of central-local government relations were all part of an attempt to deal with, amongst other things, the external politics of local authorities embracing their relationships with social classes, local party organizations, economic interests, voluntary bodies, professional bodies, party headquarters and Whitehall departments...

In moving from closed politics towards open politics, local government might also find itself undergoing a further change in addition to the move from adminstrative to ideological politics. If service delivery through privatization and decentralization to wards or neighbourhoods were to gather pace and if local authorities were increasingly to become sources of contracts, franchises and grant funding, then the tasks of co-ordination and resource allocation and of dealing with clients and agents might begin to look remarkably like the bargaining politics which Hill (1972, pp. 217-26) noted as particularly characteristic of US local government; they might also take on overtones of that other traditional feature of US local government — patronage politics. Such developments might be anticipated particularly in those urban areas where ethnic, religious and other minorities exist in sufficient numbers to make them worth wooing by local politicians impressed by their potential voting strength...

Bibliography

Alt, J. (1971), 'Some social and political correlates of county borough expenditures', *British Journal of Political Science,* Vol. 1, No. 1.
Beer, S. (1965), *Modern British Politics,* Faber.
Boaden, N. (1971), *Urban Policy-Making,* Cambridge University Press.
Boddy, M. and Fudge, C. (eds), (1984), *Local Socialism?,* Macmillan.
Bristow, S. (1978), 'Local parties after reorganisation — the homogenisation of local government in England and Wales', *Public Administration Bulletin,* No. 28.
Bulpitt, J. (1967), *Party Politics in English Local Government,* Longman.
Butler, D. and Stokes, D. (1975), *Political Change in Britain,* Macmillan.
Dearlove, J. (1973), *The Politics of Policy in Local Government,* Cambridge University Press.
Dunleavy, P. (1981), *The Politics of Mass Housing in Britain, 1945-1975,* Oxford University Press.
Elcock, H. (1981), 'Tradition and change in Labour Party politics: the decline and fall of the city boss', *Political Studies,* Vol. 39, No. 3.

370 Local political organisations

Fraser, D. (1979), *Power and Authority in the Victorian City,* Blackwell.

Game, C. and Skelcher, C. (1983), 'Manifestoes and other manifestations of local party politics', *Local Government Studies,* Vol. 9, No. 4.

Greater London Council (1984), *Responses by GLC Committees to the Government's White Paper 'Streamlining the Cities',* GLC.

Green, D. G. (1981), *Power and Party in an English City,* Allen and Unwin.

Gyford, J. (1984), *Local Politics in Britain,* 2nd ed., Croom Helm.

Hampton, W. (1970), *Democracy and Community,* Oxford University Press.

Hampton, W. (1980), 'Introduction' in *Party Politics in Local Government: Officers and Members,* Policy Studies Institute.

Hanham, H. J. (1959), *Elections and Party Management,* Longman.

Hill, M. J. (1972), *The Sociology of Public Administration,* Wiedenfeld and Nicholson.

Johnson, R. W. (1972), 'The nationalisation of English Rural Politics: Norfolk Southwest 1945-1970', *Parliamentary Affairs,* Vol. 26, No. 1.

Jones, G. W. and Norton, A. (eds) (1979), *Political Leadership in Local Authorities,* Institute of Local Government Studies.

Lee, J. M. (1963), *Social Leaders and Public Persons,* Oxford University Press.

Lipsey, D. (1982), 'Labour's new (non-manual) breed of councillor', *Sunday Times,* 19 September.

Livingstone, K. (1982), Report of speech to the Chartered Institute of Public Finance and Accountancy, *Publi Finance and Accountancy,* September.

Maud, J. P. R. (1967), *Report of the Committee on the Management of Local Government,* HMSO.

Rhodes, R. A. W. (1981), *Control and Power in Central-Local Government Relations,* Gower.

Rose, R. (1980), *Politics in England,* Faber.

Schofield, M. (1977), 'The "nationalisation" of local politics', *New Society,* 28 April.

Sharpe, L. J. and Newton, K. (1984), *Does Politics Matter?,* Oxford University Press.

Walker, D. (1983), 'Local interest and representation: the case of "class" interest among Labour representatives in inner London', *Government and Policy,* Vol. 1.

Walsh, K. (1982), 'Local government militancy in Britain and the United States', *Local Government Studies,* Vol. 8, No. 6.

Wiseman, H. V. (1967), *Local Government at Work,* Routledge & Kegan Paul.

Young, K. (1975), *Local Politics and the Rise of Party,* Leicester University Press.

Young, K. and Mills, L. (1980), *Public Policy Research: A Review of Qualitative Methods,* Social Science Research Council.

Index